To Be at Home

Work in Global and Historical Perspective

———

Edited by
Andreas Eckert, Sidney Chalhoub, Mahua Sarkar,
Dmitri van den Bersselaar, Christian G. De Vito

Work in Global and Historical Perspective is an interdisciplinary series that welcomes scholarship on work/labor that engages a historical perspective in and from any part of the world. The series advocates a definition of work/labor that is broad, and especially encourages contributions that explore interconnections across political and geographic frontiers, time frames, disciplinary boundaries, as well as conceptual divisions among various forms of commodified work, and between work and 'non-work'.

Volume 5

To Be at Home

House, Work, and Self in the Modern World

Edited by
Felicitas Hentschke and James Williams

DE GRUYTER
OLDENBOURG

ISBN 978-3-11-057987-1
e-ISBN (PDF) 978-3-11-058276-5
e-ISBN (EPUB) 978-3-11-058013-6
ISSN 2509-8861

Bibliographic information published by the Deutsche Nationalbibliothek
The Deutsche Nationalbibliothek lists this publication in the Deutsche Nationalbibliografie;
detailed bibliographic data are available on the Internet at http://dnb.dnb.de.

© 2018 Walter de Gruyter GmbH, Berlin/Boston
Coverphoto: Algeria © Maurice Weiss
Satz: SatzBild GbR, Sabine Taube, Kieve
Druck und Bindung: Hubert & Co. GmbH & Co. KG, Göttingen

www.degruyter.com

This book is dedicated to all those who are on the move and still struggle to find their one corner in the world to make themselves a home.

Table of Contents

Acknowledgements

To Be at Home came into being at the international research center Work and Human Lifecycle in Global History (re:work) at Humboldt-Universität zu Berlin. We would like to thank re:work's director Andreas Eckert for his trust in this project and his generous support.

re:work is one of ten Käte Hamburger Centers funded by the German Federal Ministry of Education and Research (BMBF). It is part of the BMBF 'Freedom for Research in the Humanities' initiative and we are grateful for the unique space of scholarship and collegiality this has provided to develop this extraordinary project.

Special thanks must go to Sebastian Marggraff, Farah Barakat, and the re:work team for their editorial and logistical assistance, as well as Helen Veitch for her thoughtful copyediting. We particularly thank Maurice Weiss for the photographs he has contributed to this volume taken from his incredibly rich archive.

We spoke with many people on the journey of producing this book and received wide-ranging support and much-appreciated advice. While it would be difficult to name everybody, a few must be mentioned: Phil Bonner, Frederick Cooper, Daniel Eisenberg, Theresa Grieben, Jens Kleihauer, Damian van Melis, Shalini Randeria, Seth Rockman, Ellen Rothenberg, Michal Warshavsky, and Severin Wucher. Marie, Modi, Moussa, and Nilsa inspired us with their youthful spirit and their clarity about where home is – and where it is not.

We are grateful for the support of Noor Nieftagodien, Filip de Boeck, and Jürgen Kocka (who accompanied the development of this book with his favorable advice), as well as all others who participated in the workshop, *Home-Making as Work: Photographic and Ethnographic Portraits of Houses and Homes in Global and Historical Perspective*, which took place at re:work on May 27–28, 2015.

We would like to thank Rabea Rittgerodt for her constant encouragement, and De Gruyter Oldenbourg and the editors of the 'Work in Global and Historical Perspective' series at De Gruyter for their support.

Finally, we are delighted to be able to thank all of the contributors to this volume. Without their commitment, this experiment would not have succeeded!

In the words of Gaston Bachelard, we believe that 'Our house is our corner of the world ... our first universe.'

Felicitas Hentschke and James Williams

Preface

"You can kill a person with a flat like with an axe," the German illustrator and photographer Heinrich Zille noted with reference to the districts of the so-called ordinary people and immigrants in Berlin around 1900. Even today, vast numbers of people all over the world find it challenging to secure a roof over their heads. All too often, people are displaced and have to search for a place to live under harsh and hostile conditions. For new generations of affluent mobility experts and managers, meanwhile, 'up in the air' seems to be the preferred home, supplemented by expensive hotel suites. Glossy magazines celebrate elegant and lavishly furnished homes that reflect the status of their inhabitants and serve as a source of aspirations for others. "To be at home," as the contributions to this volume so aptly show, thus means a lot of different things. The authors emphasize the complex relationship between home and work, and situate houses and homes in a broad historical perspective as the crossroads between the self, work, and the world.

The field of labor history related to the North Atlantic realm already offers a solid set of studies focusing on workers' housing and on state, municipal, and company projects to provide accommodation. Housing projects for the 'new' working classes have also been crucial to late colonial development, for instance in Africa, and have been studied accordingly. Early on, segregationist ideologies and practices caught the attention of a critical historiography of colonialism. Since Pierre Bourdieu's seminal studies on the theory of practice based on fieldwork in Kabylia, Algeria, we know that relations of power and social stratification are reflected in space, in which we can discern something like a lived map of daily life. Space is an important and contested area of colonial and post-colonial daily life. Power structures are inscribed in space, and space reflects social organization and defines the people in it. Space is a central object of rule. In this context, an important aspect is the keeping of distance. This is especially, but by no means exclusively, true in the colonial context, where a small European minority faced a large indigenous majority. The thin foundations of colonial control made urban planning and architecture an important symbol of colonial hegemony. Colonial planning did not promote integration: it did not even pretend to be willing to integrate. On the contrary, it emphasized difference and hierarchy.

Numerous essays in this book explore the issue of segregation, as well as other themes familiar to the history of housing, houses, and homes. What makes this volume unique, however, is its attempt to translate ongoing discussions about the fuzzy boundaries between work and 'nonwork' into richly textured miniature studies that shape our understanding of work. Another aspect that adds to the originality of the approaches developed here is the effort to take into account the dimension of life course and to carefully consider the multifaceted connections between life and work through the lens of home and housing.

Both life course and histories of work and non-work have been at the center of debates at the Käte Hamburger Collegium Work and Human Lifecycle in Global History (re:work) since its inception in 2009. This volume represents an impressive cross-section of the work of numerous fellows who over the last few years spent up to ten months at the collegium in Berlin or participated in some of our conferences or summer academies. Felicitas Hentschke and James Williams deserve our credit for having brought together such a splendid collection of essays and for making them speak to each other. *To Be at Home* is a most welcome addition to a fast-growing library in the field of global labor history. It places often very local histories into a global framework. It invites the reader on an exciting journey to many geographical sites and time periods, and addresses situations, constellations, and challenges that are arguably more topical today than ever before.

Andreas Eckert, Director of re:work

Foreword

There is a certain irony in the interest being shown in the twentieth-first century by a European university in my work on the politics of space.[1] I undertook this work to promote greater understanding of the complex legacy of colonial conquest and apartheid in South African society. Unfortunately, the post-apartheid government has yet to vigorously tackle the ugly colonial and apartheid geo-spatial wounds that mark our country.

Flying into any airport in my beloved nation provides a 360-degree view of the spatial legacy of apartheid cities and towns. The poorer you are, the darker your skin, the further you are likely to live from the city centers where the major urban assets are located. The politics of space continue to play out in the post-apartheid era as policy makers avoid the tough decisions needed to transform our lived environments into ones every citizen can feel at home in. Disrupting enclaves of privilege has yet to occur in our society.

I am particularly grateful that this book has taken a global focus to an aspect of the human community that has major implications for the well-being of everyone. My original work was inspired by Dolores Hayden's book, *Redesigning the American Dream*, in which she emphasises the importance of home:

> Human beings need nurturing, aesthetic pleasure and economic security ... To a large extent, inhabited space has a major impact on the self-image of individuals and their perception of their place in society.[2]

Twenty-four years after the end of apartheid we are learning just how deeply the wounds of the politics of space are embedded in our social fabric and in the psyche of its individual members. The limitations of physical, political, psychosocial, and ideological-intellectual spaces over more than four hundred years are playing out at every level of our society.

On April 14, 2018, a horror movie played out on our television screens during a news broadcast. A man in Joe Slovo Squatter Camp in Port Elizabeth, in the Eastern Cape, was seen on the roof of his shack holding his infant daughter. He then dangled her upside down, threatening to throw her off the roof unless the municipal authorities stopped demolishing his shack. In desperation, a member of the police climbed onto the roof to rescue the child, but just then the man threw the crying infant off the building. Another policeman caught the infant. The infant immediately stopped crying. The father was arrested and the child was taken to a place of safety.

What could have happened to a make an adult, let alone the father of a child, bargain for a place to stay by threatening to kill his own offspring? Was he so humiliated by his inability to be an effective provider of a safe, dignified home, as men are expected to be in a patriarchal society, that he took this drastic step? We now know from greater understanding of neuroscience that humiliation inflicts deep wounds on the human psyche, which register on brain imaging scans in the same areas where pain receptors are located.

Emotional pain according to experts is in some ways much more painful than physical pain. We know that emotional trauma is transmitted across multiple generations. The man in the horror story above is most likely to be a product of a disrupted migrant labor family, and he may himself be

---

1 Mamphela Ramphele, "The Politics of Space: Life in the Migrant Labour Hostels of the Western Cape" (Ph.D. thesis, University of Cape Town, 1991).
2 Dolores Hayden, *Redesigning the American Dream: The Future of Housing, Work, and Family Life* (New York: W.W. Norton, 1984).

a migrant laborer suffering the humiliation of being unable to provide a proper home for his family. His pride is wounded. His response reflects the self-sabotage response of frequently wounded people, who tend to respond to frustration with rage and destructive anger that undermines their own interests even further.

South Africa, like much of post-colonial Africa, has yet to acknowledge and address the multi-generational wounds of the legacy of colonial conquest and apartheid. The gap between the human rights set out in our celebrated constitution and the lived reality of the majority of citizens is creating moral and ethical dissonance in our society. The continued violation of the human dignity of the majority of citizens by the failure of society to meet its commitments to a progressive realization of those citizens' socio-economic rights is a betrayal of the promise of freedom attained in 1994.

What is missing from our society, as is the case in many post-liberation countries in Africa and elsewhere, is investment in mindset change from the inequities of past authoritarian governance to a mindset that enables people to make the journey from subjects to citizens. Those in public office also need this mindset change to break the authoritarian model of power relationships that characterize colonial relations.

There is much to learn from the example of the Nordic region captured in the book, *The Nordic Secret: A European Story of Beauty and Freedom*.[3] The transition of the Nordic region from a feudal system in the 1860s to a social democratic one enabled it to develop from the poorest in Europe to among the richest in the space of seventy years. This change was underpinned by investment in developing the inner person in each citizen through *Bildung*. *Bildung* is a German concept elaborated by Johann Gottfried Herder to promote a coherent identity and sense of common destiny. It is defined as a moral, intellectual, and emotional transformation and development characterized by the creation of shared values and ethics. In the Nordic context, values are attained through what locals call 'inner work,' which involves each citizen working on linking the body, mind, and soul.

Transforming mindsets of feudalism that sustained hierarchical authoritarianism and abuse to help citizens attain emotional freedom and self-authorship is an essential, complex, and painful process. Herder believed that philosophy should have a practical result, which he summarized as human growth, and that philosophical ideas have to be understood within their social context.

Healing the wounds of humiliation suffered by the majority of citizens in our country will take no less of an effort than that undertaken by the Nordic countries. Transforming the physical and spatial environments in which people live will take much longer than we had hoped due to the failures of those in public office. Post-apartheid governments in South Africa have added insult to injury by inflicting a housing model on poor people that is of even lower quality than those of the apartheid era.

Inner work needs to be tackled in the following areas. First, free high-quality education and training focused on bringing out the best in each individual while inculcating the values of respect for human dignity, equality for all, and the responsibilities of citizenship. Campaigns promoting adult basic education and training infused with human rights values are needed to eradicate illiteracy and unskilled labor.

Second, we need to establish a secure social net accessible to all citizens with free high-quality health and welfare services. We need to build solidarity in our social fabric beyond just providing minimalist social grants. Accountability, transparency, and efficiency of government and public

---

3 Lene R. Andersen and Tomas Björkman, *The Nordic Secret: A European Story of Beauty and Freedom* (Copenhagen: Det Andersenske Forlag, 2017).

officials will ensure that citizens are able to see the tangible benefits of higher taxation and accept making such contributions.

Third, we need to inculcate a deep culture of nurturing the inner core of each individual, including leaders in both the public and private sectors. Regular retreats and youth camps need to be promoted to bring the young and old close to nature and nurture harmony between mind, body, and spirit. The fruits of this hard work would help heal the wounds of humiliation and bind families and communities together.

Being at home is the most urgent task facing South Africa and many African cities. The majority of citizens on our continent live on the margins: physically, politically, emotionally, and economically. Our interconnected world needs to participate in the healing work essential to enable a sense of being at home for our global community.

There is now much more appreciation in our global community of the importance of an inclusive, sustainable, regenerative socio-economic system, so that every citizen can take ownership of contributing to the protection of our planet. Healing the wounds of humiliation and promoting the kind of development that makes every citizen feel at home is essential to the well-being of all of humanity.

Mamphela Ramphele
Co-Founder ReimagineSA

Felicitas Hentschke and James Williams

Introduction

To Be at Home: House, Work, and Self in the Modern World examines structures, experiences, concepts, and memories of houses and homes in relation to work and the life course from global historical and comparative perspectives. Drawing from research conducted in Africa, Asia, the Americas, Europe, and the Middle East, the essays in this book consider how people living in different societies and historical periods have endeavored to make and keep houses and homes under varied conditions: migration, redundancy, political upheaval, displacement, economic and social change, impoverishment, forced labor, racial discrimination, and violence. These conditions speak to the profound challenges of life in the modern world.

Houses and homes are dynamic and complex spaces within and through which people work to secure and organize their lives, livelihoods, and relationships. The following essays and interviews attest to the complexity and variousness of these labors. They also show how 'house' and 'home' prove multifarious, powerful, and often elusive ideas, invoking places, persons, objects, emotions, attachments, and aspirations. Yet within our respective fields of study – labor history, global history, economic and urban anthropology, and migration studies – we note how houses and homes tend to assume peripheral places, are interrogated insufficiently, and take on conventional forms. We are struck, too, by how the houses and homes that abound in the scholarly literature recurrently reflect preconceived and often specifically Western and bourgeois norms and fantasies: home as a naturally given space marked for reproduction and by privacy, for example; the modern house as a site or life-sphere distinct from work.

To Be at Home positions houses and homes as vital "nodal points" between the self, work, and the world.[1] Formulating home, work, and the self as interconnected and mutually constitutive life projects, we suggest, provides a new way to explore people's creativity, agency, and labor. *To Be at Home* is an experimental attempt at rethinking house-building, home-making, and the myriad activities that take place within and around houses and homes from the perspectives of work and the life course. It asks what we might gain by suspending a normative approach to home, work, and life that sees home and the self as in contrast or conflict with work and the outer world – a separation with serious theoretical and methodological consequences.[2] We hope to open fresh possibilities for thinking through ways in which houses, homes, work, and the life course bind together.

The essays within this book explore how life and work histories are shaped by the rhythms, spatiality, and temporalities of houses and homes. They scrutinize the roles of gender, age, race, and class in determining how work and home entwine or pull apart. Separately and together, they demonstrate that relations between houses, work, and the self have transformed dramatically under conditions of capitalism and modernity – and continue to change today. The essays frequently challenge *a priori* assumptions that work and home inherently or necessarily stand apart or in opposition. Textual and visual materials we have assembled in this volume capture the radically varied possibilities and impossibilities of being 'at home' in modern societies from local to transnational scales.

---

1 We borrow the concept of "nodal point" from Fiona Ross's rich and critical ethnographic work on housing and home life in contexts of urban poverty in South Africa. See Fiona Ross, *Raw Life, New Hope: Decency, Housing, and Everyday Life in a Post-Apartheid Community* (Cape Town: University of Cape Town Press, 2010).

2 A dominant paradigm in labor history, for example, assumes work to be an activity performed predominantly outside of the home (and often paid), and fails to sufficiently investigate the labor involved in social reproduction, primarily performed in homes and by women. We are grateful to Nitin Varma for articulating this point.

Origins

This book grows out of the work undertaken at Work and Human Lifecycle in Global History (re:work), an international research center housed at Humboldt-Universität zu Berlin, Germany. Through conferences, symposia, and an international fellowship program, re:work facilitates comparative and global historical research and analysis on the interdependent relationship between work and the life course, and on the imaginaries surrounding work and the life course.

An avenue of inquiry that has been especially fruitful at re:work emerged out of examining boundaries between work and 'non-work.' Houses and homes surfaced often in doing so as places, expenses, endeavors, and abstractions. We were intrigued by how common understandings of work mutate or destabilize when we 'provincialize' work and accept it as a necessary aspect of life, and focus instead on the efforts of building a house, organizing a household, and making a home. We began considering how the tasks of house- and home-making overlap and sometimes compete with the demands, places, and temporalities of formal and informal work *per se* and with wider historical, economic, and political processes. A two-day workshop in May 2015, *Home-Making as Work: Photographic and Ethnographic Portraits of Houses and Homes in Global and Historical Perspective*, generated conceptual and methodological ideas for this book and convinced us that houses and homes in relation to work and the life course begged deeper examination.

We embarked on this project by asking historians and social scientists affiliated with re:work to consider how homes, work, and life histories intersect within their research fields. We pushed them to reflect on how houses and homes interrupt or complicate their objects and subjects of study. Contributors were encouraged to take spaces and structures sometimes marginal and unchallenged in their work – houses, homes – and place them center stage. What might we learn about work, the self, and the dynamics and transformations of modern societies by focusing on houses and homes people work to make and maintain? How does work figure in people's lives, historically and contemporaneously, when houses and homes are positioned at the center of human action? How does the reproductive and economic work of houses and homes contribute to the social or political reproduction of capitalism and inequality? To what extent can houses and homes open new perspectives on the cultural and social meanings of work, labor, and the life course?

To Be at Home also traces its origins from a path-breaking ethnography from South Africa published twenty-five years ago this year. Mamphela Ramphele's *A Bed Called Home: Life in the Migrant Labour Hostels of Cape Town* is a powerful study of migrant workers in South Africa residing in hostels tied to their employment, perhaps the archetypal urban space in which the apartheid state merged work and home for many thousands of black South Africans.[3] Ramphele's ethnography foregrounded complex interrelationships between the hostels' infrastructure and the lives of their dwellers. The book impressed and intrigued us as colleagues, further convincing us of the relevance of houses and homes in labor history, migration studies, and global history.

Among its many insights and accomplishments, Ramphele's ethnography provides a way of thinking about home, work, and their intersections as dually political and emotional, and thus of how selves are made, unmade, and remade in fraught spaces such as migrant hostels, where work and home collide while concurrently being kept apart. Ramphele's study also advocates methodological plurality and interdisciplinarity in studying work and home together. Ramphele exemplifies how important it is to consult varied sources and gather many kinds of evidence to interrogate

---

3 Mamphela Ramphele, *A Bed Called Home: Life in the Migrant Labour Hostels of Cape Town* (Cape Town: David Philip, 1993), with photographs by Roger Meintjes.

how macro political and economic processes intersect with intimate projects of sustaining relationships and self-making in and around houses and homes. Such an assortment of approaches and disciplines is evident in this book, too. Our contributors draw from a wide range of archival and ethnographic sources, including literary, poetic, aural, visual, governmental, and legal materials, to glimpse at houses, homes, and home-making in relation to work and the life course.

We are immensely privileged that Mamphela Ramphele has graced this book with such a generous foreword. Her participation in our project affirms our belief that the insights and mode of scholarship she put forward twenty-five years ago continue to generate productive and responsible questions. And like all of Mamphela Ramphele's work before and since *A Bed Called Home*, we trust the essays, photographs, memoirs, vignettes, narratives, and drawings assembled here convey historical depth and acumen but speak as well to current events in our world.

Houses, Home, and the Work of Photography

A Bed Called Home was significant for its innovative alliance between an ethnographer and a photographer. The collaboration between Mamphela Ramphele and Roger Meintjes moved us greatly: for the conversations provoked between the book's written and visual ingredients; for how Meintjes's photographs might be thought of as not just supplementing or illustrating Ramphele's ethnographic and historical description and analysis but offering different ways of seeing and imagining the world as well. Through a preoccupation with space, the photographs in *A Bed Called Home* offer a glimpse of the dynamics between political power, violence, and discrimination from the perspective of places of reproduction and intimacy.

Stimulated by the complementarities, dissonances, and interactions between text and image in Ramphele's book, our project is similarly collaborative. Esteemed photographer Maurice Weiss's striking, arresting, evocative, and puzzling images interlace the essays in this book. They speak to and across the essays, augment ideas and stimulate imaginations, and in turn raise questions about how history, social science, and photography, as analogous descriptive practices and forms of portrait-making, can supplement and destabilize each other in capturing, staging, or remembering scenes of everyday life. In editing the essays, we have been struck by the consistently visual language used by the authors as they have attempted to depict the activities and struggles of house- and home-making. In the footsteps of *A Bed Called Home*, we trust our that curatorship of essays, interviews, and photographs likewise prompts reflection and questioning from its readers.

Ramphele and Meintjes's model of collaboration has influenced other ethnographers and historians. Anthropologist Filip de Boeck and photographer Marie-Françoise Plissart, for example, recently published *Kinshasa: Tales of the Invisible City*.[4] Through an interchange of text and intriguing pictures, de Boeck and Plissart forge a means of focusing not only on visible and representable portraits of the Congolese capital; they also shed light on the invisible and unspeakable. They show collective memories and imaginations, as well as individual predispositions and deviations, which they examine as strategies Kinshasa's residents use to cope with their difficult living conditions. Speaking at our workshop in Berlin in 2015, Filip de Boeck described photography's potential in terms of the "getting inside" of something to reach its hidden darkness – a form of "urban acupunc-

---

4 Filip de Boeck and Marie-Françoise Plissart, *Kinshasa: Tales of the Invisible City* (Leuven: Leuven University Press, 2014).

ture." We too believe that photography allows us to talk about the simultaneity of different times, sequences, and paradoxes, and their relations and interdependences, and thus to how photography can help uncover concealed truths of the necessities for self-preservation.

We have therefore not only asked historians and social scientists to draw on their distinct disciplinary lenses, regional and temporal foci, sensibilities, and histories of documenting and interpreting worlds to capture scenes of home-life and house-making. Maurice Weiss's photographs also form an integral visual architecture of this book and scaffold its ideas. Through the gaze of his camera, Weiss reflects on the meanings and importance of houses and homes as points of intersection between the material, social, and imaginary dimensions of human existence. Like the book's essays, Weiss's protagonists are on the margins, from forgotten spaces. He likewise offers unconventional glimpses into visible and invisible lifeworlds. Weiss's kaleidoscope of images crafts what Susan Sontag calls a "collection of the world."[5]

Photographs have the potential to conceptualize relations between work and the life course beyond words and scientific theories. Mediating distance and context, photography can identify relations between individuals and social structures and highlight aspects and details that remain disregarded in real life. Photography helps our thinking. Our book aims to provoke future dialogue between scholarly research and photography.

Themes

Our book's scope is ambitious. The book in your hands might be read as an eclectic mosaic of insights, images, arguments, descriptions, and voices produced by a diverse collective of scholars and artists that takes its reader into a multitude of worlds and historical periods. We have organized the book's contents loosely into themed sections, but we welcome readers to find alternate overlaps and connections across essays and sections (as well as disconnects, tensions, and disagreements), and between the issues and subjects the essays explore.

Homes and Mobility: Borders, Boundaries, Thresholds, the book's first section, considers efforts by individuals and families to make houses and homes amid movement and migration. Houses and homes, whether real or imagined, play vital roles in helping stabilize the lives, relationships, and life-projects of people on the move. Even if the future is uncertain for most of the individuals and families described in these four essays, the promise of a new home ahead sustains them through their present-day challenges of living in unfamiliar places, under conditions of deprivation or unmeant impermanence, and away from kin and friends.

Heike Drotbohm's ethnographic essay begins this section by recounting the life of a Cape Verdean mother, Susana, as she attempts to sustain herself and her family, split between Cape Verde and the United States, by building a house 'at home' through the remittances she sends to her parents in Praia, while also attempting to stay present in her children's lives as a mother far away. Her protagonist's resilience and vulnerability bears resemblances to the account of Nestor, a young Mozambican migrant who traveled to work in East Germany in the 1980s, by Eric Allina. Allina likewise recounts the personal sacrifices migrants are prepared to make to create a future home for themselves and others. Allina's account is striking for how young Mozambican migrants perceived their economic journeys to Europe as pathways toward both home- and self-making. For

---

5 Susan Sontag, *On Photography* (New York: Farrar, Straus and Giroux, 1977).

Nestor, work and the house his work will one day fund provides a way for him to negotiate the life course as well.

Contexts of long-term migration place economic and emotional pressures on individuals and families. These pressures surface most vociferously around houses and homes, a challenge explored in James Williams's essay on children's lives in a camp for displaced persons in postwar Liberia. As in Drotbohm's essay, Williams shows that the routines of home – the everyday acts that make houses homes – do not collapse in contexts of transnational migration, severe economic impoverishment, or in the presence of violence. Indeed, maintaining the continuities of home may assume greater significance in the wake of migration and movement, as shown here through the giving of gifts at a child's birthday (Drotbohm) or the convening of family meals when food is scarce (Williams). Houses and homes are thus projects, emotional and economic investments, and activities that help to stabilize and sustain relationships over time and space.

Alla Bolotova writes the life histories of two women in Soviet Russia who traveled as children to new industrialized towns in the Arctic in the 1920s and 1950s as part of state relocation programs. As with the East German case, these processes of long-distance migration were steered by the state. But Bolotova and Allina both describe migrants becoming attached to their new homes and communities in unintended ways. Countering the state imaginaries that brought them there, Nestor, Maria, and Nina – whose new houses or hostels, however imperfect, index a degree of stability and provide pathways towards meaningful work – came to consider East Germany and Kirovsk-Apatity home. Developing a theme that cuts across this book, we start seeing houses and homes as prominently political objects and projects, but which exert a force or power over individuals, families, and communities that always extends beyond the grasp of the state.

The essays in the second section, *Houses, Work, and Everyday Life: Rhythms, Ruptures, Cycles,* describe major transformations to houses and home-life in Asian, African, and European societies in the eighteenth, nineteenth, and twentieth centuries. Developments in houses and homes relate and reflect greater social, cultural, economic, and political changes that have arisen with the onset of modernity. Houses and homes serve here as historical objects, lenses, and figurative devices that narrate great stories of social transformation. The chapters in this section remind us that houses are often composite sites of work, production, and social and economic reproduction.

Age, class, and gender are explored especially in these five essays and, like houses and homes, are shown to become more differentiated, distinct, and specialized over time. Mary Jo Maynes and Ann Waltner compare the divergent histories of younger women's work in Europe and China to consider the contrasting options for young women in two changing societies; they chart in detail how the work of spinning yarn moved outside of the home in Europe during the nineteenth century but was typically retained within households in China. Two other essays in this section, by Josef Ehmer and Thabang Sefalafala, concern the intersections between work and home for younger people – young men especially. While Ehmer considers the many economic opportunities that arose in Central European cities for young people during the nineteenth century, which led to increased social and economic mobility for these rapidly growing populations, Sefalafala charts the contrary demise of economic opportunities for men in northern South Africa following the closure of the gold mines, where devastating unemployment has led not only to deep moral unease at being workless but has thrown houses and households into disarray as men's masculinity and personhood are undermined.

As much as houses and home life change profoundly over time, the essays in this section focus also on ordinary household routines, cycles, and everyday working and living activities. The classic anthropological concept of the 'development cycle' is worth recalling here to note temporalities and sequences that houses and homes assume already, which external processes of social and historical change thus disturb, rupture, or restructure.[6] David Warren Sabean captures these multiple dynamics in his examination of changing kinship relations in eighteenth-century German society. Using biographies of German academics and medical professionals, he dwells on the efforts taken by wealthy German households, particularly women, to cultivate a rich type of 'sociality' (*Geselligkeit*) in bourgeois homes, which he argues helped reproduce elite family networks. Attentiveness to the rhythms, ruptures, and cycles of houses and homes over time can help us better understand what changes and what stays the same – for Sabean and Ehmer, this relates to the continuities and discontinuities of houses and homes during a critical period of European class formation.

Anthropologist Gerd Spittler complements this section by providing a rural case-study from the Sahara. Spittler invites us to consider the materiality, spatial and social organization, and everyday activities such as sitting, eating, and sleeping in the houses and homes of the Kel Ewey Tuareg to challenge our assumptions about what constitutes a proper house and household. Like Sabean, Maynes and Waltner, and Ehmer, Spittler is attentive to the minute ways in which people and objects in houses and homes are stabilized during times of profound change. Status, class, and culture, we learn, are made and retained primarily through houses and homes.

We next turn to houses and homes as built structures. *Construction, Demolition, Relocation* tracks the impact of five major industrialist housing projects in Africa, India, and Europe on the workers, families, and individuals they housed. The life courses of these housing projects are hurried and dramatic, but short-lived. Focusing on episodes, policies, and processes of house building, moving, and destroying, the authors consider forms of exclusion and vulnerability that emerge in their aftermaths. In many cases, buildings that have not been destroyed continue to serve as places for living – in some cases for the same families who once lived there as workers. These essays consider ways in which both dwellings and capital delimit space and the social world.

Thaddeus Sunseri and Christian Strümpell separately consider the lives of workers of companies that have passed their zeniths. In the aftermath of a building boom, triggered by economic upswing, once-settled migrant workers – meat packers in Dar es Salaam and steel workers in Odisha – end up staying in their workers' residential neighborhoods, right next to the abandoned factories, despite their economic and legal precariousness. Slum dwellers in contemporary Bombay, however, live with the rhythms of new kinds of construction and destruction around them; they move, settle, and resettle in ways that this essay's author, Anupama Rao, experiences herself. As a European example from a similar period, Felicitas Hentschke describes the dynamic development of a single village in northern France over the course of a century from a remote rural settlement into an iron-producing town with five blast furnaces, which develops into an industrial zone between the 1870s and 1930s, and then declines almost as rapidly as it was built. Anupama Rao suggests a mode of 'disjunctural' reading in her essay – "reading across specific histories of housing deprivation" – to examine global logics of segregation at work and the impact of these logics on social exclusion. Her insight is helpful in seeing connections and juxtapositions. These different essays speak together to the trajectories and speed of capitalism in the modern world. They reinforce how the lives of houses and the lives of people, particularly the poor, rarely synchronize.

The essay by the curator Anne-Katrin Bicher reflects on an exhibition project on contemporary life in urban hostels in Johannesburg, South Africa. This exhibition at the Worker's Museum in downtown Johannesburg, which re:work staff visited in 2008, dealt with the single-sex housing structures built for migrant workers during apartheid. The exhibition, *Closed Constructions,*

---

6 See Jack Goody, *The Development Cycle of Domestic Groups* (Cambridge: Cambridge University Press, 1958).

represented hostel life through countless tiny photographs. These were placed in poster form, two meters square, and arranged like the cards of a memory game, grouped with labels such as 'soccer fields,' 'beer mats,' 'bedrooms,' and 'lavatories.' Spectators saw not only one specific space, but the prototype of whole concepts that made up the logics of institutions of discrimination and suppression. In a Benjaminian mode of collecting and sorting daily life objects, the exhibition at the Worker's Museum resembled a laboratory. It made observable what it meant to live in a Gauteng hostel in the nineteenth and twentieth centuries. It visualized the darkness, as well as the physical, psychosocial, and political struggles of the everyday lives of hostel dwellers under the constraints of apartheid rule. In her essay, Bicher contextualizes the exhibition through discussions with the hostel residents, many of whom documented their living conditions by participating in the exhibition.

The fourth section explores houses, homes, and work in explicitly political terms. *The Power of Place: Space, Exclusions, Vulnerability* begins with Gadi Algazi's essay on Bedouin in the Naqab, who have faced a long history of home demolitions and forced displacement since the formation of the state of Israel. In her legal example from Botswana, Anne Griffiths elaborates on land as a key to integration and sovereignty. Renu Addlakha challenges conventional concepts of domesticity used by state and non-state actors by examining instances of the care and neglect in 'welfare homes' in India. Vincent Houben and Stephen J. Rockel present contrasting cases of the housing experiences in Southeast Asia and East Africa in the nineteenth century.

Homes are key sites of personal and collective dreaming and reflecting, and houses are layered by national and personal histories. *Houses and Selves: Nostalgia, Imagination, Memory* considers ways in which houses, work, and life are often told and remembered through each other. Ju Li gives a female industrial worker a voice to reflect upon her life between work and home and how her work competes with her family's expectations in communist China. Sidney Chalhoub, Jonathan Hyslop, and Nitin Sinha describe intersections between history, literature, and popular culture. They use literary and musical sources to explain relations between people and their homes via spatial distances, gender, and migration.

Networks, Neighborhoods, Communities includes essays related to public space and house-building projects in Brazil, Germany, and India. Housing systems and neighborhoods are often acknowledged as extensions of the working environment. Inhabitants may use their communities and neighborhoods as political spaces for organizing change against the dominant political order. Paulo Fontes positions boarding houses in Brazil as a main hub of information, sociability, and job exchange. These were the first points of contact for newly arriving migrant workers in urban centers such as São Paulo. An alternative perspective on civil society is explored in Felicitas Hentschke's essay set in contemporary Berlin. Hentschke describes how a million refugees were received in Germany in 2015 and the efforts of volunteer groups, charitable organizations, and local activists in Berlin in providing supplies and care for them, which surpassed and sometimes challenged the role of the state. Two essays in this section speak about neighborhoods in nineteenth-century Germany and contemporary India. Despite their apparent differences, both Jürgen Schmidt and Rukmini Barua explore how work and people's appropriation with certain workplaces or work practices impact political struggles for the appropriation of territories.

The final set of essays, *Being at Home in the World: Thinking with Houses and Homes,* invites imaginative considerations of houses and homes as spaces, fantasies, and memories. We are invited here to interact with houses and homes directly – to listen and think with them. We learn how 'being at home' is not a straightforward pursuit or even a guaranteed possibility for many individuals, families, and societies, but requires ongoing effort, skill, a commitment to open secrecy, hope despite futility, or spiritual practice.

This section includes an essay on the lives of Bulgarian seafarers by Milena Kremakova, perpetually at home and not at home, whether on land or at sea. Set against a backdrop of the decline of seafaring as a national industry, Kremakova draws our attention to how people decorate their homes with objects and keepsakes from other places to keep some semblance of 'home' at hand. Isaie Dougnon considers the growing importance of home ownership in contemporary Mali, recounting the frightening prospect for many in Bamako that not owning a house, merely renting one, not only diminishes one's status in society as a second-class citizen, but jeopardizes one's life after death. Charlotte Bruckermann's ethnographic essay from China similarly points to the life courses of people and houses in Maoist and post-Maoist China. Like the politically sensitive documents governing these houses, kept hidden so as not to reveal illicit transfers of ownership during the Maoist era that may threaten social cohesion and individual safety, Bruckermann returns us to a tension raised throughout the book of a house's visibility and a home's invisibility. Finally, Cláudio Pinheiro considers how the works of Indian novelist Rabindranath Tagore assumed their own 'unhomely' afterlives as they became translated across the world. Eventually, new texts by 'Tagore' emerged in other states and societies after the novelist's death.

Kremakova, Bruckermann, Dougnon, and Pinheiro all inquire as to how houses and homes make memories and identities. Houses and homes are actors in these essays as much as people. Bruckermann and Dougnon in particular show how ancestors, spiritual powers, and nonhuman agents are often integral to individual life stories, reminding us how the life course may not be limited to individual human timespans between birth and death. Among other ideas, the essays in this section explore the interplay between the life course of houses and homes and the life course of people; they consider a kinship between property and people.

Three *Reflections* conclude the book. Nitin Varma uses the testimony of a female Indian servant who spoke in an English court in a case of marital infidelity between her British employers to craft a portrait of life inside an Anglo-Indian home in the early nineteenth century. Varma's chapter is accompanied by a drawing by graphic artist Theresa Grieben, who has attempted to recreate the interior of a colonial bungalow based on the descriptions provided by this domestic servant under oath. Like our collaboration with Maurice Weiss, the experimental teamwork between Varma and Grieben suggests one direction in which scholars and artists might partnership in the future.

Two interviews with colleagues who have generated vital conceptual ideas for *To Be at Home* follow. Prabhu Mohapatra and Alf Lüdtke offer insights from their own research sites and beyond to help weave the threads of our book's conversations together. Mohapatra draws connections between houses, homes, work, and the life course to reflect on precariousness and personhood from comparative and global historical perspectives. He suggests that relations between house, work, and the self are only just beginning to be taken seriously by historians and social scientists. Alf Lüdtke cautiously considers the place and role of photography in writing the history of everyday life (*Alltagsgeschichte*). Reminding us that written sources will always be limited in reaching a full understanding of social practice – workers' expressions, gestures, and poses, for example, are hardly documented in archival material, and are even often absent from workers' own narratives – Lüdtke suggests a more prominent and critical place for photography in historical research. For example, he argues that visual records may help us move beyond the dominant historical discourse on institutions, economic structures, hierarchies, and production, and show instead workers' pursuits of happiness that gives impetus to their work.

Laurent Fourchard provides a closing accompanying piece to both our book and to Mamphela Ramphele's foreword by considering the continued relevance of *A Bed Called Home: Life in the Migrant Labour Hostels of Cape Town* twenty-five years since its original publication.

Section 1
Homes and Mobility: Borders, Boundaries, Thresholds

Heike Drotbohm
Shoes Painfully Small: Material and Maternal (Dis)comfort in Cape Verdean Remittance Houses

Emilia (17), Luisa (14), and Edilson (9) live with their grandparents in one of the best houses in São Filipe. I met the three children while carrying out anthropological fieldwork on the island of Fogo, Cape Verde, in 2007 and 2008. Their house had been built by their mother, Susana, who has been living in Dorchester, close to Boston, in the United States since 2001. The extravagant two-story building looked exactly how most Cape Verdean transmigrants – migrants who live their social lives between their country of origin and country of destination – would describe *uma casa bonita*, a beautiful house. It was painted in pastel colors and metal fences surrounded the front lawns, with a gate allowing entry only for certain neighbors. There was a garage and a satellite dish on the roof. It was equipped with air conditioning, large leather suites, and a flat-screen TV. The kitchen had a modern stove and various cooking utensils. And despite Cape Verde's chronic water shortage, the house had three bathrooms, all with several sinks and bathtubs. "Just like she has it in Dorchester," Luisa commented when she showed me around, hinting proudly at her mother's achievements abroad.

In the anthropological literature on transnational migration, 'remittance houses,' i.e. houses built with money remitted by migrants living abroad, are considered important for understanding how family members dispersed across several countries or continents create a sense of togetherness, belonging, and intimacy despite physical separation. A *kasa d'emigrant*, as such houses are called in the Cape Verdean creole language, is understood as a tangible link that connects migrants' lives in their country of destination to their country of origin and thus as markers of identity and stability. By investing materially in their countries or communities of origin, migrants manage to affirm their responsibility and co-presence.[1]

During my fieldwork, which began on the Cape Verdean islands and extended to family members living in various locations as part of the Cape Verdean diaspora, I read this acceptance of obligations – through the building of remittance houses – as an act of care to complement other modes of transnational support, such as remittances, gifts, phone calls, or visits. As Leah Schmalzbauer has shown regarding transnational Honduran families, parents living abroad often try to improve the socioeconomic status of their children remaining behind by concentrating on status-relevant investments, in addition to covering their basic needs such as health and education.[2] At the same time, however, the material comfort flowing from the diaspora back to the country of origin is accompanied by differences and divisions that are likewise part of cross-border family lives. This essay concentrates on the '(dis)comforts' of remittance houses. I refer here to a term introduced by Daniel Miller, who used the objects assembled in households to reflect on the 'comfort of things' – the expectations, accomplishments, and frustrations of the inhabitants of a

---

1 Paulo Boccagni, "What's in a (Migrant) House? Changing Domestic Spaces, the Negotiation of Belonging and Home-Making in Ecuadorian Migration," *Housing, Theory and Society* 31 (2013): 277–93; Iris Levin and Ruth Fincher, "Tangible Transnational Links in the Houses of Italian Immigrants in Melbourne," *Global Networks* 10 (2010): 401–23.
2 Leah Schmalzbauer, "Family Divided: The Class Formation of Honduran Transnational Families," *Global Networks* 8 (2008): 329–46.

single street in London.[3] Complementing these theoretical premises, I argue that things not only comfort, but also discomfort, when they gloss over the misunderstandings and misrepresentations that are part and parcel of lives extending across national borders.

The Challenges of Leaving and Remaining Close

Susana had left her children and parents, like so many other Cape Verdean women before her, at a moment when she did not have much of a choice. Since the 1970s, which marked a new phase in the history of Cape Verdean migration, Cape Verdean women have increasingly begun to find employment abroad as nannies, housekeepers, and cleaners, but also in the health and elderly care sectors. Comparable to many other societies in the Global South, the so-called feminization of migration saw thousands of women travel to the United States, Canada, Europe, Australia, and wealthy Asian countries to find gainful employment in order to support family members left behind in their countries of origin. According to Arlie Hochschild, who introduced the critical notion of 'global care chains,' the exodus of women from the Global South is accompanied by a shortage of women to perform the same duties for their own families back in their countries of origin.[4] In Cape Verde, the absence of women in the middle generation follows the same migration pattern of their male compatriots, who have been migrating from Cape Verde to the United States since the nineteenth century to work as whalers, cranberry pickers, or in the garment industry. Cape Verdean women are likewise considered reliable, diligent, and sociable workers, who make a valued contribution to closing the care gaps generated by the increasing withdrawal of the state from North American or European welfare programs.[5]

When an opportunity arose at the end of 2000, Susana had to react. The father of her first two children had died in a car accident, the second had left her immediately after Edilson's birth, and she had to move back into her parents' house. When a cousin, who had been living in Boston for some years, found her a job, the pressure was unbearable. Everybody in their crammed little stone house knew that they would all profit from Susana's emigration and she could not ignore their expectations and excitement. She decided to apply for a tourist visa and leave her three children with her parents, where they would, she was sure, be taken good care of.

The very first weeks after Susana's departure were very difficult, her children and their grandparents told me. She called every day on the phone to talk to each of them. She checked whether everything was alright, asked about school, their friends, and health, and tried not to cry too much. She told them it wouldn't be for long. For the children, though they remained in their familiar environment, it was also a big change. The two girls in particular had to take over many household duties in addition to their schoolwork. However, merely weeks after her departure, Susana began to organize their material improvement, which started with the house.

---

3 Daniel Miller, *The Comfort of Things* (Cambridge: Polity, 2008).
4 Arlie R. Hochschild, "Global Care Chains and Emotional Surplus Value," in Will Hutton and Anthony Giddens, eds., *On the Edge: Living with Global Capitalism* (London: Jonathan Cape, 2000): 130–46; Nicola Yeates, "Global Care Chains: A State-of-the-Art Review and Future Directions in Care Transnationalization Research," *Global Networks* 12 (2004): 135–54.
5 Marzia Grassi and Iolanda Évora, eds., *Género e Migraçãos Cabo-Verdianas* (Lisbon: Imprensa de Ciências Sociais, 2007).

In a social setting shaped by constant mobility, departure, absence, and the hope for someone's return, a house built by those who managed to leave the islands, live successful lives abroad, and reinvest into their country and community of origin has always received attention and appreciation. The caring aspect of houses goes far beyond the mere act of providing a living space. Since most migrants live abroad during the building phase, they have to collaborate and communicate with the others who are present. They need to cooperate with construction contractors and middlemen, negotiating costs and supervizing their working hours, and possibly also bribing local officials for the necessary permissions.

Within months of her departure, Susana and her father had identified an ideal plot of land close to the village center. She contacted the owners, organized the acquisition through a local notary, and contracted the construction workers. She saved the respective sum over the summer, and then they started to lay the foundations. The ground floor was finished within a few months. In their weekly phone calls, Susana discussed every decision with her parents, including the materials to be purchased and the conflicts to be solved. By early 2002, immediately after the basic interior works were finished, her family was able to move from the little stone house up in the hills into this modern, fancy house close to the main road.

Coping with Unforeseen Contingencies

When I met them in 2008, Susana's children appeared to be doing very well. Their mother's financial and material investment in their education had enabled them to continue at secondary school during the years of her absence. Emilia, the eldest, attended the only private high school in town, where she took classes in business administration. The younger two were ambitious high school students; Luisa was part of a theater group and Edilson played for the school soccer team. Thanks to a steady stream of money from the United States, they had been able to adopt a lifestyle that differentiated them from their poorer peers, many of whom had no family connections to the diaspora.

Often the two girls talked about their future plans, which were fixated entirely on emigration. Emilia wanted to continue her studies and work in a bank, and Luisa planned to study medicine at a top American university. Although they had never left their home island, the transnational flow of money, information, and ideas had stimulated a precise imagination of a life abroad. Contrary to his two older sisters, however, Edilson did not yet harbor any professional ambitions, which can be considered typical of a boy of his age. In one of our talks, he told me that he liked his life on Fogo island and that he would rather stay where he was. Edilson felt particularly close to his grandmother, Maria, with whom he had developed a relationship akin to mother and son, as often happens in constellations of transnational child fosterage.[6] Unlike his sisters, he hardly remembered his mother and did not feel particularly attracted by promises of an unknown life abroad.

During their mother's absence, each child had developed their own ideas and visions. They also had doubts and fears, which they did not discuss openly. A longer interview with their grand-

---

6 Heike Drotbohm, "The Promises of Co-Mothering and the Perils of Detachment: A Comparison of Local and Transnational Cape Verdean Child Fosterage," in Erdmute Alber, Jeannett Martin, and Catrien Notermans, eds., *Child Fosterage in West Africa: New Perspectives on Theories and Practices* (Leiden: Brill, 2013): 217–45; Heike Drotbohm, "Horizons of Long-Distance Intimacies: Reciprocity, Contribution and Disjuncture in Cape Verde," *The History of the Family: An International Quarterly* 14 (2009): 132–49.

mother, Maria, revealed the bumpier side of their transnational family life, which the children seemed to find harder to expose:

> We all thought this would go faster. I am not young anymore. I have already raised my kids, now I am a mother again. Susana said she would take them to the US as fast as she could, but this is so complicated! She already has a nice house in America, and she earns well, everything is well prepared. But apparently doing the papers is still very complicated ... She never managed to come for a visit. This was very hard, especially for the little one. And in the meantime, the kids fear that their mother could forget about them. She has a new child now; did they tell you? This [she points at a picture of a little baby] is Junior, the last one, he was born a bit more than a year ago. So, she was not able to work for a certain while, I guess she even lost her job. This complicated everything.

Indeed, the three children had not mentioned their little brother, whose picture on the living-room shelf had always gone without comment. As migrants can only sponsor remaining family members once their economic and legal situation in the host state is properly established, postponed visits and unintended delays in the bureaucracy of family reunification are routine occurrences that transnational families have to bear. Interestingly, children left behind are usually well aware of the risks and contingencies associated with their desire to be reunited with their parents or other family members living abroad. While they may be confident and optimistic just after their parent's departure, many develop fears and frustrations over the course of a prolonged separation. Edilson, who always, and sometimes even stubbornly, refers to the island of Fogo when discussing his own future, provides an exemplary case. Teenagers in particular tend to hide their vulnerability and their disappointment behind layers of distance and protest. There are several cases of such children referring to their foster mother as 'mother' and calling their migrant mother by her given name as a way of expressing their psychological wounds.

Evidently, the birth of a new sibling – in this case the child of their mother's still-unknown new partner – complicated the trust felt by the three siblings in their transnational family arrangements.

Concealing Inconsistencies

In late 2008, I decided to travel to Boston to include the perspective of the family members who had been physically absent in Cape Verde during my research and whom I had not yet met in person. When I called Susana's number in São Filipe and asked her about potential addresses for accommodation in the Cape Verdean neighborhoods in the Boston area, she immediately invited me to stay at her place. When we sat at her kitchen table and talked about *a vida nas ilhas*, life on the islands, it became clear that Susana's reality in the United States differed considerably from the success story that her loved-ones imagined back on the islands.

Just like her partner, also a Cape Verdean migrant, Susana was working double shifts in two food factories in Dorchester United States. It was difficult for her to talk about the years that had passed since she left Fogo. At the beginning, she said, she had been optimistic, but then all types of problems arose. She had taken out a loan to finance not only her life in the US, but also the construction of her family's house in Cape Verde. With the housing and banking crisis that began in 2007, it became nearly impossible to cover the mortgage repayments. After losing her previous job in the elderly care sector, she had to move into a smaller apartment in Dorchester. Of course she missed her three children a lot, but she also considered them to be in a good, safe, 'traditional' environment where they would be protected. Many of the Cape Verdean diaspora struggle with precarious living conditions in neighborhoods shaped by gang and police violence, and tend to romanticize their lives back on the Cape Verdean islands, where children can grow up within a larger, caring island community. For Susana, it turned out to be a much more complicated and lengthier process than she expected to legalize her stay. It was only through her recently born child that she was able to obtain full US citizenship and file a petition for family reunification with her other three children.

Susana's trajectory, including the complications she faced in legalizing her stay and the unintended family reunification delay, is typical of migrants who are neither fully undocumented nor documented, but often straddle both statuses by means of a series of temporary permits spanning more than a decade. Evidently, these legal constraints and bureaucratic complications have severe consequences for their parenting capacity.[7] Those left behind have to cope with unclear decisions, unforeseen, long-term, and sometimes even indefinite separation, and a general lack of information, which obviously also has an effect on their emotional attachment.[8]

During the months and years of separation, Susana had filled her small apartment with memories, such as family pictures, traditionally embroidered tablecloths and bedspreads, and paintings of the Cape Verdean islands, its little villages, and the Atlantic ocean. She cooked with Cape Verdean spices and took her coffee with typical *bulaxas* biscuits, bathing in the memories of home. Besides this, she focused her material investments entirely on her family life in Cape Verde. At least three times a week she went shopping and looked out for 'something special,' as she put it, to send back to Cape Verde.

One day, she was sitting in her kitchen trying to organize the several pairs of sneakers, DVDs, bed linen, and cosmetics she had bought to send off to the islands. She told me that she had just come from the service center which was helping her file the petition to bring her children over. Again, one document was missing, and it was still unclear how she would be able to support the final costs. She also needed to help her mother apply for passports and visas as well as organize the interviews in the American embassy in Praia, the capital of Cape Verde. "We're almost there," she said firmly. Susana allowed herself to feed the optimism that had carried her through the last six years, while continuing to mourn the lost time.

I did not comment that the sneakers she was about to put into the huge plastic box were far too small for Edilson. Susana caught my eye. "I remember well how fast he was," she said shyly, "I was hardly able to catch him ... I am so proud of him." I sensed her embarrassment about the obvious loss of tacit intimacy. In this peculiar moment, we were both aware of the enormous gap that this unintentional period of separation had produced between her and her children, as well as her growing inability to accommodate their bodies, sizes, styles, and tastes. I also assume that Edilson and his sisters are very aware of the conflict between their own ideas and desires and their mother's attempt to produce co-presence, and their diverging experiences of prolonged separation.

Concluding Thoughts

While Cape Verdean immigrants are working hard to support their families in the United States as well as back home on the islands, they have become an underprivileged underclass who can hardly

---

7 Cecilia Menjívar, "Transnational Parenting and Immigration Law: Central Americans in the United States," *Journal of Ethnic and Migration Studies* 38 (2012): 301–22.
8 Lisa Åkesson, Heike Drotbohm, and Jørgen Carling, "Mobility, Moralities and Motherhood: Navigating the Contingencies of Cape Verdean Lives," *Journal of Ethnic and Migration Studies* 38 (2012): 237–60.

afford to make ends meet. Susana, who economizes on her own existence every day, constructed an oversized house in Cape Verde to transmit a sense of security as compensation for her physical absence. Evidently, the process of building and maintaining a house is to be valued as a means of demonstrating her vital co-presence and remaining socially involved. Especially for children, this material continuity demonstrates reliability and connectedness on a sensual and aesthetic level, which they need in order to make sense of their particular situation, especially during uncertain times.

The stability and abundance of transmigrants' houses give the impression of success – and have played a key role in the production of a new middle-class identity in Cape Verde. But it would be an oversimplification to see 'remittance houses' simply as part of an uninterrupted border-crossing space or as an economic investment that serves to close the gap between 'here' and 'there.' Rather, these houses gloss over the legal instability facing migrants and the vulnerability of an everyday life juggled within and between several places. They are also part of a middle-class identity produced in the country of origin that does not correspond to the migrants' reality in the country of destination. 'Remittance houses' thus raise expectations among the family members left behind, who try to envision a future in an unknown place. In the case of the two girls, it led them to project their future onto an unknown and as yet inaccessible place abroad, which will certainly fail to meet their expectations. This is particularly true of the requirements for a professional career, which many young people going abroad tend to underestimate. The incongruity between their plans and the reality they will face can also be explained by the asymmetric character of transnational communication, in that migrants living abroad try to paint a positive image and omit the hardships of a life overseas.

The quality of Susana's island house that is produced through her long-distance care also conceals the emotional sacrifices that migrants and their relatives have to endure. When Edilson receives the huge box of gifts, he may understand the love his mother felt when she chose and wrapped them carefully. However, the shoes he receives, painfully small, may also bring into sharp relief the conflict between the assumed and the real, between himself and the inappropriate gift sent by a mother whom he hardly remembers.

Eric Allina
Hostel, Home, and 'Life-Rhythm' for African Workers behind the Berlin Wall

With adventure on his mind, eighteen-year-old Nestor Matusse (a pseudonym) left Mozambique for East Germany in 1987. Never having been away from home before, he was determined to learn something of the world and of other people. Nearly thirty years later, as we sat in the garden of the German cultural center in Maputo, the Mozambican capital, Nestor described his life in Orschatz, a small German town midway between Leipzig and Dresden, where he had been sent to train and work at a fiberglass plant. Nestor recalled to me how he spent his free time: having bought a bicycle with savings from his salary, he took long weekend rides out of town. "Riding my bicycle, passing through the woods and over the hills, I could feel almost like a German," he remarked. Nestor felt most at ease while alone, away from the rhythm of the factory and the workers' hostel, a reality somewhat at odds with a cooperation agreement based on solidarity and the Eastern bloc's espousal of a "friendship of peoples" that had brought him there.

Nestor and the 20,000 or so other Mozambicans who traveled to East Germany (the German Democratic Republic, or GDR) between 1979 and 1989 were chosen chiefly for their youth. The agreement between the two states that brought young Mozambicans to Germany on four-year contracts to train as industrial workers was conceived as an investment in the future for both nations, with younger people – those selected were between seventeen and twenty-five years old – imagined to provide the greatest return. The training program provided the GDR with an infusion of much-needed low-cost labor and a chance to prove itself as a friend to states in the Global South within the socialist bloc.

For Mozambique, newly independent from Portuguese colonial rule in 1975 and aiming to put what the country's first president called "colonialism's heritage of misery" behind it, sending young people to East Germany was a step toward building a new nation.[9] The new African-led government had the population at large in mind, rather than only a white minority. Above all, the benefits of "modernity" – higher education, technical knowledge, and improved living standards – were to be brought to "the people." Young Mozambicans viewed the trainee-worker program as an opportunity to gain valuable skills and knowledge, the likes of which had long been denied to Africans during the century or so of white rule.

Leaving home and traveling for work far away was a familiar life experience for Mozambican youth. In Mozambique and elsewhere throughout southern Africa, long-distance labor migration was a well-established step taken by young men on the cusp of adulthood. Engaging in labor migration was part of a process of establishing physical and symbolic distance from their parents. The separation from home life and the workplace encounter with new forms of social and cultural interaction were vital mechanisms that helped them develop a distinct identity and shed their dependent status. Migration offered opportunities for an income and education, both less plentiful at home. Emerging out from under the shelter of the family unit and acquiring the capac-

---

9 See Maria-Benedita Basto, "The Writings of the National Anthem in Independent Mozambique: Fictions of the Subject-People," *Kronos* 39 (2013): 185–203; Margaret Hall and Tom Young, "'Anything Seemed Possible': The Transition to Independence," in Margaret Hall and Tom Young, *Confronting Leviathan: Mozambique since Independence* (Athens: Ohio University Press, 1997).

ity to provide for themselves and others, they became adults. That these young Mozambicans were on the verge of taking such a step was not something that figured in government officials' planning, extensive though it was. Nor did they imagine the ways in which these young Africans would become adults behind the Iron Curtain.

Home | Island

Recruited from throughout Mozambique, Mozambican migrants worked in enterprises all over the GDR, from fisheries on the North Sea to textile plants on the Czechoslovakian border. The majority worked in a wedge of territory extending east and southwest of East Germany's divided capital. After completing four-year contracts in German factories, living amid 'real existing socialism,' they would return home to put their skills and knowledge to work for the collective good: to build industry, advance the principles of scientific socialism, and continue the revolutionary transformation of society. Their German sojourn brought both challenges and opportunities. As well as coping with cold and dark winters, life in East Germany meant managing sometimes strange cultural norms, living in highly homogeneous communities not always welcoming to foreigners, and enduring an extended separation from family. But it gave these migrants a degree of freedom too: independence from one's elders, a chance to enjoy the adventures of a strange land and make new relationships, and the autonomy associated with a steady income.[10]

On arrival in East Germany, the worker-trainees had six months of intensive language instruction and technical training. Most had no experience of living away from family or managing the minutiae of domestic life on their own. A strong gender-based division of domestic labor in Mozambique meant that the young women, perhaps ten to fifteen percent of some groups, had some familiarity with household work, but the autonomy of life in Germany was something new. The German staff at the workers' residence taught them how to plan, prepare, and cook their own meals. As Nestor put it, "They taught us how to live." Yet as much as such training aimed to give them the knowledge and skills to navigate life in Germany, strict controls ensured it was a life with limits – above all in the workers' hostel, their home away from home. With a chronic and acute housing shortage in East Germany, many enterprises struggled to provide adequate conditions for the foreign workers eagerly sought by production staff. In some instances, administrators raced to renovate badly dilapidated buildings in time to receive the workers who would live there. Ministry officials enforced minimum housing standards. If a hostel might be a home, it certainly did not offer all of its comforts.

The migrants' hostels were typically two or three-story buildings (though in Berlin, higher-rise hostels were common), where worker-trainees lived two or three to a room with shared cooking, washing, and recreational facilities. Access was strictly controlled: the entrance was staffed around the clock and residents were required to sign themselves in and out. Visitors were permitted only with advance notice and were restricted to common areas. Overnight stays were prohibited, as were unauthorized stays outside the hostel for residents. The effect was to isolate the African workers, unsurprising in a state whose capital was emblematic of Cold War separation. That one group of

---

10 See Eric Allina, "'Neue Menschen' für Mosambik: Erwartungen an und Realität von Vertragsarbeit in der DDR der 1980er-Jahre," *Arbeit-Bewegung-Geschichte: Zeitschrift für Historische Studien* 15 (2016): 65–84; Eric Allina, "Between *Sozialismus* and *Socialismo*: African Workers and Public Authority in the German Democratic Republic," in Mahua Sarkar, ed., *Work out of Place* (Berlin: De Gruyter, 2017): 77–100; Marcia Schenck, "From Luanda and Maputo to Berlin: Uncovering Angolan and Mozambican Migrants' Motives to move to the German Democratic Republic (1979–90)," *African Economic History* 44 (2016): 202–34; Birgit Weyhe, *Madgermanes* (Berlin: Avant-Verlag, 2016).

sixty-seven Mozambicans working in a paper mill near Karl-Marx-Stadt (today Chemnitz) lived in a hostel called "Island" struck no ironic note for the mill managers. With its communal character and unconcealed surveillance, the hostel produced a peculiar intimacy that was far from home-like. Making a home in a conventional sense was all but out of reach for most Mozambicans.

Notwithstanding these rigid protocols, however, some of the young worker-trainees found ways to circumvent these rules and, as the manager of a railyard explained, challenge what he referred to as the "discipline and good order" of the hostel. There were sometimes "disturbances of the night's rest" involving loud music, fisticuffs, or other hullabaloo little appreciated by those due at work on the early shift. Regulations "were not always respected." Some workers left the residence for the evening and returned only in the morning. "All come and go as they see fit," he lamented.

"Good contact"

The friendship and socialist solidarity that drove the cooperation between East Germany and Mozambique were, at least in principle, meant to promote close relationships. However, the regulation of worker-trainees' hostel life reflected the East German state's suspicious stance toward foreigners and general desire to keep them separate from German citizens. Authorities frowned upon close degrees of intimacy between Germans and Africans, but the extensive controls on and surveillance of workers' movements were not always effective in maintaining their separation.

If some Mozambicans, like Nestor, found the quiet of the countryside a place to be at home, others made that connection in the company of others, in closer quarters, and at least nominally outside the boundaries established by the state. The young workers eluded official efforts to control their movements around the factory and residence, engaging in unauthorized activities that were both a means and an end. Some outings made for self-evident good fun, satisfying and enjoyable in themselves: Mozambicans went out in the evenings to clubs or pubs, where they socialized with young Germans and drank and danced far past the residence curfew, returning only in time to show up for a morning shift. By spending time in bars and clubs, they found spaces that were less closely monitored by the state, where they could establish relationships, especially with other young people – African and German – of their own choosing.

Beyond being entertaining as such, these evenings also were the basis on which the young women and men could establish close, lasting friendships and intimate relations. Such "good contact," as one German factory administrator blandly referred to the fact that two African workers had founded their own families, complete with Afro-German children, was the foundation on which some of the migrants could ground themselves firmly in East Germany. Notwithstanding the requirement that they live in the workers' residence, some lived largely with their German partners, with whom they had children and created family homes. These arrangements were forbidden, but were nonetheless often tolerated by factory and government officials, perhaps because these individuals tended to be content, socially stable, and perform well at work. Analogous to Nestor, though in a different manner, they found a way to feel at home away from the hostel.

So it was with Rafael Medeiros, who, having returned to Mozambique at the end of his contract in August 1985, sought to return to the small German city where he had lived for four years, where he had "felt at ease" and made many friends. He very much wanted to rejoin his German girlfriend, with whom he had a son, now two years old. "Please allow me to return to the GDR," Rafael wrote in a letter sent from Maputo to the local office of the Ministry of Wages and Labour in Erfurt. He noted that the German Postal Service had agreed to hire him. Indicating his familiarity with the political economy of the labor market, he said he was willing to take shift work, which was disliked and avoided by those who had a choice. He also pointed out that he would not require housing, because he could live with his girlfriend, even providing her street address. This may have been the strongest factor in Rafael's favor, given the housing shortage. That he had already made a German home for himself meant that the authorities would not be burdened with securing him one.

Homeward-bound?

Numbers are elusive, but enough of the young workers remained in unified Germany to motivate Mozambican politicians to travel there in 2014 to campaign for their now-middle-aged votes. By some estimates, perhaps exaggerated, some 8,000 children of German-Mozambican relationships live in Germany. The fall of the Berlin Wall and the authoritarian 'People's State' that had built it gave way to more open expressions of racial hostility, including sometimes spectacular violence against foreign workers whose skin color marked them plainly as 'other.' The shock of such violence has clouded the post-*Wende* vision of just how hostile GDR society was, where racial hostility with its veneer of anti-racist socialist solidarity was only unevenly and episodically expressed. Mozambican youth usually shrugged it off as the alcohol-fueled indiscipline of their German counterparts or the latent discomfort of an older generation less ready to embrace a wider world. After all, for most of the twentieth century, their home country had been wedged in by white minority regimes whose notions of white supremacy had few peers. For young African worker-trainees, never meant to have a long-term place in German society, the greater obstacle was an institutional context that worked powerfully to keep them in motion and prevent settling into any space that might feel like home.

There was little appreciation for other meanings of youth – neither its potential as a launch pad for political change nor its rebellious tendencies, let alone its intractable movement into adulthood. To the extent that officials recognized that latent energy, they aimed to keep it tethered to socialist production and safely under state tutelage. Still more, there was scant attention to the social and cultural significance of an extended stay abroad at their stage of life. Reflecting on the challenges the young workers faced, one GDR labor ministry official noted the "wholly different life rhythm" they encountered in Germany. The officials who negotiated and managed the agreement that governed their lives recognized that the young Africans would need support in the totally new environment. Yet socialist planners gave little thought to how the trainees might create their own support, or to the ways in which they might seek to establish themselves as newly independent adults. Above all, planners were blind to the prospect that the hostel might be not only a site of production, but also reproduction.

For young Mozambicans who reached this point in their life rhythm, leaving home far behind for work was fundamental to engaging in reproduction – acquiring the resources necessary to establish adult independence and have children, inseparable from conventional meanings of home. In this sense, an East German hostel could never be a home, and making it into one was far from what any imagined for the young trainees from southeast Africa. German officials refused to contemplate what it would take to accommodate a family. Mozambicans' time in Germany was meant to be a moment in between an insignificant past and a portentous future, not an alternative path toward the future.

Little wonder then that soon after his return to Mozambique, Nestor left home once again, illegally entering South Africa in hope of finding work and the wealth he needed to prosper as an independent adult. His effort was unsuccessful. Caught by a border guard who, on paging through his passport, saw the German entry and exit stamps, Nestor found himself explaining how Germany had once, almost, been home.

James Williams
Kinship and Displacement in Post-War Liberia: Children's Lives in an IDP Camp

The displacement of individuals and families during and since the civil wars in Liberia (1989–2003) encompasses a terrain of experiences shared by many children and adults: journeys between villages, forests, and urban centers, flights to neighboring countries as refugees, and pauses and waiting in camps for internally displaced persons (IDPs).

This essay describes some of the ways Liberian children's lives and homes are organized in IDP camps. It looks particularly at how large family networks divide up and organize themselves into discrete camp households spread intentionally across several different camps (often many miles apart). It also describes inter-household strategies that Liberian families have adopted that allow for a continuity of resources over time and an availability of persons to fulfil important tasks.

I want to show how these family groups manage to make homes 'work' in the context of a displaced person camp, under conditions of insecurity and extreme impoverishment and in the face of the suspicion and restrictive rules of UN and humanitarian agencies. In this regard, my ethnography contrasts with other anthropological accounts of migrant and refugee families that frame kinship relations as dysfunctional or as having broken down under such conditions, and blanket descriptions of camps as sites of bare life and survival struggles.[11]

Context and Methods

My analysis draws from fieldwork conducted in three IDP camps in Monrovia between May and August 2004. At this time, 400,000 Liberians (approximately twenty-five percent of the population) were residing in ninety-seven displaced person camps, most of which were located close to the capital. The UNHCR estimated that the total displaced camp population comprised some 80,000 households. Though many Liberians had stayed in displaced person and refugee camps numerous times since the start of the war, the majority of this population had arrived in Monrovia during its final stages and in the months following ceasefire, between June and October 2003. The end of the war was marked by the signing of peace agreements between the government of Liberia, political parties, and armed opposition groups, and followed the departure of Charles Taylor to Nigeria. Shortly after this, in September 2003, a United Nations Mission to Liberia (UNMIL) was deployed with the mandate to disarm combatants, facilitate humanitarian operations, and establish a transitional government. The scale of international efforts reflected urgent stakes in Liberia as a central instigator in the destabilization of West Africa.

---

11 There is a growing literature on refugee camps and the patterns of sociality that emerge within them. See Lisa H. Malkki, *Purity and Exile: Violence, Memory, and National Cosmology among Hutu Refugees in Tanzania* (Chicago: University of Chicago Press, 1995); Jennifer Hyndman, *Managing Displacement: Refugees and the Politics of Humanitarianism* (Minneapolis: University of Minnesota Press, 2000). On refugee camps as new geographies of resource extraction and forms of governmentality, see Achille Mbembe, "At the Edge of the World: Boundaries, Territoriality, and Sovereignty in Africa," *Public Culture* 12 (2000): 259–84.

During my fieldwork, I worked in three IDP camps. The camp where I spent most of my time was one of the largest IDP camps in Liberia (36,000 residents), located near the capital. This camp had been a refugee camp for Sierra Leoneans in the early 1990s, later a displaced person camp for Liberians, next a returnee camp for Liberians from Guinea and Sierra Leone during Taylor's early years, and had been re-established as a displaced person camp in early 2003. Sustained residency by large populations over this time period had depleted local resources and now required residents to walk for over ten kilometers to collect wood for fire and shelters. The camp was sprawling with traders and markets and many occupants sold food items or bulk-bought goods (batteries, drugs, shoes) from their porches. Poro and Sande groups were operating there and there were traditional healers in residence offering circumcisions for boys and girls. It housed two schools, three churches, and a mosque. Nigerian UNMIL soldiers policed its main entrance, though, as with all displaced camps, there were no fences or guarded checkpoints restricting people's movements.

I worked with eleven families in total, taking an individual child as the center of a camp household and moving outward to chart their wider kin and social networks. The largest of these networks was a Gola family, which comprised over sixty people spread across four camps (presented below). The smallest was a Vai youth who lived alone, whose seven-month daughter, born in his camp, lived with her Kissi mother and grandmother three shelters away. I met with family members together and with the children separately during my days in the camps. I participated in household tasks as we talked (cooking, dressing and washing children, preparing meals). The children were keen to take me on tours of their camps and its environs, and though I hoped my presence would not disrupt their routines and prevent them from fulfilling their domestic tasks, our meetings often allowed the children to leave their shelters for substantial periods of time. I accompanied a child to a camp clinic when another adult was busy and supervised younger children if their guardians needed to be elsewhere.[12]

Kinship by Family and Residency

All of the children I worked with lived with other people, and most were related as kin. I learned the composition of these camp households (by which I refer to the mud and stick camp shelters where children and adults lived, as well as where they are registered as official dwellers) and the wider family networks they were part of.

My use of 'household' here in some ways mirrors the definition used by humanitarian agencies, who term 'household' a place where a group of people sleep and share meals (though humanitarian groups also take the household as a given structure and equate its membership with family). Households should also be seen as constructions of camp governance. When families arrive at the camp to seek residency, the camp manager allocates a plot of land to a group of people to build a shelter. This is when personal information is recorded (names, sexes, ages) and non-food items are distributed (blankets, cooking equipment, plastic sheeting for a roof). Population records are passed to the World Food Program (WFP) for the allocation of food rations. Camp residents

---

12 Deepak Mehta and Roma Chatterji's use of "walking narratives" proved salient in my fieldwork. See Deepak Mehta and Roma Chatterji, "Boundaries, Names, Alterities: A Case Study of a 'Communal Riot' in Dharavi, Bombay," in Veena Das, Arthur Kleinman, Margaret Lock, Mamphela Ramphele, and Pamela Reynolds, eds., *Remaking a World: Violence, Social Suffering, and Recovery* (Berkeley: University of California Press, 2001): 201–49.

meanwhile collected their own records of household residency through camp committees, which enabled residents to mediate with the management and the WFP over food ration discrepancies.

The recording of population numbers, specifically household membership, was one of the most visible concerns of the WFP because they saw the displaced camp population as fluid. People, officials complained to me, "moved constantly" between camps to eat and sleep in other shelters at regular intervals. As there were no identity documents held by displaced people in Liberia other than a WFP card given to the mother of a family (describing the number of adults by age and sex within a shelter, and the number of children by age), it was not uncommon for individuals to be faced with "food cuts" if residents within a shelter were considered impermanent. Disputes over rations and residency rested almost entirely on how an individual presented their case to officials and were very hard to negotiate. In late June in the camp, for example, 33,579 people were recorded on WFP records as residents and only this number of food rations was allocated for distribution that month. Resident committees claimed the population was over 36,000 and that the WFP records were incorrect, and that at least 2,100 people had not received rations during the June distributions because their status as residents was considered "illegitimate" by WFP staff. Agencies claimed that their actions were justified because of the clandestine checks they undertook in the camps – sending staff to svisit shelters outside of food distribution days, asking residents to account for who lived there, and checking numbers by counting bodies. Ensuing protests were met with claims by the WFP and camp management that the extra persons had been deleted from their records because they were claiming food rations in multiple camps. Tensions became violent in early July and UN agencies were called in to mediate. During these discussions, camp residents also pointed to an absurdity within WFP's recording system. As Liberia's rainy season had begun by this time (which would last for seven months), shelters in the camp were collapsing rapidly, and the WFP's policy of giving rations only to individuals with shelters left many IDPs without food, who would have to stay with relatives while their shelters were rebuilt.

The children helped me to understand how these heated confusions over residency came about and how defining households solely as 'shelters' obscures important details. I take the residency of one household here as an example to show how formulations of kinship by household and family intertwine.

James' family had come to Monrovia from their village in the diamond-mining forests in the northwest and had relatives in four camps in the area. James' shelter had two rooms: one for James, his younger sister, and his mother and father, and one for his mothers' friend who had worked for James' mother's parents back home, his mother's sister, Elizabeth (who spent half her time between James' shelter and the shelter where her brother's three sons lived), and Elizabeth's daughter, Miatta. I present these relationships in two ways: Figure 1 shows James' family by relationships of kinship, detailing marriages, parentage, and siblingship; Figure 2 maps his network by household, by the shelters and camps where kin and others live.

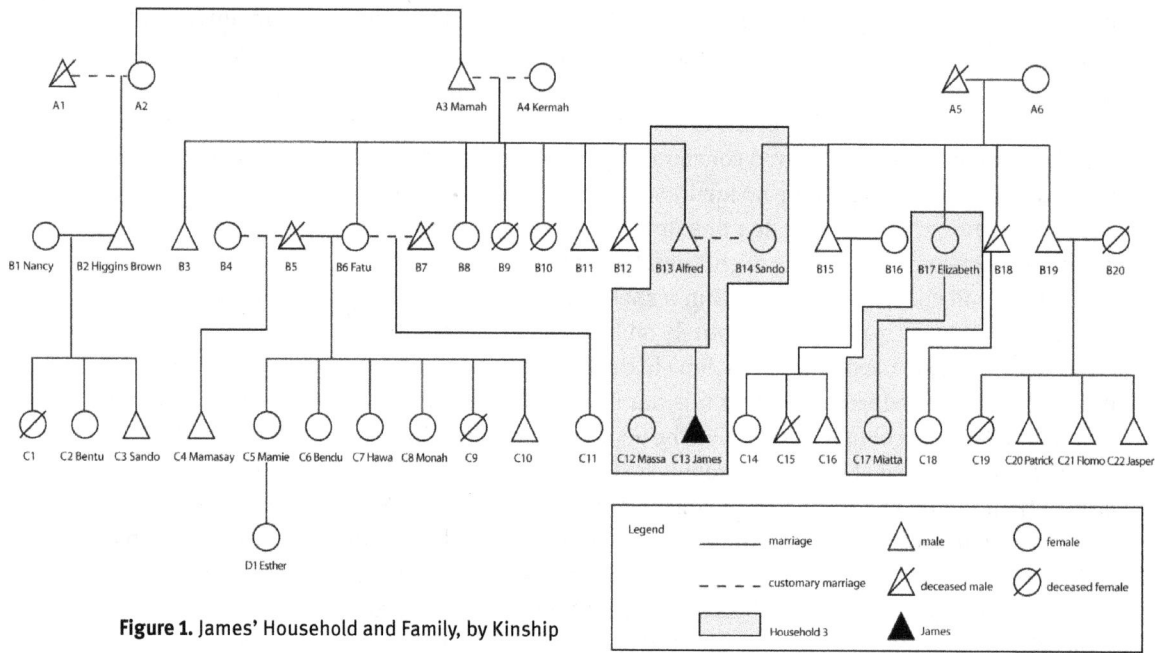

Figure 1. James' Household and Family, by Kinship

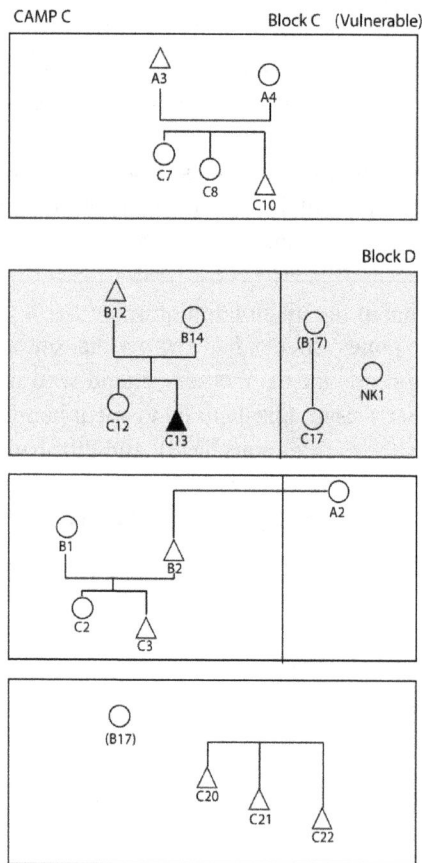

Figure 2. James' Household and Family, by Residency

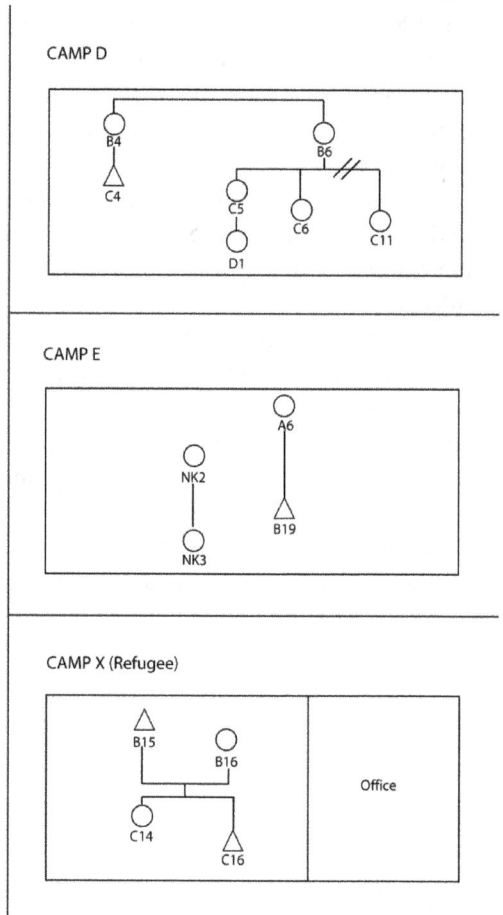

Contrasts between Figures 1 and 2 make explicit distinctions of kinship by family and household and show two ways that people in complex kinship networks in displaced person camps are related.

We might make four points on the distinctions. First, the composition of camp households can be read as lived experiences of war. Camp households include individuals whose parents, children, siblings, or spouses had died during the war or were absent, and incorporated people not related by marriage or parentage.

Second, children are seen and used as one of the most salient and physical markers of 'family.' Their inclusion within a group of adults, however related, tended to lend the household-structure a stronger sense of legitimacy from the perspective of an outside agency. Displaced children constitute a high-risk group for many agencies and are the recipients of the greatest number of humanitarian services in camps. Child protection teams operated in many camps I visited and they based their inventions upon claims that the conditions of life in displaced person camps make children more vulnerable to violence and exploitation within the home. Groups of only older people within a shelter who did not conform to the rigid skeletons of 'family' were subjected to questioning and suspicion, whereas an assortment of individuals that could hold up children as members often gave more weight to claims to being kin-related and, or in other ways, legitimated their need for shared residency.

Third, I observed how families' residency patterns within camps were based on dividing up members of a family network into separate household units (into shelters) – notably children and the elderly – with particular adult individuals kept apart to move between them. The movements of adults contrasted with the fixedness of children and revealed how children of the same parent or parents were sometimes separated into several shelters. James' father's sister's daughters were split between shelters in two camps, while his mother's sister lived for some of her time in James' shelter and at other times with James' mother's brother's sons in another shelter within the same camp; these boys' father lived in another camp with James' grandmother and a non-kin mother and daughter.

Children commonly explained such divisions in terms of the restrictions on a shelter's size by its UNHCR tarpaulin roof. Another way of thinking about these seemingly laborious arrangements lies in seeing each household member as capable of performing particular roles. Strong adults in a family network were distributed between households so that shelters could always be built, rebuilt, and repaired quickly. The movements of elderly women demonstrated their valuable role within the household (preparing food, cleaning, taking care of children and the shelter, escorting children to the clinic), which gave other adults time to perform tasks outside of the camp, such as collecting timber or attending markets in Monrovia. Children themselves were productive in terms of the tasks they could perform, and even a child of three or four years could clean a shelter or keep guard. The notion of what it might mean to be a productive child or adult and the value of ensuring a child has a fixed residency to sustain a wider network introduced me to the ways adult men and women commanded its choreography. It also explained why individuals moved so often as messengers and carriers between households to ensure the network's maintenance.

Fourth, locating people in different households, even over large distances and between several camps, serves the family network's wider need to maintain basic food provisions. Given that food rations are allocated to shelters based on the number of people, and all people (regardless of age) are allocated the same number of items, it was initially confusing as to why networks of kin did not often reside within the same camp, as they could do. A network of households divided across several camps made for long traveling times for family members. Camp management explained these arrangements in terms of individuals and families using residency across camps to maximize resources; as WFP documents do not have photographs or detail the names and sexes of children, children could move from one camp to another on the days food was distributed as a key strategy for accumulating as much food as possible. A discourse of corruption surrounded the families that operated these expansive networks.

In contrast to official explanations, I learned that having family members in a number of camps increased relationships of reciprocity and allowed for resources to be shared in times of need. It was also advantageous for a large family network to have reliable individuals to call upon in another camp because food distribution days were never known with certainty – they were spread out over the IDP camps to fall on different days every month. Household networks strategized amid great uncertainty to incorporate the contingent timings of food distribution, and the utility of many relationships (and an expectation of helping one's kin) allowed for a continuity of resources and food throughout the month, reducing the chances of any single household finding itself without food at any given moment. I observed how children's visits to relatives in other camps to bring back a cup of rice or some fish to their shelter increased significantly during the days before food distribution, when a household's food supply was always at its lowest. As many of these families had lived in displaced person camps several times before, adults within the households explained these arrangements as an important, learned strategy of camp living.

Conclusion

This essay has suggested ways to unpack relationships between children, kinship, and displacement in the daily lives of Liberian children in displaced person camps – by distinguishing between adults and children related as members of families and between those who share or form a household, and by being mindful of family routines (the tasks and roles of individuals critical to maintaining a home in conditions of displacement). It showed how children's residencies, family networks, and daily routines are connected in ways beyond any child or family's control, and thus how the interconnections between all aspects of children's lives are difficult to pull apart.

The repatriation of the displaced population I came to know was scheduled to commence in August 2004, according to the UN, as soon as the disarmament of 70,000 combatants, including 15,000 children, had been completed. Voluntary repatriation was to begin by November 2004. Forced repatriation should have ended by April 2005. By the end of May 2005, however, a population of 250,000 remained in the Monrovian camps.

Alla Bolotova
Making Home in the Industrialized Russian Arctic

Before the Soviet period, the Russian Arctic was scarcely populated, with very few cities. Today, the Russian Arctic is the most industrialized and urbanized polar territory in the world. Numerous industrial towns were built in the Russian Arctic during Soviet industrialization. Their populations comprised voluntary and forced migrants and their descendants. In this essay, I present the family histories of two women who settled as children in newly established towns in the north. They grew up in very different historical periods. My aim is to look at the history of the towns of Kirovsk and Apatity through the life stories of women from different generations. I explore how these women and their families adapted to new places in different historical and social contexts, paying special attention to the beginnings of their life in the north.

This essay is based on ethnographic fieldwork conducted in the Kirovsk-Apatity urban agglomeration in Murmansk Oblast.[13] Kirovsk and Apatity, fifteen kilometers apart, were founded at different stages of Soviet industrialization. Kirovsk started to grow in the 1930s, at the foothills of the Khibiny mountains. Apatity was established in the 1950s in close proximity to Kirovsk. In 2016, there were 26,971 people living in Kirovsk, and 56,730 in Apatity.

Kirovsk: A New Town in the Khibiny Mountains

Industrial development in the Kirovsk-Apatity area started with the discovery of a huge deposit of mineral apatite, which is used in the production of phosphorus fertilizers for agriculture. The deposit was found in an almost-unpopulated area of the Khibiny mountains.[14] The city of Kirovsk was the first large-scale Soviet industrial construction in the Arctic, and its founding was reported proudly in the national and regional press. The city grew extraordinarily quickly. The decision to establish a new city to produce apatite ore was made at the end of 1929. The same year, a railroad connecting Kirovsk with the existing St. Petersburg-Murmansk line was built by Gulag prisoners. Within just six years, by 1935, the population of the new town had reached 44,292.

The population of Kirovsk was very diverse, comprising thirty-two different nationalities. Most were Russians and Ukrainians.[15] Almost half of the population consisted of exiled peasants, so-called *spetspereselentsy* ('special settlers'). They had been forcibly deported from various regions of the USSR under the framework of *dekulakization* ('liquidation of the *kulaks* [affluent peasants] as a class').[16] Other settlers in Kirovsk were specialists and professionals who had come to the region

13 Between 2007 and 2010, I worked in Kirovsk and Apatity on the project "MOVE-INNOCOM" (supported by the Finnish Academy of Sciences, funding decision N118702), and, between 2014 and 2016, on the project "Children of the 1990s in Contemporary Russian Arctic: Assessing the Present and Aspirations for the Future" (funded by the Russian Science Foundation, Grant 14–18–02136). The life stories used for this essay are drawn from a large archive of biographical interviews I collected for these projects.
14 Nomadic tribes of Saami migrated nearby, but there were no permanent settlements in this area.
15 Other nationalities in Kirovsk included Estonians, Belarusians, Germans, Latvians, Tatars, Finns, and Poles. See Viktor Shashkov, *Spetspereselentsy v istorii Murmanskoi oblasti* (Murmansk: Maksimum, 2004).
16 Michael Kaznelson, "Remembering the Soviet State: *Kulak* Children and *Dekulakization*," *Europa-Asia Studies* 59 (2007): 1163–77.

as contract workers. Several Gulag camps were also found in the area; prisoner labor was used in construction sites and mining.

The extraordinarily rapid growth of Kirovsk involved extreme suffering for the first settlers. Builders had to overcome practical difficulties on a very tight schedule. All groups of settlers experienced harsh conditions during the early period of city construction, particularly the special settlers and Gulag prisoners. The special settlers enjoyed relative freedom compared with the prisoners: they were not guarded, they lived with their families, and received salaries. Still, their rights were limited compared with the specialists and contract workers. The settlers had to re-register regularly with the local administration and were not allowed to leave town.

The Life of Special Settlers in the New City

Maria came to Kirovsk as a child of one of the first special settler families. She was born in 1925 in Stavropolsky Krai, in southern Russia. When she was four years old, her family were deported to Khibinogorsk-Kirovsk, a place with a very different climate. All of their belongings were confiscated in the process of *dekulakization*. There were four children in this family, two sisters and two brothers. Initially, the family received a place in one of the huge tents in a small industrial settlement next to the mine:

> There were so many families living in our tent, it was very crowded there. We did not get any allowance, no opportunities, it was very hard to survive, but we did survive.

Soon after arrival, any special settlers who wanted to improve their living conditions were allowed to build wooden shed-barracks during their free time. Maria's father and oldest brother took part in the construction work, which enabled her family to eventually obtain a small room within a barrack.

> We were sleeping on the floor, everywhere. The heating was in the corridor, they were for common use. There were sixteen rooms on the first floor and sixteen rooms on the second floor. Two kitchens and two toilets were on both sides of the corridor.

Later, the families got permission to put stoves in each room, which made it warmer and easier to cook.

Special settlers made up the main workforce on all construction sites in Kirovsk, but they were very poorly qualified. Maria's parents were uneducated peasants from southern Russia, and the Arctic was their first encounter with urban life. Maria's father worked as an unskilled laborer in the mine. Her mother was a street cleaner, which was an important job in Kirovsk because of the extreme amount of snow each winter. Maria's mother earned additional income whitening ceilings in the houses of the specialists. The family used skills from their previous rural life, and whitening houses was a summer tradition in southern Russian villages. All of the children worked from a very young age, earning money for their school uniforms and shoes. They cleaned the rooms after their mother had whitened them, collected dry wood in the forest for heating and selling, and picked and sold berries.

The children felt a great difference between their lives and the lives of the specialists and contract workers in the new town:

We called them *vol'nye* ('free people'). They came and got the best conditions, they even had special food allowances. You know, we help our mum with cleaning after whitening and sometimes they invited us to join them for lunch. And we saw what they had on the table! Batter! And bread! And everything! We did not have this, there was nothing in the shop then.

The family's life changed after 1938 when the settlers gained permission to have a garden and keep cattle. They started to grow potatoes and keep goats and chickens. This combination of rural and urban lifestyles helped the family survive. Their mother also soon found employment as a mining worker at the apatite enriching plant within the flotation process. However, later she developed silicosis as a result of working there for many years.

Prisoners and resettled peasants continued to be the main workforce in Kirovsk during and after World War II, until the death of Stalin in 1953. During World War II, Maria's family was evacuated to Archangelsk with other special settlers. After the war, the family returned to Kirovsk. In 1946, Maria's mother died from silicosis. Her older sister died from tuberculosis, and one of her brothers died soon after the war.

While in Archangelsk, Maria started vocational training in medicine. After graduation, she returned to Kirovsk and started working as a nurse at an orphanage. In 1948, she married a geologist who often went on long-term expeditions. Due to the shortage of housing in Kirovsk, the new family started off sharing a room in a wooden barrack with Maria's husband's parents and siblings. After the birth of their first child, they received a separate room from the state. Maria then started to work at the local hospital. Her husband resigned from his expeditionary job to spend more time with the family. He was later employed at the Apatite mining enterprise in Kirovsk, but died young. Since her two children have grown up and left home, Maria has lived alone in a three-room apartment in Kirovsk.

The New City, Apatity, and the Change in the Workforce

After World War II, during a second wave of industrialization, new industrial towns were established in the Murmansk region. One of them was the city of Apatity, which was founded in the early 1950s very near to Kirovsk. It was a base for housing industrial workers from the Kirovsk mines and the location of a new apatite enrichment plant.[17] The Kola Science Centre was built in Apatity to support the mining and chemical industries.

There was a significant change in the northern workforce after Stalin's death in 1953 and the gradual dismantling of the Gulag system that followed. Apatity was no longer populated by forced workers, but by voluntary migrants from different regions of the Soviet Union. The post-Stalin state encouraged migration to northern settlements through various policies, most of which were directed toward young people. As a result, workers who came to Apatity in the 1950s and 1960s were different from the settlers who had moved to Kirovsk in the 1930s. Most newcomers were young people who had grown up in rural areas. Some of them had recently finished their professional education and had been distributed to Apatity.[18] Others found employment as contract

---

17 By that time there was no space for growth in Kirovsk: the city is situated at the foothills of the Khibiny mountains and space for housing is very limited.

18 The system of centralized distribution of graduates after receiving diplomas (*raspredelenie*) was implemented in the Soviet Union to cover state demand in the workforce at various distant locations.

workers, hired by recruitment agents who had been sent by industrial enterprises to various central and southern regions of the Soviet Union. Many young people were fascinated by the prospect of going to distant territories; the north was seen as a challenging and romantic place for self-realization and adventure.

Most new migrants to Apatity saw their move initially as a temporary solution. In time, however, many decided to stay longer. Compared with the rest of the Soviet Union, it offered higher wages, longer vacations, better housing and food supplies, earlier retirement, and larger pensions.[19] The system of 'northern benefits' which was created to attract workers to the circumpolar regions transformed the northern settlers into a distinct and superior social class within the Soviet hierarchies of privilege.[20] This led to a rapid rise in both geographic and social mobility, and significantly influenced the life course of this generation. Many people who populated Apatity could maintain close connections with their regions of origin.

The Lives of Migrants in Apatity

Nina, whom I met in Apatity in 2010, was seven years old when she arrived in Apatity in 1957 with her family. Both of her parents were originally from Penza. Before coming to Apatity, they lived in Siberia and several other places. The family migrated to different localities because her father, who was a coalminer, searched for better earnings and a good place for the family. Nina remembers some details about life in Kemerovo in Siberia and the reasons why they decided not to stay there:

> We lived there not for long. Life was difficult; there were coal mines around the town. I just remember that it was very difficult work, and we were breathing this coal dust and everything was black. Even laundry hanging outside got black, you know ...

After this experience in Siberia, Nina's father decided to try going north. He initially went alone and found employment as a shaft man at the central mine in Kirovsk, which belonged to the mining enterprise, Apatite. His brigade was building shafts in underground mines and he was responsible for electric works.

The 'city-forming enterprise' of Apatite was state-owned, as were all institutions in the Soviet Union. It controlled all spheres of life and community institutions in Kirovsk, not only industrial production. The enterprise provided the majority of jobs in two localities, organized social activities, and coordinated housing construction and distribution. Soon after arriving, Nina's father received a one-room apartment in Apatity and was able to invite his family to join him. There were already two children in the family:

> We came to join him here, all three of us. It was such a happiness – to get a separate one-room apartment for four people at that time! And we lived there for long time ... In the beginning it was rather easy to get an apartment, but it was very difficult to move to a bigger apartment later, though the city was growing extremely fast.

19 Samuil Venediktovich Slavin, *Osvoenie Severa Sovetskogo Sojuza* (Moscow: Nauka, 1982).

20 Niobe Thompson, *Settlers on the Edge: Identity and Modernization on Russia's Arctic Frontier* (Vancouver: University of British Columbia Press, 2009).

At first, Nina's mother took care of her youngest children, but she later found work at the industrial railroad line, which was used to bring apatite ore from Kirovsk to the central line that connected Murmansk and Leningrad.

Nina remembers how her parents always planned to move from Apatity once they retired:

> In fact, they always wanted to leave here, even though they really liked the climate and nature. My father is a fisherman, and he knew all places around here. [...] He was going fishing to Kandalaksha and to Karelia, to the White Sea. He is also a hunter, so we always got a lot of meat and fish. We weren't rich, so this was good support.

As a child, Nina and her brother often joined their father when he went fishing. For 1950s and 1960s settlers, going fishing, hunting, or berry-picking was not a matter of survival. Spending time in nature, outside of the industrial cities, became a favorite leisure activity for most labor migrants in the north. Nina and her siblings had an obligation to share some of the catch with neighbors and friends. She described to me the atmosphere of mutual help as an important characteristic of the Apatity community. This was a common feature of the narratives of individuals from newly established towns in the north: people were actively supporting each other and helping newcomers become accustomed to northern life.

Housing was one of the most important factors connecting recent migrants to their new towns in the Arctic. Housing was allocated by state institutions and enterprises. By the late 1950s, housing in the Kirovsk-Apatity agglomeration had improved, and, in her later school years, Nina's family received a three-room apartment from the enterprise where her father was employed. Unfortunately, the flat was in Kirovsk. Nobody in the family wanted to move to Kirovsk, because they preferred Apatity:

> Kirovsk is not a cozy town, it is rather uncomfortable. It is situated on the hills and it is higher above sea level compared with Apatity, so the perspective to live there was not very pleasant. We absolutely did not want to move there and we wanted to make an exchange for Apatity. But nobody wanted to go there, nobody even wanted to exchange our three rooms in Kirovsk for a two-room apartment in Apatity.

Despite their efforts, the family did not succeed in securing this exchange. Her father worked until he was fifty-three years old, her mother until she was fifty years old, and both retired in 1982. After retirement, her parents bought a house in the home village of Nina's mother in Penza and moved back there, as they had always wanted to. Nina went to Murmansk to study pedagogy. Her brother lived alone in their big apartment in Kirovsk while completing his vocational training in mining at the local technical school. Nina later finished her studies in Murmansk, returned to Kirovsk, and got married.

Staying or Leaving? Feeling at Home in the North

After the collapse of the Soviet Union, the Kirovsk-Apatity agglomeration experienced a drastic change. State subsidies to northern industry towns were cut significantly. Many towns experienced large-scale out-migration and downsizing. The state implemented relocation programs aiming to reduce the non-working urban populations in the north: the cost of maintaining northern towns was too high.[21] Between 1989 and 2006, seventeen percent of the population migrated out of the far north to more temperate regions.[22] The population of Kirovsk fell from 43,500 in 1989 to 26,900 in 2016. Apatity's population shrunk from 88,026 in 1989 to 56,730 in 2016.

Such a large outflow of people prompted everyone in the northern industrial communities to consider leaving. While both Maria and Nina's families participated in the state-sponsored relocation programs, neither women wanted to leave the north.

Maria initially joined the relocation program thinking that her daughter or grandson would move south with her. However, when after several years she received an apartment in Kostroma in central Russia, nobody in the family wanted to go there. Maria's family eventually sold the apartment in Kostroma and gave the money to Maria's grandson so he could move to Murmansk and buy a flat there. When I asked Maria if she ever wanted to leave the north, she replied, "I do not have any other place. My parents died here. I have five graves to take care about."

Nina's family also participated in the relocation program. Nina and her husband were still working and were too young to join the program themselves, so they convinced Nina's husband's parents to participate. The old couple did not have any plans to leave the north, but they agreed to apply for resettlement on behalf of their children and grandchildren. After several years of waiting, they received an apartment in Vologda, but again, nobody in the family wanted to move there.

The planners who developed the relocation programs continue to see former migrants as newcomers with no attachment to the place, as opposed to indigenous populations following the traditional lifestyles and with deeper, longer ties to the north. However, the inhabitants of the northern industrial towns who arrived as temporary migrants have developed very strong connections with their localities.[23] The state underestimated people's sense of attachment in planning population mobility. Despite ongoing discussions about leaving or staying that take place in most families due to the region's economic instability, many interviewees in Kirovsk and Apatity, including Maria and Nina, have come to consider the northern towns to be their home, feeling attached to the northern people and to the northern natural environment.

---

21 Fiona Hill and Clifford Gaddy, *The Siberian Curse: How Communist Planners Left Russia Out in the Cold* (Washington: Brookings Institution Press, 2003).
22 Timothy Heleniak, "Changing Settlement Patterns Across the Russian North at the Turn of the Millennium," in Vesa Rautio and Markku Tykkylainen, eds., *Russia's Northern Regions on the Edge: Communities, Industries, and Populations from Murmansk to Magadan* (Helsinki: Aleksanteri Institute Press, 2008): 25–52.
23 Alla Bolotova and Florian Stammler, "How the North became Home: Attachment to Place among Industrial Migrants in the Murmansk Region of Russia," in Lee Huskey and Chris Southcott, eds., *Migration in the Circumpolar North: Issue and Contexts* (Edmonton: CCI Press, 2010): 193–220; John Round, "Rescaling Russia's Geography: The Challenges of Depopulating the Northern Periphery," *Europe-Asia Studies* 57 (2005): 705–27.

Section 2
Houses, Work, and Everyday Life: Rhythms, Ruptures, Cycles

David Warren Sabean
Constructing Middle-Class Milieus in Nineteenth-Century Germany: The Labor of *Geselligkeit*

The restructuring of kinship relations in Europe during the late eighteenth century was characterized by the fundamental importance of endogamy.[1] Through marriage and friendship alliances, people became active in constructing milieus that brought together those with the same cultural attitudes and styles.

Endogamy occurred through repeated marriages into the same families or into circles of families that constituted complex alliances among each other. The Delius family from Bielefeld and Bremen, for example, married into the same families over many generations.[2] Marriages between cousins were structurally prominent in nineteenth-century familial endogamy, but there were other ways for families to link themselves repeatedly over time without a particular couple being related by blood. The Göttingen historian Reinhold Pauli, for instance, described how Karl Richard Lepsius's son Bernard had studied in Göttingen and frequented their house, falling in love with one of his daughters. Because the boy's mother was the only daughter of the long-deceased sister of his old friend Parthey and the closest friend of Reinhold's mother, "old connections were renewed again through this marriage."[3]

But the endogamy that was characteristic of nineteenth-century kinship also (and perhaps primarily) referred to marriage within the same cultural and social circles. Marriage was oriented toward finding someone 'familiar.' There are many examples of young men developing a close relationship with a particular family before seeking out one of the daughters for a spouse. Christopher Johnson has characterized this new kinship structure in terms of 'horizontalization.'[4] It is one where the intense sibling, cousin, and in-law relations proliferated along horizontal axes, enveloping wide nets of interacting kin, who reinforced particular cultural styles, guided social reproduction, supported entrepreneurial and political activity, and provided aid and counsel during periods of celebration and crisis. Intense family life was decisive in the creation of cultural understanding and practice, and the social intercourse between groups of families was crucial for the formation of social (*Schichten*) consciousness.

I have previously offered an account of the structural aspects of European nineteenth-century kinship systems and how these systems worked to preserve social boundaries, form and maintain alliances, and inculcate implicit understandings:

---

1 For discussions about nineteenth-century endogamy, see David Warren Sabean, *Kinship in Neckarhausen, 1700–1870* (Cambridge: Cambridge University Press, 1998); David Warren Sabean, Simon Teuscher, and Jon Mathieu, eds., *Kinship in Europe: Approaches to Long-Term Development (1300–1900)* (Oxford: Berghahn, 2007); Christopher H. Johnson, "Die Geschwister Archipel: Bruder-Schwester-Liebe und Klassenformation in Frankreich des 19. Jahrhunderts," *L'Homme: Zeitschrift für feministische Gesschichtswissenschaft* 13 (2002): 50–67; David Warren Sabean and Christopher H. Johnson, eds., *Sibling Relations and the Transformations of European Kinship, 1300–1900* (New York: Berghahn, 2011).

2 *Deutsches Geschlechterbuch*, vol. 193 (Limburg an der Lahn, 1987), edited by Uta von Delius.

3 Elisabeth Pauli, *Reinhold Pauli: Lebenserinnerungen nach Briefen und Tagebüchern zusammengestellt* (Halle a. S., 1895): 335.

4 Christopher H. Johnson, "Die Geschwister Archipel": 50–67.

Kinship and the alliance system of the nineteenth century were crucial for concentrating and distributing capital, providing strategic support over the life course of individuals, structuring dynasties and recognizable patrilineal groupings, maintaining access points, entrances, and exits to social milieus through marriage, god-parentage, and guardianship, creating cultural and social boundaries by extensive festive, ludic, competitive, and charitative transactions, configuring and reconfiguring possible alliances between subpopulations, developing a training ground for character formation, shaping desire and offering practice in code and symbol recognition ("something in the way she moves"), training rules and practices into bodies, and integrating networks of culturally similar people.[5]

Life Trajectories through Houses: Male Autobiographies

Karl Ewald Hasse, professor of medicine and teacher of Robert Koch and Wilhelm Wundt, came from an academic family, and both he and his brother became academics.[6] His father arranged for him to live with one of his friends when he went off to university, primarily because this 'house' was the center of a constant stream of local and foreign guests, not unlike the house he grew up in. Such a house was a meeting point for cultural figures of all kinds: artists, literati, scientists. He makes it clear that his sense of taste and his own style of life was deeply rooted in the kinds of houses that he lived in and had access too. There was an easy flow from houses where he encountered family and kin to houses where he was introduced into the intellectual life of the university and the towns and cities he passed through. Everywhere he went he found the same familiar milieus. In the Leipzig he grew up in, he was surrounded by relatives, something he thought of as crucial for his socialization. He mentions a series of houses that were key to the construction of the kind of milieus in which he and the rest of his family felt at home. He talks about close relations with several houses into which his relatives eventually married. He himself was surrounded by cousins, and his uncles and aunts configured the life in which he, his siblings, his cousins, and his friends took part. As he grew up, there were groups of young people around the core group of relatives busy with music, dancing, living pictures (*tableaux vivants*), and intellectual games. Throughout his time as a student and when he was developing himself professionally, he spent a great deal of time in the various houses of his brothers-in-law. And every week, his father gathered together all of the wider family.

Not all families or houses were alike. One house Hasse visited had medical professionals in constant attendance, and it was here that Hasse developed the contacts and found the support for his later career as a doctor. In another house, that of the Brockhaus family, he found a meeting point for writers, and like many other middle-class young men of the period, he cultivated relationships over an extended period with the house into which he eventually married. Heinrich Brockhaus's ward was an intimate friend of his sister and Brockhaus was anxious to be allied with the Hasse family. After completing his education, Hasse found employment in Zurich. He remarks about the difficulty of leaving an environment of friends and relatives for a city where he was a stranger. But then he was immediately taken up by a series of 'houses.' The whole time he was there, a constant stream of relatives passed through, and he and his wife did the rounds of kin-visiting throughout the year. He later took up a position in Heidelberg, where once again *Geselligkeit* (sociality)

---

5 David Warren Sabean, *Kinship in Neckarhausen*: 451.

6 Karl Ewald Hasse, *Erinnerungen aus meinem Leben* (Leipzig: Wilhelm Engelmann, 1902).

structured the rich and varied life he describes. Finally, in Göttingen, kinship and *Geselligkeit* provided constant subjects for consideration. Indeed, his autobiography is devoted less to his work or scientific breakthroughs than to the contacts he cultivated in the many houses he spent his time and how these connections played a role in his career. He has little to say about his teaching, preferring to list students who were professionally successful – one of whom married his daughter. Kin even show up in his circle of clients. His nephew studied with him and, through his patronage, ended up as a professor.

Hasse's autobiography is fascinating for the transitions it demonstrates in his reflections on professional milieus and family networks. The key intersection for him seems to lie in *Geselligkeit*. When he lived in Switzerland, people from all over Europe liked to visit. Medical professionals from abroad used their contact with him to show up for vacations and collegial interaction. While he frequently lists some of his famous contacts, his recollections center on the houses where he was welcomed and on the openness of his own house to visitors. More important than narrow contacts with others in his own discipline were houses providing a variety of cultural entertainment, particularly music. 'House-sociality' offers the possibility of networks extending well beyond his own profession. Many of his closest friends were colleagues, and they entered his family life in many ways, including by becoming godparents to his children. As soon as his sisters or daughters married, Hasse immediately talks about the brother- or son-in-law and his house, pointing out how long-term relationships even among kin are structured through the idiom of the house.

Cultivating the House, Cultivating Relationships: Women's Work

There are significant silences in men's autobiographies. Hasse, for example, wrote very little about his wife and much more about his father-in-law and brother-in-law. He lists this or that person whom he met, but seldom locates them in a particular space – in the particular house where he encountered them. A house might be given a name, that of the man who headed it, but the most important figure for him, often unnamed, is the wife or 'mother' of the house. It is precisely she who was responsible for the house's style.

For such women, we also see a seamless transition between kin, friends, and neighbors, with kin offering the structural center around which other networks were constructed. Characteristic of women's activities were 'cousin circles' or groups of sisters and sisters-in-law who coordinated family news and information and configured larger kin networks. Of course, much of the family-visiting involved men, even if most of the planning and organization was carried out by women. All of the cooking, cleaning, washing up, directing the household servants, nursing, and the like was done by women.

Quite central to the dynamics of kinship cultivation was the hospitality provided by wives, sisters, and daughters. Hospitality provided by women, as well as their planning activities, was at the heart of integrating extensive kinship networks and the sociability of professional and entrepreneurial men. Lorenz von Stein considered the role of wives to be critical in the ability of men to create social networks, referring abstractly to male "social thought" and female "social feeling."[7]

---

7 Lorenz von Stein, *Die Frau auf dem socialen Gebiete* (Stuttgart: Kessinger, 1880); Lorenz von Stein, *Die Frau; ihre Bildung und Lebensaufgabe* (Berlin: Diedmann, 1890).

Ernst Brandes made the same distinction as von Stein between public and private spheres and observed the fundamental importance of wives and mothers in bridging them. Mediating between the public and the private was a sphere where men and women met on an equal basis, an area he called *Geselligkeit*.[8] In such mixed society, he argued, everything orbited around women. Women framed the spaces in which such gatherings took place, as well as the forms of interaction.

There are not many accounts of the actual work that women carried out, but the autobiographies and collections of correspondence from the nineteenth century provide hints to allow us to piece together a sense of what was involved. It is important to distinguish three aspects of women's labor in terms of the presentation of the house: the physical work, the development and cultivation of networks, and the development and maintenance of the particular culture, manners, and style of the family. The rich house-sociality that Hasse and others participated in was the subject of extensive planning, networking, and physical labor on the part of the women of the house.

Louise Otto provides an authoritative description of the associated household labor.[9] During the 1830s and 1840s, she explains, the household economy involved far more complex labor than when she was writing, in the late 1870s. Taking on more servants later in the century did not reduce the labor, but rather changed the nature of household management. First of all, she pointed out that most households were larger at the start of the nineteenth century, so that even a craftsman had journeymen, helpers, and apprentices living and boarding in the house. She describes the complex labor requirements, from baking, cooking, and preserving and drying fruit, to making and mending clothing and doing the laundry, all of which could involve weeks of labor. The list of actual tasks should be fairly clear, but what Otto stresses is the *Geselligkeit* of the work among all the women of the household, and that the many activities were tied up with the openness of the house to the larger network of kin, friends, and acquaintances. The point here is that women's labor should not be taken for granted. What is interesting is that all of the autobiographies by men that I have read take it for granted. And they reduce it to the symbolic figure of the mother of the house – her graciousness and style – mentioned only in passing. What matters to men for the most part is the tone of the houses that they frequented.

The creation of a *Bildungsbürger* lifestyle in the nineteenth century had a great deal to do with the familial dynamics and house-sociality created by women. Emil Fischer, the Berlin professor of chemistry and Nobel Prize laureate, spent his long bachelorhood on professional development in the presence of male friends and colleagues. The lecture hall, laboratory, meals, walking tours, and visits played a core role in developing his network. But all of his lasting relationships seem to have been filtered through house-based *Geselligkeit*. Once he was married, he could not conceive of his professional life outside of maintaining a "great" house, though here his wife unfortunately failed him; he quickly found a more suitable female companion to take her place after her premature death. There seems to have been two parallel networks for a man like Fischer, though patronage and academic political discourse could not be separated from the social life of the home. Throughout his academic career, from his time as a student to his retirement, women controlled access to the kinds of venues where he was anxious to spend his time. Women were busy weaving professional and marital networks. His autobiography reveals a dense network of academic marriages. Fischer was the patron of at least four of his closest kin for chemistry professorships and he was

---

8 Ernst Brandes, *Betrachtungen über das weibliche Geschlecht und dessen Ausbildung in dem geselligen Leben*, 3 vols. (Hannover, 1802): vol. 1, 76–83, 91; vol. 2, 27–8; vol. 3, 172ff.
9 Louise Otto, *Frauenleben im deutschen Reich: Erinnerungen aus der Vergangenheit mit Hinweis auf Gegenwart und Zukunft* (Leipzig, 1876).

likely instrumental for many other contacts through the rich and varied networks in the houses he frequented.

It was commonplace for people in the nineteenth century to talk about friendships opening up the door to a whole family and extending to a family's larger circle of friends and relatives. At crucial points in his autobiography, the Hamburg patrician Emil Lehmann describes the way new acquaintances introduced him to the social life and friendship of their whole families.[10] *Freundschaft mit unserer ganzen Familie* ("friendship with our whole family") repeats itself throughout his account. The Swiss anatomist Wilhelm His develops the theme of visiting houses at each stage in his career – as a student in Basel, Berlin, and Vienna, as a young academic in Basel, and as a professor in Leipzig.[11] He relates how he entered Berlin society through two particular families. Especially attractive for him was the Friedländer house, the center of literati, intellectuals, and artists. By the time he got to Vienna, the mother of one house had decided to invest in his self-presentation, although given his upper-bourgeois background and his seamless transition from circle to circle, he must have already been quite presentable in the first place. Everywhere he lived and throughout his career, families and houses were of central importance and enabled him to enter society. Each of them was dominated by a 'house mother' and each had its own style. The Göttingen historian Georg Gottfried Gervinus provides a contrasting account.[12] His youth had been spent preparing to be a merchant and reading Romantic novels. By the time he was about to set off to study in Heidelberg in his early twenties, he clearly had not developed the requisite manners for the academic circles he now aspired to. At that point, two women who had married into *Beamtenfamilien* decided to take on the task of making him socially respectable. They worked on overcoming his bashfulness and ridding him of his ill manners. As he put it, visiting their houses on a regular basis and learning to act properly around women was crucial to his cultural and social development. Indeed, for a year, he joined them in their house every single evening. Marriage was just as much a door to a larger family as friendship was. Socially, culturally, and economically, friendship and marriage provided bonds not just between individuals but between houses, families, lineages, dynasties, and networks.

People of the nineteenth century had to learn to manage quite different kinds of networks, and this delicately choreographed system involved the presentation of each family and its members according to the rules of the particular stratum and cultural sphere in which they wished to operate. The private house and its activities were intricately articulated with a larger network of social connections and aesthetic assumptions. The education of both men and women in open and fluid systems where couples had to cooperate in tasks of social representation required protracted drilling in taste, morality, sentiment, and style.

Houses, Families, and *Geselligkeit*

Male autobiographies from the nineteenth century describe the many aspects of work that relate to the construction of the nineteenth-century bourgeois house. These accounts include a constant refrain about houses, families, and *Geselligkeit*. The aspect that I want to underline here is the dual

---

10 Emil Lehmann, *Lebenserinnerungen*, 3 vols. (Kissingen, [1885]–1895), vol. 1: 29, 61.
11 Wilhelm His der Ältere, *Lebenserinnerungen und ausgewählte Schriften* (Bern: Verlag Hans Huber, 1965).
12 Georg Gottfried Gervinus, *G. G. Gervinus' Leben: von ihm selbst 1860* (Leipzig: Engelmann, 1893).

role of the house – a stage for *Geselligkeit*, on the one hand, and to create and sustain networks of family and friends, on the other. Both of these tasks involved complex forms of labor that were largely in the hands of women. They acted as the doorkeepers, controlling who had access to the space in which the social interaction of like-minded people took place. In this way, women's work was fundamental to patrolling the boundaries of class. They determined access and exclusion, and were crucial to the formation of political, familial, and cultural alliances. Studying this kind of work tells us about the formation of class *habitus*.

The house was central to the configuration of milieus. It was here that a sense of taste and style was established. Mediating the public and the domestic sphere, the house was a place for women to impose form and configure networks. Hospitality was a result of considerable effort, integrating kin, friends, colleagues, and strangers. This laid the foundation for like to find like, which supported nineteenth-century kinship construction and class formation.

Gerd Spittler

Home-Making among the Kel Ewey Tuareg in the Sahara

Many people in today's Western world see home-life and work as opposites. The former is associated with feelings of love, care for others, and free communication, while the latter implies impersonal rationality, purposeful calculations, and self-interest. People often speak of the difficulty they face finding an equilibrium between their career and their family. From an anthropological and global historical perspective, however, divisions between work and family are not as obvious as they seem to us today. In most societies, the institution of the domestic economy unites the worlds of work and family. Men, women, children, and the elderly work together not only on domestic tasks but also on production. This type of economy predominated from the beginning of the Neolithic period until capitalist industrialization. While the domestic economy has largely lost its central place in Western societies, the worldwide spread of capitalism has not undermined home-based economies everywhere. In many countries, above all in Africa, the domestic economy is still the most widespread form of economic organization. This holds true not only in rural areas, but also in cities.

The Kel Ewey Tuareg

The Kel Ewey Tuareg have lived for centuries in the Aïr Mountains of the Sahara, in what is today the country of Niger.[13] Their economy is based on the caravan trade, camel and goat herding, and horticulture. Their economic center is the oasis of Timia. Although the caravan trade covers an area the size of Germany, it is operated entirely by families, rather than big merchants. When the caravans arrive in Bilma and Dirkou, the caravaneers buy salt and dates after traveling six hundred dangerous and demanding kilometers through the desert. With these goods, the caravan travels south to Kano, Nigeria. In Hausaland, they sell the salt and dates at local markets.

Of all the goods acquired by the Kel Timia in the south, millet, their staple food, has the highest priority. Other goods, such as cloth, are bought only after this has been accomplished. The goods they buy are not for resale, but are all destined for individual households.

Sitting on the Ground and on Mats

In Western civilization, a home means not just a house but also an assortment of furniture. We would consider a dwelling without tables, chairs, or beds – where all the tasks of the home have to be done on the floor – as deficient, poor, underdeveloped, or uncivilized. 'To go down' means to suffer a defeat. We say that someone is 'feeling down' when they are unhappy.

---

13 See Gerd Spittler, *Hirtenarbeit: Die Welt der Kamelhirten und Ziegenhirtinnen von Timia* (Cologne: Rüdiger Köppe, 1998); Gerd Spittler and Michael Bourdillon, eds., *African Children at Work: Working and Learning in Growing Up for Life* (Münster: Lit, 2012); Gerd Spittler, *Anthropologie der Arbeit: Ein ethnographischer Vergleich* (Wiesbaden: Springer VS, 2016); see also www.deva-research.uni-bayreuth.de.

The Tuareg do not have tables, chairs, or sofas. Does this mean they are poor? Are they unhappy? They don't think so. If a visitor comes, they say *awud amadal* ("sit on the ground") as an invitation to stay a while. In the eyes of the Tuareg, many European visitors behave like uncivilized barbarians who do not know better: they do not take off their shoes when they enter a home, they extinguish their cigarettes in the sand, and they drop food on the mat when they eat. The Tuareg treat not only the mat, but also the sand inside and in front of their tent or hut, as we would a carpet. They don't walk on it with shoes or sandals. They keep it clean and keep their goats off it.

At night, a young husband goes to visit his wife in her tent (*ehan*). He creeps up to avoid being seen by his mother-in-law. The tent is close to her mother's compound, but it is portable. When the young woman takes a herd of goats to the pasture, she takes her tent with her and her husband goes to visit her there.

A bride's tent contains a portable wooden bed, consisting of poles laid across movable legs and covered with finely woven mats. This is often given by the mother to the first of her daughters at marriage. A bride's tent lasts a long time, but not all her life. At first any wear or tear is repaired, but eventually it is replaced by a stationary hut (*iberkan*). This hut is not made with woven mats, but with straw from desert grass and is very durable. It is produced by a group of older women.

A home also includes a storage area, which can only be entered by women, and a fence around the whole compound. All of this constitutes a home (*aghiwan*). A dwelling without women is inconceivable, but there can be dwellings without men. Outside the compound the wilderness, the bush, begins. A visitor does not enter the compound before announcing his arrival and only takes a seat after being invited to do so.

What does taking a seat mean if there are no chairs? The visitor is asked to sit either on the ground or, more usually, on a woven mat that is spread out in front of him. Women and men sit on separate mats. It is a great honor for a visitor to be invited to share the host's mat. Children do not sit on mats, but on the bare ground.

It is important not only where people sit, but also how they sit. This depends on the situation. At a formal meeting, such as a council or Islamic instruction, the participants sit cross-legged. For relaxed conversation, there are several possibilities. People may sit, crouch, or lie on the ground or on a mat. A person may sit cross-legged or with one or both knees raised, or with his legs stretched out. If he lies down, there are even more possibilities: one may lie on one's back (men only), on one's side, or on one's stomach. Or one can rest on one's elbows and place one's legs in different positions.

These are not just theoretical possibilities. All of these positions are practiced and often have special names. Photographs in my books and on my website show that very few sitting, crouching, or lying positions are identical and that there are in fact hundreds of variants. Individuals will have their favorite positions, but they may adopt dozens of different positions, sometimes in the course of one evening.

Whether sitting or reclining, any person who is close to the ground shares the same status. A hierarchical difference can be expressed by one person sitting on a mat while the other sits on the ground. In a group, everyone is on the same level: men and women, host and guest, an Islamic scholar and his pupils, and visitors, adults, and children.

However, there is a big difference in height between camel riders and people standing or sitting on the ground. Camels are bigger than horses, especially if the saddle is on the hump. A person on the ground has to look up to a camel rider. If he wants to greet him with a handshake, he has to stretch his hand up and the rider has to bend down. On festive occasions, spectators sit or stand on the ground. Behind them are the camel riders, who have a better view, high up on their camels. Their height is increased by the saddle, which requires them to sit in a stiff, unchanging position.

Sitting on a saddle gives them authority and dignity, but it is not comfortable. During the strenuous Bilma caravan, the caravaneers do not sit on a saddle, but prefer to ride on a pack camel so that they can choose the most comfortable position: sitting; or lying, on their back or on their side, or with their legs drawn up.

Most Europeans are not particularly impressed by the woven, straw-colored mats. But they are prized by the Kel Ewey and it is impossible to imagine their life without them. The roof of the bride's tent is made with big mats woven from doum palm leaves. Inside the tent, the ground is covered with different kinds of mats. The finer mats are not woven from doum palm leaves, but from the leaves of the date palm, which is much more time-consuming to produce. The bed is covered with several layers of mats. The top one is the finest, which takes several months to make from fine straw interwoven with leather strips. Complicated patterns are produced by specialists. One mat is equal in value to a camel.

Most mats are kept rolled up in the tent and are unrolled when needed, for example, for visitors to sit or lie on. Mats should not be exposed to the sun or the rain. People may step on a mat with bare feet, but not with shoes or sandals. They must not be soiled by goat droppings or children's urine.

The Tuareg do not understand why, instead of sitting on a mat, I prefer to upend a mortar and sit on that in the absence of a chair. For them, the different sitting and reclining positions are much more comfortable than a chair or a mortar. When I asked a shopkeeper why he had placed a bench in front of his shop, he told me that this wasn't because he wanted to offer people a comfortable seat, but exactly the opposite. A bench is uncomfortable and it was meant to deter people from sitting there too long. If he were to put mats down in front of his shop, they would sit there and block the entrance for other customers.

Chairs are considered uncomfortable. You cannot change position all the time. The seat is hard, you slide off it, your legs hang down, and your back aches. There were several chairs in my house in Timia, but none of my local visitors ever sat on them. Chairs signify a different lifestyle, and most importantly they are signs of power and political change. The village chief sits on a chair in front of his house, the members of the local council sit on chairs round a table, and the children sit on benches at school.

Homemaking by Women

All family members – men and women, children, and the elderly – contribute to the family's livelihood through their work, whether they herd camels or goats, cultivate the garden, lead caravans through the desert and into Hausaland in order to obtain food and clothing for the family, or stay at home to prepare meals. In this way, each helps to secure the family's material well-being.

The tent and the mats belong to the women. They are a material symbol of matrilocality among the Kel Ewey. The home (*aghiwan*) is primarily the home of the women, while a husband is a visitor who lives in the tent and on the mats of his wife. This becomes clear in the case of a divorce. Ghayshwan explains to me: "The husband takes his sword and his tea things and departs. He leaves the house [tent] and the children behind." This is not always what happens in real life and it does not correspond to Islamic law, but it shows how the women think. For children, both boys and girls, their mother's house is their home. Even after a man has married, when he says he is 'going home,' he usually means to his mother's house, at least in the early years of his marriage while the children are still small.

Not only are the women the owners of the mats and tents, but they are also the ones who make the mats on which everyone sits and lies, and which are used to construct the tents. Women often sit around weaving strips for mats, either alone or in the company of other women. When a woman takes her goats to the pasture, she combines the work of herding with that of weaving strips to make a mat. But women also gather in groups: they sit in a tent or in the compound, each working on a strip. They chat with each other while they work. Sometimes they sit and work together on a mat by sewing or weaving the strips together.

Walking, Sitting, Working

The work of the camel herders (men) and the goat herders (women) consists mainly of walking and running. The women roam from sunrise to sunset, leading their goats to good pastures or watering places. The work of camel herders is more irregular. They do not stay in the pasture with the camels all day, but have times when they go out to look for their camels and round them up. If they cannot find a camel, they may spend whole days and nights following its tracks. The longest period they spend working is when they travel on foot with a caravan to Bilma or Hausaland. The caravan to Bilma keeps moving for sixteen to eighteen hours every day for a whole week – without a break.

Sitting is in contrast to the walking and running typical of herders and caravaneers. 'Sitting' is often used in a figurative sense to mean resting. But people also work while they are sitting, crouching, or kneeling. Caravaneers sit in the market to sell salt and dates. To perform activities like pounding millet, cooking, milking the goats, or making cheese, women sit cross-legged, or crouch or kneel on the ground. Women sit to weave strips for mats, and men sit to make the ropes they need for the caravans. Working in a sitting position allows people to use not only their hands, but also their feet or their knees as an aid. A lot of work can be done while sitting down. Nevertheless, it is considered more comfortable than the mobility of the camel and goat herders. People sometimes say that activities performed while sitting down are not work.

Afterword

I conducted research among the Kel Ewey between 1976 and 2006. Since the end of my fieldwork, the Kel Ewey and Timia have undergone changes which also affect the way homes are constructed. The bride's tent and hut are increasingly being replaced by mud brick houses that are built or financed by the husband. Together with an increase in polygamy (traditionally the Tuareg were monogamous), this reflects a new male dominance in gender relations. In the case of a divorce, it is unclear what should be done with the brick house. It belongs to the husband, because he built it, but the land it stands on belongs to the wife because land is passed down through the maternal line.

Today, in the homes of school-educated Kel Ewey, you can sometimes find chairs. However, even the educated Tuareg prefer the more comfortable traditional way and continue sitting and lying on the ground. This is true above all for common meals. Every Tuareg higher civil servant living in a city possesses sofas in his home. But for dining, if there are no Europeans among his guests, he and his friends will not go to the table but will sit on the ground for the common meal.

Josef Ehmer
Living in Homes, but What Kinds and Whose? Single Young People in Nineteenth-Century Central Europe

In the modern world, the home seems to have an unambiguous meaning, clearly distinguished from homelessness.[14] But nowadays, a significant number of people worldwide live somewhere between these two poles: in institutions such as boarding schools, hospitals, care homes, army barracks, jails, or refugee camps. Throughout European history, the grey zone between living in one's own home and being without a home was much broader. Its historic climax came during the long nineteenth century, during the transition toward modernity. Most of such ambiguous living arrangements were closely related to specific labor relations and working conditions, and to life course stages. This essay looks at nineteenth-century homes as they become visible in a wide range of Central European historical sources, such as population censuses, social surveys, autobiographical memories, and literary texts, but also in photographs and artistic drawings.

My starting point is the observation that in the rapidly growing nineteenth-century Central European cities, a large majority of young people of both sexes spent considerable amounts of their lives not in their own homes or in those of their parents or relatives, but in the homes of their employers or as boarders or lodgers in households of other poor people. 'Being at home' had ambivalent meanings in both cases. Homes were often shelters where young people slept at night and stored their few personal belongings, if they had any at all. This was a far cry from homelessness, but these young people lacked privacy, stability, and self-determination. Living in this way implied subordination to the authority of employers or landlords. These homes were anything but a "Haven in a Heartless World," as Christopher Lasch phrases the ideal of the bourgeois family home.[15] Rather, they were spaces of multiple dependencies and intensified exploitation, and therefore part and parcel of the severe living and working conditions of the laboring population in the early stages of industrializing capitalism.

Homes, Work, and the Life Course

Such living and working conditions in Central Europe were not created by nineteenth-century industrialization and urbanization. They were key elements of early modern modes of production and their respective life-course regimes. To a considerable degree, the labor force of the peasant family economy and artisanal commodity production was based on the so-called 'life-cycle servant,' in which children would leave their parents at an early age – typically before the age of twelve – to become live-in servants in husbandry, apprentices and journeymen in the households of master artisans, or maids or domestic servants in homes across the social hierarchy.[16] They would remain

---

14 I would like to thank Mel Greenwald for his help with the English version of this chapter and particularly for the translation of the literary texts.

15 Christopher Lasch, *Haven in a Heartless World: The Family Besieged* (New York: W.W. Norton, 1958).

16 The notion of the 'life-cycle servant' was introduced into social history by Peter Laslett in the 1970s and subsequently experienced a highly successful academic career. See Peter Laslett, *Family Life and Illicit Love in Earlier Generations: Essays in Historical Sociology* (Cambridge: Cambridge University Press, 1977): 13, 34.

in such an inferior social position until their late twenties, when they tried to marry and form a family and household of their own, and if possible establish themselves as independent farmers or as master artisans, be it as an employer or self-employed. Part of this life-course regime involved a late first marriage, the so-called European Marriage Pattern, and a specific household formation system in which marriage was tied to the ability to establish and maintain a household by one's own means – in other words, to create one's own home.[17]

During the years spent living in the homes of strangers, the status and agency of young people changed. Young children were most strongly exposed to the authority and the quite often despotic rule of their 'housefathers' and 'housemothers.' Adolescents and young adults had better opportunities to resist or leave a tyrannical employer or landlord and look for better conditions elsewhere. Particularly in cities, living as a boarder or lodger offered young adults an alternative to the overlapping of workplace and home. Their increasing autonomy, however, did not lead to more stability, but rather to short-term working and housing arrangements. Those young men and women living away from home formed the core of the high geographical mobility and labor market fluctuation of early modern and early industrial Europe.

Living in Which and Whose Homes: Statistics

In European history, the amount of people not living in a home of their own peaked in the nineteenth century. Particularly in large Central European cities, traditional modes of production and life courses merged with the dynamics of industrialization and urbanization. In cities such as Berlin, Vienna, Zürich, and Zagreb from the 1830s to the 1860s, between one-half and two-thirds of all gainfully employed men and women lived in the homes of others. But a statistical analysis of a sample of census listings for Central European cities and towns in the middle decades of the nineteenth century shows remarkable variation.

Among apprentices (*Lehrlinge*), only twenty-eight percent lived with their family or relatives, compared with sixty percent in their employer's household and twelve percent as boarders or lodgers.[18] Among journeymen (*Gesellen, Gehilfen*), twenty-seven percent of young people lived in a shared family home, fifty-one percent lived in their employer's household, and twenty-two percent lived as boarders. Those who were registered as workers (*Arbeiter*) in population listings were on average older than apprentices and journeymen, and worked not only in small crafts and trades but also in industrial factories; forty-two percent managed to live in their own home. This was more than those who lived with their employers (fifteen percent), but still not as many as those who lived as boarders (forty-three percent). Living in one's own home was commonplace for the upper

---

17 The 'European Marriage Pattern' and 'household formation system' are basic terms in historical demography. Both concepts were developed by the English statistician John Hajnal in the 1960s to 1980s; see John Hajnal, "European Marriage Patterns in Historical Perspective," in David Glass and D.E.C. Eversley, eds., *Population in History* (Chicago: Aldane, 1965): 101–43; John Hajnal, "Two Kinds of Pre-industrial Household Formation System," in Richard Wall, Jean Robin, and Peter Laslett, eds., *Family Forms in Historic Europe* (Cambridge: Cambridge University Press, 1983): 65–104. For discussion and critique see Josef Ehmer, "Marriage," in David I. Kertzer and Marzio Barbagli, eds., *Family Life in the Long Nineteenth Century 1789–1913* (New Haven: Yale University Press, 2002): 282–321.
18 Both German and English terminology to designate nineteenth-century rental arrangements are fuzzy, overlapping, and have regional differences. In the sources used for this chapter 'boarder' (*Kostgänger*) includes some kind of meals, while a 'lodger' or 'bed-lodger' (*Bettgeher, Schlafgänger, Schlafbursche*) rents nothing more than the (often-shared) use of a bed. Subtenants (*Untermieter, Aftermieter*) usually rent a chamber of their own.

classes – for employers and the self-employed, civil servants, and people with a higher education – but it was clearly exceptional for large segments of the working class.[19]

Table 1: Housing Conditions, Occupational Status, and Social Position of Residents in Central European Cities, 1774–1880 (as a percentage of social position)[20]

Social position	Living in one's own home (or with parents or kin)	Living in the home of one's employer	Living as boarder or lodger
Master artisan	96	0	4
Other employer/self-employed	78	0	22
Worker (*Arbeiter, Arbeiterin*)	42	15	43
Apprentice (*Lehrling*)	28	60	12
Journeyman (*Geselle, Gehilfe*)	27	51	22
Other employees	25	54	21

One has to keep in mind that wage labor and belonging to the working class in Central European cities in the mid-nineteenth century was not a lifelong experience.[21] Which or whose home one lived in varied greatly through the life course.[22] Most people born into working-class families undertook some kind of wage labor at an early age, but many had a realistic prospect of establishing themselves later on as master artisans, shopkeepers, or businesspeople – positions of relative economic independence – and thus forming and financing their own house and household.

Housing conditions reflect this life course. In a Viennese industrial suburb in the 1850s, for example, almost all children under the age of ten lived at home, but as soon as boys and girls started to enter the labor market – between the ages of ten and fourteen – they also began to leave the parental home. In the fifteen-to-nineteen age group, the majority lived either with their employers (forty-five percent) or as boarders (fifteen percent). Living away from one's own home peaked in the twenty-to-thirty age group: roughly one-third each lived at home, in an employer's household, and in boarding houses or lodgings respectively. The share of those who lived in their own home increased with age, reaching eighty percent in their late forties. After fifty, with the onset of old age, another transition took place as people moved out of their own home and into other people's homes as boarders.

---

19 Josef Ehmer, *Soziale Traditionen in Zeiten des Wandels: Arbeiter und Handwerker im 19. Jahrhundert* (Frankfurt: Campus Verlag, 1994): 52–100.

20 Based on population and census data from Konstanz in 1774, Zürich in 1836 and 1870, Zagreb in 1857, Salzburg in 1857, Perchtoldsdorf in 1880, and various Viennese districts in 1827–1880. Total sample population: 46,206. Number of people with clear occupational status provided: 8,351. Note that nineteenth-century occupational titles are highly gendered. Most of the masters, journeymen, and apprentices in this sample are male, while a third of other employers/self-employed and the majority of workers and other employees is female. Source: Ehmer, *Soziale Traditionen in Zeiten des Wandels:* 66, 100.

21 For more intensive discussion see Josef Ehmer, "Lohnarbeit und Lebenszyklus im Kaiserreich," *Geschichte und Gesellschaft* 14 (1988): 448–71.

22 Ehmer, *Soziale Traditionen in Zeiten des Wandels:* 64.

Table 2: Housing Arrangements over the Life Course, Gumpendorf, Vienna, 1857 (as a percentage of age group)[23]

Age group	Living in one's own home (or with parents or kin)	Living in the home of one's employer	Living as boarder or lodger
5–9	91	1	8
10–14	76	16	8
15–19	40	45	15
20–24	34	35	31
25–29	39	27	34
30–34	58	15	27
35–39	74	7	19
40–44	76	5	19
45–49	80	5	15
50–54	78	3	19
54–59	76	3	21
60 and above	69	3	28

Experiences and Evaluations

How was living away from one's own home experienced and evaluated? Until the early nineteenth century, living with one's employer was a relatively typical experience for young people of both sexes. This was praised by the authorities as a means of social control for potentially unruly young men and women. However, during the nineteenth century, this was viewed increasingly negatively. Housing conditions of the poor contradicted new ideals of bourgeois family life and the demand for privacy, as well as rising working-class aspirations for self-determination. Autobiographical writings, social surveys, and literary texts from this period paid close attention to the various forms of living away from home. They consistently painted a very dark picture of employers' households and boarding homes. In the late nineteenth century, the perception of living away from one's own home was almost unanimously negative.

A literary text helps us understand children's experiences of these housing conditions. Christine Lavant (1915–1973) grew up in a valley hemmed in by mountains in the Austrian province of Carinthia. Her stories provide realistic accounts of the social conditions in this rural region during her youth in the 1920s and 1930s.[24]

One of her most poignant works, *Das Wechselbälgchen* ("The Little Changeling"), is the story of Wrga, an unmarried farmhand, and her mentally disabled daughter. In one episode, Wrga recalls her own childhood. She could not have been much older than five or six:

---

[23] Total sample population: 13,322. Source: Ehmer, *Soziale Traditionen in Zeiten des Wandels:* 64.
[24] Christine Lavant, *Das Wechselbälgchen* (Göttingen: Wallstein Verlag, 2016).

When she was sent to work for a farmer up in the mountains. At the time, her mother was hospitalized with consumption, and a stranger ... brought her to the farm ... that became her hell on earth – for years, the bitterest torment imaginable for a little girl left completely on her own. No, even to this day, she still couldn't think about it without her hair standing on end! The dread! The horrible, never-ending dread!

By day, dreading the coarse hands of the farmer's wife and the wooden-clogged feet of the farmer, the sharp nails of the little children that she had to constantly lug around with her despite being scarcely a head taller than they were. And the nights were ever worse! How often she had had to scrub down the big kitchen while the others were already asleep and then, over and over again, despite the dread, how often had she fallen asleep in the middle of the job, simply nodding off atop the damp rag. Never had she been awakened with anything besides blows or kicks, sometimes even with ice-cold water, which was even worse. No, a bed was something she never had then. She was permitted to sleep on the damp, cold bench behind the oven where they stored the water vats and tubs, which she first had to remove before she could make her bed out of a few old feedbags. And that's where she had her first attack of rheumatism before she was even old enough to go to school. She was permitted to attend school for only a few months, but that had been the short-lived paradise of her whole childhood, where she could sleep and dream, and where she wasn't beaten all that often – and when she was, then only by the other children.[25]

Lavant's account may well be an extreme example, but it is not unique. In Switzerland, orphans, children of poor families or single mothers, and children of families suspected by the authorities of immoral conduct were transferred by national childcare authorities. This practice continued until the 1980s. Only a few years ago, a critical public debate started in Switzerland in which these so-called *Verdingkinder* (indentured child laborers) increasingly became regarded as 'child-slaves' and as victims of exploitation and forced labor. In April 2016, the Swiss parliament passed a law that condemned this traditional social practice and granted financial compensation to the approximately 15,000 former *Verdingkinder* still alive.[26]

Adolescent farmhands were in a better position than little children to look after themselves. As a rule, they had regular sleeping quarters – traditionally, in the stalls with the cattle and horses, strictly separated by gender. It was not until the late nineteenth century in Central Europe that it became common, at least on prosperous farms, for male and female farmhands to be assigned separate sleeping chambers where each servant had his or her own bed as well as a place for a chest to store their belongings, and thus to be accorded a modicum of privacy in the peasant family economy that had previously been a privilege reserved for married peasant couples.

Young Workers in Fin-de-Siècle Vienna

Housing conditions and the various meanings of home for the urban working classes can be illustrated by Viennese sources from the late nineteenth century. Those who lived in their employer's household usually had no room to themselves and often no bed either. In these cases, female domestic servants might have had to sleep on the floor of the kitchen and male apprentices in the workshop. Alfons Petzold, who got his occupational start in 1896 as an apprentice in a large shoemaker's workshop, shared a small bed chamber with seven fellow apprentices:

---

25 Christine Lavant, *Das Wechselbälgchen:* 46–48; translated by Mel Greenwald.
26 http://www.spiegel.de/panorama/justiz/schweiz-beschliesst-entschaedigung-fuer-verdingkinder-a-1089557.html, accessed June 25, 2017.

The beds were similar to berths on a ship, bunk beds stacked on top of each other, and this was a pretty clever arrangement since the room was so tiny that there was hardly space for two beds. The 'bedding' consisted of … beat-up mattresses and foul-smelling blankets crawling with fleas.[27]

In one of his subsequent workplaces, a tavern, his so-called bed was a crate with a lid that was closed by day to serve as a bench.[28]

For those who could avoid living with their employer, boarding was an alternative. In Vienna, as in all other Central European cities, two forms of lodging existed. The cheapest and most widespread one was for bed-lodgers (*Bettgeher* or *Schlafgänger)*, who simply rented a bed, be it alone or sharing with another lodger.

Fourteen-year-old Johann Böhm traveled to Vienna in 1900 in search of work with his father, a mason. They rented a shared bed in the home of a railway worker: "Our shared sleeping place was in a dark kitchen adjacent to the hallway – a cot set up in the evening and removed the next morning. There was so little room that, to avoid falling on the floor, we had to nestle up against one another the whole night." The landlord specified that Johann and his father could remain in the flat only for the purpose of sleeping there. "Since *Bettgeher* were otherwise unwelcome guests, we went for long walks on Sundays …, which is how I got to know the city. Or, when we got tired, we hung around in parks."[29] A social survey of the conditions of female garment workers came to a similar conclusion. "Most working women who only rented a sleeping place enjoyed neither peace and quiet nor any other sort of comfort."[30]

More comfortable accommodation was enjoyed by *Untermieter*, subtenants who could afford to rent a chamber, either on their own or together with others. Franz Grillparzer, one of Austria's most famous writers, describes in his short story *Der arme Spielmann* ("The Poor Fiddler") a poor, old street musician who rented a small chamber with two journeymen.[31] A visitor to his chamber was struck by a chalk line straight through the room. "'My home extends to here and no further,' said the old man, pointing to the line across the floor. 'Two young craftsmen live over yonder.'"[32]

Admitting a lodger of course changed the homes of landlords. Usually, working-class families rented out a place to sleep to supplement their household income. As Böhm remembered, "Notices were posted on the entryways to all the residential buildings advertising sleeping places for rent within."[33] However, the average working-class home in Vienna around 1900 was a very small flat, typically consisting of one room and a small kitchen. A survey based on the household accounts of 119 better-off Viennese working-class families in 1912–1914 revealed that only forty-two percent of all family members slept in a bed of their own; the majority shared a bed with one or two others.[34] These spatial conditions, highly confined in any case, were exacerbated by the admission of lodgers. As a rule, members of the landlord's family and lodgers slept in the same room. However, even these conditions were regarded as preferable to the housing estates affiliated with

---

27 Alfons Petzold, *Das rauhe Leben: Autobiographischer Roman* (Wien: Wiener Verlag, 1947): 87.

28 Alfons Petzold, *Das rauhe Leben:* 113.

29 Johann Böhm, *Erinnerungen aus meinem Leben* (Wien: Verlag des Österreichischen Gewerkschaftsbundes, 1953): 18, 29.

30 Josef Ehmer, "Wohnen ohne eigene Wohnung. Zur sozialen Stellung von Untermietern und Bettgehern," in Lutz Niethammer, ed., *Wohnen im Wandel: Beträge zur Geschichte des Alltags in der bürgerlichen Gesellschaft* (Wuppertal: Peter Hammer Verlag, 1979): 145.

31 Franz Grillparzer, *Der arme Spielmann* (Wien: Wilhelm Frick Verlag, 1847).

32 Franz Grillparzer, *Der arme Spielmann:* 22

33 Johann Böhm, *Erinnerungen aus meinem Leben:* 61.

34 Josef Ehmer, *Soziale Traditionen in Zeiten des Wandels:* 91.

large factories such as the brick plants on the outskirts of Vienna. There, single young workers were accommodated in huge dormitories in barracks. As a Social Democratic weekly reported in 1888, "In these places, there are forty, fifty, up to seventy people sleeping in one huge hall. Wooden bunks covered with wretched old straw; the bodies upon them laid out haunch to paunch ... No sheets, no blankets – old rags served as under layers; their own dirty clothes were their covers."[35]

Such descriptions may be particular examples, and indeed one hardly knows whether and to what degree they can be generalized. What we know, however, is that the cozy home was far removed from the nineteenth-century working class experience, and even more so for children and young people. Among the upper segments of the working classes, the ideal of the bourgeois family home, as a well-ordered space of privacy, solidarity, and love, was very slowly taking shape, but, for many others, the harsh realities of life and work were very different.

---

35 Josef Ehmer, "Wiener Arbeitswelten um 1900," in Hubert Ch. Ehalt, Gernot Heiss, and Hannes Stekl, eds., *Glücklich ist, wer vergisst ...? Das andere Wien um 1900* (Wien: Böhlau Verlag, 1986): 205.

Thabang Sefalafala
Experiences of Wagelessness and the Meaning of Wage Work in the Free State Goldfields, South Africa

I interviewed retrenched Goldfields mineworkers in Welkom, the second-largest city in the Free State province of South Africa. The mineworkers' unemployment had had a profound impact on their sense of self and their place in their homes and community. They experienced deep moral unease at being workless.

The Free State Goldfields

The Free State Goldfields are located in the South African province of the Free State, in the Matjhabeng local municipality of the Lejweleputswa district. The discovery of gold in the Free State in 1946, with an assayed gold content ninety-two times higher than that discovered on the Witwatersrand, led to the emergence of a spectacular mining industry in the 1950s and 1960s, which directly employed hundreds of thousands of workers. The Free State Goldfields rapidly became a significant attraction for migrant labor. By 1968, there were eight gold mines with over forty-six shafts in operation, which accounted for approximately thirty-five percent of total gold production in South Africa, and twelve percent of the global total.[36]

1988 is regarded as the peak of the Free State Goldfields mining development. At this time, over 150,000 mineworkers were employed. Gold mining and its support industries and services underpinned Welkom and the area's rapid development. It sustained white-owned businesses and economic growth for over thirty years. By the 1980s, over eighty percent of the jobs in the area were mine-related.

Odendaalsrus was the only already-existing town when gold was discovered in the area.[37] Welkom was founded in 1947 as a private town of the Anglo-American mining company. The towns of Allanridge and Virginia were also developed to accommodate the mining population. Welkom is named after the farm on which gold was discovered and was officially declared a city in 1948. It is now the second-largest city of the Free State province after Bloemfontein.

Welkom was planned as a modern 'garden city' and developed in accordance with the best standards of town planning at the time. The city has no traffic lights, only a host of traffic circles containing beautiful gardens. Welkom is spacious, with a number of parks and gardens. There is one long street through a central business district, which also houses the civic theatre. Ernest Oppenheimer had envisaged Welkom as a permanent place of beauty and wealth. According to Max Fleischer, "What Sir Ernest had in mind was not a mining camp which would disappear when the

---

36 Etienne Nel and Tony Binns, "Decline and Response in South Africa's Free State Goldfields: Local Economic Development in Matjhabeng," *International Development Planning Review* 24 (2002): 249–69.

37 Lochner Marais, Deirdre van Rooyen, Etienne Nel, and Molefi Lenka, "Responses to Mine Downscaling: Evidence from Secondary Cities in the South African Goldfields," *The Extractive Industries and Society* 4 (2017): 163–71.

mines were finished but a town of permanence and beauty such as men could not believe in at the time and which they thought that even the millions of Anglo-Americans could not create."[38]

The city of Welkom and its surrounding towns are accompanied by townships planned for black labor. The township closest to Welkom is Thabong. In Sesotho, 'Thabong' loosely translates as a 'place of joy or a place of refuge.' Thabong was established in September 1951 as the official Bantu residential area in the Welkom municipality. The township was established to service the labor needs of the new mine-related industrial enterprises and respond to the rapid influx of African migrant workers to mine compounds mushrooming around the city.

In 1968, there were 3,200 dwellings in Thabong, housing a population of 22,800 African male laborers living with their families. Today, Thabong has an estimated population of 126,013, comprising 39,710 households.

Welkom and Thabong since the 1990s

Mine downsizing and closures have been particularly devastating in the Free State Goldfields. Black low-skilled mineworkers with little or no prospect of shifting to other sectors were the worst affected.[39]

The closure of Rand Mine's Harmony mines in 1991 was the first spectacular blow to Matjhabeng. It resulted in the loss of over 10,000 jobs. In 1996, the total employment in mining was estimated at 97,914. It dropped to 36,505 in 2001 and then to 27,494 in 2011. The Free State Goldfields currently employ less than 30,000 staff (down from the 150,000 in the late 1980s). In the late 1980s, mines had up to eight shafts each, but, by 1999, the remaining operating mines had no more than two shafts each. Many of the remaining mines have been sold off to smaller emerging black players, such as African Rainbow Minerals.

The following table provides sectoral employment figures for Matjhabeng between 1996 and 2011. These figures highlight the spectacular decline of the mining industry and the related performance of other industries in the municipality, such as agriculture, manufacturing, construction, services, and trade.

Unemployment in the region today is approximately thirty-seven percent. Youth unemployment is estimated at just under fifty percent. According to Statistics South Africa, Matjhabeng currently has negative growth of approximately −0.04 percent.

---

38 Classic studies of mining in South Africa's Free State include: Max Fleischer, *Welkom: Capital of the Orange Free State Goldfields* (Johannesburg: Felstar Publishers, 1968); Paul Klempner, *The Orange Free State Gold Mines* (London: South Shields, 1956).

39 See Lochner Marais, "The Impact of Mine Downscaling on the Free State Goldfields," *Urban Forum* 24 (2013): 503–21; Gay W. Seidman, "Shafted: The Social Impact of Down-Scaling in the Free State Goldfields," *South African Sociological Review* 5 (1993): 214–34.

Table 1: Sectoral employment figures (percentage) of Matjhabeng between 1996 and 2011[40]

Sector	1996	2001	2011
Agriculture	5.3	8.4	3.7
Mining	55.6	31.0	29.4
Manufacturing	4.4	7.8	6.1
Utilities	0.4	0.3	0.5
Construction	3.9	3.3	5.5
Transport	1.8	2.4	3.4
Trade	9.3	18.1	17.4
Finance	7.8	9.6	10.4
Services	11.5	19.2	23.6

Unemployment: Economic Insecurity

Globalization has produced chronic economic insecurities for the working class, both unemployed and employed. But unlike the working poor, the unemployed lack any meaningful prospect of a predictable income to meet their basic needs. This is particularly profound in Thabong.

Scrap-metal collecting, waiting for jobs at the side of the road, and grants and family remittances were three main responses of unemployed men to their insecurity. However, scrap-metal collecting and waiting on the road were seen as humiliating activities and undertaken out of desperation, and remittances from family members were an unpredictable and embarrassing source of income. Grants were often the only source of predictable income. Ex-mineworkers benefitted indirectly from child, old age, and disability grants.

Mineworkers' experiences of economic insecurity were often shaped by the masculine gender identity associated with mine work, including the role of a breadwinner. As Raseboko declared, "Unemployment has taken away my status as a man. A man gets his status from providing for his family. If I cannot provide for my family, what status is there?" These men are unable to fulfil their social and economic obligations and so they lose confidence and feel ashamed and worthless.

Family expectations do not adjust to these new challenges, leading to pressures and household tensions. Letsie declared, "You cannot provide for your family as a man. The pressure from my family was too much, I even thought about committing suicide. I felt that I was nothing, no one important to my own family. Useless. I cannot see what I am still living for."

Economic insecurity also breeds other forms of insecurities. Men accuse their wives of having affairs with employed men because when they can no longer provide for them. Molakolako stated, "When you work you can stand up for yourself. You can do things for yourself. I was retrenched in 2002 and divorced in 2010. When I ran out of money, it affected my marriage. She was cheating on me with a working man. We decided to divorce because I was going to kill her. She left me when I was sick [with silicosis]."

---

40 Marais et al., "Responses to Mine Downscaling"

New forms of financial and social envy emerge that have a polarizing effect on good neighborliness and threaten social solidarity. Ex-mineworkers experience envy when neighbors unload grocery bags while they have nothing in their homes. Their children report severe hunger and worry about food. They sometimes eat *pap* (maize meal) with water or peaches, and sometimes they drink only water before going to sleep.

Some ex-workers are given rotten food by their extended families. As Manketsi said, "My uncle brought rotten meat to give us here at home. Maybe in his eyes, we are dogs. He thinks he is better. Poverty brings a lot of disgusting things."

Participation in community burial and saving schemes is also eroded.

Ex-workers did not mention the Unemployment Insurance Fund as a source of economic security. This is not surprising given the high number of ex-mineworkers that the Department of Labour is trying to track down so they can submit qualification assessments. High illiteracy among ex-mineworkers discourages them from following through on their benefits.

Unemployment: Social Insecurity

Work plays an important role in bringing people together and providing social solidarity. Unemployment can dilute or break work friendships making it more difficult for people to meet or form friendships because of their isolation.

Unemployment is widespread in Welkom, meaning that many workless people are present in and around the community during working hours. This is social isolation of a different type. There is a sense of social blemishing through stigma, insults, and disrespect that ex-workers feel targets them because they are unemployed.

Stigma removes people from social acceptance and puts the moral status of a person in question. That unemployment is common does not de-stigmatize it because wage-work remains central.

Unemployment however also provides new possibilities for social solidarity. A group of ex-mineworkers gather regularly to challenge mining companies to re-employ them or employ their children. The gathering also plays another important role. Ex-workers re-unite to share old experiences and humor, to give advice and talk about what is happening in their lives, and to discuss politics. These gatherings help them to overcome the social isolation they suffer. Bonds of reciprocity and mutual obligation make it possible for these men to imagine new forms of solidarity without wage-work.

Unemployment as Psychological Impairment

Stress is a common experience of the unemployed. Economic and social insecurities contribute to the psychological distress of the wageless. These men constantly worry about keeping alive and they experience social stigma through the lens of lost masculinity.

Loss of masculinity includes the inability to provide for the family, a diminished sense of dignity and respect in the community, and an inability to ensure the sexual satisfaction of their spouse.

Some men felt that psychological distress and lack of confidence impacted negatively on their sex lives. They used a Sesotho metaphor to make sense of this situation: *kgomo esa kgorang ha e tlolele* ('a bull that has not eaten properly is unable to mate'). Their distressed sex life was more pronounced with their spouse, than their *nyatsi* or girlfriend. They often relied on *pitsa*, a traditional concoction to treat ailments including sexual problems.

To make sense of why their sexual drive was intact with their *nyatsi*, they said, *"Lapa le se nang Nyatsi lea shwa"* ('A third party strengthens a marriage'). The reason they gave for the variation in sex drive between their wife and *nyatsi* was that constant arguing, bickering, and tensions with their spouse made their *nyatsi* more appealing because there was nothing to argue about. It was an easy and mostly sexual relationship.

Dreams are important in understanding unemployment. They are not just about an individual's psychological state but are also collective and social because they are often based on social realities.

Ex-mineworkers with similar experiences of wage-work in the gold mines and abrupt mass retrenchments had similar dreams when unemployed. Dreams reveal things about the individual but also about the social conditions in which they exist.

The nostalgia for work was revealed in dreams. Nostalgia means loss and displacement, and ex-mineworkers felt abruptly displaced from a world of employment and lost in new forms of anxiety. Through dreams, solidarities forged in wage-work underground, the ability to provide, and a strong social status were evoked.

Bodily Meanings

Two ideas of the body emerged in this research.

First, the black body has been an instrument of production to create wealth in the South African gold mining industry and economy. After it is used and injured, it is disposed of. But it continues to bear the brutality of mine work through deep scars inflicted by sharp falling rocks and occupational diseases such as phthisis.

Secondly, the black body is a metaphor to describe a fractured social and moral order. Ex-workers described their experience of unemployment through strong images of incomplete, unrecognizable, and sick bodies with missing and injured parts. Sickness and disability were used to describe unemployment as a condition of moral dysfunction.

Through ideas of the body, it is possible to see unemployment as a symptom of a much deeper problem. Unemployment reflects a condition of loss, a moral loss.

Future Hopes for a Decent Wageless Life

What happens when full employment becomes impossible? How else can we ensure that the working class meets its basic needs, attains a decent life and overcomes a moral abyss when unemployed? One way to approach this would be through a Basic Income Grant (BIG).

Ex-mineworkers saw the positive impact of the BIG in reducing the insecurity of unemployment. They still preferred employment as a way of earning a living rather than handouts. Handouts could not resolve the social isolation and stigma. They also believed that such a grant would make people lazy. Their partial rejection of the BIG was underpinned by the moral commitment to wage-work.

The BIG is a guaranteed, unconditional sum given to all citizens to use however they choose.[41] The findings affirmed the centrality of wage-work. People want jobs, not grants. Yet jobs are unattainable for millions of work-seekers who struggle daily to meet their basic needs. Grants were not an acceptable policy response for ex-mineworkers. The challenge is that ex-mineworkers and various sections of South Africa cannot imagine a decent life outside of wage-work. For the BIG to become a viable policy solution, ex-mineworkers, policy makers, and analysts would have to imagine a world where workers no longer rely on wages for basic needs.

---

41 James Ferguson, *Give a Man a Fish: Reflections on the New Politics of Distribution* (Durham: Duke University Press, 2015); Liz Fouksman, "Universal Basic Income: A Radical Post-Labour Agenda," *South African Labour Bulletin* 41 (2017): 28–30; Guy Standing, *Basic Income: And How We Can Make It Happen* (London: Pelican Books, 2017).

Mary Jo Maynes and Ann Waltner
Spinning Yarn: The Changing Place of Girls' Work in Chinese and European History

The work of producing textiles crossed the threshold of the home in the early modern era in both China and Europe. Spinning yarn, our particular focus here, was typically a female occupation, and a skill that many girls learned at home as they grew up. Married women also span, of course. But younger, unmarried women had the potential to spin full-time, uninterrupted by the increased domestic responsibilities brought on by marriage and childbearing. In 1800, girls in both China and Europe span mostly at home; the yarn they span was destined for the market as well as for use by their own household. By 1900, however, young spinners in Europe were mostly working outside the home, often at large mechanized mills, where they produced exclusively for the market. Girl spinners in China, meanwhile, were much more likely to still be working at home, though they too increasingly produced yarn for the market. This comparative difference in the age- and gender-specific history of spinning interests us. What significance might the location of girls' work have for patterns of economic development as well as for young women's options?

Answering these questions involves the challenge of finding traces of working girls in the historical record, which has definitely marginalized them and their activities. The history of the census is an important example of this invisibility. Government censuses began to appear with some regularity in Europe in the nineteenth century. However, census takers were far more likely to name the occupation of the male household head than that of his wife or children. Trends in occupations that were self-reported by young women, such as in marriage registers, can help to counter their invisibility in the census, as we shall discuss below. Finding girl spinners in the sources is even more challenging in the case of China. As we develop our argument here, we indicate the types of sources through which we have been able to get a glimpse of this elusive but important labor.

Girls' Textile Work at Home around 1800

Let us begin with China. In textile-producing regions of Jiangnan in southeastern China around 1800, it would take four hours of spinning cotton to produce enough yarn to occupy a weaver for an hour. To maximize the efficiency of cotton weavers, who in the prevailing system of home cloth production were often adult married women, other members of the household – younger girls or older women – would spin the needed yarn. Kenneth Pomeranz notes that since there was little cotton yarn for sale at this time in China, weaving households relied on family members to spin.[42]

Spinning was introduced very early into a girl's socialization. Educational advice manuals suggested that a girl should begin working with textiles at about the same age that a boy should begin to learn to read. The late sixteenth-century writer Lü Kun claimed that a ten-year-old girl was old enough to spin.[43] Other sources linked the labor of producing cotton or silk yarn to particular

---

42 Kenneth Pomeranz, *The Great Divergence: China, Europe, and the Making of the Modern World Economy* (Princeton: Princeton University Press, 2005): 249.
43 Chu-bin Liang, "Mingdai nügong yi beifang funu wei zhongxin zhi tantao" ("An Exploration of Women's Work in the Ming Dynasty, focusing on the North") (Ph.D. thesis, National Central University, Zhongli, Taiwan, 2001): 66–7.

stages of the female lifecycle and to the home as a textile workplace. In Jiangnan, women typically married much younger than their Western European counterparts – at seventeen or eighteen – and they usually joined their husband's father's household.[44] Gender and generational authority based on household and kinship systems also structured production; spinners might include the daughters, daughters-in-law, wife, or mother of the male household head. Analyses of production cannot be separated from family and lifecycle history. It was not uncommon in China for a very young girl to join a household as a 'little daughter-in-law,' who might be incorporated into her future husband's household and its workforce long before the marriage was consummated.

The Chinese state encouraged this form of production and labor, in a variety of ways. One way was through illustrated texts, such as the *Gengzhi tu* ("Pictures of Spinning and Weaving"), a series of older paintings and poems, revised and reissued by the Qing court at the end of the seventeenth century, and circulated with the aim of encouraging silk production in the empire. This source offers rich depictions of textile work at home. We cannot, of course, read these images as representations of actual practices, but we can read them as ideological statements about normative gendered and generational divisions of labor in peasant households in the early modern era. The *Gengzhi tu* depicts girls and women of different ages involved in household silk production, and moving seamlessly between the work of childcare and the work of producing silk.[45]

In eighteenth-century Europe, we find the same gendering of the spinning workforce. There were important differences between China and Europe, however, in the marriage system. Women in major textile regions of Europe typically married in their mid-twenties. Moreover, they were more likely to set up a new household with their husband when they married than move into their father-in-law's home. Spinning full-time could continue for a longer phase of the young woman's lifecycle in Europe, and she was unlikely, upon marriage, to be incorporated into the workforce of an established household run by her husband's family.[46]

French silk production offers a good example. Eighteenth-century French sources generally associate spinning and silk reeling with unmarried or young women, though not, as in China, exclusively so. The original caption for the image of silk reeling in the 1772 edition of *L'Encyclopédie* was explicit in regard to the personnel it depicted: "This vignette shows the process of drawing silk from the cocoons and two girls (*filles*) so occupied – one at the crank of the reel and the other at the cauldron." The former is later referred to as the *tourneuse* and the latter simply as an *ouvrière*. The French words employed for these occupations, as well as that of spinner in general (*fileuse*), use the feminine form.[47]

---

44 Tsui-jung Liu, "The Demography of Two Chinese Clans in Hsiao-shan, Chekiang, 1650–1850," in Susan Hanley and Arthur Wolf, eds., *Family and Demography in East Asian History* (Stanford: Stanford University Press, 1985): 28.

45 *Yuzhi gengzhi tu* ("Imperially Commissioned Pictures of Tilling and Weaving") (Beijing: Imperial Press at Wuyingdian, 1696); https://artsandculture.google.com/asset/gengzhi-tu-pictures-of-tilling-and-weaving-hand-coloured-woodblock-prints/aQGhDXXcUkBuGA, accessed July 10, 2018.

46 John Hajnal, "European Marriage Patterns in Perspective," in D.V. Glass and D.E.C. Eversley, eds., *Population in History: Essays in Historical Demography* (London: Edward Arnold Publishers, 1965); Hans Medick, *Weben Und Überleben in Laichingen. Lokalgeschichte Als Allgemeine Geschichte* (Göttingen: Vandenhoeck and Ruprecht, 1996); Sheilagh C. Ogilvie, *A Bitter Living: Women, Markets, and Social Capital in Early Modern Germany* (Oxford: Oxford University Press, 2003).

47 Denis Diderot and Jean le Rond d'Alembert, eds., *Encyclopédie, ou dictionnaire raisonné des sciences, des arts et des métiers, etc.* ("Encyclopedia: or a Systematic Dictionary of the Sciences, Arts, and Crafts") (University of Chicago: ARTFL Encyclopédie Project); see http://encyclopedie.uchicago.edu/, accessed July 10, 2018.

At this point in time, most silk thread production was done in households or small sheds in rural areas near where the silkworms were raised. An 1839 household budget analysis from the Department of the Gard, a region involved in protoindustrial silk production, featured a household that combined agricultural production with work in silk. Almost half of the family's income in this case came from the labor of the wife and her two 'post-pubescent' daughters who were engaged in spinning silk. Although few census enumerators in silk-producing regions of southern France listed the occupations of women or children, young women often self-reported their occupations when they married. For example, in the small town of l'Isle-sur-la-Sorgue in the 1820s, ten percent of the city's brides claimed to be either a spinner (*fileuse*) or a silk worker (*ouvrière en soie*). In the city of Avignon, one of the older silk centers of southern France, during the 1820s, over forty percent of brides reported themselves to be silk workers (*ouvrières en soie*; *devideuses*).[48] The protoindustrial spinning labor force in Europe relied heavily on female workers, most of whom had learned the necessary skills as girls or young women and practiced them before leaving home for marriage. Young women were also heavily engaged in spinning the flax, wool, or cotton yarn that eventually made its way onto weavers' looms across Europe.

Patterns of Change, 1800–1900

Young female labor was significant in the household production of textiles in both China and Europe around 1800. The composition of the labor force and the relations between home and work changed in the following century. In China, textile production expanded rapidly after 1800. Bozhong Li estimates that cotton production in Jiangnan doubled between 1700 and the mid-nineteenth century. Silk production also more than doubled during the same period. Both finished cloth and raw silk were exported; raw silk (or silk thread) was an especially important export to Europe as Europeans began to develop their own silk-making capacities.[49]

Cotton thread and cloth continued to be produced in rural households, although the households involved in the spinning did not necessarily grow the cotton they span.[50] Household-based production for market distribution as well as for domestic use dominated the cotton industry in China well into the twentieth century. Some cotton factories in China were launched toward the end of the nineteenth century; the first one opened in Shanghai in 1889. By 1920, there were over 30,000 cotton workers in mills in Shanghai, about half of whom were women. However, most of the cotton cloth used for ordinary consumption was not factory produced. Xinwu Xu has estimated that, in 1860, 99.5 percent of the cotton worn in China continued to be produced in rural households. As late as 1920, sixty-five percent of the cotton consumed in China was what he calls "rural native cotton." Chinese peasant households produced textiles for their own use well into the twentieth century, a phenomenon which Xu labels "a distinctive phenomenon in world history."[51]

The story of silk in China was somewhat different. In this sector, production began to move into urban factories toward the end of the nineteenth century. Girl workers eventually moved as

48 Archives Départementales de Vaucluse, Série E Etat Civil, L'isle-sur-la-Sorgue.
49 Bozhong Li, *Agricultural Development in Jiangnan* (New York: St. Martin's Press, 1998): 33.
50 Harriet Zurndorfer, "Cotton Textile Manufacture and Marketing in Late Imperial China and the 'Great Divergence'," *Journal of the Economic and Social History of the Orient*, 54 (2011): 701–38.
51 Xinwu Xu, "The Struggle of the Handicraft Industry against Machine Textiles in China," *Modern China* 14 (1998): 39–43.

well. According to Lillian Li, the introduction of large-scale spinning mills around Shanghai in the late nineteenth century meant that the household system altered. Peasants increasingly sold silk worms to the mills, rather than selling reeled silk, and so silk reeling was no longer a largely domestic enterprise. Household reelers were thus displaced and either had to change the work they did or move to the filatures. According to Li, in Shanghai reeling mills, "girls from eight to twelve years old" were assigned the most "unpleasant" tasks – tending the basins and finding the cocoons' threads – while older women did the actual reeling.[52]

This evidence suggests that it was possible to move girls and young women workers into factory settings in China by the very end of the nineteenth century. However, it is a notable comparative difference that girls who worked in textile production in China continued to work predominantly in small household production units long after such young spinners had moved out of the home in most regions of Europe.

Female textile workers 'left home' much earlier in Europe. As textile production moved gradually and at a regionally varied pace from cottages and sheds to mills during in the eighteenth century, young unmarried women on the move played a key role in the transition. They arguably comprised the majority of Europe's earliest factory labor force and were taken for granted as an available workforce. Young women's labor brought competitive advantages to factory entrepreneurs in the global struggle for domination of various textile markets. New technologies that revolutionized British textile production, for example, were developed with an eye toward a workforce that was often explicitly imagined as young and female. According to Maxine Berg, "In calico printing, processes were broken down into a series of operations performed particularly well by teenage girls who contributed manual dexterity (learned at home) with high labor intensity. The spinning jenny was first invented for use by a young girl, its horizontal wheel making it uncomfortable for an adult worker to use for any length of time."[53]

Similar thinking influenced the economic development strategies of German states in the early nineteenth century. For example, between 1817 and 1829, Württemberg's Ministry of the Interior solicited ideas for encouraging the state's linen industry in the face of a prospective flood of British machine-produced goods. One proposal makes explicit the author's imagined labor pool as he describes a spinning machine "recently invented" in Munich: "This machine is operated by one person who requires the assistance of eight twelve-year-old girls; they then do the work of seventy-two people (*Menschen*). In that seventy-two threads flow out of the machine from the prepared flax."[54]

What was distinctive at this point was not the age- and gender- division of labor in Europe's textile industry, but rather the presumed mobility of a pool of young, unmarried female textile workers. As we have seen, until around 1800, Europe's young women workers worked mostly in households and small shops. But those among them who were still unmarried began to leave home to move to nearby or more distant factories or silk reeling sheds, following a pattern that was not so different from the older routine of engaging in lifecyclic domestic service on farms or in cities. They eventually moved into large factories whose spinning and weaving machines were powered

---

52 Lillian Li, *China's Silk Trade: Traditional Industry in the Modern World, 1842–1937* (Cambridge: Harvard University East Asia Center, 1981): 29.

53 Maxine Berg, "What Difference did Women's Work Make to the Industrial Revolution?" in Pamela Sharpe, ed., *Women's Work. The English Experience, 1650–1914* (London: Arnold, 1998): 161.

54 Baden-Württemberg Landesarchiv, E14 Bü1170: 3–5.

by water or steam. This pattern of labor force migration by young, unmarried women remained a key distinction between Europe and China from around 1800 until around 1900.

The early textile industrial centers of Europe were filled with young women: "The image of factory and workshop labor is the 'mill girl' ... eighty-two percent of the female textile workers of Roubaix were under thirty. In Lancashire, seventy-five percent of female workers were single ... The factory became an alternative route, instead of service."[55] In the large cotton spinnery established near Waterford on the south coast of Ireland in 1835, forty-two percent of the mill's employees were girls under the age of twenty-one.[56]

This pattern prevailed in many modern textile mills elsewhere in Europe. Jean Bonnet, a self-made man who owned silk mills in Jujurieux in southern France, recruited young girls from the poor agricultural families of the region, promising "to give them board, lodging, clothes, and all that they required, together with small wages, and to teach them not only the art of silk making, but to give them a general education." According to Edward Watherston, a British journalist writing in the 1870s, Bonnet's establishment boasted dormitories staffed by members of religious orders who maintained strict discipline, a useful weapon, according to Watherston, in the struggle "to tame these little savages into order."[57] In Bonnet's mill, the very young girl workers were provided with a new 'home' and lived under the factory owner's disciplinary regime. But most girls who worked in factories had to fend for themselves and make new homes in factory towns.

The long-term consequences of these new labor patterns for young women in Europe were mixed. Certainly, the relatively low wages they commanded precluded economic independence. Moreover, in many textile-producing regions of Europe, the late eighteenth-century promise of prosperity was often darkened or interrupted by crises, for example, a protracted depression in Württemberg's linen industry in the first half of the nineteenth century or the silkworm disease that devastated cocoon production and silk reeling in southern France beginning in the 1850s. The young woman spinner was thus an economically and socially vulnerable, if pioneering, figure when she crossed the threshold of the home to leave for work.

The Place of Girls' and Young Women's Work across Time and Region

The role that girls' spinning played in regional and global economic development is undeniable. But the problematic character of female labor in general, the cultural tendencies in both China and Europe to absorb female labor into the realm of 'reproduction' as opposed to 'production,' and the special marginality of the labor of younger and older women all serve to make spinning an especially complex and thus telling form of work. How do notions like 'women's work' or 'girls' work' relate to and refine conceptions of work more broadly in different historical contexts? How did the place where the work was done (especially inside or outside of the home) affect its meaning as well as its economic value?

55 Deborah Simonton, *A History of European Women's Work* (London: Routledge, 1998): 139.
56 Tom Hunt, *Portrait of an Industrial Village and Its Cotton Industry* (Dublin: Irish Academic Press, 2000): 59.
57 Edward J. Watherston, "French Silk Manufactures, and the Industrial Employment of Women," *Good Words* (1879): 107.

Since the pioneering work of Louise Tilly and Joan Scott, who posed these questions in European historiography in the late 1970s, historians of Europe have grappled with the problem of assessing women's economic contributions in domestic and non-domestic workplaces, in the past and in the present.[58] Feminist historians and economists have continued to grapple with these questions in Chinese history as well.[59] Huge questions remain about gendered relationships to the market in both regions. Normative sources from both regions, ranging from household manuals to economic theory, suggest that elite observers were suspicious of the moral consequences of women's involvement in market transactions even as they observed the market's expansion. For example, Shangpeng Pang's household instructions (written in Guangdong in the sixteenth century) insisted that members of his household should make garments for family members at home but could purchase clothing for servants, establishing a distance between family and the market.[60] This suspicion is echoed in English- and German-language sources such as advice manuals for girls dating back to the late eighteenth and early nineteenth centuries, which warned girls against the tyranny of fashion and the obsession with acquiring new clothing at the risk of their virtue.

Such gendered and moralistic dimensions of economic history are illuminated by attention to the relationship between home and workplace, and the related but separate question of the work of producing goods for household use and for the market. For example, the fact that Chinese girls and women began to do less outdoor farm work and more work indoors spinning and weaving when it became more profitable to do so may have encouraged normative depictions of 'indoor' activities as virtuous and respectable for women, even though they connected women more directly with market production.[61]

In both areas, early modern age- and gender-based divisions of labor changed in response to developments in markets for agricultural products, labor, and textile goods, but they did not change in the same way. These varying temporal and regional patterns of household labor in agriculture and textile work, and their relationships to space and to the market, are at the core of our comparative observations. These patterns held consequences for the history of gender, generational relations, and, we suggest, for long-term patterns of economic development. In particular, the different relationship between the households and the market that we have sketched out here may have contributed to the longer viability in China of the combination of household-based protoindustry and farming. In Europe, the earlier concentration of textile production in urban mills was built upon the expectation that rural youth, including girls, could leave home – an expectation that undermined the strategy of rural households to base their livelihood on a combination of agricultural and industrial production.

---

58 Louise A. Tilly and Joan W. Scott, *Women, Work, and Family* (New York: Holt, Rinehart and Winston, 1978).

59 Melissa Brown, Laurel Bossen, Hill Gates, and Damian Satterthwaite-Phillips, "Marriage Mobility and Footbinding in Pre–1949 Rural China: A Reconsideration of Gender, Economics, and Meaning in Social Causation," *The Journal of Asian Studies* 71 (2012): 1035–67.

60 Shangpeng Pang, *Pangshi jiaxun* ("Pang's Family Instructions") Baibu congshu jicheng, no. 93 (Taipei: Yiwen shuguan, 1968).

61 Li, *Agricultural Development*: 142–3.

Section 3
Construction, Demolition, Relocation

Anupama Rao
Subaltern Urbanism, or Dwelling and the Unhoused: Histories of Housing in the United States and India

This essay begins with a set of personal observations about the relationship between the physical house and the intimate experience of space as the point of entry into broader questions about the intersection between built form and social experience across cities in India and the United States – between Bombay and Chicago in particular. I use my own personal history of moving from Bangalore to Chicago's south side, where I encountered the effects of spatial segregation, to reflect more broadly on the politics of comparison; to ask what is shared and what is distinct about the social life of housing in the north Atlantic and the Global South. To do so I adopt the mode of 'disjunctural' reading, of reading across specific histories of housing deprivation that are nonetheless reflected in urban form and in shared logics of how spatial segregation impacts (and is itself the consequence of) social exclusion. My focus is on the presence and perspective of the homeless, the evicted, the self-housed, and those relegated to public housing (tenements, ghettos, projects). Their experiences illuminate the significance of housing as a key site where state policy, ideologies of social difference, and forms of capital accumulation converge.

Desiring Home

My partner and I began to discuss moving out of our subsidized university housing some years after I had begun conducting historical research on urban Bombay, subaltern neighborhoods, and the question of social housing. Our search for housing in New York City culminated with the purchase of an apartment in 2014, which we then gutted and renovated.

The bureaucracy we encountered along the way was extensive and suggested that efforts to standardize real estate property are not conflict-free. Attempts to make the home into an asset are subject to multiple challenges – for owner and renters, and for housing activists and state authorities. Like everyone else who buys property in New York City, we found ourselves negotiating a maze of legal regulations that elaborated a fundamental contradiction between viewing one's home as an economic asset, on the one hand, and viewing housing as a universal right, as shelter or refuge, on the other.

The process of 'making home' through destruction and renovation was pleasurable but fraught. It brought back vivid memories of the home I had left behind in 1979, when my family moved from India to the United States. Every nook and corner of that house in Bangalore was etched in my mind. This was no doubt the consequence of a semi-solitary childhood that had sharpened my powers of observation and recall, but it was also aided by the vital experience of social interconnection in a 'joint family' that included my paternal grandparents. The house occupied a large corner plot. It was designed by my engineer father, who had returned from England with a taste for natural ventilation and quality materials. I remember the polished teak and rosewood inside, as I do the coconut, pomegranate, and guava trees outdoors.

I arrived in Chicago when I was ten. For the next decade, it was the geography of the city's south side that constituted my mental map. This was the world of the Prairie Shores and Lake Meadows high-rises along Lakeshore Drive; the once-stately homes now burned out or boarded up along Indiana Avenue as one made one's way into Hyde Park; and the one-way streets and brown-stones that surrounded the University of Chicago, where there was always talk, in hushed tones, about 'no go' areas like Midway Plaisance. It was as if the city's segregated history indexed a deep violence that could incapacitate thought unless we kept it at arm's length. And so we did. Many of us embraced European thought and theory. In the process we forgot that the University of Chicago was the birthplace of urban sociology, the famous Chicago School. In fact, the first department of sociology in the United States was founded here in 1892. The Chicago School's focus on the city as a social laboratory and its investment in ethnographic methods produced a number of fine-grained studies of unions, race relations, housing, and transport. The university's own efforts at racial engineering was rarely acknowledged, however, even though evidence of its destruction of a once-thriving African-American neighborhood was all around us.

My memories of Bangalore only make sense when placed against the contrasting experiences of Chicago's south side, much as the story of our real estate acquisition in New York called to mind ongoing research on housing in Bombay. The cross-referencing of historical geographies and personal itinerary, not to mention the apparent convergence between historically distinct and logically disjointed spatial processes, constitutes a mode of critical reading. It is a mode of reading that sees comparison as both politically necessary and methodologically insufficient. Such reading is insufficient because comparison always introduces the idea of a developmental norm against which objects are compared. Yet comparison also enhances political perception: when we compare x with y, we are also asking how x was produced, why x appears to be lacking when it is compared with y, or how it is that x and y, though they are different, appear to have been produced by similar processes.

I utilize this disjunctural mode of reading to explore two distinct, yet equally stigmatized, forms of housing, the American ghetto and the Indian slum, which allows us to see that the question of housing is at heart a question about managing subaltern populations through the regulation of space.

Housing and Historical Comparison

What links India to the United States? What links Chicago and Bombay? Is it possible to trace moments of historical convergence when the two spaces came to be constituted by similar social forces and economic processes? The restructuring of the colonial economy was one such moment when loss of British access to American cotton spurred the growth of Bombay as an important imperial hub that developed around the cotton economy and linked the city with its hinterland through technologies of travel, labor migration, and environmental transformation. Chicago's rise as a modern city was enabled by the fire of 1871 that created a rare opportunity for urban zoning and modern planning, as did Bombay's bubonic plague of 1896. The connections are conjunctural but the consequences are visible and long-lasting: in the aftermath of their natural disasters, both Chicago and Bombay came to be associated with forms of stigmatized housing, the ghetto and the slum, respectively, which reflect broader processes of mobilizing labor and regulating social difference through spatial politics.

The political geographer David Harvey has suggested that we expand our understanding of political activism to include what he calls "urban revolutions," especially struggles around housing.[1]

---

1 David Harvey, "The Right to the City," *New Left Review* 53 (2008): 23–40.

Harvey links urbanization with the absorption of surplus (labor and capital). He argues that in the aftermath of efforts to produce the modern city as a space of political pacification to prevent revolutionary action, urban dispossession has entailed "repeated bouts of urban restructuring through 'creative destruction,' which nearly always has a class dimension since it is the poor, the underprivileged, and those marginalized from political power that suffer first and foremost from this process."[2] My observations about urban segregation in Chicago and the history of black housing in the United States more generally certainly bear this out, as do the failures of social housing in Bombay. Let me elaborate.

Negro Housing

The mass migration of African-Americans from Mississippi and the Carolinas to urban centers in the Midwest and Northeast numbered 1.5 million in the period between 1910 and 1930. A further three million migrated from 1940 to 1960. This led to housing scarcity in the northern cities. The legislated right to property ownership was secured via practices of red lining and racial covenanting. These were financial instruments that enabled the social exclusion of African-Americans and precluded their accumulation of private property through exclusion from credit markets. Financial exclusion and the imposition of a tax for black homeowners in the form of an inflated monthly payment that counted towards eventual home ownership enabled conditions of financial precarity and led, ultimately, to home foreclosures. Indeed, the politics of home ownership and the desire for residence in non-segregated or mixed-race neighborhoods continues to structure the anxious everyday of a socially mobile black bourgeoisie.[3]

Meanwhile, the African-American working poor and the underclass was largely concentrated in the ghetto, a symbol of urban outcasting and a consequence of the structured exclusion of African-Americans from the housing market.[4] By the 1960s, the ghetto was on its way to becoming functionally obsolete and unviable. Landlords decided to burn their buildings and take the insurance money as profit. For instance, an article in *Time* from 1977 noted that there had been over 7,000 fires in New York City's South Bronx, that Chicago's Humboldt Park area had some 400 charred, abandoned buildings, and that 10,000 burned-out houses in Detroit stood vacant.[5] This was followed by the War on Drugs and mass incarceration, while resources were diverted to urban peripheries through highways, infrastructural transformation, and suburbanization. This led to a reterritorialization of American cities.

The connection between the problem of so-called 'Negro housing' and worker housing in Bombay is counter-intuitive. It suggests divergent outcomes for what was in essence a global problematic: urban pacification in the context of industrial unrest in the interwar. Urban exclusion in North American cities was produced by the ways in which the right to housing was racially regulated between the protection of private property rights, on the one hand, and complemented

---

2 Harvey, "The Right to the City," 33.

3 Ta-Nehisi Coates, "The Case for Black Reparations," *The Atlantic*, June, 2014.

4 The sociologist Loïc Wacquant locates the plantation, the project, and the prison as sites for aggregating black bodies, which are then subject to distinctive routines of discipline and dehumanization. In his account, the American ghetto is a key intermediary destination in racializing processes. Loïc Wacquant, "From Slavery to Mass Incarceration: Rethinking the 'Race Question' in the US," *New Left Review* 13 (2002): 41–60.

5 "Arson for Hate and Profit," *Time*, October 31, 1977.

by racially demarcated spheres of containment on the other, which was used to justify the violent policing of the ghetto. Meanwhile Bombay's urban landscape was distinguished by policies that produced scarcity of housing. These generated practices of self-housing, with the working poor engaged in the production of informal housing for themselves in the context of government apathy for social housing. Efforts to control labor produced distinctive infrastructures of inequality; they produced housing types and urban landscapes that reproduced the logic of spatial segregation with enduring consequences.

The Urban Question in Bombay

The history of modern Bombay is linked with the rise and fall of the region's cotton economy. Problems faced by British industry in procuring cotton from the American South during the American Civil War led to the opening of colonial markets in Egypt and India, which was aided by steam shipping across the Suez Canal. The rich black soil of the Khandesh and Berar region was given over to cotton, while technologies for rationalizing production and accelerating the circulation of Bombay cotton created new linkages between the rural hinterland and the city, and between Bombay and the British empire.[6] However, the end of the Civil War saw a sharp drop in demand for global cotton. This intersected with excessive revenue demands on the peasantry. Famine and the infamous Deccan Riots of 1877 followed.[7] Rural dispossession was a major cause of migration to Bombay at the turn of the twentieth century.

Meanwhile an epidemic of the bubonic plague in Bombay (1896) provided colonial administrators with an alibi for demolishing large swaths of the central city. The plague allowed planners and government officials to conduct mass demolitions, which were followed by extensive experiments in urban governance and industrial housing. Unhygienic housing was razed. The Bombay Improvement Trust was established to oversee the construction of poor and working-class housing. An important experiment in public-private partnerships between state and indigenous capital to finance housing construction was undertaken. Money to purchase land in working-class areas by the government was realized through the sale of areas beyond the city's limit to individual investors who land-banked and later used the land to erect middle-class housing colonies in the interwar period. However, the immediate result of urban social engineering through authoritarian policy was a scarcity of worker housing; more homes were demolished than constructed after the plague. As the 1921 Industrial Disputes Committee observed, "The heaviest burden which Labour has to bear in Bombay arises from the deficiency of housing accommodation and the low quality of much that is available."[8] The *chawl* [tenement] became the symbol of worker housing and a sign of the city's ongoing housing scarcity.

---

6 Sandip Hazareesingh, "Chasing Commodities over the Surface of the Globe," Commodities of Empire Working Paper No. 1, http://www.open.ac.uk/Arts/ferguson-centre/commodities-of-empire/working-papers/WP01.pdf; For an account of why American cotton did not "take" in the cotton growing districts of southern Maharashtra; and "Cotton, Climate, and Colonialism in Dharwar, Western India, 1840–1880," *Journal of Historical Geography* 38 (2012): 1–17.
7 While western India's peasants suffered, Bombay's merchant communities shifted capital to cotton mills, which could be converted to textiles for the domestic market following the opening of railroads in the middle of the century, rather than playing a subordinate role in the international market, which was dominated by European finance and shipping.
8 Kanji Dwarkadas. *Forty-Five Years with Labour* (Bombay: Asia Publishing House, 1962): 27–9.

Chawl

The scarcity of housing in Bombay was a consistent theme among colonial officials, mill owners, and native elites, even though their policies routinely contributed to un-housing people, or else pushing the working poor into episodic encounters with homelessness. The *chawl* embodies the contradiction between the abundance of labor and Bombay's housing scarcity – a marked feature of industrial capitalism in urban India.

Most *chawls* were three to five stories high. They comprised single rooms, typically ten-by-ten feet, with a small drain in one corner for washing. A verandah ran along the length of the room.[9] The bulk of them were constructed between 1922 and 1928 in response to a wave of organized strike action by textile laborers. They thus had a distinct association with working-class protest.[10] Indeed, central Bombay, also known as *Lalbagh* (lit. red garden), came to be associated with working-class radicalism and union politics.

Overcrowding was justified through recourse to racial stereotypes about the natives' penchant for dirt and crowded living. These stereotypes became a powerful alibi to support the steady defor-mation of laboring life. Yet their social effects were often unintended. Given their human density, *chawls* were also spaces of thick sociality and interaction, desired and undesirable.

Water taps and public toilets were sites of everyday violence. Accidents were frequent: women's saris caught fire while cooking in ill-ventilated and poorly illuminated rooms, and men could be run over if they slept outdoors on the pavement, which they often did in order to make space for women and children inside.[11] Spaces in and around *chawls* were used for communal purposes: as *khanavalis* (canteens) for single working men; as drink shops and gambling dens, which were freely scattered in mill areas with *chawl* owners often keeping their own shops patronized by resi-dents; by hawkers, especially women selling vegetables and other daily necessities; as community centers; reading rooms, and *vyayamshalas* (exercise halls) created through residents' initiatives. Other practices of street sociality arose from precarious employment, which created a continuum between work, street, and home.[12]

Dalits ('untouchables') lived in tin sheds created by hammering out kerosene tins after they were opened and fitted together, or in *zavlis*, huts made of dry leaves of coconut or date palm. Built in long rows like warehouses, their roofs covered with rubbish, and a thin tin wall providing privacy between sheds, these places had no water, taps, or lavatories. The co-presence of the *chawl* and these more numerous, makeshift shelters were a constant presence in laboring areas, and a precursor to the slum as the modal housing form in contemporary Mumbai.

---

9 CRIT Team, *Housing Typologies in Mumbai*, http://urban-age.net/0_downloads/House_Types_in_Mumbai.pdf, accessed June 25, 2017.
10 By then, the Bombay Development Directorate had replaced the Bombay City Improvement Trust as the authority tasked with the provision of social housing.
11 Radha Kumar, "City Lives: Workers' Housing and Rent in Bombay, 1911–1947," *Economic and Political Weekly* (June 25, 1987): 47–56; Vanessa Caru, "Where is Politics Housed? Tenants' Movement and Subaltern Politicization: Bombay 1920–1940," *Revue d'histoire moderne et contemporaine* 4 (2011): 71–92.
12 Alexander Robert Burnett-Hurst, *Labour and Housing in Bombay: A Study in the Economic Conditions of the Wage-Earning Classes in Bombay* (London: P.S. King, 1925).

Slum

It is significant that there was no comprehensive policy for the provision of social housing in Bombay after Independence. Instead, slum services, rehabilitation, and now resettlement in high-rise buildings are retroactive efforts (by planners and politicians) to address the social fact of self-housing by the urban poor.

Today, those places once stigmatized as slums are sites of enormous value generation. Ironically, those areas of the city such as the notorious M-Ward in east-central Mumbai, which has a long history of receiving populations displaced by slum eviction and housing demolition (especially from historic working-class areas), now generates the largest quantum of TDR (Transferable Development Rights). TDR allows builders to provide sub-standard housing for slum-dwellers, in return for the right to build taller buildings – luxury housing – in wealthy parts of the city through a complex calculus.

Slum rehabilitation entrenches the logic of private property through slum-dwellers' desire for home ownership. But it also provides land in the virtualized form of the TDR necessary for building middle and upper-class housing at market rates. Real estate speculation in Mumbai is predicated on the social fact of the slum.

Conclusion

A brief snapshot of the infrastructure that governed the social life of Bombay labor and the lives of urban African-Americans reveals something significant. In each case, the state was an active player in managing social difference through the politics of space. In one case, this process worked by producing the scarcity of housing as matter of urban policy. This led to the emergence of the slum as the quintessential urban form associated with poor housing in Bombay. In the American case, spatial incarceration prevailed.

Unlike European cities, which generally built up a city core and then put slums out on the periphery, American cities followed an opposite pattern, with resources diverted to urban peripheries. This means the 'urban crisis' in the de-industrializing United States bore a strange resemblance to the 'urban crisis' in the industrializing Global South. In both spaces, industrializing urban cores that had drawn on socially stigmatized labor and settled them in low-income enclaves began to extrude these populations to the outskirts of the city, or, as in the American context, to incarcerate them and remove them from the labor force altogether. Today, those same urban centers where social housing was created to provide a stable labor force for industrial capital – sites of 'white flight' in the United States, or dense zones of deindustrialization in cities like Bombay – are thriving. Rather than laboring bodies, however, it is the land on which labor was housed that is valuable for speculative activity the world over.[13] In this contest between land and labor, housing forms the key mediating term: it is the site where surplus is extracted and the space where it is parked.

Housing politics – struggles to secure housing and evade high rents; the experience of episodic evictions that most of the working poor experience; establishing informal settlements proximate to formal housing; struggles to secure tenurial claims – are projects of making home and securing

---

13 Saskia Sassen, "A Savage Sorting of Winner and Losers: Contemporary Versions of Primitive Accumulation," *Globalization* 7 (2010): 23–50.

urban belonging. It is worth rehearsing the different valences of the idea of housing that makes it so worthy of attention. As property, housing is enmeshed in property regimes; as infrastructure, housing is subject to government planning and regulation; as inhabitation, the house attains symbolic significance as a space that is rendered habitable through practices of care and intimacy. Because the movement between house and home is also a movement between collective social projects and the desire for sociality and intimacy, we cannot afford to think housing without also imagining new ways of living together.

Thaddeus Sunseri
Evicted in Dar es Salaam: From Tanganyika Packers to Uptown Kawe

In modern Tanzania, a new program of urban restructuring is underway that threatens to cause substantial social upheaval by uprooting and relocating millions of impoverished city dwellers castigated by the state as invaders (*wavamizi*). According to the 2015 Master Plan for Dar es Salaam, Tanzania's principal city, as many as 3.6 million residents (out of a population of 4.5 million) live in squatter settlements or unplanned areas. Many houses have improper land titles or exist in non-surveyed areas. All are potential targets of eviction.[14] The Master Plan for the next ten years has lofty goals, seeking to restructure the city to ease transportation gridlock, create new satellite cities closer to residential townships, and remove squatters and unplanned houses from flood-prone areas, swampy lands, coastal lands, open spaces, and industrial zones. It aims to create "a competitive economic environment... attractive to investment and business," which will "provide opportunities for all to develop socially, politically, and economically."[15] Because eighty percent of the city's population lacks proper titles, city residents need to brace themselves for massive evictions beginning in June 2016.

These evictions are often justified by warnings of climate change that make it urgent to protect watersheds and coastlines, and prevent invasion of protected spaces, such as forests, whose destruction contributes to global warming. According to the Environmental Management Act of 2004, "No human activities of a permanent nature or which may, by their nature, [be] likely to compromise or adversely affect conservation or the protection of ocean or natural lake shorelines shall be allowed."[16] Unplanned settlements are said to compromise urban infrastructure, threaten eruption of diseases like cholera due to flooding and poor drainage, harm communal lands, and deter tourism. Much of the discourse on evictions is couched in the language of protecting the environment and defending environmental law. For example, more than eight thousand homes in the Msimbazi watershed of Dar es Salaam were targeted for destruction by January 2016. Because the houses were built in a restricted area, no compensation is expected.[17] Much of the bulldozing in river valleys was by order of the National Environmental Management Council, backed up by riot police after some people protested the demolition of their houses. An opposition member of parliament warned that "under the pretext of environmental conservation, the government is mercilessly demolishing innocent people's houses. They are now going homeless and helpless."[18]

In Africa, eviction is not unusual in urban settings. Besides material deprivation and loss of movable property, evictees experience depression, psychological stress, and a decline in health. Eviction often leads to breakdowns in community, social, and family bonds. Yet a high proportion of Africa's urban residents live in unplanned settlements, an outcome of rapid urbanization

---

14 Aisia Rweyemamu, "New Dar Master Plan to Render Millions Homeless," *The Guardian* (Tanzania), December 27, 2015.

15 Ministry of Lands, Housing and Human Settlements Development, *Dar es Salaam Masterplan, 2012–2032* (Rome: Fontanari, 2013).

16 Deogratius Kamagi, "Demolitions in Flood Prone Areas Halted," *Daily News* (Tanzania), December 23, 2015.

17 Devota Mwachang'a, "Mayhem as Mkwajuni Demolition Victims Block Dar Roads," *The Guardian* (Tanzania), January 19, 2016.

18 "House Demolitions are Legal," *Daily News* (Tanzania), February 5, 2016.

since Independence and the failure to provide adequate affordable housing. African governments have viewed urbanization as undesirable, discouraging migration from the countryside.[19] This has sometimes meant the repatriation of jobless men and women, often young people, to rural villages, and in the most blatant cases, it has resulted in the bulldozing of whole townships. Urban restructuring and destruction might have a racial basis, as in apartheid South Africa, or aim to undermine political opposition, as in Robert Mugabe's *Operation Murambatsvina* – "clearing the rubbish" – in which up to 700,000 urban homes of 2.4 million Zimbabweans were bulldozed, mostly in areas that had supported the opposition Movement for Democratic Change party in the 2005 elections.[20] Likewise, because Tanzanian opposition parties are strong in Dar es Salaam, evictions serve to shore up the ruling Chama cha Mapinduzi, in power since independence in 1961.

Creating a Working-Class Suburb

Although there may be good environmental reasons for evicting tens of thousands of people from flood plains and destroying their houses and property, some of which took decades to construct after painstaking savings, this was not so with the Tanganyika Packers Limited (TPL) house demolitions in the Kawe ward of Dar es Salaam, which in many ways was a harbinger of the current rush to evict.[21] The TPL case, coming shortly before the Msimbazi River demolitions noted above, suggests other motives at play besides environmental protection. One motive is to build residences and urban spaces for middle-class and elite Tanzanians and expatriates, who are able to pay far more for housing than the squatters living in informal settlements. Another is to generate income for the parastatal National Housing Corporation as well as private investors in the new Tanzanian economy, including politically connected Chinese and Gulf State companies.

Consider the Tanganyika Packers case.[22] In 1947, the British colonial government invited Britain's Liebig's Extract of Meat Company (Lemco) to open a beef-canning factory in Tanganyika to market hundreds of thousands of indigenous cattle, which the colonial government believed caused environmental destruction. TPL was created out of a partnership between Lemco and the Tanganyika government. TPL's canned beef filled protein deficiencies in post-war Britain and supplied British military needs. The Kawe suburb of Dar es Salaam was selected as the site of TPL, about a kilometer from the Indian Ocean, because it was sparsely populated, had adequate grounds for cattle, and the smells and effluvia of a slaughterhouse could be kept at a distance from the city center, about thirteen kilometers to the south. The TPL factory anchored a new working-class suburb in Dar es Salaam, built from the ground up after buying out and relocating local Zaramo farmers, who were resettled to the west.

Although TPL managers in 1950 had a vision of migrant housing for single men based on established colonial models, two forces mandated family-style houses for married men with children. One was the Labour government in Britain that advocated social welfare for colonial sub-

19 Andrew Burton, *African Underclass: Urbanization, Crime and Colonial Order in Dar es Salaam* (Oxford: James Currey, 2005): 220.

20 Richard Bourne, *Catastrophe: What Went Wrong in Zimbabwe?* (London: Zed Books, 2011).

21 Devota Mwachang'a, "Frail 80-Year-Old Appeals for Special Consideration in Face of Demolition," *The Guardian* (Tanzania), January 6, 2016.

22 Thaddeus Sunseri, "Working in the Slaughterhouse: Tanganyika Packers Ltd., from Colonialism to Collapse, 1947–2014," *Labor History* 59 (2018): 215–37.

jects, seeking to preserve colonial rule by improving conditions and creating a loyal African middle class.[23] Another was the aspirations of workers themselves, who, by the end of the 1950s, sought to bring their wives and children to the city and worksite. TPL provided family housing for its core workers – men on the factory floor, who controlled the rhythms and pace of factory work – alongside barracks for casual workers, who were laid off seasonally. On the eve of Independence in 1961, TPL workers, backed by a vibrant trade union movement, brought their vision of family housing to factory management.[24] TPL officials acceded to the family housing model, even as the workforce tripled between 1950 and 1970. The TPL housing estate, located close to the factory, included a beer hall, sports fields, a cinema, and a store selling basic necessities. Eventually, land was made available for a mosque, a Catholic and a Protestant church, and a primary school.[25] Company housing provided leverage over the workforce, since disorderly workers and their families could be evicted. Kawe emerged as a working-class neighborhood that spawned ancillary businesses to cater to non-factory residents. By the early 1970s, TPL's workforce peaked at 1,200, mostly men and some women from cattle districts of the distant inland. Most new workers spilled across the factory road into makeshift houses that became unplanned settlements, or commuted from outlying townships, reflecting the experience of most new urban inhabitants of Dar es Salaam.[26]

Although meatpacking is a highly gendered industry, favoring men for most jobs, TPL followed industry patterns in hiring women for less-skilled stages of the production process, especially sorting meat and packing cans into cartons for shipment overseas.[27] By the late 1960s, about ten percent of the workforce were women, meshing with the new independent Tanzanian state's vision of modernizing its population and creating a socialist work environment. As a government parastatal, TPL management, increasingly Africanized, publicized the 'smart [well-dressed] girls,' who were a visible part of the workforce, even though they were most likely to be laid off seasonally or during periods when the production process was disrupted. For many women, seasonal layoffs may have meshed with lifecycles of marriage, child rearing, and eventual return to more permanent employment. Some of the women hired in the mid-1960s were still employed by TPL a generation later, even though most of the workforce had been laid off by then.

From Socialism to Neoliberalism, Company Housing to Eviction

The high tide of TPL production was short-lived, cresting in about 1970. Shortly thereafter, the Tanzanian government increased state control in order to force the company to supply fresh meat to the state-run butcheries of Dar es Salaam. The fresh meat side of the business competed with the more profitable export of canned beef, but also provided concrete benefits to vocal urban residents

---

23 Frederick Cooper, *Decolonization and African Society: The Labour Question in French and British Africa* (Cambridge: Cambridge University Press, 1996): 323–60; Tanzania National Archives (TNA) ACC460/4/49/26, Inspection Reports TPL, Broadhead-Williams to Resident Manager, TPL, 25 February 1950.
24 TPL Archive, "Minutes of the Fifty-Fifth Meeting of the Directors of Tanganyika Packers Limited," Tangombe Estate, 23 June 1959: 4.
25 G. Rwiza, "Tanganyika packers na mchango wake katika uchumi wa Tanganyika," *Mwananchi*, October 6, 2011.
26 Wilbard Jackson Kombe, "Land-Use Dynamics in Peri-Urban Areas and their Implications on the Urban Growth and Form: The Case of Dar es Salaam, Tanzania," *Habitat International* 29 (2005): 113–35.
27 "The Tanganyika Packers: A Pillar of Progress," *The Nationalist,* June 9, 1966: iv–vi.

demanding cheaper meat. By then, TPL's capitalist orientation conflicted with the socialist development ideals of Tanzania's founding president, Julius Nyerere. In 1974, the Tanzanian state fully nationalized TPL, breaking the partnership with Lemco, which was the global leader in canned beef. The Tanzanian state in turn became the new landlord for TPL workers. But nationalization came at a bad time: a severe drought in Tanzania forced TPL to buy up tens of thousands of emaciated cattle at a loss, while a world glut in cattle drove prices down. Mismanagement and corruption over the next few years – common to all Tanzanian parastatals – ensured that TPL would not be profitable and the loss of the Lemco affiliation deprived the company of an international market. Between 1978 and 1982, TPL laid off more than half of its workforce. But TPL management directed that workers should not be evicted from their houses, even as factory production declined steadily during the 1980s. It was hoped that production would be revived, and resident workers would have first claim to jobs. In this way, many TPL workers retained access to housing even after they had ceased to work in the factory.

By late 1991, Tanzania was well into the neoliberal turn that reflected the end of the Cold War. The finance minister announced that parastatal restructuring would begin the following February, involving the privatization of many moribund industries. He warned that the future of each parastatal depended on "rehabilitating themselves and the attitude of their workers."[28] TPL clearly represented the worst of parastatal performance. In December 1991, its workers had gone two months without pay.[29] The Industrial Court ordered the company to reinstate eighty-four workers who had been laid off six years earlier and pay them all their benefits. In November 1992, some two hundred remaining TPL workers occupied the Kawe factory, blocking managers from entering and preventing canned goods from exiting.[30] By then laid off for seven months, they accused TPL managers of mismanagement and corruption, and called on the agriculture minister to suspend the managers and reopen the ailing factory.[31] The workers demanded salary arrears and termination benefits to the amount of sixty million shillings (about 273,000 dollars). Efforts by the Tanzanian government over the previous years to find private investors to revive the factory had failed when it was discovered that the company carried a debt of over two million dollars.[32] In May 1993, the police forcibly removed the workers, and managers prepared to close the factory for the foreseeable future.

Despite the loss of their jobs, disputes over pensions and severance pay meant that TPL workers continued to live on the Kawe housing estate, not far from the closed factory. This toehold in the urban economy allowed them to survive by seeking new jobs or casual work, renting out rooms, or selling small stocks of household goods like soap and matches. So important was this continued access to company housing that in 1998 some three hundred former employees of TPL petitioned to buy the houses that they occupied.[33] Moreover, some of their neighbors formed an NGO in 2004 called *Nyumba ni Mama* ("Housing is Motherhood"), a self-help group made up largely of single mothers, who sought land on the TPL estate with access to electricity, sewage lines, and clean water to raise their living standards from a squatter settlement in a slum to stable households.[34] Unlike

---

28 Mkumbwa Ally, "Restructuring Starts Soon," *Daily News*, December 4, 1991.

29 "Dar Meat Plant in Doldrums," *Daily News*, December 19, 1991.

30 Chiku Lweno, "TPL Workers Still Say 'No' to Managers," *Daily News*, November 5, 1992.

31 "Makwetta to Meet Packers Workers," *Daily News*, January 6, 1993.

32 "Tanganyika Packers: Potential Investors Pull Out," *Daily News*, December 8, 1992.

33 Bob Karashani, "Tenants Add New Twist to Sale of Meat Company," *East African*, June 30, 1998.

34 Kenneth Ruwaichi Sinare, "Housing Finance: The Case of Kawe Women Development Trust—*Nyumba ni Mama* Self-Help Housing Group" (M.A. thesis, Southern New Hampshire University and the Open University of Tanzania, 2005): 4–6.

the TPL long-term residents, *Nyumba ni Mama* resembled the eighty percent of Dar es Salaam citizens living in unplanned settlements, families of second-generation workers lacking clear housing rights.

The government rejected both the TPL workers' bid for titles to their houses and *Nyumba ni Mama*'s request for land. Both interfered with various proposals for the TPL estate, including a luxury shopping mall owned by the Al Ghurair consortium of the United Arab Emirates, a sports stadium, and a revived meat factory, which some progressive figures in government favored. By 2014, the government devolved ownership of TPL land to the National Housing Corporation (NHC) to construct an upscale housing, shopping, and recreation complex to be called Uptown Kawe. Although the NHC slogan is *Nyumba ni Maisha* ("Housing is Life"), it is unlikely that ordinary Tanzanians, let alone the impoverished residents of Kawe ward, will be able to afford to live there.

In August 2014, two decades after the closing of TPL, the NHC moved to evict former TPL workers from the Kawe housing estate.[35] The Tanzanian High Court ruled that the NHC was the legal owner of the property and that the workers must leave. The NHC agreed to pay residents between 150,000 and 550,000 shillings each as compensation (approx. 60–220 dollars). Some expressed defiance. One was an elderly woman named Mwatatu Mwasi, who had started working at TPL in 1966. She said to a reporter, "I have worked for the company since 1966, but in May 1992 more than 200 workers were laid off, and to date we have not got our pensions... I am not going to leave this place, I have lived here for more than forty years, and the government has not given me my payments... When they pay me, I will leave but not before then ... if they kill me then let me die." Her neighbor, Syrilo Muganyizi, stated, "We are not against the eviction order, but what we want is reasonable compensation of at least one million shillings (about 400 dollars) or more." In August 2014, bulldozers arrived unannounced to level the houses of more than one thousand residents who had refused to leave. In October, President Jakaya Kikwete was expected to lay the foundation stone for the construction of the new Kawe Satellite City.

I visited the land of the former TPL houses in May 2016 to find empty fields and little evidence of the former housing estate. Construction cranes surround the neighborhood, the first signs of Uptown Kawe, although the shell of the TPL factory still stands. I asked an official of TPL what had become of the former residents. He said he didn't know.

Conclusion

For half a century, the TPL neighborhood had anchored a stable community that included homes, churches, a mosque, schools, and sports fields, surrounded by shops and businesses that catered to the community. Although TPL workers never had secure title to their houses, they were not an unplanned community or a squatter settlement. Far from it, their neighborhood was planned painstakingly and with worker input to be a backbone of blue-collar Dar es Salaam. If the government could demolish such a community, despite the opposition of residents on the ground and in the courts, then what hope is there that the millions of unplanned informal settlers who make up most of Dar es Salaam today will have better success in holding back the bulldozers that are the current symbol of urban planning in modern Tanzania?

35 "Evicted Kawe Residents Refuse to Leave as they Demand Due Pay," *The Guardian* (Tanzania), August 8, 2014.

Felicitas Hentschke
The Changing Faces of a Village:
Italian Migrant Workers' Families in Lorraine

Between 1870 and 1930, northern France, especially Lorraine, was heavily transformed by the fast growth of heavy industry. Small villages turned into industrial sites with a wildly growing rail network connecting mines, furnaces, and iron manufacturers – industrious, densely populated, noisy, and polluted. The owners of these factories – the 'iron barons' – were massively recruiting low and unskilled workers, many of them of Italian origin.[36]

Today, in contrast, Lorraine is structurally weak, and the iron and steel industry is less important. Apart from minor companies, derelict industrial buildings, dead railway lines, and countless workers' housing estates, the villages of the region are silent witnesses to golden times gone by. The Italian names on the door plates of residential allotments point to the massive settlement of Italian migrant workers about one hundred years ago.

Saulnes is such a place in Lorraine on the border between Luxemburg and Belgium. In 2010, I met Monsieur Adrian Zolfo in Saulnes. He was sixty-nine years old and had been the mayor of Saulnes for many years. I interviewed him for my research on Italian migrant workers in the region.

We sit in his office in the tiny town hall. He is a man of good values. He makes no secret of his leftist disposition. His office is decorated with a large poster of Che Guevara. Stacks of brochures, bunches of small flags, and collections of trophies clutter the room. Looking out of the window, numerous reproductions of historical photographs of industrial buildings and men at work adorn the white-washed wall surrounding the parking lot, testimonies from a time when Saulnes was still an industrial site. These photographs, coarsely pixelated in large format, catch the eyes of passers-by.

From Village to Industrial Site:
A Noble Man and the Reconstruction of Saulnes

The industrial history of Saulnes spans just three generations. For a mere one hundred years, iron ore was mined here, and iron, steel, and cement were commercially processed.[37]

In 1873, Gustave Raty, partner in the Luxembourg company Raty et Cie, purchased 261 hectares of land and a concession in Saulnes-Longlaville to build four blast furnaces in the years 1874, 1880, 1882, and 1896. Within a very short period, the rural village of Saulnes boomed into a small industrial town of more than two thousand inhabitants. The iron industry was on the rise. The new Thomas-Gilchrist process made it possible to produce versatile steel from local, comparatively-inferior phosphorus-rich iron. In Lorraine, blast furnaces were erected like mushrooms sprouting from the ground. A dense railway network for the transport of coal, iron ore, liquid iron, and steel

---

36 Gérard Noiriel, *Workers in French Society in the 19th and 20th Centuries* (New York: Berg, 1990): xiv.

37 Company archive, Saulnes Municipal Archive, Departmental Archives of Nantes (ADMM); Christina Pasina, *Saulnes, One Hundred Years at the Feet of the Blast Furnaces* (Diplôme de Maitraise, Université de Nancy II, 1984).

was created. The rural region developed into an important location for the French iron and steel industry.

The new entrepreneur, Gustave Raty, urgently needed labor, like all other iron barons of this period, and was forced to create living spaces for the many migrant workers. To this day, numerous worker settlements dominate the town and the region, fifty years after the closure of the last blast furnace.[38]

The first worker settlements were built when the mines were opened and the blast furnaces erected. The families of the company owners themselves lived in two palaces: the main palace, a three-story castle-villa surrounded by a large garden, and the 'Château-Neuf' not far from the first. The smaller Château-Neuf was bombed by the Germans and destroyed in World War I. The villa has since been converted into apartment housing.

Construction of the workers' houses was a process that lasted several decades. All of the houses looked alike and were ordered along the street in rows, like pearls on a string. The units usually had two stories and a surface area of approximately thirty-five by sixty meters. Each had a kitchen, three rooms, a pantry, and two rooms in the cellar. Some had small attic rooms.[39] The construction of these settlements owed nothing to any profound piety or philanthropic commitment on the part of the Raty family, as far as can be detected. Rather, there were two constraints that prompted the entrepreneurs to take action. First, there was the never-ending influx of workers, often from neighboring regions, but also directly from Italy, who initially crowded into tight living spaces around the plant, the cellars, and stables of what had originally been a rural village. While elsewhere it had been possible to support the workers by providing a small amount of credit to build their own homes, this did not work in Saulnes.[40] Second, many workers were mobile, and as long as they were free of ties and unsettled, they moved from factory to factory, and stayed wherever the living conditions proved most favorable. To recruit workers and to guarantee a stable number of workers on the plant, the Ratys took matters and their own money in hand. Between 1900 and 1930, they planned to build numerous dwellings, with yards for vegetable gardens, in order to bind their workforce to the factory and lock down their loyalty. Other iron barons in the region built up small industrial towns as well. They built worker settlements with shops, schools, halls, and sports fields. But they had little interest in investing in churches. The conventional combination of church and state in neighboring Germany was eyed with skepticism, and French secularism was invoked in local company policies.[41] Meanwhile, however, manufacturers were afraid of strikes and did everything to satisfy in particular the many Italian immigrants within the workforce, who insisted most strongly upon Catholic churches in their communities.

---

38 On April 30, 1968. By the end of 1968, the whole ironworks facility was closed.

39 See blueprints from the company archive.

40 Gérard Noiriel, *Workers in French Society*: 68–9.

41 In the German Reich, religious and nationalist interests were deeply entangled. See Laurent Commaille, "Ein neues Bild der Arbeitersiedlungen in Lothringen," in Hans-Walter Herrmann, Rainer Hudemann, and Eva Krell, eds., *Forschungsaufgabe Industriekultur. Die Saarregion im Vergleich* (Saarbrücken: Merziger Druckerei, 2004): 361–68.

Three Generations of Italian Immigrants: Protagonists of Transformation

The industrial history of Saulnes can be read in the company documents, which Mayor Zolfo has kept in the basement of the town hall for many years. He found them in 1982. As president of his soccer club, he had decided to build a new bar in the clubhouse. They needed wood for the floor and Zolfo recalled the vacant office buildings of the old Raty factory. He and a few former miner friends from the ironworks set to work taking up planks from the old factory floor, where he discovered a large archive of company documents. He took the wood, but left the documents. Curiosity finally got the better of him and he returned to the archive. By the light of his headlamp, he rummaged through the documents, stumbling across old accident reports, instances of child labor, and testimonies of the German occupation during both world wars. In 1985, a fire broke out in the old factory building. Many documents were burned or destroyed by the flood of water from the firemen's hoses. Only a fraction could be saved, yet still a huge amount of material remained from the early days of iron and steel production in Saulnes (1870) until its decline in the 1960s. At first, he stored the documents in his private home. After becoming Mayor of Saulnes, he moved the documents to the town hall basement. In 2010, they were handed to historians in Berlin.[42]

We are now standing with Adrian Zolfo at the window of his office, looking out at the photographs along the parking lot wall – scenes from life long gone: miners and carts filled with ore; the tangle of piping and conduits from a billowing blast furnace; strikers marching. "The man in the middle is my father," Adrian Zolfo tells us, pointing to a black and white shot from the 1930s. It shows three ore crushers, together holding a heavy hammer high up above their heads with straight arms and proudly looking into the camera. Their task back then was to shatter into small pieces the iron ore chunks that had come in from the mines in the Lorraine region.

Adrian Zolfo's father, Icilio Zolfo, was a carpenter. He was the son of a simple communist farmer near the city of Bologna, Italy. Adrian Zolfo laughs as he tells of his illiterate grandfather, Primo. Like many of his comrades, his grandfather subscribed to *L'Unità*, a newspaper affiliated with the Communist Party, until 1924, when it was prohibited by Mussolini. While he couldn't read the words on the page, his subscription demonstrated his distance to the new fascist movement.

Icilio Zolfo, also a communist, was politically active too, but quite differently to his father. He faced increasing pressure from the right after Mussolini's 1922 rise to power, such that he decided to leave Italy in 1923. He fled to France. He moved, as many Italian migrants did, to the border between Belgian, Luxembourg, and France. Here, workers were desperately sought and Italian refugees were welcomed with open arms.

After World War I, the French side of the iron and steel industry in the Lorraine region experienced rapid growth. It benefited greatly from the Versailles Treaty of 1919. German industry had collapsed and the Lorraine steel companies, briefly annexed by Germany, recovered. Moreover, the upgrading of technical facilities as well as investment by newly formed joint-stock companies led to an increase in productivity.

Meanwhile, steel was a large industry due to the creation of countless iron and steel products and by-products from the processing of slag and residual metals of semi-finished products, which were processed outside the region. The French workers experienced a division of labor. Icilio Zolfo belonged to the mass of immigrant and still-migrating workers who were employed throughout the

---

42 The company archive is currently on loan to re:work, Humboldt-Universität zu Berlin.

Lorraine in the tunnels and furnaces without any special qualifications. They formed the lowest layer of the new working class. Above them was the expanding workforce in the service industry such as transportation, as well as in mechanical engineering and electrical engineering.[43]

But unskilled workers were still needed in the factories of the iron barons. So, Icilio Zolfo easily found his first job as an ore crusher in an ironworks in Villerupt, a site situated near Saulnes. While there was much work available, living space was critically sparse. Many unmarried migrant workers lived in boarding houses, where the beds were often rented out in the rhythm of day and night shifts. One worker would leave his bed at the boarding house in the early morning to make it to the shift change at the factory just as another returned from his night shift and laid down to rest in the same bed until his shift began in the evening. It was in such a situation of need that Icilio met the daughter of the boarding household, who would become his wife.

In 1938, the French-Italian couple moved to Saulnes. Meanwhile, they had five young children. At fourteen the sons were old enough to follow their father into the factory. It was common for sons to labor in the tunnels and ironworks like their fathers. At times, even the wives worked. But most of the time they worked in the agricultural enterprises and farmed their own gardens, from which they nourished their families. They kept the household, and looked after the children and often lodgers. They had to take account of the men's shift patterns.[44] On Sundays, everyone gathered for soccer, music, and convivial get-togethers in the ballroom, and also regularly in the church. Like most Italians in the Lorraine, the Zolfos joined the local Catholic congregation.

The Church had great influence on the identity formation of the workers and helped them retain their 'Italianness.' Already in the nineteenth century, it had supported the formation of Catholic workers' associations, leading to the emergence of the French Confederation of Christian Workers in 1918, which advocated economic and social democracy according to Christian principles.

In addition, Catholic communities, such as in the case of Saulnes, were engaged in the social integration of its members. Due to their political activities, the Italians were feared by the company heads of the factories and ironworks. There was a striking tendency of communist and union activists to be quite strong wherever there was a dominant proportion of Italian workers. The company heads therefore attempted to isolate the Italian workers, and thus relations between the Italian and French workers remained mostly rather aloof. In their niche existence, the Italian workers increasingly depended on their Church communities.[45]

Adrian Zolfo's father must have experienced this firsthand. In the 1950s, according to his son, Icilio Zolfo had to leave the town of Saulnes. A local priest had beaten one of Zolfo's sons for a harmless mischief, in response to which the ore crusher had used his strong arms when it came to blows. As consequence of this incident he had to leave the town in shame but stayed in the region.

Adrian Zolfo leans back in his chair and raises his arms to cross them behind his head. He closes his eyes and seems to sink back into the images of his memory. He is still a regular player with the Catholic soccer club in Saulnes – wearing purple jerseys against a team of non-religious workers in red jerseys.

---

43 Gérard Noiriel, *Workers in French Society*: xiv.

44 See Susanne Nimmesgern, "Am Herd wie am Hochofen. Saarländische Frauen zwischen Hausarbeit und Industriearbeit im 20. Jahrhundert," in Hans-Walter Herrmann, Rainer Hudemann, and Eva Krell, eds., *Forschungsaufgabe Industriekultur*: 273–99.

45 See documents in the company archive. The expression of 'Italianness' was a form of resistance (*Eigensinn*). However, in contrast to Alf Lüdtke's observations in Germany, their Catholicism helped them to underline their control of themselves. Alf Lüdtke, *Eigen-Sinn: Fabrikalltag, Arbeitererfahrungen und Politik vom Kaiserreich bis in den Faschismus* (Münster: Westfälisches Dampfboot, 2015): 128–29.

The youngest son worked like his father in the ironworks. He went into the cement plant of the factory in Saulnes. For twelve years, from 1957 to 1968, he dealt with the slag that was processed into cement made from the waste product of iron smelting, glass wool, and even paving stones. His two oldest brothers worked in the factory management. His oldest brother benefited from the accidental experience he gained during World War II at the age of fourteen, when he sought shelter along with the wave of refugees fleeing the Lorraine to Gironde, the stronghold of the French resistance. His stenographic skills enabled him to be of use as a clerk. Keeping lists of the refugees, he became qualified for administrative work back home in Saulnes later on. Only one Zolfo brother broke with generational tradition to become a baker.

The iron and steel industry in France collapsed in the 1960s. The factory in Saulnes was shut down in 1968. In the face of unemployment, many took their families to other regions like Normandy, where iron and steel workers were still needed. Those who were over fifty applied for early pensions. Their children oriented themselves, insofar as they stayed in the region, towards Luxembourg.

After three generations, the iron rush was over. The Raty family had always prioritized the family over economic necessity and could not respond to the rapidly changing needs of a rapidly changing economy and politics to keep the company afloat in the long term.[46] The same fate thus befell the Ratys that had befallen their workers' families. Gustave Raty had come to Saulnes in 1873. In 1957, his grandson and final owner of the factory, Jean Raty, passed away. The Raty family of Saulnes disappeared with him. Jean Raty had two sons, both of whom lost their lives in World War II. No further relatives ever came back to Saulnes, something that the communist Adrian Zolfo is certainly not sorry about.

The founder's villa and the worker settlements that sprung up over the decades as well as the old train station are the only remnants of the Raty legacy.

The conversation with Adrian Zolfo ends as seamlessly as it began, with more and more people dropping into the brightly lit office to arrange lunch. We bid each other a warm farewell and I head over to the last steel hall in Saulnes, which stands today where the slag from the iron ore production was once processed. It still exudes an industrial aura and gives off an impression of the din, dust, smoke, and steam that filled this valley for about a hundred years. The modern hall stands directly adjacent to the old Saulnes cemetery. Thick iron dust now envelopes the Raty family's mausoleum.

---

46 Jean-Marie Moine, *Les Barons du Fer. Les Maîtres de Forges en Lorraine* (Metz: Editions Serpenoise, 2003): 120–21.

Christian Strümpell
Remaking Homes and Reproducing Inequalities in an Eastern Indian Steel Town

It is estimated that around fifteen million people worldwide lose their homes each year to economic development projects such as large dams and irrigation projects, urban development projects, and the building of rail, road, and other transport facilities. Much of this takes place in Asia. Around forty-five million people were displaced in China in the second half of the twentieth century and over sixty million in India. In the latter case, official and semi-official figures reveal that displacement affects particular groups of people disproportionally. Displaced populations in India include large numbers of people who belong to communities the state has classified since late colonial times as 'scheduled tribes' and identified as in need of special protection with regard to land rights, access to education, government employment, and parliamentary representation. These people describe themselves as *Adivasi* (a Hindi neologism connoting autochthons or indigenous people), and though they make up eight percent of India's total population, forty percent of those whose land the state has acquired for development projects since Independence in 1947 are *Adivasi*. Furthermore, it is not only particularly vulnerable people whose land is targeted in processes of economic development; most development projects also have a poor record when it comes to the resettlement and rehabilitation schemes they offer the displaced. After some time, those in charge are often unable to tell you where the displaced have relocated and what their new means of livelihood are.

This essay sheds light on one case of displacement and resettlement in eastern India that dates back to the 1950s. It started under relatively favorable conditions. The government of India established the Rourkela Steel Plant (RSP) in the state of Odisha as a flagship for its larger modernization-cum-nation-building project. RSP was a public-sector undertaking intended to provide mass employment as well as relatively good salaries and working conditions. RSP was envisioned to attract workers from all over India and to act as a 'melting pot.' Through working together in a modern, public-sector industry and through living together in its attached modern township, workers' disparate identities of caste, region, and religion would be inevitably and irrevocably transcended; indeed, RSP would transform the workers into a pan-Indian citizenry.[47] Simultaneously, the local *Adivasi* population was to be integrated into this nation-building project. However, as I will show in what follows, the notions steel plant management held of *Adivasis* inadvertently rendered them particularly exploited at work. One generation later, the ideological foundations of the whole undertaking had shifted; the public sector was now supposed to primarily produce profits, not mass employment, and RSP's workforce was drastically reduced. In its wake, local *Adivasis* were deemed unfit for regular employment because they lacked higher education qualifications. Those in charge took this lack almost for granted, even though, in fact, it was largely produced by the way local *Adivasis* were made to rebuild their homes after their displacement in the 1950s.

---

47 For further information on India's industrial modernization project in the 1950s, see Sunil Khilnani, *The Idea of India* (London: Penguin, 2003): 61–106. For a case study of another public-sector steel town in India, see Jonathan Parry, "Lords of Labour: Working and shirking in Bhilai," in Jonathan Parry, Jan Breman, and Karin Kapadia, eds., *The Worlds of Indian Industrial Labour* (New Delhi: Sage Publications, 1999): 107–40.

Industrial Work under Nehruvian 'Socialism'

Rourkela today is a town of 550,000 inhabitants, a six-hour train journey southwest from Calcutta. Rourkela appears not unlike other towns of a similar size in India. People describe the neighborhoods around the railway station, or Rourkela proper, as a densely populated and congested urban area with multistoried buildings housing Rourkela's merchant families and their businesses, slums of informal sector laborers, and small workshops that repair equipment for the local ancillary industries or the steel plant itself. The sight becomes less familiar at the southern end of this bustling area. Here, the massive ovens and furnaces of RSP reach high into the sky.

Until the mid-1950s, when RSP arrived and transformed the place so thoroughly, Rourkela was a relatively isolated village of a little less than two thousand inhabitants. In 1954, on the advice of the West German steel manufacturers Krupp, who had been contracted to build a state-of-the-art steel plant with an attached, equally state-of-the-art, township, the government of India decided that it would establish here the first in a series of large integrated steel mills.

Soon after the location was fixed, the government of India founded the public-sector company that was to own and operate RSP as well as other steel plants elsewhere in India. These would be the 'temples of modern India,' as the country's first Prime Minister Jawaharlal Nehru expressed it. RSP was to produce a key commodity without which the young nation-state would remain dangerously dependent on imports from advanced industrial nations. RSP was also envisioned to produce a working class that would stand as a model for the nation as a whole. In addition to the local population, RSP would draw on labor from all over the country and hence unite India's diversity of castes, regions, and religions.

RSP requested the state government of Odisha to acquire approximately 20,000 acres of land for the construction of the plant and township. The state government announced the compulsory acquisition of land from around 2,500 families – approximately 15,000 people – two-thirds of whom belonged to one of half a dozen scheduled tribes settling locally. Villagers protested against their displacement and the terms of their compensation. After protracted negotiations and violent confrontations, an agreement was reached that promised each displaced household compensation at the market rate of the requisitioned land to which they were constitutionally entitled. The state promised to establish three resettlement colonies on the periphery of the township and provide housing plots and building subsidies to them. Villagers were also assigned unbroken land for cultivation in one of a dozen or so 'reclamation camps' within a one-hundred-kilometer radius of Rourkela and an allowance for breaking it. Finally, the villagers were promised jobs in the regular RSP workforce: one able-bodied member from every household from which land was requisitioned. Though the package might sound generous, there were many complaints.

The authorities in charge of land acquisition were accused of lacking sympathy for (or even being suspicious of) the concerns of those affected by land acquisition. A candid account by a West German social worker on the misbehavior of West Germans in Rourkela vividly describes the fate of the local population.[48] He described the agony with which the locals sat in the resettlement colonies drinking away the cash they had received for their land – in sums that often exceeded what they had been given so that many soon ran into debt. Eye-witnesses I met in Rourkela also spoke of displacement as a very traumatic experience. Japun, a man from the Mundari scheduled tribe who was around sixty-five years old when I first met him in 2004, explained that one afternoon, state

---

48 Jan Bodo Sperling, *The Human Dimension of Technical Assistance: The German Experience of Rourkela, India* (Ithaca: Cornell University Press, 1969).

government officers arrived on the small veranda of his parents' mud hut and yelled at them to pack their belongings within an hour and load it onto the truck they had brought along. They had already brought along the bulldozers that would erase their homes. Others told me about elderly relatives who had died of desperation at an unforeseeable future.

Though many were hired by RSP as regular workers, they were usually posted to what are known as RSP's 'hot shops.' These were the coke ovens, blast furnaces, and steel-melting shops, where working conditions are the most hazardous because of exposure to heat, dust, and fumes. In the hot shops, the local displaced *Adivasis* toiled together with *Adivasis* from the same and other scheduled tribes who had come to Rourkela from all over eastern India in search of wage-work. Retired personnel managers claim that it was their lack of education that explains why *Adivasis*, few of whom were literate, were concentrated in these areas of work.

When RSP recruited its first workforce in the 1950s and 1960s, there were few workers available who already possessed industrial skills. All others were unskilled and this included migrant workers from elsewhere in Odisha and India who were not *Adivasi*, but belonged to various other castes and communities. There were other reasons why *Adivasis* were concentrated in the plant's most hazardous work environments. One is that they lacked contacts with people higher up the echelons. An old Brahmin told me that he pleaded with some officers from the same high-caste background to not assign him a job in the furnaces. Equally important is the fact that members of higher castes often assume that *Adivasis* have a natural propensity for hard manual work, partly because they are also thought to have a particular propensity for hard-drinking. Allegedly, the consumption of a local rice beer, which people refer to as an 'Adivasi cold drink,' makes it easier to bear the heat; local liquors are said to clean dust from the throat. Since those holding these beliefs largely staffed the personnel department, they had a pronounced impact on staffing.

Japun, as well as other *Adivasis* I met in Rourkela, took pride in their capacity for hard work and dismissed others as lazy *kām chor gudā* ("work thieves" or shirkers), who are only good in *tela māribā* ("endearing themselves to seniors," lit. anointing oil) and therefore manage to escape hard tasks. Accordingly, Japun and others emphasized that it is their labor that keeps the plant running. However, when they talked about their everyday work in the coke ovens, blast furnaces, and other hot shops, they described it as an endless grind. They often called the way they were made to work there as torture.

Industrial Work under Neoliberal Capitalism

The situation turned from bad to worse in the 1990s. Under pressure from global financial institutions as well as domestic forces, the government of India shifted away from Nehruvian 'socialism' and embraced economic liberalization. Public-sector undertakings such as RSP were now supposed to compete in a global steel market. As a result, management cut the regular RSP workforce from around 39,000 in the late 1980s to 19,500 in 2009. The first generation of RSP workers retired during that period and fewer new workers were recruited. RSP still offered secure, relatively well-paid employment to its regular workers, and even on the lowest pay scale, a regular RSP worker earned wages and perks that placed him in the ranks of the Indian middle class in socioeconomic terms. But among the new hires, there was almost none of the local displaced people. In the 1990s, RSP also modernized its equipment and claimed to now require an educated workforce with vocational training or diplomas from engineering colleges. The sons and daughters of the displaced people usually lacked these qualifications and were excluded from the workforce. Just like their parents and grandparents in the 1950s, they looked to an uncertain future.

During the years of my research in Rourkela between 2004 and 2009, I witnessed how Japun's nephew Ladra tried desperately to find respectable employment. As an adolescent, he told me, he had always taken it for granted that he would become an RSP worker, just like his father had been until his premature death. He had done a variety of odd jobs, but after his marriage in 2004 and the birth of his son a year later, he became concerned about his working life. For someone like him, with just ten years of schooling, the RSP gates would remain closed. He could work *bahar* ("outside") as a daily-waged construction laborer, but that would mean that all his former school-mates would see how low he had stooped. He could also hide from the public and work in one of the dozens of sponge iron plants that private industrialists had established around Rourkela after India's economic liberalization.[49] However, he was sure he would get sick there. His cousin's brother had worked there for some time and within one week, thick black liquid started dripping from his nose. What further aggravated his anger about being barred entry to the 'temple of modern India' was the fact that, as he said, RSP stood on the former houses and fields of his grandparents.

Ladra joined the demonstrations on the town's main roads that an association of the displaced people regularly organized between 2004 and 2006. The protests demanded that Odisha state and RSP kept the promises they had made ten years earlier in the wake of large-scale protests by a pre-cursor displaced people's association. Back then, protests struck a deal that granted around one thousand displaced households that had not yet received compensatory employment the right to nominate one member from each household to be employed by RSP. By the mid-2000s, RSP had employed less than five hundred of them, because the process of verifying the nominees' identities and relationships to the one thousand households was tedious. Ladra and most other displaced people suspected this was simply a case of negligence. They now aimed to vociferously remind the state and plant authorities of their promises and demand new negotiations. Ladra, as well as many others, had fathers or grandfathers who had been regular RSP workers. However, they had been recruited because RSP was then in urgent need of workers, not primarily as compensation for displacement. They further claimed that the compensation the state and RSP had provided for their forefathers' land was inadequate. Their land, they said, was inheritable, but regular RSP jobs were not. The courts had rejected the corresponding writ petition as violating the principle of constitutional equality of all citizens.[50]

The usual response from Rourkela's non-*Adivasi* middle class – RSP managers, civil servants, lawyers, and regular RSP workers – was to brush away the displaced people's claims. They never tired of saying that "there had been nothing here before," about which local people could complain. In their eyes, the comparatively low level of education of the children of local RSP workers was self-evident. In their eyes too, it is in their 'tribal' nature to live for the moment, drink and dance, and not care about the future, let alone save money or educate their children. Ladra and other descendants of the displaced people shared the idea that their elders drank too much and they sometimes blamed them for their lack of school education. However, I often heard them ending such contemplations with the words, "They didn't know [better]." This captures their dilemma very well. Given the promises of industrial modernity that had been made to them in the 1950s, how could they have

---

49 These plants turn iron ore into sponge iron or direct reduced iron by means of natural gas or coal, not coke. It is therefore significantly cheaper than the usual way of steel-making in blast furnaces that requires coking coal.

50 For further information on this and other court cases, see Christian Strümpell, "Law against Displacement: The juridification of tribal protest in Rourkela, India," in Julia Eckert, Brian Donahoe, Christian Strümpell, and Özlem Biner, eds., *Law against the State. Ethnographic Forays into Law's Transformations* (Cambridge: Cambridge University Press, 2012): 202–27.

known that RSP would later cut its regular workforce to half its former strength? How could they have known that vocational training or engineering diplomas would be required in the future to become a RSP worker?

Remaking Homes and Reproducing Inequalities

The situation Ladra and others like him find themselves in has its roots in the ways they remade and were made to remake their homes after displacement. One of the outcomes of the negotiations around the original land acquisition was that resettlement colonies were established around Rourkela for the displaced people. The differences between the resettlement colonies and the public-sector company township are stark. The latter is a generously laid-out urban space, with parks, sports grounds, and above-standard schools and hospitals, all well maintained by the public-sector company. In the resettlement colonies, by contrast, the Odisha state authorities provided a few showcase houses in what they considered a 'traditional tribal' style. However, these models plus some paved roads and water pumps were all they provided. Schools and other civic amenities were opened only later, in the 1970s. And because it was the Odisha state government that was in charge, not the public-sector company, they remained notoriously poorly equipped and funded. Since the displaced people were largely *Adivasis*, so were the inhabitants of the resettlement colonies. Here, they were joined by *Adivasis* who had migrated to Rourkela in search of wage-labor. By contrast, migrant workers from Odisha's coastal lowlands and other Indian states settled in the RSP township. Even more stark than the contrast between the township and resettlement colonies is the contrast between the township and the slums. The state-of-the-art township for RSP was designed as a garden town with lots of green bordering onto neighborhoods. These greens had often been former village sites and, once they realized that it had remained vacant, the former villagers reoccupied it. Japun had done that, too, because the house he could build himself here was larger than the company quarters assigned to low-grade RSP workers in the township; it also allowed him and his wife to still plough some of their old fields.

Furthermore, rebuilding their village house allowed them to partly rebuild their village community. However, the *bastis*, as the rebuilt villages are called, were considered illegal occupations of government land and no schools were opened at all. The comparative lack of education of those growing up in the resettlement colonies and the *bastis*, like Ladra, thus goes back to the way they and their parents were made to rebuild their homes and lives after displacement, not to their inherent 'tribal' nature. However, it was only after the 1990s, when India liberalized her economy and RSP reduced its relatively well paid and securely employed workforce, that the differences between resettlement colonies and *bastis*, on the one hand, and the township, on the other, became apparent. Until then, the largely *Adivasi* inhabitants in the former could usually count on a regular RSP wage. Since then, they have struggled to survive as precarious informal sector workers.

Anne-Katrin Bicher

Closed Constructions: The Apartheid Architecture of Migrant Hostels in Gauteng

Can a single bed in a prison-like building designed on principles of spatial segregation, political control, and labor exploitation become a home? What are the aspirations, living conditions, and familial biographies of the women and men who live with the heritage of apartheid architecture in South Africa today? These were some of the questions that a team of young photographers and historians sought to answer in 2008 with *Closed Constructions*, a visual and oral research project on migrant workers' compounds and hostels in Johannesburg and the surrounding region.

Workers' compounds and hostels formed a cornerstone of colonial and apartheid housing policies that fueled the country's migrant labor economy: an economy that principally deprived black Africans of their land and propelled them by means of racist and segregationist legislation into capitalist industries and services owned by whites. Compounds and hostels are large-scale, single-sex housing facilities for African workers that exist across the urban centers of the country in large numbers. Although they have been the subject of photography since the 1890s, anthropologist Mamphela Ramphele noted that they have been kept "largely invisible" since their first emergence in the 1880s on the diamond fields of Kimberley.[51] This can be explained by their mainly isolated geography informed by the apartheid ideal of racially divided cities, as well as the fact that several stereotypes have solidified around hostel communities over time, adding various social barriers and taboos to the physical walls and fences. In the past, much like today, public perceptions of hostels tend to call up images such as "dilapidated and infested," "labor batteries," "civic disgrace," or "sites of injuries" that "breed anger and violence."[52] This association is rooted in their complex social, economic, and political history.

Rather than primarily counteracting this one-sided imagery, the *Closed Constructions* project team was first of all driven by a desire to record and create greater 'visibility' of the seventy-plus compound and hostel structures in the area through systematic photographic documentation and interviews with female and male residents. A unique archive of images and voices was created over the course of three years, revealing the diverse strategies employed by hostel-dwellers to deal with the challenges and opportunities presented by spaces that were never meant to serve as homes. The project findings clearly support research perspectives that stress the heterogeneity of hostel 'communities' and highlight the gendered aspects of hostel life and the heteropatriarchal nature of

51 See Svea Josephy, "Fractured Compounds: Photographing Post-Apartheid Compounds and Hostels," *Social Dynamics* 40 (2014): 444–70; Mamphela Ramphele, *A Bed Called Home: Life in the Migrant Labour Hostels of Cape Town* (Cape Town: David Philip, 1993).

52 Pamphlet by Councilor Hilda Watts, "They Work for You: How 15,000 Non-European Municipal Workers Live," 1946, Johannesburg City Council Archives; G.H. Pirie, "Public Housing as a Device for White Residential Segregation in Johannesburg 1934–1953," *Urban Geography* 9 (1988): 571; Kenichi Serino and Nqobile Dludla, "An Apartheid Legacy: South Africa's Hostels Breed Anger and Violence," www.uk.reuters.com/article/uk-safrica-violence-hostels/an-apartheid-legacy-south-africas-hostels-breed-anger-violence-idUKKBN0O50KP20150520, accessed February 13, 2018.

apartheid policies.[53] At the same time, the project acknowledges the uniformity and persistence of compound and hostel architecture, and the impact it still has on its population today.

Closed Constructions was initiated by Khanya College, a non-governmental organization based in Johannesburg that has been educating and training workers and community activists since 1986. The aim was to assess the transformation of hostel structures and living conditions in the Johannesburg and Tswahne (Pretoria) areas. Khanya's focus on council and provincial compounds and hostels was informed by the college's wider engagement in preserving the Newtown Compound, which was built in 1913 in Johannesburg's former municipal power station precinct. When designing *Closed Constructions* as a capacity-building, exhibition, and cultural education project, the college looked for project partners who shared its values of 'bottom up' historical research, writing, and participatory education. Consequently, we began to work with the Newtown-based Market Photo Workshop (MPW), which has played a pivotal role in the development of politically engaged documentary photography in South Africa, and the History Workshop of the nearby University of Witwatersrand. The Gauteng Provincial Housing Department's hostel eradication program was also underway, seeking to demolish all hostels in the province and replace them with family units that would better suit the needs of their occupants. While Khanya generally supported the idea of improving conditions to mitigate the injustices of the apartheid era, these most recent improvement plans failed to give consideration to preserving the heritage of the hostel and township communities it affected.

With regard to the heritage of hostels, it is important to understand that the core aim of apartheid politics of segregation was to have a steady peri-urban African workforce engaged in circular migration yet excluded from permanent settlement in the city by means of pass laws and influx control. The 1913 Natives Land Act, which provided only 7% of the country's land in reserves for blacks, together with the Native Urban Areas Act of 1923 set the stage for a series of confining legislative developments. Despite these restrictions "that made criminals out of ordinary Africans who dared to seek for job opportunities in white urban areas,"[54] migration out of the homelands for economic reasons rose rapidly after World War II, when the rural population was increasingly battling poverty and industrialization was growing. Accommodation was notoriously scarce. With the National Party in charge, massive hostel schemes boomed in the Johannesburg area from the mid-1950s onwards. The first was built in Dube in 1955, part of the South Western Township (Soweto). Today, most of the compounds and all of the hostels in Gauteng that were established during the twentieth century are still in use and largely overcrowded.[55]

After a lengthy process of locating the sites and securing the support of *indunas* and resident committees, the launch of *Closed Constructions* coincided with the xenophobic violence of 2008 that targeted black migrants from outside South Africa.[56] While the launch was not sparked by the attacks, unlike other documentary image productions on migrants from this time, the events

53 Glen S. Elder, "Malevolent Traditions: Hostel Violence and the Procreation Geography of Apartheid Author(s)," *Journal of Southern African Studies* 29 (2003): 922; Makhosi Xulu, "From Hostels to CRUs: Spaces of Perpetual Perplexity," *South African Review of Sociology* 45 (2014): 140–54.
54 Mamphela Ramphele, *A Bed Called Home*: 16.
55 Holly E. Reed, "Moving Across Boundaries: Migration in South Africa, 1950–2000," *Demography* 50 (2013): 92.
56 See, for example, Matthew J. Smith, "Violence, Xenophobia and the Media: A Review of the South African Media's Coverage of Xenophobia and the Xenophobic Violence Prior to and Including the Events of 2008," *Politikon: South African Journal of Political Studies* 38 (2011): 111–29.

encouraged the team to continue its work: processes of exclusion and xenophobia against migrants were embedded in the history of hostels.[57]

Three different teams were formed. One examined built heritage for the "Architectures of Exclusion" section, meticulously photographing the distinctive architectural physiognomy of each hostel. The late David Goldblatt, who founded the MPW in 1989, contributed an eye-opening body of aerial photographs.[58] The second team worked on "From Hostels to Homes?" MPW students of documentary photography worked with students and trainees from the History Workshop to produce portraits and interviews from five compounds and hostels in Soweto and Alexandra, two of which were women's hostels.[59] Fifteen freelance photographers living and working inside or close to hostels formed the third team, "Ubambiswano Lwabashuti" (isiZulu for "us photographers holding together"). They participated in the *Closed Constructions* capacity-building program and collectively curated their own work of event and studio photography for the exhibition.

For "Architectures of Exclusion," the photographers created a visual inventory of each site, working his or her way through from the outer walls to the single units. The consistency in the perspectives allows the viewer to concentrate on the differences and similarities each space reveals. The remarkable uniformity of the core elements of the compound and hostel designs – informed by capitalist efficiency and apartheid power structures – becomes evident. But beyond just making these repetitive patterns visually legible, the images go further. They reveal the strategies used by residents to make the available space their own. Spaces are beautified, used, reused, used for different purposes, added to, re-built, destroyed, neglected, or allowed to go to waste. Temporary structures, such as the barracks that housed the constructions workers who originally built the hostel, have since become permanent housing. Permanent structures, such as administrative offices and community and beer halls, are temporarily or permanently used for new purposes: mostly sleeping quarters, but sometimes gyms, shops, or religious or childcare facilities.[60]

The architectural images of this series not only demonstrate how differently residents deal with the very similar phenomenon of scarcity of space, depending on their available resources, familial situation, individual motivation, and communal needs, but also show the changed economic realities that hostels face today. As sociologist Makhosi Xulu stated in 2014, the term "migrant worker" no longer accurately describes the work and life of a "hostel dweller." Many are not formally employed, but rather are either seeking work or are informally employed and thus see themselves as "casuals" than as "workers." Several are self-employed, running their own "spaza" kiosks and other small businesses that form an integral part of the present-day economic infrastructure at the hostel. As manifest in the photographic material, the scope of these small-scale enterprises goes far beyond the spaces historically earmarked for trade purposes on the hostel premises.

57 Marietta Kesting, *Affective Images: Post-Apartheid Documentary Perspectives* (New York: State University of New York Press, 2017): 7.
58 As described recently by art historian Marietta Kesting, MPW "educators and students are at the forefront of the discussions on the shortcomings of post-apartheid society" providing photographic skills and visual literacy to neglected and marginalized parts of society. Marietta Kesting, *Affective Images:* 138.
59 In total the project included three hostels originally built for women.
60 The decline of service delivery by the government had already begun in the mid-1970s as the state radically reduced its already low investment in the living conditions of the black population. It worsened with the growing influx to the hostels in the 1980s and the ethnic and politic conflicts of the 1990s that set the stage for today's overcrowding and structural decay. See report by Noor Nieftagodien, "An Oral History of Hostel Dwellers in Gauteng" (2009): 38, 46.

Familial and cultural ties with rural home regions and customs are present in the photographic works of the "Ubambiswano Lwabashuti" team. They provide evidence of the rituals and celebrations that take place during visits to the villages or are acted out on the hostel grounds. But not all residents have a rural family home to regularly migrate back to. Their bed at the hostel might be the only living space available.

A particular insight into the complex familial and gender relations of hostel residents is provided by the oral history material. Especially for the women who live in the female-only hostels, democracy seems to have had little impact on their inability to integrate their family life with being a hostel resident. Beatrice Nkomana, for example, lives at the Helen Joseph hostel in Alexandra township. She has two daughters and two sons, but only lives with one of the girls in the hostel, as her fourteen- and fifteen-year-old boys were "chased out." She explains that the city council would forcefully relocate all male children from the hostel when they reached the age of seven. Beatrice has lost all contact with her teenage boys, stating that if she had an alternative place to stay, she would have continued to live with all her children. Still, for Beatrice, moving to the hostel in 1979 meant a change for the better. Others, like Pauline Thiti from the Orlando West women's hostel, were forcefully removed to the hostel. She was working for the inner-city Carlton Hotel as a cleaner when she was one of the many domestic workers who were forced to leave their staff quarters as a result of the 1955 "Locations in the Sky Act." This legislation prohibited white employers from housing more than five African workers at a time on their premises.[61]

While some residents stay at the hostels by choice and many because they don't have a better option, one of the striking ambivalences of hostel life is the question of safety. While almost all of the female residents interviewed for *Closed Constructions* regarded the hostel a safer place than the township, women also face severe levels of sexual harassment there. Two residents of the Helen Joseph women's hostel recall that several rape incidents happened in the 1990s. They describe how they only managed to put an end to them by mobilizing against the offenders. Also, all men interviewed for the "Hostels to Homes?" project identified crime (e.g. robberies and murder) as pressing matters for the resident committees. Ethnically rooted processes of conflict resolution and social control mediated by traditional leaders are still in place, but as *induna* George Shamase from the George Goch hostel states: the importance and acceptance of elected committees has grown in recent years.[62]

The committees play a pivotal role in representing residents' sometimes-diverging interests on the conversion of hostels into family units.[63] In the three years that the team worked on *Closed Constructions*, several developments were underway, but progress was slow. It is only in three places in the province – where re-development schemes had already begun the previous decade – that families are living in units that are adequate for family occupation. The units constructed more recently under the hostel eradication program were all still unfinished when the exhibition was launched in October 2011. Some of them have remained vacant shells, reminding passers-by of the empty promises made by government officials to hostel and township communities, which generated anger and protest among those who applied for an upgrade a long time ago. While the trans-

---

61 Hendrik Verwoerd enforced the Natives (Urban Areas) Amendment Act from 1956 when an increased number of domestic workers after World War II came to live in staff quarters in urban areas. Many of them were housed on the rooftops of the multi-story residential buildings of their employers.

62 Nieftagodien, "An Oral History of Hostel Dwellers": 42.

63 Since the 1980s, Inkatha Freedom Party followers in particular have frequently objected to plans to upgrade hostels into family units, which they saw as an assault on their way of life.

formation of hostels into homes is a contested process that some regard as an impossible mission and others long for, one should heed the closing words of George Goch hostel resident Mthuliseni Ndebele:

> We are people here and deserve to be taken like people. I would like to tell the journalists and the writers out there to take the stories of the hostels as normal because we are all people.

Section 4
The Power of Place: Space, Exclusions, Vulnerability

Jenny

$4.000

Gadi Algazi

The Naqab/Nagev, Israel:
Rebuilding Demolished Homes

This is Ḥākma after her home had been demolished. She is sitting under a tree with some of her children and relatives, encircled by piles of sand.

It is June 21, 2014. Ḥākma Abu-Mdighem A-Tūrī has eight children and lives in Al-'Araqīb, a tiny Bedouin village. As an 'unrecognized village,' officially it does not exist: there is no electricity, no water or sewage, and no social services; only repeated demolitions of the shacks people have built for shelter. The village is located in the northern Naqab/Negev, the semi-desert region of southern Israel, some ten kilometers north of Beer Sheba. Worse things happen in the Palestinian Occupied Territories, in the West Bank and Gaza. Arab inhabitants of the Negev/Naqab, however, are Israeli citizens.[1]

Nine days earlier, on June 12, 2014, a large force – police, special squads, and bulldozers – arrived in the village. By then, after seventy demolitions of the improvised shacks, the few remaining families of Al-'Araqīb were living within the cemetery compound. Now the bulldozers tore down

---

1 I have seen many demolished houses in the West Bank and Gaza. This piece engages with one aspect of the life of Palestinian citizens within Israel, often rendered invisible. The report is based on activities undertaken by members of Tarābut–Hitḥabrūt – an Arab-Jewish movement for social change, including myself. Photo: Michal Warshavsky.

the cemetery fence and the security forces marched in. The inhabitants, including old women and a young mother with her baby, joined by some thirty activists, gathered in the only structure still standing – the village mosque. We were surrounded for hours, while the bulldozers razed everything to the ground in front of our very eyes.[2]

It seemed at the time that this shock treatment would spell the end of the struggle of the people of Al-'Araqīb. The following weeks brought constant harassment by riot police and the special police unit trained to secure house demolitions. It was a very hot summer, a few days before Ramadān. From a distance we could hear Gaza being bombed: another 'military campaign' began and no one paid any attention to the plight of a few Arab citizens. During the demolition, the only water tank had been confiscated. Agriculturalists in the area were warned not to sell any water to the people of Al-'Araqīb. The families whose shacks had been torn down gathered under two trees and tied a net between the branches to provide shade. Before noon, 'Green Patrol' inspectors – a government unit entrusted with protecting state land from encroachers – came to report the continued presence of these 'encroachers.' They also cut the net with scissors. On several occasions, police cars entered the compound. They drove up and down on the sandy ground, blowing up as much dust as possible in the direction of the families gathered under the trees, causing coughing and shortness of breath, especially among the children.

Slightly further afield, right in front of the area where the police cars were patrolling, Ḥākma sat under her tree, surrounded by the sand heaps created by the bulldozers, joined by her youngest children, Ali and Sujūd, her adult children, and other relatives. She was fearless. She shouted and cursed at the policemen. When two of the boys, aged thirteen and fifteen, were illegally detained for two days, she protested with all her might that they had no right to take her children into custody. It was clear she was at the forefront of the conflict; it was not always easy for the men to accept this.

I have known Ḥākma and her family since 2010. I recorded her talking that day, sitting under the tree:

'Each time you come here, you shall see my eyes'

"If they come to evict us, I'll be sitting up in the tree. I'll wave to them 'hello' from up there. This tree is my new home at Al-'Araqīb. I'll make a sign saying: 'My New Home,' with words about what happened here and how they demolished the place, in Hebrew, English, and Arabic, and I'll hang it on the tree. So that everyone can read and know.

"They [the policemen] come here in their cars to cover the children with dust. I told them, they can blow as much dust as they please. I'm ready. The dust of my land won't hurt me. When my strength leaves me, I breathe in the air of my land. This gives me strength. I'm ready to live under the sun, me and my family. I have two married children, and six are here, sleeping under the tree, homeless. This land is my mother, it has kept me, it will keep me all my life. Who would sell his own mother? Only a mad person would. [As if speaking to an Israeli policeman:] 'How long have you been here? 70 years? My grandmother was here before me. This tree is a gift from my grandmother. It has been here more than 120 years.'

2 See the photo essay by Silvia Boarini, "In Photos: Israeli Bulldozers raze Bedouin Community," *Electronic Intifada*, https://electronicintifada.net/content/photos-israeli-bulldozers-raze-bedouin-community/13478, accessed July 10, 2018; the video: https://www.youtube.com/watch?v=5rNv_zBixJ0.

"They now demolish [our shack], so that when the Supreme Court decides whether Al-ʿAraqīb belongs to the Bedouins, they can say: 'There are no longer homes in Al-ʿAraqīb.' This is why we stay here. We won't let them decide over our land.[3]

"They [the police and the special squads] come during the night, they disturb us in the morning; all night I did not sleep. They put pressure and more pressure, so that the women and the men leave the village. But we don't go away. We shall either live here as we should, properly, or [as I live now] under the tree, or we die here. [We shall live] Under the tree, in the valley, in a car – no difference, I'm ready for anything. I shall not move. I told the officer of the riot police: Each time you come here, you shall see my eyes. In your dreams you'll see Ḥākma.

"I won't forsake my village. No power in the world can make me leave my village. [...]. I said it time and again: I don't need a fancy house in Tel Aviv, I want a little tent for me and for my children. Let us build a small tent. What does a person want? To live peacefully. Jews and Arabs are brothers. Why should they treat their brother like this? [...]

"They don't want just Al-ʿAraqīb. I wish it was only Al-ʿAraqīb. They don't want the Bedouins. I used to work, my children were working hard, I worked until the eighth month of my pregnancy to pay for a lawyer to stop the demolition [of my home]. What's the point? In the end they lied and demolished everything.

"And then [when all the village is demolished] they'll say: 'Nothing ever existed here ...' You know, they clean everything [after demolitions the debris and remnants are removed].

"The policeman told me: 'I am under pressure from above' [to demolish]. [I tell him:] 'Is this how you make your living? Off people?'

"I could talk for a whole month about what they did this week, and it won't be enough."

Nomadization and Expropriation

Al-ʿAraqīb is not a new squat. Bedouins lived here before the founding of the State of Israel. Some of them managed to stay after the War of 1948; those who remained were subject to a sustained campaign of deportation by the military, which took place mainly between 1949 and 1952 and went almost completely unnoticed. The Bedouin were cut off from the media and means of communication, their movement restricted by the military governor. Since many of the Bedouin remaining in the Negev occupied its northwestern, most fertile part, they had to be evicted to make place for new Jewish settlements. The people of Al-ʿAraqīb were among them.

Even though the Bedouin in this area had been practicing extensive agriculture and were integrated in regional economic networks as workers and traders, after 1948 they were routinely represented as free-roving nomads. Nomads cannot own land. Prior to the founding of the State of Israel, however, Zionist organizations bought land from the Bedouin. This stopped after they assumed power: Bedouin land could now be confiscated, or rather 'acquired' by the state. The new doctrine – not unanimously adopted – was that Bedouins, as such, have no land rights. Most of Israel's southern half was now officially defined as 'state land,' to be allocated to Jewish settlements. The state occasionally signaled its readiness to offer Bedouins some partial compensation

---

3 The people of Al-ʿAraqīb, led by Sheikh Sayāḥ Abu-Mdighem A-Tūrī, are involved in a long and protracted legal battle for recognition of their land rights.

as an act of grace, to subdue resentment, but refuses to recognize – other than in few exceptional cases – their land rights.[4]

Bedouin 'unrecognized villages' did not emerge until 1965, with the enactment of the Planning and Building Law, which regulated land-use in Israel for the first time. By almost completely ignoring existing Bedouin settlements in the Negev, they were retroactively transformed into 'illegal settlements.' After some hesitation, the official policy adopted was to drive the Bedouin into new townships by promising them access to infrastructure and education. Those who refused would be denied access to all services. But 'modernization' turned out to be illusory: the townships became synonymous with unemployment, high criminality rates, and oppressive social conditions. As the Bedouin realized that moving from their ancestral lands to townships paved the way for the alienation of their land – the little that remained – many decided to hold on to it: to stay in the 'unrecognized villages' and pay the price. Every Bedouin mother knows what this means in terms of raising children, access to medical services, and schooling. As this form of orderly production of suffering proved insufficient, the state turned to demolishing Bedouin homes built without a permit. In an 'unrecognized village,' construction is forbidden and all houses are hence 'illegal.' By 2008, there were more than 50,000 such houses. It is estimated that about a third of the Bedouin population now still lives in thirty-six 'unrecognized villages.'[5]

Al-'Araqīb is such a village. Its people enjoyed two important advantages when reclaiming their land rights: some of them were evicted to a location just a few kilometers away and they were able to re-assemble around their cemetery, founded in 1914. The state has conducted a long war of attrition against them. In 1999 the Jewish National Fund began forestation works on their land, using trees to mark ownership claims and make Bedouin land uncultivable. Aerial spraying with herbicide was also used between 2002 and 2003 to destroy Bedouin crops and drive them away, with long-term implications for their health. This was followed by demolitions, law suits, fines, and harassment. In July 2010 the whole village was demolished. In an act unheard of since 1949, some 350–400 people lost their homes. I still remember M., a school teacher, showing me his children's toys and the broken pieces of their computer in the debris. The shock was supposed to bring an end to their resistance, but the families of Al-'Araqīb held on and built improvised shelters again and again, after each subsequent demolition. In January and February 2011, the authorities sought to solve the problem through an intensive series of daily attacks on the remaining inhabitants: tear gas, beatings, sponge bullets, and detention. Most families with little children left the site; a few remained and sought refuge in the Muslim cemetery compound. June 2014 was another escalation in a long campaign.

So, this is not just about having a home, a roof over one's head. Home stands for much more. Refusal to relocate to a township, stubbornly holding on to one's land, living without essential services and under the imminent threat of demolition and harassment is a way of asserting rights and struggling for dignity. Of making a home.

As I write these words, four years later (February 2018), three families are still holding on in Al-'Araqīb. Ḥākma is among them. By now, the shacks have been demolished more than 125 times, only to be rebuilt anew each time. The people of the village are required to pay a horrendous sum

---

4 See Alexandre Kedar, Ahmad Amara, and Oren Yiftachel, *Emptied Lands: A Legal Geography of Bedouin Rights in the Negev* (Stanford: Stanford University Press, 2018).

5 For a map, see Negev Coexistence Forum for Civil Equality, 'On the Map: the Arab Bedouin Villages in the Negev-Naqab', https://www.dukium.org/map/. 10 of among 46 'unrecognized villages' won recognition, but their situation hardly improved as a result.

to cover the costs of the demolition of their own homes. The case for recognizing their land rights in Al-'Araqīb is still pending, but they are persecuted as encroachers of 'state land' facing imprisonment.

A Common Home

For several years, mostly between 2010 and 2016, we focused our grassroots work on bringing together people without a home in Israel: Palestinian citizens in poor neighborhoods suffering from discrimination and gentrification, Jewish single mothers struggling to make ends meet as neoliberal policies erode the little that remains of Israel's public housing, and Arab residents of 'unrecognized villages' paying with deprivation and demolition for their attachment to their lands, their water wells, and trees.

Their suffering was comparable, perhaps related, but far from identical, shaped by very different histories, truly and often tragically entangled. Some believed they that they were denied essential rights as citizens, mothers, human beings. Some claimed that they were entitled to a home because they were Jewish, because they were not Arabs, because they served in the army, served the state. Others, mostly Palestinian citizens, often just hoped the state would forget about them for a while, let them be, and stop destroying their fragile existence. It took us a while to realize that 'home' was an image, a memory, a yearning at once connecting people and dividing them. Access to a home was conditional, blatantly unequal, and depended on the mercy of rulers and the willingness of subjects to exhibit loyalty: a gift dispensed by those up above (the Hebrew expression is to be 'bound' or 'trapped' by gratefulness) rather than an equal and universal right. Above our heads, the outright nationalist party of the Neo-Zionist right gathered force and adopted a new name for itself: 'The Jewish Home.' Unlike our own, this was more than just a fragile vision for a different future. Jewish citizens without a true home and unable to rely on democratic and equal entitlement had good grounds for yielding to this vision of an exclusive fortress, armed to the teeth, in which you trade loyalty for some consideration.

Homes in Israel do not have a similar shape across ethnic divisions. Palestinian citizens often cling to privately owned houses in over-crowded settlements. They have never had significant access to public housing. Privately owned one-family houses remain the privilege of the Jewish middle class and its upper echelons. But traditionally, most Jewish citizens have not lived in privately owned houses; rather, they would work years to buy, rather than rent, an apartment in an apartment block. Such a communal residential building is called in Hebrew a 'common home' or a 'shared home' (*bayit meshutaf*). It often means endless quarrels among residents about paying bills and renovation work and over shared responsibilities. There are always some who do most of the talking at residents' assemblies and get to shape decisions, to be sure, but the 'common home' knows no institutionalized privileges and no single owner dominates the rest.

This would indeed be something: for all people of this torn, bleeding country, without distinction, to have a home, a common home – not an exclusively Jewish state, not a settlers' bastion with green lawns and a stolen Arab olive tree for authenticity's sake. A common, shared home.

Renu Addlakha

Public-Private Continuities and Alternate Domesticities: Welfare 'Homes' in India

This essay examines how discourses of home, family, and domesticity configure the structure, management, and daily routines of social welfare institutions such as asylums, children's homes, beggar homes, juvenile observation homes, old age homes, shelter homes for destitute women, and homes for the disabled. Although these establishments differ in the populations they target and in their aims (ranging from treatment and care to rehabilitation and correction), there are historical, structural, and organizational similarities between them. One of the common features of these 'homes' is that they are residential institutions where age- and sex-based segregation is the norm. They fulfil one of the definitions of 'home' as institutions for people needing professional care or supervision. Using a historical, gender-based approach, I would like to ask what is it about these places that enables them to be referred to as 'homes'? How are the everyday lives of residents governed by ideas of home and family? The social welfare paradigm strategically makes use of the terms 'home' and 'houses' when dealing with the management of deviant, different, and non-normative individuals, including disabled people, beggars, delinquents, homeless women and children, and the elderly. This paradigm has a global historiography going back to the Great Confinement and the Poor Laws in Europe, yet it is very much part of contemporary state policies. I write with particular reference to social welfare institutions in India.

Why is the term 'home' used in the management of heterogeneous populations through a network of social welfare institutions? What is a 'home' in these contexts? Do such establishments create an alternate domesticity? How are their daily rhythms and routines instituted to mimic an idealized household or home? Think of the medieval workhouses in Europe that housed a diverse range of economically and socially dependent individuals: These shelter arrangements subsequently migrated into asylums, hospitals, and schools, which became the sites of both confinement and knowledge production. Colonial states such as India created similar residential welfare structures to those that existed in the Western world. With minimal changes, this administrative architecture continues to be part of the welfare system in India today, both in the public and private spheres. Within a conceptual framework of marginality, domesticity, and the public-private interface, this essay asks what makes it necessary to deploy ideas of home, house, and homemaking in the ideological understanding and day-to-day functioning of these institutions.

The Ubiquity of Home

Capitalism is conventionally understood to have created a binary between home and work, where work is defined almost exclusively in economic terms as labor, employment, or livelihood. But work is not just an economic category; it extends far beyond the narrow definition of production. In its widest ramifications, work is survival, and in that sense, it is central to the subsistence of all life forms. Instead of analyzing work only within the economic paradigm, let us look at work in terms of broader goals such as socialization, moral improvement, or personality development, which are some of the functions of the establishments under consideration. Needless to say, home and work are both embedded in contexts in which other variables such as gender, age, class, and caste come into play. Provincializing work is not enough – we need to look at work in the making of the home and work at home. Feminist scholarship has amply demonstrated the importance of women's work in the form of reproductive work, housework, and care work. It is the contention of this essay that there are direct connections between economy, society, intimacy, and morality in the constitution and functioning of social welfare institutions, which immediately call into question the taken-for-granted opposition between home and work in the West.

In an earlier work on psychiatric hospitalization in India, I have shown how Erving Goffman's concept of the 'total institution' cannot be used even as a heuristic device in under-resourced contexts like public hospitals.[6] A chronic paucity of resources, an acute model of treatment, and a family-dominated social system combine to create a treatment context based on continuities, rather than discontinuities, with the patient's home world, giving rise to a distinctive hospital-family alliance. This alliance constitutes a pragmatic approach to the management of psychiatric disorders in a situation that rules out long-term institutionalization. It also shields the patient's identity from being eroded by typical procedures of degradation experienced upon admission into a total institution-like setting.

During the course of my fieldwork, I made home visits to a young woman, Sita, who had been hospitalized for a few months and who described her stay in the psychiatry ward as follows:

> Yes, of course I liked being there. There is no work. One eats, chats, and sleeps the whole day. But one has to leave, because it is not home.

My case study also highlighted the strategic utilization of periodic psychiatric hospitalization as a way of avoiding indigence in a family context where a chronic, psychiatrically ill elderly female patient was being looked after by her siblings, none of whom were willing or in a position to offer her permanent shelter during periods of remission. Sita's case history showed periodic relapses accompanied by regular sojourns in the same psychiatry ward for a couple of months at a time, a pattern observed over more than ten years.

Psychiatric hospitalization is very different from penal incarceration in a juvenile home or confinement in a children's home on account of homelessness, yet all these arrangements are constituted against the backdrop of an actual or imagined family support system mediating between the resident and the outside world.

The idea that home is the converse of the workplace – not a site of economic production but the locus of biological and social reproduction – is central to its creation and routines. Home is a place for feeding, resting, cleaning, and grooming the body in a secure environment. Physical and emotional security are the prerequisites of an ideal 'home.' Establishments like juvenile homes and children's homes try frequently to create the figment of the family by designating key functionaries as house-parents. There, as in any normative home, all residential establishments have to necessarily make temporal divisions between sleeping, mealtimes, and body-care activities. If housekeeping involves residents' participation on a considerable scale (as it often does in the case of under-resourced institutions), then sweeping, mopping, cooking, and washing dishes and clothes may also become part of the daily routine. My contention is that in any arrangement involving

---

6 Renu Addlakha, *Deconstructing Mental Illness: Psychiatry, Women and the Family* (New Delhi: Zubaan, 2008). Goffman defines a total institution as "a place of residence and work where a large number of like-situated individuals, cut off from the wider society for an appreciable period of time, lead an enclosed, formally administered round of life," in Erving Goffman, *Asylums: Essays on the Social Situation of Mental Patients and Other Inmates* (Harmondsworth: Penguin, 1961): 11. For Goffman, such institutions include prisons, mental hospitals, monasteries, and boarding schools.

residence, self-care, and domestic activities in a particular space invariably renders that space a home in form if not in spirit. You may not feel homely there, but it is still a home.

The historical role of capitalism in the creation of institutionalization is too well known to be repeated. Suffice to say that industrialization, with its long working hours and factory-based system of production, required some mechanism to manage those who could not or did not participate in the production process due to reasons ranging from ill-health, perceived lack of intelligence, or criminal or any other deviant behavior. Such individuals had to be separated from the social mainstream, controlled, and if possible re-socialized into the norms and values of capitalist society. Liberal utilitarianism, medicalization, eugenics, and social Darwinism provided ideological ammunition for this process. The development of democratic governance systems was concomitant with the provisions of taking care of the needy and the destitute. Even though capitalist developments ran parallel to democratic thought processes, cultural, social, and political contexts influenced the way the individual in society was conceived. Each individual as a citizen was entitled to certain rights associated with certain obligations. The negative effects of industrialization on sections of the population were analyzed in depth via social surveys on the poor and marginalized.[7] Such research provided a rationale for the development of provisions for the welfare of these populations. Associated with these were developments in the profession of social work.

People in society have inherently tried to take care of destitute and underprivileged individuals either out of moral benevolence or religious and customary obligations. As governance systems evolved, there was an effort to institutionalize welfare. In more modern times, the welfare discourse has evolved from charity to needs, and to rights-based approaches. Social welfare is an organized system of social services and institutions, designed to aid individuals and groups, particularly those belonging to the deprived sections, to attain satisfactory standards of life and health.

Social welfare seems to be a backup mechanism that comes into play when a family is absent, unwilling, or unable to manage a situation at the individual level. The external agency taking over family functions may be temporary or permanent. The care of children, the aged, and the disabled is considered the responsibility of the family, but the state steps in to fill this gap when the family fails in its 'natural' role to care for its members. Politics, economics, and ideology variously determine how the welfare system is managed. After Independence in 1947, social welfare was built into the Indian Constitution, which empowered the state to promote the welfare of citizens and meet the basic needs of the underprivileged in society. These programs, including the establishment and management of social welfare institutions, were included in the five-year national economic plans. The Central Ministry of Social Justice and Empowerment and state ministries of social welfare are currently charged with the provision of social welfare. The voluntary sector is a major player in service delivery and management, singly or in partnership with the state.

Life in the 'Home'

All nations developed social welfare services as they moved from agrarian to industrial economies. The role of the extended family in addressing the needs of its members declined in the modern complex societies, necessitating the development of extra-familial institutions and organizations

---

7 See, for example, Charles Booth, *Life and Labour of the People in London* (London: Macmillan, 1902); Benjamin Seebohm Rowntree, *Poverty: A Study of Town Life* (London: Macmillan, 1901).

to provide welfare. Even though welfare is the concern of both public and private agencies, it is accorded ham-handed treatment in terms of the allocation of financial and human resources. A standard narrative is evoked through anecdotal and media accounts: the paucity of materials and trained human resources, dilapidated buildings, overcrowding, insanitary living conditions, inadequate and poor-quality food, inadequate bedding, the lack of clothes, soap and other essential articles of daily living, abuse and violence. With few exceptions, a sub-standard, if not sub-human, residential environment is more the norm than the exception. But how different is this situation from the 'normal' homes of the majority of the residents in poor and under-developed societies? Indeed, some residents may find the living conditions in the institution more comfortable than their home outside.

Apart from the material environment, one of the most frequently reported features of such institutions is the almost total lack of constructive activity to fill the day. Whether a person is institutionalized to give treatment, provide safety, or mete out punishment, the ultimate aim is their reintegration into the social mainstream. But is this possible in the absence of a daily structuring of time into a set of routine activities? The oft-reported temporal emptiness that characterizes the lives of residents of most social welfare institutions is highlighted in a recent Human Rights Watch Report on the lives of women in mental hospitals in India. Women with psychosocial or intellectual disabilities reported having no meaningful activities to keep them engaged. Aparna, a woman with bipolar disorder and epilepsy, told Human Rights Watch:

> I have studied a little and can read a book if you give me one, but they don't give books here. Nothing happens here. You wander around, eat, drink, sleep, that's all.[8]

While this report confirms popular depictions of such institutions as dumping grounds, with congested and unhygienic living conditions and rampant sexual abuse and violence by staff and other residents, what stands out is the absence of meaningful activities to keep the residents occupied. This leads to apathy, boredom, and unhappiness. Without meaningful activity, there is no self-worth or dignity. Residents sleep, wander around aimlessly, and get drawn into fights with each other as an outlet for their aggression. It is not that activities are not woven into the conceptual structure of these establishments – basic education and vocational training, recreation, and entertainment are a part of the daily routine – but it is more in theory than practice. While a television will invariably be available more for distracting the residents into submission than for providing wholesome entertainment, the provision of other facilities is more ad-hoc. Very often, the shortage of staff to manage the teeming numbers ensures that the tenor of life is maintained at the basic minimum. Such a situation is particularly disturbing in the case of children's homes, since the absence of a daily structure has particularly deleterious consequences for their growth and development.

Conclusion

This essay has tried to question the common-sense perception that the idea of home is naturally and necessarily associated with the household and family. Social welfare institutions in under-

8 www.hrw.org/report/2014/12/03/treated-worse-animals/abuses-against-women-and-girls-psychosocial-or-intellectual, accessed September 15, 2016.

resourced contexts such as India are useful examples to focus on the permeability of the separation between home and institution, particularly because they incorporate facets of the home and the family into their structure and day-to-day functioning. Indeed, the heuristic tenability of the inside-outside binary that is the hallmark of the total-institution framework, and which serves as the template for the design of social welfare establishments, prisons, and hospitals, is particularly questionable in the case of female residents, whose sphere of operation is normally restricted within the confines of the domestic. Long-term residence in public institutions is a ripe context for querying the boundaries between 'home' and 'non-home.' Home is not only where the heart is, as the age-old proverb goes; home is where life is. Any space that is the place of self-maintenance, self-care, and self-regeneration over an extended period of time is home. Physical location, familiarity, and duration are the architecture of the home. Whether a home is homely or not is another matter.

This essay has painted a fairly drab picture of social welfare institutions in India, with the focus largely being on state-run institutions where chronic shortages of material and human resources and rampant corruption contribute to their corrosion. However, a ray of hope is provided by the participation of NGOs in the management of social welfare work, both singularly or in partnership with the state. While the former is an offshoot of charity and philanthropic work, which is as old as human civilization, the latter, known in India as the public-public private partnership model, is a major tool deployed by the neoliberal state to manage vast aspects of the social sector, including health, education, and social welfare. Neoliberal economies may in theory advocate for economic deregulation, but in practice, governance requires active participation by agencies of the state, both in maintenance of public order and in the promotion of socioeconomic equity.

Anne Griffiths
Land as a Site for Creating a Home: A Cautionary Tale from Botswana

"Home is more than having a roof over your head."[9] Home represents a space in which social relationships acquire meaning as well as a territorial location. It is a place that embodies connections among people, including families and households, as well as to land. Land is thus a site in which both concrete and more intangible elements of existence come into being, creating associations around a nexus of relations. It is a site that has global significance, not only because it is crucial to international and transnational initiatives concerning sustainable economic and environmental development, but because it also forms a key component at a micro-level in providing families and households with shelter and a base to pursue their livelihoods, as well as the potential for capital accumulation. As a foundation on which a home is constituted, encompassing security, sustenance, work, and labor, land is central to families' and households' existence and well-being.

Who has rights to land – to create a home – raises important questions about legitimacy, authority, vulnerability, and exclusion. Without recognition of land rights, families may find themselves evicted, their land repossessed, and their home destroyed. This essay explores these issues by examining the power of the law in determining and enforcing rights to land in the *Murima* case from Botswana, a country where I have carried out fieldwork for many years. The case highlights the pressures and contestations over land that exist in Botswana and elsewhere in Africa, and is especially pertinent with regard to debates over 'illegal' occupation and squatting.

Global and Local Dimensions of Land

Land has become an ever more sought-after resource in light of the unprecedented growth of urbanization around the world. It raises questions about human security in relation to the growing market in land and its commodification. In Botswana, the demand for land has been exacerbated through migration towards urban centers, such as the capital city, Gaborone, where many citizens flock to live and work.

Botswana (formerly the Bechuanaland Protectorate under British indirect rule) has seen a transformation from the agrarian base that was in place at independence in 1966, when most of its citizens engaged in subsistence activities, to a situation where the majority of its population are classed as urban dwellers engaging in or looking for other forms of work. It is not surprising that today about one-third of the country's population is located in and around Gaborone and its catchment area in the southeast of the country. It is in this area that Mr. Murima established his home, on land that was at the heart of the dispute in the *Murima* case.[10]

---

9 This was the title of a set of performances undertaken by students in the Women's Law program at the Southern and Eastern African Women's Regional Law Centre at the University of Zimbabwe in the early 2000s.
10 *Murima and Another v Kweneng Land Board* 2002 (1) BLR 18 (HC). All quotations in this essay are drawn from this case report, unless otherwise noted.

Mr. Murima's Circumstances

The land in question was situated at Tsolamosese in the Mogoditshane area. When he was given the land by Mmapula Mokgalagadi in 1968, it formed part of a ploughing area where he built a house for himself and his family. The land in this area, like most in Botswana, was held under land tenure governed by oral, unwritten customary law and did not involve any written formalities. Working as a self-employed motor mechanic, his family expanded over the years and he was given an adjacent piece of land in 1984, which he ploughed to feed his family. He used the land to build further homes for his family, which by the time the case came to court, consisted of nine wives and thirty-nine children. By this time, he was one of the oldest residents in the area and according to the judge who heard his case, Collins AJ, "obviously well known to all in the neighborhood."

The difficulty that Mr. Murima faced was that between 1968 and 1984 the Tribal Land Act of 1968 came into existence.[11] This Act attempted to redesign established customary land tenure by transferring powers held by chiefs over land (in pre-colonial and colonial times) to land boards. The Act originally vested land in land boards "in trust for the benefit and advantage of tribesmen of that area," but this was amended in 1993 to open up the jurisdiction of the land boards to all citizens of Botswana regardless of where they came from or their tribal affiliation. The Act handed over powers previously vested in chiefs under customary law in relation to allocation, transfer, use, and cancellation of land rights to land boards. Mr. Murima's land was located within Bakwena tribal territory in Kweneng district and therefore fell within the jurisdiction of the Kweneng Land Board (KLB). As with other land boards, the allocation or transfer of land requires a written land certificate issued by the appropriate land board. Although Mr. Murima appeared to have acquired the initial land under recognized rules of customary law and prior to the creation of the KLB, he did not have a certificate from the KLB for the land on which he had built and which he was occupying at the time the case was raised.

The position in which he found himself was not due to a lack of action on his part. Indeed, he had made several attempts to get the KLB to authenticate the donation of land to him; the court acknowledged that "positive steps were taken by him ... over a lengthy period of time to obtain approval." However, despite repeated attempts to acquire a certificate and verbal assurances that one would be forthcoming, his application was never processed. He was not alone in this experience. Given the peri-urban location of the Mogoditshane area, where the land was situated, people were desperately seeking to acquire land there to live and pursue employment opportunities. Following the KLB's failure to adequately oversee and control the allocation and transfer of land, along with any authorization required for a change of use, local people took matters into their own hands, engaging in self-allocation. Their perception of the KLB as biased in its decision-making led to those with control over ploughing fields transferring their fields, or subdividing them on their own initiative and selling on the subdivisions to those who wanted to convert these fields into residential property.

---

11 Cap 32.02

The State's Response to Dealing with Land

The situation was so chaotic that it led to the government setting up a Commission of Enquiry in 1991 that gave rise to a white paper in 1992.[12] This set out recommendations on how to deal with those occupying land in the area without land certificates from the KLB. It included the setting up of a task force to investigate claims about the rights of existing occupiers, with a view to identifying those involved in the illegal occupation of land as squatters. In an effort to deal with the situation, the government elected to impose a 5,000 pula fine on illegal occupiers who had substantial buildings on their land on the understanding that they would then acquire legal recognition of their status and an official land certificate. This proved to be unworkable, however, with Collins AJ observing that the decision backfired almost immediately. Illegal occupants lined up to pay their fines in the knowledge that their illegal acts were now sanctioned and that they would have security of tenure. For those occupants, it was not a fine but a 'purchase-price' (and well worth the money considering the alternatives).

In recognition that the situation was out of control, the government issued a presidential directive that adopted a hardline approach, pursuing the eviction of illegal occupiers of land and the demolition of buildings in order to prevent "a complete breakdown in law and order."[13]

The Destruction of Mr. Murima's Homes and the Legal Responses

Given these developments, what was the position in which Mr. Murima now found himself? By the end of 2000, he had constructed a six-room concrete building, a nine-room concrete building, four shacks used as storerooms and bathrooms, and a twenty-eight-room double-story brick-and-mortar building. All this work had, as the judge in his case acknowledged, "taken him the best part of a lifetime to construct in order to give shelter to his very large extended family." However, it was more than that; what had been built up over many years on this land provided the home base from which he and his family could conduct their relationships with one another and the broader local community, and pursue their livelihoods.

However, in November 2000, Mr. Murima found himself facing the 'yellow monsters' (as heavy building machinery and vehicles are colloquially referred to in Botswana) that were sent by the KLB to demolish the buildings on his land. He immediately contacted an attorney, who managed to halt the demolition crew; they had acquired a verbal undertaking from the deputy board secretary, Mrs. Mathake, that the demolition would not proceed until a court order was obtained. This was confirmed in a letter written by his attorney to the board that was marked urgent and hand delivered. Alas, the letter was ignored and the demolition proceeded over the next nine days until his life's work was destroyed, leaving him and his extended family exposed to the elements, desperately trying to salvage small household items from the debris and devastation.

The distress that such actions caused Mr. Murima and his family was highlighted in the evidence that during the demolition process "all [his] children and wives were crying." Unfortunately,

---

12 Government White Paper No.1 of 1992: A report by the residential commission of inquiry into land problems in Mogoditshane and other peri-urban villages.
13 No. CAB 28(b)/2000

Mr. Murima did not manage to obtain a restraining order against the KLB until January 16, 2001, by which time the demolition was all but complete. There was no explanation for his delay in pursuing court action, although the judge surmised that the first two weeks in January are a time when attorneys traditionally take their vacation, which might have impacted Mr. Murima's ability to approach the court earlier. He also opined that the delay might be attributed to the fact that Mr. Murima was so shell-shocked by the onslaught in defiance of the respondent's undertaking not to demolish without a court order that he was unable to act.

The delay meant that it was too late for the restraining order to prevent the demolition that had already taken place. It did, however, provide certain temporary interim orders prohibiting the KLB from evicting Mr. Murima and his family, from destroying their moveable goods, and from harassing, humiliating, and threatening them. These orders were granted pending the outcome of the current case brought before Collins AJ, who asserted that the KLB's actions had been unlawful.

In response to a claim of wrongful action, the KLB denied that it had ever given an undertaking to Mr. Murima's attorney that it would not proceed with the demolition without a court order, an assertion that the judge rejected, finding the board's conduct to be "deceitful, cowardly and callous." The KLB also denied destroying any structures of substance, arguing that they had only destroyed recently erected shacks in line with the terms of the presidential directive. In doing so, the KLB maintained that it was "acting pursuant to superior orders of the state."

The judge rejected the board's contention that it did not need a court order so long as the property in question was a shack and not a substantial structure. He did so, firstly on the grounds that independent evidence from one of the contractors engaged in the demolition had established the contrary, and pointed to the heavy toll that such work took on the machinery which broke down under the strain and required substantial repairs. In any event, the judge observed, "The quality of the structure is irrelevant. Why should the less fortunate among us whose meager resources will only stretch to a few corrugated iron sheets be treated any differently from those whose resources are abundant?"

Secondly, the judge questioned the legal status of the directive, noting that there had been no declaration of a state of emergency, where the ordinary laws of the land would be suspended. This being the case, it had "no force of law at all" and could not be relied upon by the KLB to justify its actions in relation to squatters or occupiers of tribal land under its jurisdiction. It made no difference that Mr. Murima did not possess a land certificate, although the KLB treated failure to exhibit a certificate of rights as being "tantamount to illegal squatting." Regardless of Mr. Murima's legal status, in acting without giving notice and without acquiring a court order, the KLB were acting unlawfully. The judge observed, "Even if the applicants were stealthy squatters (which they were not) the respondent's actions were unjustified and illegal. They took the law into their own hands with devastating consequences for the applicants." Thus, the question of whether Mr. Murima's occupation of the land was lawful was irrelevant. Indeed, the legal basis for his occupation was never discussed notwithstanding the judge's declaration that he and his family were not "stealthy squatters." This indicated that the judge recognized that Mr. Murima had some valid relationship to the land, which appeared to meet the legal requirements for transfer under customary law (at least in the first instance) before the Tribal Land Act came into effect.

Legal Uncertainty, Vulnerability, and Exclusion: The Limits of Law

What this case makes visible is the question of legality that attaches to occupation of land. It highlights the competing norms and rules that come into conflict with one another – in terms of legality being constructed on the basis of possessing a land certificate or not under the TLA – compared with older forms of land transfer that are recognized under customary law. Depending on which rules are applied in a particular context, occupation can be rendered legal or illegal, with all the consequences that ensue from such a classification. This creates uncertainty and renders families vulnerable to dispossession, even if, as in Mr. Murima's case, the relevant authority was found to have acted unlawfully.

Given the KLB's unlawful actions, what were Mr. Murima's remedies at the end of the case? Unfortunately, the court could not order the KLB to restore the demolished structures because "the damage is of such a magnitude that an order in these terms could not be enforced." Similarly, an order for compensation was incompetent because the current case only concerned a finding on the lawfulness of the KLB's actions and did not include an action for compensation. However, the court left the KLB in no doubt that "compensation is payable as an alternative remedy in damages." In stating this, the court also made it clear that the KLB could not rely, in defense to a compensation claim, on the fact that Mr. Murima did not have a land certificate. It emphasized that compensation would be due and that "it is only a question of establishing the amount." In the meantime, pending further court action, the judge made the earlier interim orders permanent. They included a special provision for Mr. Murima and his family to continue occupying the field together with the temporary structures that he had erected after the demolition had taken place, pending the outcome of his action for compensation. Finally, the KLB were ordered to pay the costs Mr. Murima had incurred in raising the action.

The judge recognized the limits of his legal power in this case, expressing the hope that the KLB, with the blessing of the Minister of Lands, Housing and Environment, would immediately set up bilateral discussions and negotiations with the applicants to redress the damage which had been carried out as a gesture of practical compassion. This was a matter of some urgency as the "families live in conditions which they should not have to endure for a moment longer than is necessary."

Unfortunately, this did not happen and an attempt was made at a later date to deny Mr. Murima and his family compensation on the basis of a legal technicality that their claim for damages was out of time. But that is a story for another day.[14]

---

14 See *Murima v Kweneng Land Board* 2007 (2) BLR 486 (HC), where the court refused to uphold the KLB's assertion that the claim was out of time.

Vincent Houben

Homes and Colonial Violence in the Dutch East Indies: The Coolie *Pondok*

From the late 1910s until the early 1930s, the Dutch East Indies went through a period of rapid economic growth. The exploitation of mines and large plantations on the Outer Islands of colonial Indonesia necessitated the large-scale transfer of indentured labor from the densely populated island of Java to remote corners of the archipelago. In the wake of the expansion of the colonial economy and the concentration of large numbers of indigenous workers in places of capitalist production, the coolie shed or barrack – the *pondok* – emerged as a key site of colonial imagination and social contestation. The *pondok* strictly confined ways of home-making.

It is difficult to surmise whether those who inhabited coolie sheds could develop feelings of 'home' there or whether there always remained a lack of identification with the place where workers sat together, cooked, engaged in leisure activities, and slept after their shift had come to an end. In certain ways, the *pondok* exemplified a non-home because its design was not specific to a particular place, the people who shared it were not family, and its social functions were severely restricted. Despite a work regime geared towards maximizing intersectional divisions between ethnicity, work, and gender, which caused occasional strife, the cohabitation of predominantly young males produced mechanisms of social solidarity. A small minority of old hands reenlisted several times as contract workers on a single enterprise may have felt their *pondok* to be home, since they eventually lost contact with their homes of origin. Others moved out of the plantation into surrounding villages, started families, and found homes there.

The Spatial and Historical Dimensions of the *Pondok*

Although communal houses were not uncommon in parts of Indonesia, the typical village house on Java was built for single families. European colonizers had separate dwellings for their servants on the courtyard of their mansions. However, the *pondok* had a different origin and was connected to the work regime via European colonizers everywhere in the tropics. They probably had a military connection, since from early imperial times onward, colonial soldiers were housed in barracks. Plantations, like barracks and prisons, entailed strict drills. This explains why, at least in the Dutch East Indies, coolie barracks were also called *tangsi*, an expression for military barracks.

Coolie sheds exemplified a global tropical format of housing which appeared when large-scale agricultural production created the demand for a concentration of workers at or near to the production site, where no regular villages were available but where the labor force had to be controlled. Most of the dwellers were transient, since workers' contracts were temporary. To save costs, employers did not invest much in the quality of these dwellings. When coolie sheds were situated at agricultural frontiers, they were hasty and make-shift properties. Once full-fledged plantation premises had been established, these temporary housing facilities were turned into more permanent constructions, since they had to function for many years without much upkeep.

Besides reflecting a global imperial format of organizing work, the coolie barrack on the Outer Islands of the Dutch East Indies also resembled forms of housing on the island of Java, where plantation agriculture had been introduced by the Dutch during the seventeenth century. The coolie shed had been a regular part of Javanese rural life since the nineteenth century, when the Dutch introduced large-scale production of sugar cane, tobacco, and indigo for the world market. A study of 1939–1940 informs us that at least one-third of families working on plantations in Java did not live in villages, but in houses on the premises themselves. The communal houses in particular were smaller in size but more solidly built than those in the village.[15]

Coolie sheds were often constructed in a rectangular form around a square, where the laborers could sit together and where cooking facilities were provided. Toilets were often simple holes behind the barracks. Coolie sheds had a clay soil, wooden walls, and palm leaf roofs (*atap*). They contained very little furniture – a set of 'sleeping tables' used for both eating and sleeping.[16] Yet the design of coolie barracks evolved over time. In West Sumatra around 1900, the *pondok* was built out of plaited bamboo (*plupuh*), consisting of one hall with two rows of plank-beds, with up to 120 coolies in one barrack. During the 1910s, new barracks were increasingly built out of wood or brick and subdivided into sections or rooms.[17] In Palembang, married coolies were housed in separate, larger rooms in one of the barracks or sometimes even in small houses with small gardens, where they could grow vegetables and plant fruit trees. In East Sumatra, a similar arrangement was made in 1928 for married contract laborers who had been in the service of a single employer for five years.[18]

In the 1920s, the Dutch Labor Inspectorate in Deli oversaw the provision of proper housing for the coolies. Guidelines were issued for their construction. Unmarried coolies (*bujang*) should be housed in dwellings consisting of two rows of up to forty rooms on both sides of a gallery. Each room was required to have an average size of three-by-four meters, offering a sleeping place for up to four men.[19] In southeast Kalimantan, unmarried males were likewise housed in large barracks with a floor in the middle. Barracks there were twenty-by-seven meters with a capacity for on average thirty-six people. For the few coolie families, separate rooms existed.[20]

Dutch labor inspectors also visited nearby colonies, where Javanese indentured laborers could be found. When British North Borneo was visited in 1927, coolie housing was found to be similar to that in the Dutch East Indies. Single and double-row *pondoks* existed, subdivided into rooms, sometimes with a gallery around the outside or an inner corridor in the middle. Unmarried coolies were given a place in sleeping halls, in accordance with the *tangsi* system. The upkeep was apparently rather bad; kitchens, toilets, and water facilities were neglected. In contrast, coolie housing in Malaya was much better. The labor codes in the Federated Malay States and in Johore prescribed a standard design for coolie housing. They had to be built on stilts, with twenty to twenty-four rooms in two rows back-to-back and a veranda on both sides. The roofs had to be of iron well-plate, with cemented trenches beneath. Drinking water was to be provided from wells with cemented walls and bucket-latrines used as toilets.

---

15 Luidolf Harm Huizenga, *Het Koeliebudgetonderzoek op Java in 1939–40 ("The Coolie Budget Inquiry on Java in 1939–40")* (Wageningen: Vada, 1958): 52–8, 257–8.

16 Jan Breman, *Koelies, Planters en Koloniale Politiek: Het Arbeidsregime op de Grootlandbouwondernemingen aan Sumatra's Oostkust aan het Begin van de Twintigste Eeuw* (Dordrecht: Foris, 1987): 90.

17 Vincent J.H. Houben and J. Thomas Lindblad, *Coolie Labor in Colonial Indonesia: A Study of Labor Relations in the Outer Islands, c. 1900–1940* (Wiesbaden: Harrassowitz, 1999): 188.

18 H.J. Langeveld, "Arbeidstoestanden op de ondernemingen ter Oostkust van Sumatra tussen 1920 en 1940 in het licht van het verdwijnen van de poenale sanctie op de arbeidscontracten," *Economisch- en Sociaal-Historisch Jaarboek* 41 (1978): 343–4.

19 Houben and Lindblad, *Coolie Labor in Colonial Indonesia*: 55.

20 Houben and Lindblad, *Coolie Labor in Colonial Indonesia*: 160–1.

Fantasizing the Coolie Home

Probably the most famous novel on the life of indentured plantation laborers in late colonial Indonesia is *Koelie* by the Dutch-Hungarian female author Madelon Székely-Lulofs, which appeared for the first time in Dutch in the early 1930s.[21] Based on personal observations as the wife of a planter, she imagined how life must be for the coolies. She adopted the perspective of Roeki, a young Javanese male recruited for work in Deli, northeast Sumatra, at that time the largest integral plantation area in Asia. Her portrait of plantation society was close to lived reality, yet the Javanese worker's psyche was put into an orientalist frame. The worker was clearly exploited and mistreated, but he remains an animal-like primitive creature in the novel, driven by lust and prone to violence.

After his arrival, Roeki was brought to sit in the middle of an empty, barren coolie square – similar to the square of a village (*kampong*). Looking around, he saw rows of coolie rooms on all four sides, small compartments under a single roof of palm leaf, with no houses in sight. Alongside there was a corridor, where a few women were cooking. At 9pm, a wooden block (*tong tong*) was beaten to indicate that everyone had to go to sleep. Roeki entered a room for unmarried males (*bujang*), a small square den with four rugged walls and a clay surface. There he found six small wooden sleeping benches (*bale-bale*), where his roommates slept on mats (*tikar*) in the light of a single little oil lamp.[22]

The activities in and around the *pondok*, as described by Székely-Lulofs, were manifold. Coolies spent part of their wages on playing dice, betting during cock-fights, and visiting females, who were married but prostituted themselves. They chatted, gossiped, played gamelan and cards, and bought sweets and tobacco. The *pondok* premises at night seemed peaceful, but the situation could tip over instantly, for instance when a Chinese male sneaked in after dark to pick up one of the females for paid sex. On one of these occasions, the Chinese man was first beaten up and then killed by a mob. From being a place of nightly quietness, the *pondok* square turned into one of screams. "In one second, out of dreamlike devout atmosphere, wild bloodthirstiness was borne. They swayed with *parang*s (chopping knives), *cankol*s (hatchets) and pieces of wood. They screamed, raged and laughed like lunatics." What started as beating (*pukul*) the 'Chinese pig' (*babi cina*) turned into a collective desire to kill (*bunuh*). After their outpour of hatred had climaxed in murdering the Chinese intruder, silence returned and all slept like animals, "silent, unconsciousness, unknowing of their own cruelty."[23]

Home and Colonial Violence

In his classic study on the tobacco plantation industry in Deli during the late nineteenth and early twentieth centuries, Jan Breman described how the physical layout of the plantation in Deli mirrored the social inequalities produced by the logic of capitalist production.[24] In the center of the enterprise (*kebon*), all the major buildings necessary for output were situated – administrative offices, warehouses, homes of the European staff, a shop, and the coolie barracks. The way these

---

21 Madelon Székely-Lulofs, *Koelie*, 6th ed. (Amsterdam: Manteau, 1985).
22 Székely-Lulofs, *Koelie*: 57–60.
23 Székely-Lulofs, *Koelie*: 117–8.
24 Breman, *Koelies, Planters en Koloniale Politiek*.

buildings were positioned reflected the power hierarchy on the plantation. The residence of the head administrator (*tuan besar*) was at the very center, but it was inaccessible to the workers.[25]

Since the *pondoks* were so different to what villagers were used to in Java, they considered it a punishment to be forced to work on a plantation. Their signing of a coolie contract was considered to be an act of selling their soul (*jual jiwa*). Solidarity among workers developed through the fact that those working together in a gang were also usually living together in the same room or barrack. The fact that coolie barracks were the place where workers rested after their shifts and where they could not be continuously monitored by the plantation staff meant that, besides being a place of leisure and play, the *pondok* could develop into a site of contestation. Coolie riots were suspected to be secretly planned here, based on feelings of revenge and stemming from, what Javanese themselves label as, a 'warm heart' (*panas hati*). European staff thus feared the *pondok*, did not enter it, and left it to Asian overseers to install some sort of surveillance.

During the late 1920s, incidences of violence on the part of coolies rose sharply, which led to an intense debate in Dutch colonial sources on its possible causes. Besides an acknowledgement of the often tactless and violent attitudes of young, inexperienced European plantation assistants towards their workers, one of the root causes was identified in the changed mentality of coolies themselves. A 1930 report of the Labor Office signaled that because of increased education and more contact to the outer world, coolies were no longer people who had not seen anything beyond their own village. The labor conditions connected to the whole system of indenture were reevaluated – the long working day, the limited number of resting days, the strict execution of orders, and the finishing of prescribed tasks. There existed too few opportunities for relaxation and life was monotonous in comparison with that in Java. The way of life in a coolie establishment had become too different to that of a village (*kampung*) on Java.[26]

Thinking Home

The coolie house was not home. The imagined home for Javanese coolies existed on the island of Java or in the Javanese village to which he or she longed to return. Feelings of *rindu* – the craving for something lost – could not abate completely. Another kind of longing had led the Javanese to enlist themselves for contract work – the wish for a better life in future, away from poverty, debt, and lack of security. But once resettled and subjected to the harshness of the work regime on the plantation, this longing was reversed into nostalgia for an imagined better life back home. Yet home in this sense was also a fantasy, since many coolies did not previously own or live in a village house. Among these were temporary migrant workers, who moved between places in Java and who had lived in *pondok*s before. Many came from the margins of rural society.

Photographs of coolie barracks are scarce. Somehow they escaped the colonial gaze, except when they needed to be displayed to contemporary Western viewers, possibly investors, or maybe officials of the labor inspectorate. The picture of a Javanese barrack on the Padang Boelan planta-

25 Breman, *Koelies, Planters en Koloniale Politiek*: 63.
26 Nationaal Archief Den Haag, Ministerie van Koloniën: Geheime Mailrapporten, inventarisnummer 2.10.36.06 no. 78, mailrapport 1930 no. 91x.

tion of the Amsterdam Deli Company is a case in point.[27] This is clearly a model *pondok* – with a fresh roof, partly consisting of palm leaf and partly of corrugated sheet iron, freshly white-washed walls, open windows, and a veranda to the outside. This photograph appears to have been taken during working hours, as females and children are sitting around idly awaiting the return of the men. This photographic representation is supposed to render well-kept orderliness and a peaceful atmosphere which could convey, at least for colonial onlookers, the feeling of home. In the end, it is a fantasy too.

---

27 Collection KITLV, Universiteit Leiden, The Netherlands, digital image library, image code 78313, *Kampong van de Javanen op een tabaksplantage van de Amsterdam Deli Compagnie te Padang Boelan bij Medan* (C.J. Kleingrothe, circa 1900).

Stephen J. Rockel
The Home and the World: Slavery and Domestic Labor in a Nineteenth-Century East African Caravan Town

On January 24, 1861, the exploration caravan of John Hanning Speke and James Augustus Grant arrived at the trading settlement and caravan town of Tabora, in the powerful Nyamwezi chiefdom of Unyanyembe in what is now western Tanzania.[28] The journals of the two explorers provide a wealth of information about the regions they passed through, in particular those where they resided for lengthy periods of time. While Speke concentrated on the political and geographical issues central to the expedition's mission, Grant, in his still unpublished journal, had the task of recording aspects of the cultures and lives of the peoples among whom they resided, including household and domestic life.[29] This essay utilizes Grant's journal to examine the nature of domestic work, the making of homes, and the lives of slaves and their owners in the houses and households of the big coastal and foreign traders resident in Tabora.[30]

The journey by foot along paths across savannahs, through river valleys, and over mountain passes, perhaps 1,200 kilometers in all from Bagamoyo on the coast opposite Zanzibar, had taken almost four months. Grant described the scene in his journal as the caravan approached the town:

> Kazeh [A misnomer for Tabora] ... is a large settlement of Arabs living in the ordinary tembe of the country with verandahs, holding women slaves and servants. Almost a mile befor[e] arrival a host of natives led by a man in ostrich feather ... & scarlet robe with guns &c. awaited us under a tree. Our caravan was well drawn up & looked formidable as seen when the path wound about. We discharged complementary salutes – they returned it & we (S[peke] & I) in the end nearly of the string [of porters] – passed this mob saying salaam. Moossah our host was amongst them but so modest did not come forward & I did not recognize him. On we went & passed by huts & tembe planted almost together with high Indian corn about, reminding me much of India, & women howling in complement. Moossah came up ... & was recognized. I introduced [myself] – [He is] a benevolent like old man – fair, tall, large eyes, long face & little grissly beard, head clean shaved & a white skull cap embroidered jacket & long white shirt. He ... said little but conveyed us by a back entrance (to avoid the rush of our own porters in front) to the front & and raised verandah of his house.[31]

28 My research has been supported by the Social Sciences and Humanities Research Council, Canada, and the Office of the VP Research at the University of Toronto, Scarborough. The story of the search for the sources of the Nile, a prologue to European colonialism in East Africa, is well known. Recent literature includes John M. MacKenzie, ed., *David Livingstone and the Victorian Encounter with Africa* (London: National Portrait Gallery Publications, 1996); Felix Driver, *Geography Militant: Cultures of Exploration and Empire* (Oxford: Blackwell, 2001); Stephen J. Rockel, "Decentering Exploration in East Africa," in Dane Kennedy, ed., *Reinterpreting Exploration: The West in the World* (Oxford: Oxford University Press, 2013): 172–94.
29 John Hanning Speke, *Journal of the Discovery of the Source of the Nile* (New York: Harper, 1864); James Augustus Grant, Journal, National Library of Scotland, Edinburgh.
30 For slavery in the East African interior see François Renault, "The Structures of the Slave Trade in Central Africa in the 19th Century," in William Gervase Clarence-Smith, ed., *The Economics of the Indian Ocean Slave Trade in the Nineteenth Century* (London: Frank Cass, 1989): 146–65; Marcia Wright, *Strategies of Slaves and Women: Life Stories from East/Central Africa* (New York: Lilian Barber Press, 1993); Henri Médard and Shane Doyle, eds., *Slavery in the Great Lakes Region of East Africa* (Oxford: James Currey, 2007).
31 Grant, Journal, January 24, 1861. Henceforth all quotations are from Grant's journal, January 24 to March 16, 1861.

After a welcome party with Moossah (Musa Mzuri; 'the handsome,' due to his fine silk *dotis*) – a senior Khojah trader from Kutch, India, and one of the founders of Tabora – and some of the powerful Arab resident traders,[32] where the prevailing succession crisis in the chiefdom was discussed, Speke and Grant settled into their quarters in Musa's *tembe*:

> On adjoining to our quarters which formed the last side of his tembe we found capital rooms but had to light a candle to see in them ... Gave some directions to Esau a man who seems to be about Moossah very much & he ... made whatever alterations we desired. Milk was brought, a basin (black wooden) full of butter, a bowl of all ready to eat ground nuts, plantains &c. a [dish?] of rice of this country – in fact we were overwhelmed with kindness.

A few days later further supplies of livestock and foodstuffs were presented to Musa's guests, despite the shortages which prevailed in the civil conflict in which Tabora's resident Arab population had foolishly involved themselves. Mshima, a friend of Burton and Speke's at Ujiji during the first expedition of 1859–1860, had sent "a fatted & very savage cow – a splendid goat as fat as butter – and immense sack of rice (3/4 of a bushel) & 15 eggs – most handsome really, & no return can be made for it."

Grant was quick to notice the domestic arrangements in Musa's comfortable home: "Lots of clean slave women all about the house. Some making butter this morning by shaking or rolling the gourd ... The head woman [likely Musa's wife] is a perfect rolling mass of fat, but laid up now." The next day Grant observed, "This is an immense establishment of Moossah's, his tembe being surrounded by a circle of small [dwellings?] which are servants' houses, (300 people probably), cattle, detached garden enclosures & plantains." Underlying these apparently calm pastoral and domestic arrangements lay the violence toward and commerce in human beings of the East African slave trade, to which we will return.

Musa and the other Muslim traders had founded Tabora a few kilometers from the chiefdom's center of power at Itetemia. They had maintained residences there for approximately twenty years by the time of Speke and Grant's visit.[33] They had established large homesteads centered on their *tembe*s, with associated villages of Waungwana retainers as well as slaves and servants of varying origins who tended gardens and managed herds of cattle.[34] A little further away lay the various villages and settlements of the Nyamwezi people of the Unyanyembe chiefdom, with their own households consisting of the free and servile inhabitants of *tembe*s and rondavels, who worked their gardens and fields and managed their livestock. Close to Itetemia, a third center of trade and military power was emerging: Kwihara, settled mostly by Swahili traders from the coast. Kwihara became known through the writings of Henry Morton Stanley and David Livingstone, over a decade later.[35]

---

32 For Arab traders see Norman R. Bennett, *Arab Versus European: Diplomacy and the War in 19th-Century East Central Africa* (New York: Africana Publishing Company, 1986).

33 On nineteenth-century towns see Beverly Brown and Walter T. Brown, "East African Trade Towns: A Shared Growth," in William Arens, ed., *A Century of Change in Eastern Africa* (Geneva: Mouton, 1976): 183–200.

34 For the Tutsi, their Nyamwezi hosts, and the Waungwana, see Stephen J. Rockel, "The Tutsi and the Nyamwezi: Cattle, Mobility and the Transformation of Agro-Pastoralism in Nineteenth-Century Western Tanzania," *History in Africa* (Forthcoming); Stephen J. Rockel, "Slavery and Freedom in 19th Century East Africa: The Case of Waungwana Caravan Porters," *African Studies* 68 (2009): 87–109.

35 David Livingstone, edited by Horace Waller, *The Last Journals of David Livingstone* (New York: Harper, 1875); Henry M. Stanley, *How I Found Livingstone* (London: Sampson Low, Marston, 1872).

Different historical contexts and settings come to mind where the need to form new homes and labor in and around the homestead has been a central experience. For example, homemaking in colonial and frontier settlements across the globe, or conditions of forced labor and slavery in which people were wrenched from their original homes and communities and by necessity had to make new homes and ties under conditions of great hardship. We are also reminded of the enormous numbers of refugees expelled from their homelands in the crises of world wars and postcolonial conflicts, and their struggles to recreate a home in unfamiliar and often hostile surroundings. Cathrine Brun and Anita Fabos have described this process as "making homes in limbo."[36]

In African studies, the themes of home, dwelling, and household labor have been established in several streams of scholarly work over the last few decades. Concepts of household and community, notably in Jane Guyer's early work, have stimulated a wide range of studies by historians and social scientists on issues such as domestic labor, slavery, migrant labor, gender relations, and women's oppression. At the same time, the history of the family in Africa received renewed attention in the 1980s. In recent decades, feminist scholars have gendered the study of the household and increased our knowledge of African and colonial domesticity.[37] South Africa in particular has provided numerous examples of fine-grained social history and sociology, often dealing with the experience of migrant labor and the need for migrants to reconstruct home and domestic relations in the world of the mine camp, plantation, compound, or hostel during the segregation and apartheid eras. Recent work on African communities, sometimes with mission stations as the historic core of apartheid townships, highlights struggles over domesticity and the making of homes in the most oppressive of circumstances. Nowhere else has the question of space and home been so central to politics and social construction.[38] Compared with this, the history of slavery has not received sufficient attention in narratives of home, household, and domestic labor. Indeed, perhaps no other single institution has had such a powerful effect on the creation of places, ties, households, and families as shown, for example, in John Mason's exploration of the new bonds brought into being by slaves in the harsh conditions of the early nineteenth-century Cape Colony. Other studies, particularly of the Muslim societies of northern Nigeria as well as the Swahili coast, examine harem domesticity and work in the homes and households of the Muslim elites, which were dominated by concubines and other slaves.[39]

---

36 Cathrine Brun and Anita Fábos, "Making Homes in Limbo: A Conceptual Framework," *Refuge* 31 (2015): 5–17.

37 Jane I. Guyer, "Household and Community in African Studies," *African Studies Review* 24 (1981): 87–137; Shula Marks and Richard Rathbone, "The History of the Family in Africa: Introduction," *Journal of African History* 24 (1983): 145–61; Karen Tranberg Hansen, ed., *African Encounters with Domesticity* (New Brunswick: Rutgers University Press, 1992).

38 Examples include Sheila Meintjes, "Family and Gender in the Christian Community at Edendale, Natal, in Colonial Times," in Cherryl Walker, ed., *Women and Gender in Southern Africa to 1945* (Cape Town: David Philip, 1990): 125–45; Deborah Gaitskell, "Housewives, Maids or Mothers: Some Contradictions of Domesticity for Christian Women in Johannesburg, 1903–1939," *Journal of African History* 24 (1983): 241–56; Mamphela Ramphele, *A Bed Called Home: Life in the Migrant Labour Hostels of Cape Town* (Cape Town: David Philip, 1993); Meghan Healy-Clancy and Jason Hickel, eds., *'Ekhaya': The Politics of Home in KwaZulu-Natal* (Pietermaritzburg: University of KwaZulu-Natal Press, 2014).

39 John Edwin Mason, *Social Death and Resurrection: Slavery and Emancipation in South Africa* (Charlottesville: University of Virginia Press, 2003); Heidi J. Nast, *Concubines and Power: Five Hundred Years in a Northern Nigerian Palace* (Minneapolis: University of Minnesota Press, 2005); Abdul Sheriff, "Suria: Concubine or Secondary Slave Wife? The Case of Zanzibar in the Nineteenth Century," in Gwyn Campbell and Elizabeth Elbourne, eds., *Sex, Power, and Slavery* (Athens: Ohio University Press, 2014): 99–120; Francesca Declich, "Domesticity as Socio Cultural Construction: Domestic Slavery, Home and the Quintal in Cabo Delgado (Mozambique)," *Gender and History* 27 (2015): 628–48.

Caravans, Trading Settlements, and *Tembes*

Western Tanzania in the nineteenth century combined several of these scenarios: it was a frontier of commerce, trade, and settlement rocked by occasional violence and populated by a very energetic and mobile Nyamwezi and foreign population. Commerce in ivory, imported cloth, beads, livestock, foodstuffs, guns, and metal goods fueled the emergence of new market towns and villages, as well as entrepreneurship, wage labor, and slavery. Mobile and itinerant newcomers, including coastal and foreign traders, caravan porters, and eventually colonial soldiers, relied on local female partners, clients, and slaves to establish new homes in far off regions along caravan routes and then colonial frontiers.[40]

The economic boom in nineteenth-century East Africa was revolutionary. Far-flung parts of the region became integrated into the global capitalist economy for the first time, as rapid industrial growth in Europe and North America led to a constantly rising demand for tropical products, including ivory. Elephant hunters, ivory traders, and their caravans pushed further into the East African interior, often undertaking journeys of several years. They put down roots, establishing settlements under the protection of commercially minded chiefs. Caravan stops and market places, houses and caravans formed the basic infrastructure. Frequently they were combined in a unique central and east African architectural form, the *tembe*, with its compound-like structure. The making of new houses, households, and homes in traders' modified *tembes* took place in an increasingly commercialized and sometimes violent environment. Merchants and chiefs, slaves owners and patrons built *tembe* houses and homes for themselves and their domestic entourages, while slaves, clients, and employees built wattle and daub villages close by. The character of these large households with their domestic and ancillary inhabitants highlights questions of work, intimacy, gender, patronage, and dependence. The stabilizing and at the same time changing role of these homes and households facilitated a new kind of multiethnic East African urbanism in the second half of the nineteenth century. Thus, the work of making houses, households, and homes in this context signifies an entirely new development in farming and pastoral communities in the same region. It also prefigured and differed from the introduction of western constructs of home, household, and domesticity during the colonial period.

The *tembe* of the East African interior, an African dwelling unique to central and western Tanzania, is a compound-like structure favoured by mixed farming peoples including the Kaguru, the Gogo, the Nyaturu, and the Nyamwezi. The *tembe* and its adjacent spaces were both the residence and workplace where most social relations of the home were born and expressed. In Nyamwezi and other settlements, each *tembe*, itself virtually a village, was a long, low, flat-roofed quadrilateral timber and mud building containing many rooms in which several related families and their dependents lived. Sections of the *tembe*, usually facing onto an enclosed courtyard, were reserved for domestic animals.[41] Like most important settlements and towns in the East African interior, Tabora was a collection of many dispersed villages, with one or more *tembes* at the center of each. Most of the *tembes* of the Arab, Swahili, and Indian traders were concentrated around the market

---

40 Stephen J. Rockel, "Enterprising Partners: Caravan Women in Nineteenth Century Tanzania," *Canadian Journal of African Studies* 34 (2000): 748–78; Stephen J. Rockel *Carriers of Culture: Labor on the Road in Nineteenth-Century East Africa* (Portsmouth: Heinemann, 2006).

41 Henry M. Stanley, *Through the Dark Continent* (Toronto, London: Dover Publications, Vol. I, [1899] 1988): 77; Stephen J. Rockel, "Forgotten Caravan towns in Nineteenth Century Tanzania: Mbwamaji and Mpwapwa," *Azania* 41 (2006): 13.

area in the center of the town, and at Kwihara. The coastal traders with their trading and defensive requirements adapted the basic design and added numerous modifications for reasons of comfort and defense. The spatial features of the *tembe*, with its surrounding rondavels, gardens, fields, and more distant grazing lands defined the working and domestic lives of household members.

The modified *tembe* design perfectly suited the purposes of large traders with their entourages of askari, wives and concubines, servants, slaves, clients, and their considerable stores of goods including manufactured cloth, ivory, beads, metal goods, food stocks, weapons, ammunition, and tools. Lockable storerooms, a kitchen, and bedrooms were built into the structure. A well might be dug in the *tembe* courtyard or outside. The bigger traders, chiefs, and local caravan leaders added features such as verandahs. Grant found the verandah at Musa's *tembe* "being levelled and dressed by a fellow who talks Hindustani."

Households, Slavery, and Domestic Work in Tabora

Although secondary to the ivory trade, large numbers of captives and slaves were accumulated in the trading chiefdoms and towns of the East African interior, probably far more than were exported to the coast and overseas. According to one (exaggerated) early colonial estimate, they numbered as many as 233,000 in Tabora district alone around 1890, corresponding to roughly two-thirds of the population of about 350,000.[42] Many – perhaps the majority – of the members of Musa's household were women, most of them almost certainly of slave origin. In nineteenth-century East Africa, there were various categories of slaves, one being the relatively favoured concubines of powerful and wealthy Muslim men such as Musa Mzuri. These were the *suria*, and we may assume that this is who Grant is referring to in the following paragraph:

> Just as we were finishing up breakfast with a plantain a troop of women came to call – no men with them – cleanly dressed modest … creatures. We asked them to sit down or squat on the raised matted floor in the corner of the room & they did so but covered their faces which were next turned to the wall. We wished them not to turn their heads to us in this way but suddenly they bolted laughing. Some were Moossahs.

Grant was also impressed with Musa's domestic slaves, commenting on their hard work and efficiency.

> The slaves inside here are the most quick, good industrious like creatures I ever saw – never idle. Very clean & respectable … & as happy as the day is long – amusing to see the younger lot squatting round their dinners presided over by a grown-up woman. No fighting or squabbling all good nature.

The reference to "a grown-up woman" makes clear that the slaves were children, perhaps of adolescent age. He then listed some of the daily chores of these young slaves: "Occupations are at 5 a.m. making butter, cleaning all about the place. 8 or so, corn is ground by two of them pounding it in [a] pestal & mortar. Breakfast goes on, then clothes aired, dinner made, hair dressed & [they] retire early." Note, however, Grant's resort to the stereotype of the "happy" domestic slave, a staple

---

42 Jan-Georg Deutsch, *Emancipation without Abolition in German East Africa c. 1884–1914* (Oxford: James Currey, 2006): 58.

of pro-slavery propaganda prior to abolition in the British Empire in 1833 and in the antebellum United States.

Female household labor took place not only indoors, but in the gardens and thickets in the vicinity. Grant saw "women gathering mushrooms from amongst the green thick grass outside the tembes." Nyamwezi women, some of whom may have been attached to the *tembes* of the larger traders, were also active farmers in the neighborhood. On a walk, Grant observed "a woman wezee [a Nyamwezi woman] going to work in the fields so leisurely with little pick hoe in one hand & long pipe (smoking away) in the other."

Despite the relatively peaceful domestic scenes described by Grant, violence was never far away. The episodic violence of the Nyanyembe civil war that was taking place in Tabora's hinterland during Speke and Grant' visit was exacerbated by the interventions of the Muslim traders, the associated food shortages, and the longer-term structural violence of the ivory and associated slave trade. Grant wrote more than once about the very high price of foodstuffs and shortage of staples (which affected the Tabora elite much less than the ordinary people):

> Grain is so dear – a slave will sell for a cloth. We hear all the Karagwah people [probably Tutsis from the kingdom of Karagwe in northwest Tanzania] ... have bolted & the place plundered by a friend [of] Snay ... Snay ... plays the devil with this country which was one of the most abundant and plentiful. Now we may say there is a famine ... Had another present this morning – a cow, goat & 2 plates of sweetmeats covered with honey (latter used to be in quantities now none!)

Weeks later, the famine conditions were biting hard; a caravan on the road from Karagwe reported ten Nyamwezi had starved to death by the roadside, although Grant was skeptical. Closer at hand, in Musa's *tembe*, two children had died "from sickness" during the night, perhaps indirectly due to the poorer quality food available. Reports came from another caravan that "All the country in famine & lain waste" due to the war, with many of the Nyamwezi villages looted by the Arabs under Snay, who lived "by plunder." Snay and his followers seemed oblivious to the impact of their intervention against Mnywa Sera on their own households, followers, and businesses, and Musa was loath to assist them, contributing only a few of his slaves to the war effort. Five of them were killed in the fighting in neighboring Kigwa, as was his brother Japoo. Indeed, Grant implies that the food shortages would affect Musa's household during Ramadan, which began on March 14: "In times of plenty he feeds all his slaves, who keep it for the thirty days ... During this religious 'feast' his expenses are equal to five other months of the year as it is made a regular Xmas holiday of."

Within a week of the caravan's arrival, Grant had noticed the brutal conditions that captives frequently had to endure in Tabora: "Within the square I see two of the slave women chained round the neck – the immense connecting branch being carried by one – they work & go about all day [like this]." Treatment could be arbitrary. Some slave owners were cruel, while others, such as Musa Mzuri, relatively kind. Musa's plan was to retire to Bombay and emancipate his slaves before departure rather than sell them. In the event, he died before he was able to make the long journey to the coast.

Several weeks later, ten female slaves came to Musa's *tembe* "asking redress." They were women of the Arab trader Japoos who had passed them over to a fellow trader, Mohinna, while the former was at the coast. Grant noticed the "welts ... & bloody streaks ... visible on their backs." The issue from the women's perspective was inadequate rations, while for Mohinna, they did not work long enough. Speke's attempt to prevent further beatings failed: "He [Mohinna] promises & this is told them & and away they go, but they then received a frightful beating, we hear." Indeed, the famine itself led to the enslavement of some of the most destitute of the local population, who might end up as the lowest household or agricultural slaves of the Nyamwezi or coastal elite. Grant describes one such case, where a starving man was arrested for stealing and eating some maize, and then offered for sale by his captors. "A *naked* Wezee in charge of three ... spearmen passed the front door this morning – badly swollen with stolen I[ndian] corn – body emaciated. [He was] being taken to Sultan who may ... spear him to death, keep him as a slave or allow him be sold ... The men stopped in our tembe offering him for one dhotee! Not taken." Yet harsh punishments were not reserved for slaves alone. Grant observed fearful retribution meted out to "four runaway Wezees" – it is not clear whether they were employees or retainers of Musa or one of the other big traders – who had absconded "owing 18 cloths." They each received fifty lashes, presumably with the standard *kiboko*, or hippopotamus hide whip, and one received another sixty lashes the next day.

Brun and Farbos describe "home" as not only "the day to day practices of homemaking" but also "'[h]ome' as representing values, traditions, memories and feelings of home." Yet the experience of captives and slaves was not identical to that of refugees in our own times. East African slaves came from all kinds of ethnic backgrounds. They were mostly female and they were mostly children at the time of enslavement. Although they were in a kind of limbo, they usually remained in or near the homes of their owners even if they were freed through processes of redemption or manumission. African slaves in Tabora and other trading centers in the commercializing world of nineteenth-century East Africa were able to build new families, households, and communities, even allowing for the brutal conditions they were subjected to. Indeed, they constituted a large proportion of the founding populations and residents of the towns in the East African interior through processes of making homes and being 'at home.'

Section 5
Houses and Selves: Nostalgia, Imagination, Memory

Ju Li

A Woman and a Nation: A Story of Work and Home in China

This is a truncated life story of a seventy-seven-year-old retired engineer, whom I always call Aunt Ma, who worked in a Third Front factory, anonymously named Nanfang Steel, in China. Third Front Construction (TFC) is one of the largest industrialization projects established in China in the 1960s. It embodied China's direct response to the specific international situation at that time, especially the intensified military threat and pressure from the United States as well as China's split with the Soviet Union. The objective of TFC was to create an entire industrial system within the naturally remote and strategically secure region of China's interior, the so-called Third Front. From 1966 to 1975, thousands of institutes and enterprises were built, bringing industrialization to the area on an unprecedented scale, with Nanfang Steel as part of it. At the same time, millions of workers and engineers were assigned there from different parts of the country.[1] Aunt Ma was one of these engineers. I recorded her life story during my several fieldtrips to Nanfang in 2007 and 2008.

As the readers will see, the story I am going to tell below is a highly selective one. This is partly due to the fact that all memories are selective: we remember and narrate things subjectively, sometimes consciously, other times subconsciously. Such subjectivity also applies to the readers: we interpret the stories in such different ways according to our own understanding of the world and our own life experiences. As an individual, Aunt Ma's life story, as she selectively told it to me and as I record it selectively here, is of course particular and unique. But it exemplifies some distinctive elements shared by a generation of Chinese intellectuals who grew up during the socialist era and are now fading slowly off the historical stage. Liberals might interpret this part of her life story as an unworthy process of sacrifice (especially her sacrificing personal and family life for work) as she herself had been blindly brainwashed by a totalitarian and irrational ideology, while people who had really lived in that alternative modernity might be able to grasp something more complicated and subtle. In any case, except for some necessary explanations, I will try to restrain my voice in the narrative process, and simply expose these words on your table.

Aunt Ma's Story

Right after the Liberation in 1949, our country started to establish an industrial base in the northeast. My father volunteered, so our whole family moved to the Great Northern Wilderness [北大荒]. My father worked in a heavy machinery plant there … It was the first heavy machinery plant in New China, aided by experts from the Soviet Union.[2]

My father has always been a role model for me. I saw him working so hard. Even when he came back from work, he would spread out his design drawings on the floor after supper, thinking, calculating, drawing … Every morning at 4:30am, he would wake me up and ask me to run. Whenever

---

1 For further reading about the history of the third front, see Ju Li, "How It Was/Is Told, Recorded and Remembered: The Discontinued History of the Third Front Construction," *Journal of Historical Sociology* 28 (2015): 314–41.
2 See Zhihua Shen and Yafeng Xia, *Mao and the Sino–Soviet Partnership, 1945–1959: A New History* (Lanham: Lexington Books, 2015).

I was outside on the frozen, snow-covered land, I couldn't stop running, otherwise I might freeze. It was so cold, thirty degrees below zero in winter. My mother always said that my father was cruel to do that, but he just wanted to train my willpower: perseverance, courage, and never giving up. During my whole life, I have been courageous and perseverant, and I thank my father for that. No matter how difficult the situation was, I would grit my teeth and hold on. You just can't quit ...

I had always been the top student in high school, so in 1962, I was admitted to Qinghua University, the best university in China ... Then in 1967, the year I was graduating, I saw a job on the job-assignment list in Fulaerji, my hometown. Meanwhile, there was another job in Chengdu, where my boyfriend worked. I wrote to my father asking for his advice. I wrote, 'My teacher has told me about available jobs. If I choose Fulaerji, I can live close to you and mother. If I choose Chengdu, I can be with my boyfriend. What is your suggestion?' Do you know what my father wrote back to me? He wrote, 'I got your letter. It seems that you are struggling a lot. But your struggles have not leapt out of their small, individualist circle.' These were the exact words of my father. You know, he had never criticized me like that before. Now he was criticizing me in a very serious way. That's why I can still recite every word he wrote in the letter: 'I have told you before that we raised you not to support us in our old age, but to do your duty for our country. Haven't you considered the fact that it was our country that educated you all these years? You can say all those beautiful and loyal words in the classroom of Qinghua University. That's easy. But now is the time for the Party to test you. Why didn't you consider the place where our country needs you the most? Right now, it is a great moment for our country, constructing the Third Front. Many capable people are needed there. The circumstances might be arduous, very different from the comfortable environment you could enjoy in Qinghua University. You have to build it from nothing. Be prepared for it. It will be just like how the Soviet Union built Komsomolsk!'

I felt so ashamed and angry when I read the letter. It was as if my father was denying all I had said and done before. It seemed that he was accusing me of forgetting the needs of our country and only thinking about my parents and boyfriend in the face of the real test! So, I quickly decided that I would go neither to my hometown nor to Chengdu with my boyfriend. In 1967, after I graduated from Qinghua, I came here.

Upon arrival, I was assigned to the construction team. You know, by then, the factory was still under construction ... We went to work at 6am every morning. Sometimes we had to work until midnight. We worked from 6am in the morning until midnight! Our overalls were always wet. The sweat just soaked into our overalls with the cement dust. When we got off work and went back to the dormitory at night, we took off our overalls and hung them up. We were too tired to wash them. There was nowhere to take a shower and no hot water. We just let them be and laid on the bed to sleep. Next morning, when we got up, the overalls would be dry, as if starched. We just put them on. They felt like armor! Once they became wet again with sweat, they were soft again. That's just how it was. No time and no place to take a shower.

I felt only pride at that time. I always thought of Pavel Korchagin, you know, the main character in the book *How the Steel Was Tempered*.[3] Do you remember that part when he was repairing the road? Even when the sole of his boots fell off, he still stepped on the frozen soil with his bare feet and continued his work. How hard that must be! I thought that my situation was almost the same. I didn't mind working hard ... In a letter to my mother, I proudly described my life here. And soon

---

3 *How the Steel Was Tempered* (Как закалялась сталь, *Kak zakalyalas' stal'*) is a socialist realist novel written by Nikolai Ostrovsky (1904–1936). Pavel (Pavka) Korchagin is the central character. He is a quintessential positive hero of socialist realism.

my mother wrote back. She said, 'My child, you can work revolutionarily and with all your life, but also remember to keep your life!'

The only thing I was not happy about was that the Military Control Commission in the factory at that time always called our intellectuals the 'stinky number nine.'[4] This name made us really uncomfortable. 'Learning from the working class' was all right. The working class is great, isn't it? Our intellectuals should learn from them. But they didn't have to call us 'stinky number nine' or that we had to be 'reformed through labor' [劳动改造]. We were actually all so passionate and eager to dedicate ourselves to the factory and to our country.

Then the Cultural Revolution ended and the Spring of Science came! Deng Xiaoping said intellectuals were now also part of the working class. We were no longer the 'stinky number nine' who had to be reformed through labor. Science was also a productive force, even the first productive force! That was really something! On January 13, 1978, the technology group was established in Nanfang and we college graduates all went there … Now everything was good because now I could finally apply what I had learned at university to my work. One day, Wei Xiaonan, the factory's Party secretary, came to our technology group and asked who were Communist Party members. Another colleague and I said, 'We are.' He said, 'Since you are Party members, do you think that you can work regardless of time, pay, and fame?' I was so touched that I said, 'Of course!' I thought to myself, older generations of Party members had even sacrificed their lives for our New China. We were now living in a peaceful environment; what else couldn't we do?

I was very good at my work. Once I knew the technical requirements for the steel, I could always figure out what the whole process should be in my head and what the sample should look like under the microscope after it was complete. I would design the whole production process … After the steel was produced, I looked at the final samples through the microscope and saw that the result was exactly as I had predicted! I can tell you that that was a great feeling. That sense of accomplishment and happiness was incomparable. Whenever I was unhappy, I went to the microscope room, picked up a sample, ground it, and looked at it under the microscope. It was so beautiful that all my frustration would disappear immediately. I felt so comfortable, tranquil, and happy …

I could also feel such happiness in the workshops. As soon as I entered the workshop, climbed the steps, and stood on the elevated platform, the workers came to me and asked, 'Engineer Ma, what kind of steel are we supposed to make today, and what are the requirements?' I then began to explain, and they would take notes. You know, these workers loved to study. You told them new things and they were all eager to learn. I illustrated the process by drawing. When the red steel was hung out, I went with the workers to the rolling mill, to watch the pressing process. At last, the steel came out successfully. We were all so happy and satisfied. No matter how late it was when I returned from the workshop, I never felt tired. I rode my bicycle back home, enjoying the gentle breeze of the summer evening … As long as I was participating in the scene of mass production, working with these young workers, I felt that I would be young forever, vigorous, relaxed, and independent.

---

4 The so-called Military Control Commissions (军管会) was were established by the central government at every Third Front site at the end of the 1960s in order to suppress the populist violence caused by the Cultural Revolution, restore order, and resume construction/production. During the Cultural Revolution, there were 'Nine Black Categories' who were always the targets of the 'class struggle.' They were landlords, rich farmers, anti-revolutionaries, bad influences, right-wingers, traitors, spies, capitalist roaders, and intellectuals. Since intellectuals belonged to the ninth black category, they were called 'stinky number nine.'

I always worked overtime voluntarily. Once, I worked ten days and nights continuously, with only three hours of sleep every day. Now, if you wrote all these things down, the Americans would think that there were no human rights in China. How could people work like that? But for our generation, this was natural. This was how we got educated: dedicating yourself to your work, your factory, and your country. I never minded. During the several decades of working in the factory, I always had a sense of happiness and achievement: staying with the workers, and seeing my designs succeed. For me, the whole process was a blessing, just like you plant a tree: you sow the seeds, you nurture them, and you see them grow. Those whose only concerns are money or fame could never understand me.

No matter how exhausted I was at work, I couldn't complain at home. Once, I had stayed in the workshop for several days in a row and was very tired. So, when I went back home, I said to my husband, 'I don't want to cook or eat this evening, so you cook whatever you want by yourself.' Then, I went to bed directly. My husband shouted, 'You are tired now? But I know one call from the workshop and you will jump! Whenever you are working, you never feel tired, but whenever you come home, you are always tired!' As if I should somehow feel guilty for working hard! You know, I always had to prepare food and store it in the refrigerator for him whenever I went on a business trip. I had tried to teach him to cook, but he refused to learn. My daughter learned to be independent when she was very young: cooking her own meals and washing her own clothes, since both of us were not always at home ...

We were told that women should be equal to men and that women hold up half the sky. But is that true? Sometimes I was so angry that I thought all men were liars. When I met my husband at Qinghai University, he told me that because I was smarter than him, he would like to be the man behind me supporting me to realize my dream ... But see what happened later! Liar! He always complained that I was not like other women, bringing warmth to their husbands and their homes, and that he never enjoyed the warmth of marriage ... But why didn't he bring warmth to me and the family? Why should I be the only one who was supposed to make sacrifices for the family? He was the chief engineer at the factory and he worked very hard too, but I never complained ... What happened to those earlier promises? If there were a next life, I would definitely choose to be a man. I told this to my husband. I said that even if I was an animal in my next life, I would like to be reincarnated as a male animal!

Women in our generation are really too exhausted, much more exhausted than my mother's generation, who only needed to play one role. You know, during all these years whenever I went to work, I never thought of myself as a woman – I just thought of myself as an excellent engineer. There were some difficult research projects that male engineers dared not to take on, but I always knew I could do them and I did ... It was not until my retirement that I realized I was a woman.

The one-cut early retirement policy came in 1996.[5] All female engineers suddenly had to retire at the age of fifty-five. I wasn't prepared for that. You know, when that day came, I just returned to my office from the workshop, exhausted. Then the Party secretary of our department suddenly told me that I didn't need to come back the next day since I had to retire earlier according to the new policy. I could tell that it was very difficult for him to say these words, his face all twisted. I was so angry and sad. After so many years of dedication and hard work, it was suddenly over in such a cruel way. I had dreamed about a more honorable retirement.

---

5 This refers to the downsizing movement of the factory starting from 1996, as part of the whole neoliberal reforming package imposed on the factory by successive governments since the mid-1990s. The downsizing movement aimed to streamline the factory with huge layoffs and forced early-retirement.

The cut-off age for female engineers was fifty-five, but it was sixty for male engineers. Wasn't that gender discrimination, discrimination toward women? It didn't matter if this person was useful for the factory or not; as long as he was man, he could stay! I worked so hard, but I was sent home at such a young age! It was a loss for the factory. I was so good at my work; I felt all my talents and knowledge hadn't been used up. I could still contribute; I was still useful. What should I do with all this knowledge? Bring it to the crematorium when I die?

Even after my retirement, the young colleagues from my old workplace always celebrated my birthday with me. After my daughter died, they also celebrated Mother's Day with me.[6] They brought me carnations, telling me in such a serious and sincere way, 'This is the flower for mothers.' Tears filled my eyes …

I lived a hard life, but now I have nothing left. The older I become, the sadder I feel. When I had a heart attack in 2003, Cheng Hong, Gan Lu, and my other young colleagues were still living here in the factory community, so they helped me a lot. Now they have all moved out of the old community to Zhongba.[7] What will happen if I have another heart attack? The problem now is that since the factory withdrew its welfare programs there is no support here for older people. If the government would organize something for us, at least there would be some support. Governments in big cities like Chengdu would do such a thing, but in small places like here, the government does nothing. The factory stopped all support a long time ago.[8] I am confident about my work, but I feel like a loser in my personal life. I even lost my only daughter …

People might think that my story was one of fiction from the *Arabian Nights* and wouldn't really happen. Or they might think I am a fool. How could such a fool exist? The Americans would never understand. Americans hold different values to us. My daughter studied in the US. Once, after working extremely hard in a lab for her professor, she got the ideal experimental results. Her professor praised her highly and immediately gave her a pay rise. Afterwards, she called me, because she thought that working hard was a natural thing and because she always saw her mother working that way. She'd never thought of rewards before. Then she told me, 'Mom, this is the US. Your working performance is closely tied to your material gains. It's not like China. In China, what you did always had to be selfless dedication and you were never supposed care about fame or money. This is the US. Mom, have you ever felt that you were being fooled in China?'

So, you see, American values are different from ours. If the Americans heard my story, they would think it absurd. It might deepen their negative impressions of China, since they would use my story as proof that there are no human rights in China or that China does not respect individual values. Is that right? But to tell you the truth, I don't have any regrets even today. Americans would not understand me, but I would not understand them either. I look down on them! Why do they need so much money? You just have one mouth to feed and one body to dress. Even if you have nine luxury houses, you only need one bed to sleep in at night, right? I just could not understand them …

---

6 Her daughter committed suicide when she was a PhD student in the US, at the age of twenty-eight.

7 The previously prosperous and consolidated industrial community disintegrated rapidly since the 1990s neoliberal reform. Many people, if they could afford it, chose to move from the old factory community to the nearby city of Zhongba.

8 'Burden alleviation,' another neoliberal package that was implemented in the factory during the second half of 1990s, cut down almost all welfare programs that had been previously provided by the factory, including the senior-care service center.

Epilogue

During the Chinese New Year in 2017, I called Aunt Ma from the United States to send her my New Year greetings. A few years ago, Aunt Ma and her husband had moved to another city, closer to where their nephews and nieces live. In our phone call, Ma told me that she had had a stroke in 2015 and now she felt that her brain was not working as well as it did before: "I have always been so proud of my brain for the past seventy years. When I was working in the factory, I was the only one who dared to take the most difficult research projects that others recoiled from. You know I had dreamed of becoming the Chinese Madam Curie when I was young!" She laughed loudly on the other end of the phone.

Sidney Chalhoub

A House for a Missing Self: Nostalgia for Slavery and Its Times in Machado de Assis's *Dom Casmurro*

Dom Casmurro (first published in 1899) is one of the best-known novels of Machado de Assis (1839–1908), arguably the most important Brazilian writer of all times. A founding member and first president of the Brazilian Academy of Letters, Machado de Assis was the son of a poor Portuguese immigrant woman and a housepainter, whose parents had been born slaves but achieved freedom.

The novel tells the story of Bento Santiago, nicknamed Dom Casmurro. The neighbor who invented the nickname may have intended 'Dom' to be an ironic remark about the social decadence of Santiago and his ilk in the wake of the abolition of slavery (1888) and the fall of the monarchical regime (1889). 'Casmurro' meant taciturn, to highlight Santiago's reclusive manners, although contemporary dictionaries define 'casmurro' as stubborn, referring to people who, once convinced of something, never change their minds.[9]

In old age, Bento Santiago recollects his relations with his childhood sweetheart, first love, and wife, Capitu. Apparently nostalgic for his younger self, Dom Casmurro says that in writing the book, he intended "to relive what I lived then,"[10] thus professing to offer an impartial and trustworthy account of events in which his past self had been a central character. Nonetheless, his autobiography is influenced by a subtle and dissimulated accusation that Capitu had betrayed him and committed adultery with his best friend, Escobar. Although not disclosing to the reader at the outset that his claim to tell the truth about his past is tainted by the conviction, obtained retrospectively, that his wife and best friend connived to betray him, Dom Casmurro opens his narrative with a description of his motivations, which should be read as a cautionary tale. The passage has such a poetic thrust, not lost in translation, that it must be quoted in full:

> I live alone, with a servant. The house I live in is my own; I decided to have it built, prompted by such a personal, private motive that I am embarrassed to put it in print, but here it goes. One day, quite a few years ago, I had the notion of building in Engenho Novo a replica of the house I had been brought up in on the old Rua de Matacavalos, and giving it the same aspect and layout as the other one, which has now disappeared. Builder and decorator understood my instructions perfectly: it is the same two-story building, three windows at the front, a verandah at the back, the same bedrooms and living rooms. In the main room, the paintings on the ceiling and walls are more or less the same, with garlands of small flowers and large birds, at intervals, carrying them in their beaks. In the four corners of the ceiling, the figures of the seasons, and at the center of the walls, medallions of Caesar, Augustus, Nero and Massinissa, with their names underneath ... Why these four characters I do not understand. When we moved into the Matacavalos house, it was already decorated in this way: it had been done in the previous decade. It must have been the taste of the time to put a classical flavor and ancient figures into paintings done in America. The rest is also analogous to this and similar to it. I have a small garden, flowers, vegetables, a casuarina tree, a well and a washing-stone. I use old china and old furniture. Finally, there is, now as in the old days, the same contrast between life inside the house, which is placid, and the noisy world outside.

---

9 Marco Cícero Cavallini, "Spleen e escravidão: a melancolia senhorial em Dom Casmurro e Brás Cubas," *Revista de Letras* 48 (2008): 93–6.
10 Machado de Assis, *Dom Casmurro*, translated by John Gledson (Oxford: Oxford University Press, 1997): chapter II, page 7. All references to the novel come from this edition; hereafter, *DC*, ch. II, p.7.

Clearly my aim was to tie the two ends of life together, and bring back youth in old age. Well, sir, I managed neither to reconstruct what was there, nor what I had been. Everywhere, though the surface may be the same, the character is different. If it was only others that were missing, all well and good: one gets over the loss of other people as best one can; but I myself am missing, and that lacuna is all-important.[11]

The narrator says that, "it is of the essence of nostalgia to go over old memories again and again."[12] However, he seems aware that the reader may find it excessive to take this impulse to the point of having the house of his childhood recollections reconstructed exactly as it was, albeit in another location; he remarks he is "embarrassed" to put in print "his private motive for doing so." The motive, he confesses, is "epistemological," so to speak; that is, it is an attempt to deal with an alleged "obsession with accuracy that plagues me."[13] He expected the reconstructed house to make time and historical experience vanish, allowing him to relive the world of yesterday exactly as it was in a given period of his life. In silencing his intention to convince the reader that his wife committed adultery, he hides his true obsession, which originated in his uncontrollable jealousy for Capitu. Furthermore, while the narrator admits that rebuilding the house did not bring back the old times, he implies that writing the autobiography would serve the purpose.

There is good reason for the narrator to omit his main motivation in reconstructing the house, and, later, in deciding to write the book. His credibility would be seriously at risk if the reader understood from the start that the "truth" he had reached about his life, and the underlying theme of his autobiography, is that his wife and his best friend had committed adultery.

Pedro Luiz Napoleão Chernoviz, the author of the most famous medical dictionary that circulated in Brazil at the time, identified jealousy as one of the main passions conducive to melancholy, a condition characterized by sadness, reclusiveness, and a tendency to obsess with certain facts or impressions ("fixed ideas"). He considered melancholy to be a form of "mental alienation" whose victims became "solitary" and "misanthropic," tending to think of other people as perpetually scheming against them.[14]

Chernoviz's description seems tailored to describe Dom Casmurro's state of mind after he became convinced, on the day of Escobar's burial, of Capitu's adultery. In addition, Chernoviz developed in great detail the relation between professions and health. He described the illnesses deemed to be more common among different types of manual laborers and contrasted them with those supposedly prevalent among the "sedentary classes."[15] The latter included poets, statesmen, theologians, and artists, and also those from the privileged classes who, as another famous Machado de Assis narrator, Brás Cubas, who suffered from hypochondria himself, would put it, had "the good fortune of not having to earn my bread by the sweat of my brow."[16] In other words, the lack of physical exertion led to excessive mental activity, thus to the risk of developing melancholy or hypochondria. Melancholy was often seen as a source of "literary inspiration,"[17] thus making Dom Casmurro a writer and his autobiography the nostalgic narration of a world gone by.

---

11 *DC*, ch. II, pp. 4–5.
12 *DC*, ch. XXXIV, p. 68.
13 *DC*, ch. L, p. 93.
14 Pedro Luiz Napoleão Chernoviz, *Diccionario de Medicina Popular* (Paris: A. Roger and F. Chernoviz, 1890, 6th edition): entries for "melancolia" and "hypochondria."
15 Chernoviz, entry for "profissões."
16 Machado de Assis, *The Posthumous Memoirs of Brás Cubas*, translated by Gregory Rabassa (Oxford: Oxford University Press, 1997): chapter CLX, p. 203.
17 Pierre Larousse, *Grand Dictionnaire Universel du XIXe. Siècle* (Paris: Administration du grand Dictionnaire universel, 1873, 10th edition): entry for "mélancolie."

The reconstructed house appears to be a metaphor for Bento Santiago's sense of a lost world of economic and social privileges. Dom Casmurro's autobiography makes clear the process of economic decadence that fell upon his family in the last decades of the nineteenth century.

Let us return briefly to the first sentence of the tale: "I live alone, with a servant. The house I live in is my own." Houses and servants (formerly enslaved) were indeed the assets Bento Santiago and his family considered the best symbols of their wealth.

As was often the case in the 1830s and 1840s, the wealth of the Santiago family originated in agricultural production, either sugar or most probably coffee, which expanded enormously throughout the province of Rio de Janeiro at that time. With the accumulation of wealth came political influence, therefore Bento Santiago's father became a congressman and the family moved to the capital, Rio de Janeiro. When her husband died, Dona Glória, Bento's mother, decided not to go back to rural life. She sold the plantation and some of the slaves, bought other slaves and put them to work in the streets or hired them out, acquired "a dozen buildings and a quantity of government bonds," and "settled down in the Matacavalos house."[18] During one of Escobar's visits to Santiago, the latter seemed dazzled by the former's mathematical abilities. Given the value of the rent of each of the nine houses that belonged to the family, Escobar calculated the Santiagos' monthly rental income in a matter of seconds.[19] Regarding slaves, there were quite a few, with names that comprised "all the letters of the alphabet,"[20] an observation made by Escobar that seemed to reveal to Bento an aspect of his world that he had not really been aware of.

The 1860s and 1870s were times of sweeping economic transformation in Brazil. The cessation of the African slave trade in 1850 and the continuous expansion of coffee brought about an intense transfer of slaves from urban to rural areas, with poor Portuguese immigrants flooding the labor market in the city of Rio. The deepening crisis of slavery in the 1880s brought down slave prices dramatically. In addition, real estate in the downtown areas of the city and its immediate surroundings, as was the case with Matacavalos street, was devalued because elites were moving to the suburbs and the southern part of the city for fear of yellow fever epidemics and other contagious diseases. Finally, high inflation rates during the economic crisis of the early 1890s may have melted the value of whatever quantity of "government bonds" the Santiagos still held on to. In summary, in a couple of decades, rental income, slaves, and government papers were either gone or had diminished in value considerably. At one point, the narrator refers to Capitu's efforts to save money by controlling household expenses.[21] Elsewhere, to Capitu's observation that he seemed steeped in melancholy, Dom Casmurro replied that "business was bad."[22]

Slaveholding was the main symbol of wealth and power in the world in which Bento Santiago grew up. However, slaves were not the only people subordinated to patriarchal figures such as Dom Casmurro. There were dependents aplenty beyond the enslaved, ranging from less affluent members of the family, free or freed domestic servants, individuals who lived in the house in exchange for rendering small services, such as running errands (as was the case of José Dias in *Dom Casmurro*), and neighbors of a less privileged social position.

18 *DC*, ch. VII, p. 15.
19 *DC*, ch. XCIV, pp. 166–7.
20 *DC*, ch. XCIII, p. 164.
21 *DC*, ch. CVI, pp. 184–6.
22 *DC*, ch. CXXX, p. 219.

Houses, again, serve as a metaphor for the connections between the wealthy Santiago family and their dependents in the outside world. Bento and Capitu were next-door neighbors and grew up together. Furthermore, as one reached the backyard:

> There was a connecting door there which my mother had had put in when Capitu and I were small. This door had no lock or latch; it was opened by pushing on one side or pulling on the other, and shut itself by the weight of a stone hanging on a rope. It was almost exclusively for our use. When we were children, we went visiting, knocking on one side, and being received on the other with many bows and curtsies.[23]

However close, the two families did not relate on equal terms. Their proximity had originated in a "great flood" that had brought enormous hardship to Capitu's family.[24] The Santiagos helped the neighbors and thereafter enjoyed a certain moral ascendancy over them. Capitu's father was a public employee, who could make ends meet because "his wife spent little, and living was cheap."[25] When the employee had a setback at work and was saddened to the point of speaking of suicide, Capitu's mother asked Dona Glória to talk to him. According to the narrator, the widow did so in a commanding manner: "What lunacy was this, thinking he was going to be disgraced, just because he was going to lose extra payments ...? No, he should be a man, the father of a family ... . Pádua obeyed."[26]

The courtship between Bento and Capitu appeared likely to provoke the suspicion that the girl and her family were hoping for a marriage which would connect them formally to the wealthy neighbors next door. The stone hanging on a rope that kept the door between the two backyards permanently closed carried perhaps a symbolic weight as well. On one hand, Dom Casmurro's narration seeks to entice the reader to believe in a purely romantic involvement on the part of the young Bento Santiago. On the other hand, it subtly suggests that Capitu and her family schemed all the time to obtain the marriage they wished for.

Regarding its form, Dom Casmurro's autobiographical narration seems to be inspired by Saint Augustine's *Confessions*.[27] According to Dom Casmurro, Bento Santiago reaches "the truth" about the adultery between Capitu and Escobar through a kind of revelation, not as the culmination of experiences and observations. Bento does not learn from interacting with Capitu, Escobar, and others around him that adultery occurred. Rather, it dawned on him suddenly as God's beam of light or a curse from Hell. The moment of revelation was at the funeral:

> There was general confusion. In the midst of it, Capitu looked for some moments at the body with such a fixed gaze, with such a passionately fixed gaze, that it's small wonder that into her eyes there came a few silent tears ...

> Mine stopped immediately. I stood looking at hers; Capitu wiped them hastily, looking sidelong at the people in the room ... . There was a moment when Capitu's eyes fixed on the body, ... large and wide open, like the waves on the sea out there, as if she too wanted to swallow up that morning's swimmer.[28]

Escobar drowned while swimming at the beach in March 1871. The narrator says that, "Here and there they were talking about the recent Rio Branco ministry ... I have never forgotten the month

23 *DC*, ch. XIII, p. 26.

24 *DC*, ch. III, p. 8.

25 *DC*, ch. XVI, p. 31.

26 *DC*, ch. XVI, p. 32.

27 William Spengemann, *The Forms of Autobiography: Episodes in the History of a Literary Genre* (New Haven: Yale University Press, 1980).

28 *DC*, ch. CXXIII, pp. 211–2.

or the year."[29] Months later, Rio Branco's cabinet would enact the Law of Free Womb, seen as a decisive step towards the end of slavery in Brazil and widely interpreted by part of the planter, slaveholding class as the result of a betrayal by the Crown and its political allies. The experience of political defeat in 1871 soured the slaveholding class toward the Emperor and the monarchical regime. The regime would have to go some years later in part as a result of the process of slave emancipation. In addition, the law of 1871 granted slaves a series of rights, such as the freedom of children born to slave women, and the right to savings and to use them to buy their manumission irrespective of the masters' consent. In the following years, enslaved people, helped by their kin, friends, and abolitionists, sued slaveholders often and sought to uphold their newly acquired rights. However limited the effects of these events, they made masters suspicious of dependents in general. They became rancorous and vindictive, convinced that subaltern people around them and the Emperor himself were plotting to do away with their way of life. This is the clay from which Dom Casmurro was made.

The tale of the reconstructed house plays an important role in Dom Casmurro's narration. Its purpose is to lure the reader into believing from the start in Bento Santiago's innocence and lack of malice – to the point of his aspiring to relive the old, romantic experiences of his youth. These character traits attributed to Bento stand in sharp contrast to the mature, self-controlled, and sophisticated strategist that Capitu had allegedly been since she was a child. The narrator seeks to lead the reader to the conclusion that adultery came to Capitu naturally:

> You will agree with me; if you remember Capitu as a girl, you will recognize that the one was in the other, like the fruit inside its rind.[30]

29 *DC*, ch. CXXII, p. 210.
30 *DC*, ch. CXLVIII, p. 244.

Jonathan Hyslop
From Forecastle to Folk Club: The Homeless Seafarer

Around the end of November 1972, seventy-six-year-old Ben Bright left the two-room apartment in an outer suburb of London where he had been living and headed to Australia.[31] After a lifetime as a seaman, he said, "London was really getting me down." Somehow, on his way to the other side of the world, Bright got side-tracked to Tahiti and ended up working on an American's yacht. He eventually reached Sydney, where it was "nice and warm." When he was last heard of, in 1974, Bright was planning to "take a hike into the mountains."

We know about Bright's journey because, shortly after he left London, two researchers showed up at his door to discover that he was gone. Ewan MacColl and Peggy Seeger had been interviewing and tape-recording Bright as he talked about his life and sang some of the many songs of the sea that he knew. After winning Bright's confidence, MacColl and Seeger had conducted three long sessions with him in the flat, a "rather bare" place located at the top of two flights of stairs, which they described as having "the 'temporary accommodation' look typical of the homes of Scots travelers and old seafarers." It was more than a year later that they received a postcard telling them of Bright's subsequent travels. A little later they published a pamphlet about his life.

MacColl and Seeger were two of the leading figures of the folk music movement that had flourished in Britain during the previous two decades.[32] MacColl, a product of Depression-era working-class Salford, was a long-time Communist whose collaborations in the 1950s with the American Alan Lomax and the English folk singer A.L. Lloyd had popularized folk music among young people, generated a rash of folk clubs across the United Kingdom by the early 1960s, and galvanized a movement of musicological research.[33] Despite MacColl's vestigial Stalinism, the folk clubs were a key cultural feature in the rise of the British New Left. Young, mostly middle-class radicals found folk music irresistible in its promise of an organic connection to popular experience. MacColl possessed a magnificent voice and had composed many songs, a few of which, such as *The First Time Ever I Saw Your Face*, remain popular. The younger Seeger, who came from a family of musical American intellectuals, had emerged as a writer of a number of famous feminist lyrics. MacColl and Seeger's performances were a prominent feature of the British folk scene.

The encounter between the mariner and the folk singer is emblematic of the way in which the idea of the roaming – and therefore homeless – sailor has exerted great cultural power. MacColl and Seeger's fascination with Bright was based in his rich stock of songs about the sea, almost all of which were drawn from the world of the great sailing ships on which Bright had served in his youth. These were songs of the men who lived in the crew's quarters or forecastle (pronounced 'fo'c's'l'), the cramped interior space where sailors slung their hammocks.[34] Their repertoire can usefully be divided into work songs or 'shanties,' the chanting of which helped synchronize efforts

---

31 Ben Bright [Ewan MacColl and Peggy Seeger eds.], *Shellback: Reminiscences of Ben Bright, Mariner* (Oxford: History Workshop, 1974). All quotations from the authors and Bright are from this source, as are all lyrics, unless otherwise noted.

32 Ben Harker, *Class Act: The Cultural and Political Life of Ewan MacColl* (London: Pluto, 2007).

33 John Szwed, *Alan Lomax: The Man Who Recorded the World* (New York: Viking Penguin, 2010); Dave Arthur, *Bert: The Life and Times of A.L. Lloyd* (London: Pluto, 2012).

34 The forecastle was originally the small raised deck forward in the ship, but the term came to be used for any crew accommodation, even when the site shifted to other parts of the ship and bunks replaced hammocks.

when pulling on the ropes or turning the windlasses and capstans, and forecastle songs, sung in leisure hours and usually taking a balladic form.[35] The music initially seems to have survived the transition from sail to steam and was still being sung on some ships into the new era. It is worth noting that the original lyrics of the work songs sung by the sailors were sometimes highly sexual or scatological and a certain amount of 'cleaning up' seems to have occurred during their subsequent transmission to a wider audience.

MacColl and Seeger were also interested in Bright's time as a labor activist and his later working life on steamers. But for the mostly young followers of the folk music movement, it was the idea of the heroic yet lonely and homeless sailor that packed enormous emotional appeal. To this day, the sea shanty and the maritime ballad have a following in the folk world and occasionally surface in the broader culture. As Bright's disappearance indicates though, the seaman who had no home was not just a figment of the enthusiasts' imagination.

Maritime Romanticism

> Haul on the bowline, our bully ship's a rolling,
> Haul on the bowline, the bowline, *Haul*!
> Haul on the bowline, Kitty is my darlin',
> Haul on the Bowline, the bowline, *Haul*!
> Haul on the bowline, Kitty lives at Liverpool,
> Haul on the Bowline, the Bowline, *Haul*!
> *An old English sea shanty*

Throughout the nineteenth century and up to the immediate post-World War II period, the British Merchant Marine was the largest national fleet in the world. Only in the following years was its premier position destroyed by the rise of 'flags of convenience' – ships registered in countries such as Panama and Liberia, which enabled ship-owners to evade the financial regulation and social legislation of stronger and more prosperous nation states. In the earlier period of British dominance, the Merchant Marine (or Merchant Navy as it was later called) employed a majority of British and Irish seamen. But there was a smattering of other north Europeans (Scandinavians, Dutch, and Germans) and a substantial number of African and Asian seafarers.[36] In the mid-nineteenth century there was also a complex relationship with the Americans. The United States had a strong sailing ship fleet, and after the end of the War of 1812, a vast commerce developed between British and American ports. Seamen moved between the two merchant fleets and shared much in the way of shipboard culture, including their songs. However, when the United States turned inward for its economic growth after the Civil War, the US Merchant Marine went into relative decline.

---

35 Joanna C. Colcord, *Songs of American Sailormen* (New York: Bramhall, 1938).

36 For an overview of the labor history of the British Mercantile Marine in this period, see Leon Fink, *Sweatshops at Sea: Merchant Seamen in the World's First Globalized Industry from 1812 to the Present* (Chapel Hill: University of North Carolina, 2011). When I say British, I do not mean to convey a racial category: transnational seafaring communities did form in a number of British ports, and so some black British seamen were able to sail under British employment conditions. Nevertheless, a racial politics was at work here. White sailors did often articulate their grievances in racial terms, incited by populist union leaders to blame their problems on the competition of the cheap labor of seamen of colour, and black British workers also sometimes became the targets of this racist politics.

At least until the social and labor reforms of the 1940s, many British seamen were in remarkably marginal social positions. In a brilliant recent book on seafarers, the British anthropologist Helen Sampson has described present-day transnational maritime workers as "spectral," a category of laborers invisible to the rest of society.[37] This was true of a large proportion of the British workforce in the heydays of sail and steam. British seamen often had a very tenuous relation to 'home,' which was the term by which the British diaspora referred to the United Kingdom.

It was this very tenuousness which underpinned the sailor's cultural appeal. From the turn of the nineteenth century, the rise of the romantic cultural mode in the West began to transform a dominant perception of the sea as a frightening place into the idea that it was the quintessence of power and natural beauty. With this went a shift, in the British and American cases, in the perception of the sailor. In at least some representations, the seafarer became a heroic individual, moving freely across the world, unfettered by social convention. Older ideas of him as an insubordinate plebeian and newer ones of him as a dissolute recipient of the moral and material benefactions of church and state were always strong, but more positive, romantic sailor-images persisted. The seafarer, like the nineteenth-century notion of the gypsy, was an imaginary of freedom from convention. The long persistence of the sailing ship into the industrial age strengthened this idea. Sailing was perceived as a technology in harmony with nature, unlike steam which embodied the ugliness of industrial life.[38] To some extent, sailors themselves internalized these ideas.

Whether the romanticization of seamen was particularly strong in Anglo-American culture is an interesting issue that would bear further investigation. Images of the brave fisherman can be found in some continental European writers' work, such as Victor Hugo's *Toilers of the Sea*. But there is not a single fictional work, even a short story, by any of the great Russian writers that deals with maritime themes.[39] There does seem to be an especially powerful resonance of the idea of the wandering sailor in the Anglophone world, which is perhaps traceable to the centrality of seaborne commerce in shaping the modernity of Britain, its Dominions, and the United States, during the age of sail.

Later folk musicians' ideas of the sailor followed in this Anglophone tradition of romanticization. For many seamen, home was an aspiration rather than a reality. For others, it was something they saw as a trap and sought to avoid. And for still others, home was something they sought to create, but which the organization of work and the wider social order made difficult to achieve. To the 1950s and 1960s generations that followed their music, largely composed of the future professionals, state employees, and intellectuals of an increasingly constrained, bureaucratized, and consumerist world, the sailor represented dreams of escape from a likely suburban and domesticized future.

Ben Bright's Voyages

> And as we lollop around Cape Horn,
> Heave Away! Haul Away!
> You'll wish to God you'd never been born,
> We're bound for South Australia.
> *Clipper Ship Shanty, Nineteenth century*

---

37 Helen Sampson, *International Seafarers and Transnationalism in the Twenty-First Century* (Manchester: Manchester University Press, 2013): 69.
38 John Mack, *The Sea: A Cultural History* (London: Reaktion, 2011): 95–104.
39 I am grateful to Richard Sylvester for this information.

Ben Bright was a rather typical representative of the transitional sail-steam world. Born in a small town in north Wales in 1896, he lost his trade unionist father to a work accident in a quarry. His mother moved her four children to Liverpool, where Bright went to work at an early age. He soon got a job on a coasting schooner. Subsequently, he joined a Norwegian full-rigged ship, rounding Cape Horn at the age of fourteen. This was followed by journeys on a series of other sailing vessels around the world. Later, Bright worked on steamers. Bright developed a rich repertoire of shanties and ballads. In 1916, in America, he became attracted to the radical syndicalist politics of the Industrial Workers of the World (IWW). He participated in their campaigns in the United States, South America, and Australia, and became active in the IWW's Marine Workers Union. His interviews reflect an egalitarian racial attitude, but whether he had this through his life or whether it was a product of his later political influences is unclear. Bright's interest in music continued ashore, especially because the IWW developed a strong tradition of political songs. As an organization based largely on male migrant casual laborers, many of these songs also celebrated the wanderer. In Australia, song-borne legends of the heroic loner in the Outback appealed to him, and he learned lines like:

> A gallant young stockman lay dying
> And this was the last words he said:
> Wrap me up in my stockwhip and blanket,
> And bury me deep below,
> Where the foxes and crows won't molest me,
> Way deep where the Coolibah grows.

Bright was active in the IWW until 1932. In that year, he made a brief return to Britain, but the recording of his life story breaks off at this point, and his movements thereafter are unclear.

Because of his great global mobility, Bright never established a real home. He told MacColl and Seeger that his entire family were dead or had disappeared. He had been away from the United Kingdom for sixty-two years. Yearning for home and its actual unattainability was a theme that stretched through the sail-era songs which Bright sang for his interviewers. One song celebrated "Rolling home to merry England" and the "fond hearts [that] await you in the land to which you go." Others pulled in the very different direction of celebrating brief encounters in in tropical ports: "I will never forget you/ And the love you had for me/ O come back my lovely sailor/ O come back my dear to me."[40] There was though a harsher depiction of sexuality in the songs sung by Bright, reflecting a world in which prostitution and the accompanying misogyny played a large part. *Maggie May* tells of a sailor ashore in Liverpool who has his money and clothes stolen by a prostitute while he is asleep, but records with satisfaction that she is convicted and sent to Van Diemen's Land. With this went anxiety about sexually transmitted disease: the double-entendre lyric *Hoist Your Topsails* starts off by declaring:

> My ship is a new ship, she's free from the stocks,
> And I hope every man aboard is free from the pox.

However, in the United States, Bright later picked up a song from the Wobblies, *The White Slave*, written by the IWW's bard Joe Hill, which more sympathetically, although perhaps paternalistically, portrays prostitutes as victims of circumstances:

---

40 The tropical setting is indicated by the line "For when the palm trees they are swaying."

It's the boss that pays starvation wages,
A homeless girl can always hear
Temptation calling everywhere.

Interestingly, it is through the common condition of homelessness between the woman and the male migrant laborer that Hill's song works to create a sense of empathy in his intended audience.

The difficulty experienced by British seamen in establishing a stable home was structurally produced. This is a prime example of what would today be called precarious labor. Throughout the period of steamships, which did not end until the completion of the transition to oil burners after World War II, the majority of seamen never enjoyed the benefits of stable employment. Seamen were hired by the voyage. Typical international sailing ships or tramp steamers moved goods between ports in voyages of indeterminate length, which often lasted many months. In many cases the conditions on board were so bad that sailors deserted in foreign ports. But then they would find themselves without pay from their last voyage.[41] This would often result in their falling prey to the rackets of 'crimps,' crooked boarding housekeepers who would pay their debts, but at the price of delivering them into the hands of a new captain and taking the sailor's advance note of payment. In turn, this could lead to the seaman being trapped in a cycle of debt and structural poverty, and of course to further extending his time away from his home country.

Although some social historians have attempted to play down the role of crimps and suggest that they have been unjustly demonized, Bright's experience certainly accorded with the conventional view. "The conditions in some ships were that bad that fellas preferred to leave a ship and become beachcombers and bums. And that was where the crimps came in ... He was a crimp on the basis of getting your shipping fee out of your month's advance. He'd delude you about what the conditions of a ship was going to be." In Bright's account, the crimping system was still going strong after World War I and was highly coercive. Fifty years later, he could still name the most famous crimps of San Francisco, New Orleans, Liverpool, Newcastle (New South Wales), New York, and London.

Bright's repertoire included a song about a particularly notorious crimp, who packed sailors into his premises and specialized in passing off unskilled workers as trained seamen:

You have heard of the academy of Mister Paddy West,
For style and popularity, my school is the best,
For I've only room for forty and I'm boarding seventy-four,
And sure, by Jesus, who is that comes knocking on my door.

But for all the quite incredible dangers and hardships of their lives, sailors also bought into the sense of camaraderie and freedom that the temporary home of the ship could sometimes give. This was especially true of the sailing-ship world with its craft and collective endeavor. Despite the dirt, crowded accommodation, and bad food, Bright said that he:

Preferred the sailing ship to the tramp any day. There was always plenty to do, of course: you had the maintenance of the gear, the rigging, the setting of the sails. Oh yes, you were pretty active. It's true you worked arduous working hours and the crew discharged the cargo ... and you lived in quarters that were freezing. And there was no compensation for injuries or for illness or for shipping in malarial waters. But, in the main, when you settled down in a sailing ship it was better than being in a tramp. Once you got a decent passage and a decent slant, well, you carried on.

---

41 Archibald Cowie, "The Supply of British Seamen," *Contemporary Review* (1898): 855–65.

It was in part this enthusiasm for sail among the workers who spilled over from that time into the machine age that kept their songs alive. A pioneering role in saving sailors' songs was played by early collectors, who had a direct link with that world. The American Joanna Colcord loved the sea shanties and ballads from her days of sailing as a little girl on the ship owned by her father, a New England captain, and as an adult published a selection of them. She lived to be a prominent social worker in the New Deal era.[42] Of the two main figures in the British sea shanty revival, Stan Huggill and A.L. Lloyd had connections to this time of transition. Huggill had started work on a sailing ship at the very end of their time in the early 1920s. Lloyd, a Communist and a brilliant autodidact intellectual, had worked briefly on a mechanized whaler in the South Atlantic in the 1930s, when he seems to have acquired some of his store of songs from old hands who had served on the clippers. He played a key role in the new post-war popularity of the maritime songs as a collector and performer, and can be seen leading the singing on the deck of the *Pequod* in John Huston's 1950s Hollywood version of *Moby Dick*.

Departures

It's not the leaving of Liverpool that grieves me,
But my darling when I think of thee.
Clipper Ship Ballad, Nineteenth century

Recently, I attended a festival of sea shanties and maritime ballads at a club in a small Irish coastal town. The music was delightful and performed with great gusto by enthusiastic musicians, some of whom were extremely skillful and spirited. Among the songs I recognized were ones that MacColl and his friend A.L. Lloyd had helped keep alive. Yet the majority of performers and the audience, like me, had grown up in the 1960s and 1970s, and one suspected that the brilliant younger musicians there were going to be struggling against the tides of interest of their generation. 1960s neo-romanticism provided, at a distance, a lot of the energy of the evening. Still, as the music drifted out over the Atlantic, I felt that the old sailors' laments for the departure from home touched on a kind of tension between the agony of leaving loved ones and the excitement of new ventures that not just spoke to its own day but had a continuing appeal.

Perhaps it was not so strange after all that Ben Bright loved the sailing ships and could never find anywhere to stop. The tension between the relative security of a known living space and the promise of new places remains a real conflict for many, even when the more adventurous course may be more dangerous. Perhaps the appeal of the seamen's songs will outlast the generation that revived them, connecting the voices of sail and steam to a new generation's navigation between their home and their world.

---

42 Colcord, *Songs of American Sailormen*.

Nitin Sinha
The Home and the World in Indian Folksongs of Marriage and Migration

Move steadily, O! my Lord, I am lost and defeated ...
On the one hand, I part with my nose-ring,
On the other, O! Lord, I leave behind my mother. Move steadily ...
On the one hand, I part with my necklace,
On the other, O! Lord, I leave behind my transparent saree. Move steadily ...
On the one hand, I move away from my village and my habitat,
On the other, O! Lord, I leave behind my home and hearth. Move steadily ...
On the one hand, I part from my brave brother,
On the other, O! Lord, I leave behind all my [female] friends. Move steadily ...
On the one hand, I part with my garden and my fields,
On the other, O! Lord, I leave behind my beloved cow. Move steadily ...

This folksong is one among many that encapsulates the pangs of separation a young girl goes through at the time of her wedding. The song depicts the moment of her departure from her natal house and village to that of her husband's, which is new, unknown, and unseen. She is preparing to miss the physical place of her family home, which bears the marks of her childhood and adolescence, but also her relationships with friends and kin. The song captures how even her ornaments are invested with the emotion of home. New ornaments are given and worn at the time of the wedding. She laments taking off her old nose-ring and necklace, soaked with the memories and love of her family and natal home.

The folksong comes from the 'Bhojpuri belt' of northern India, chiefly comprising eastern Uttar Pradesh and western Bihar. The region was historically significant during the early modern and modern periods. From the sixteenth to the eighteenth century, streams of men left to join the Mughal army. In the nineteenth century, Purabiya men migrated in large numbers to the second imperial capital of the British empire, Calcutta, to work in mills and factories. Some emigrants, including women, migrated even further to work in the sugar plantations of the Caribbean or tea plantations in Assam.

Women of this region suffered from double separation. They left their parents' home at an early age only to see their husbands leaving their new home in search of work. So goes one song:

Railways have become a co-wife,
It has taken away my beloved;
It has taken away my beloved to Rangoon,
It has taken away my beloved to Bengal.
Neither the railways nor the steamships,
The real enemy is money;
It forces to wander from one to another country,
The real enemy is money.

The song ends on a touching note of affection and love. The woman is willing to suffer, to survive on very little food, but she is not ready to let her beloved go:

I don't feel no hunger, no thirst,
I just feel a swelling affection;
When I see your face,
I just feel the deep affection.

The women of these folksongs appear immobile, but their world was not static. Marriage and migration changed their lives. Movement to their in-laws' homes was both an emotional and physical journey, which forever remained incomplete. This essay attempts to capture a slice of these women's social worlds. It uses popular folksongs to capture their ideas and spaces of home. What does it mean to be 'at home' when the world is rapidly changing due to railways and steamships, and more importantly, due to capitalist (and imperialist) economy based on labor migration?

The Architecture of Emotion

> *Where do Ram and Lakshman come from, where does my beloved come from, O! Lord;*
> > *From Ayodhya come Ram and Lakshman, from Morang comes my beloved, O! Lord.*
> *Where should I sit Ram and Lakshman, where should I sit my beloved, O! Lord;*
> > *At the gate (duwari) will sit Ram and Lakshman, in the home my beloved, O! Lord.*
> *What food will I offer to Ram and Lakshman, what will I offer to my beloved, O! Lord;*
> > *Pudi I will offer to Ram and Lakshman, [and] puwa to my beloved, O! Lord.*[43]
> *Where would I put Ram and Lakshman to sleep, where would my beloved sleep, O! Lord;*
> > *At the gate (duwari) will sleep Ram and Lakshman; on my bed my beloved, O! Lord.*

Home is a graded space both architecturally and emotionally. The Hindu gods Ram and his brother Lakshman have arrived from Ayodhya, while the migrant husband arrives from Morung.

In this corpus of poetic imagination, to be at home meant marking the boundaries of intimacy and familiarity along the lines of architecture. *Khet* and *khalihaan*, the farm and the field, were the domains of men. *Khalihaan* also referred to the outer courtyard of the house where the grain and hay was stacked, where married women seldom went. In contrast, unmarried young girls had greater access to these places.

Duwari and *duwariya*, both meaning the gate or the threshold, separated the outer and inner courtyards. In houses with only one courtyard, it served as the boundary between the outer public space and the inner quarters of the home. *Duwari* marked the passage of intimacy. In spite of being a god, Ram was not allowed to cross this boundary into the inner courtyard, which was called *angnaa* or *anganwaa*. He had to sit and sleep at the *duwari*. The intimate space of home and bed was reserved for the migrant husband.

In certain situations, crossing the *duwari* was a matter of shame and embarrassment:

> *Oh! Lord, I lost my earring at this place ...*
> *I searched the bed, I searched in the courtyard ...*
> *I blushed while searching at the duwari ...*

We find an inversion of this emotional architecture in the teasing, playful songs sung at marriages, which confirm the normative, performative, and emotional meanings attached to *angnaa* and *duwari*. Here, the woman asks a series of questions about how she should treat her younger brother-in-law and her lover who have arrived at the same time. Such a comparison is again possible only in the context of men being away for work. The lover gets to sit in the *angnaa*, while the

---

43 *Pudi* means fried puffed bread and *puwa* a sweet pancake. Both are non-everyday foods and hence their use in this folksong indicates that their receiver was deserving of special treatment. *Puwa* because of being sweet is invested with greater prestige.

brother-in-law remains at the *duwari*.[44] The former gets sweets and milk, the latter plain boiled rice and water. The lover gets to sleep in the inner courtyard, while the younger claimant of the house sleeps at its boundary.

Lifecycle Homes

While men traveled to big cities in search of work and money, young girls went through mundane but powerful transformations in their lifecycle through marriage. *Angnaa, duwari,* and *khalihaan* have retained similar gendered and emotional meanings, but once we think of home from the perspective of a marriageable or married young girl, we are struck with subtle changes in how these spaces were accessed.

Naihar, the natal home of the girl, is a place of carefree and careless freedom, where thresholds of courtyards were less significant. In the opening song, the girl misses the whole habitat of her home, hearth, and village, signifying an unrestricted access to these places. The groom's house, *sasuraal*, is more ritualized and disciplined. Boundaries of access and freedom of movement are relatively fixed. Even *angnaa*, which is largely a female space, becomes inaccessible if male members are present. When it rains, goes one song, the girl complains that *angnaa* has become the homestay of the father-in-law and the elder brother-in-law. The whole day is spent touching their feet and maintaining the veil. In their presence, she finds it difficult to do the household chores. She asks how she can go and sweep the floor.

Cared for by her father and brother at her natal home, her new home means new discipline and new rituals. In many folksongs, the girl, now a wife in her new home, threatens to go back to *naihar* when confronted with arguments and displeasure by her husband and in-laws.

Women's lives spanned two homes, pointing to the complexity and ironic duality of home and home-making. Marriage makes the girl instantly *parayaa* (stranger or kinless) whereas a stranger's family, *sasuraal*, becomes her new home. Familiar becomes strange and strange never succeeds in becoming completely familiar.

Many folksongs, therefore, have a didactic tone: of mothers instructing their daughters how to behave in the *sasuraal*. Because she was adored and pampered in her *naihar*, she has not learnt any *sahur*, the proper way of self-conduct. This reflected in her inability to observe boundaries and thresholds. At the *naihar*, for example, she does not have to maintain the veil in front of her father and elder brothers. In the *sasuraal*, she must observe it meticulously.

Because marriage is pivotal in bringing about these changes, the girl pleads her father not to marry her off:

> *Hide me in the home, my father, the groom can go back to his home.*

Once married, however, *naihar* still retained the value of being an intimate space of belonging. This is particularly important when her husband insists on migrating:

---

44 *Jhumar* is a very popular genre of folksong which is sung at marriages and is excessively based on teasing and playfulness.

If you, my beloved, migrate, if you migrate;
Call my brother I will go to naihar.
If you, my love, go to naihar, if you go to naihar;
First pay the money I have incurred on you.
If you, my beloved, ask for money, if you ask for it;
First provide me the home as was my father's.

Transgressions within Homes

While the husband leaves to earn money to build an extra room or to make the house *pucca*, the domestic world of the wife revolves around her two homes.[45] None of these is static. Both *naihar* and *sasuraal* undergo changes. One is through a simple addition of new members. The wife's brother has got married and so her *naihar* has its own daughter-in-law. When frustrated in *sasuraal*, she thinks of going to *naihar*, but gets no comfort:

Sometimes I think I should have gone to naihar, [and] oh god, drown myself in a well or pond,
But on going to naihar, my sister-in-law will ridicule, and also, I have lost all my friends.

At her *sasuraal*, the biggest change is the long absence of her husband. This historical reality of migration gave rise to new genres of Bhojpuri folksongs in the late nineteenth and early twentieth centuries. In these songs, the predominant form of relationship forged between the wife and the female members of her in-laws' house is of feud and enmity. For the young wife, the flavor and tone of each woman's voice is of special bearing:

Tell me, how do the words of mother-in-law [saas] sound, they sound like the piquant of red chilies,
Tell me, how do the words of sister-in-law [gotin] sound, they sound like the burn of black peppers,
Tell me, how do the words of sister-in-law [nanad] sound, they sound like the blaze of a glowing stove.[46]

Saas and *nanad* in particular are seen as born and sworn enemies. The reasons for tussles are varied: the husband on his return has brought gifts, which have made other family members jealous; the household chores have not been done properly; the wife remains childless; the young wife threatens to transgress the boundary of sexual conduct when her husband is away. She is flirtatious and lacks decency:

I was preparing food on the Balia railway station,
And I was feeling restless in between;
First of all, I am fair, and second, young,
Third was the thrust of my youthfulness in your absence, my beloved.

---

45 Making the house *pucca* (solid, concrete) is very significant. In contemporary times, it means the transition from mud- or hay-thatched roof to concrete, cement-based. This marks a passage to relative prosperity and upward social mobility.
46 The sister-in-law of the second line refers to the wife of husband's brother; the one of the last refers to husband's sister.

Some transgressions potentially happen within the intimate and familiar precincts of the *angnaa*. In some folksongs, the returning husband finds a child born by his wife and his brother. As the following *jhumar* shows, the male gaze is widespread both inside and outside the house:

> *Wonder does the blouse spell on my youth. Wonder ...*
> *While going to the market the passer-by hoots,*
> *In the garden, the gardener pounces. Wonder ...*
> *My beloved calls me to prepare the bed,*
> *While cooking, the brother-in-law scoots. Wonder ...*
> *While sweeping the angnaa my brother-in-law calls,*
> *Showing betel leaf my beloved darts. Wonder ...*

Reflections

Reading folksongs as fixed textual sources is highly problematic. They are performative texts and a lot of meaning depends on and derives from the context of their performance. These folksongs also incorporate new symbols. The reference to railways in such songs mean that they are of late nineteenth-century origin, even if the narrative structure points to earlier periods. Similarly, the constant reference to migration to Calcutta for work is also a nineteenth-century feature. It would thus be simplistic if this poetic imagination and expression is taken at face value to make generalizing claims about gender, home, and the intervening social reality in colonial India. Many songs are full of irony and exaggerations: teasing and mischief, acceptance and subversion, and love and mockery. Sung at social functions such as marriages, the birth of a child, and other such auspicious occasions, their performance can become both ritualistic and subversive.

Folksongs do not conform to a single pattern. The figure of *dewar* (younger brother-in-law), for example, can be villainous and lecherous or obedient and a confidante. The younger sister-in-law can be a woman's most intimate friend or the most spiteful character in her life. The typologies of relationships are complex. Therefore, the poetic imagination, which is predominantly a male imagination, as these songs were usually written or composed by men, cannot be read as exact mirror images of social reality.

But what can be said with a great certainty is that, in all their playfulness and subversion, woman are the central subjects of these folksongs. Either in her idealized form or as her sexualized transgressive avatar, women come across as the main subject in representations of love and jealousy, feud and affection, separation, and curiosity. It is through her lens that we see this world of marriage, dowry, migration, and graded forms of relationships. Her woes as a young girl, her pangs of separation as a wife, her profanity, and her licentiousness are the subject of description, control, discipline, ridicule, and entertainment.

These songs are not the celebration of women's agency. She is rather the carrier of male projections, idealizations, fantasies, and desires. And indeed, of anxieties as well. The migrant male fears her having an affair in the village; the woman in the village is jealous of her man returning with a second wife. Each live in fear of the other. Distance due to migration gives conjugality and marriage a specific meaning.

But for women, marriage in itself is a form of dislocation. It is a journey from her natal to new home which accompanies the change of emotional and moral registers. While the story of nineteenth-century migration and circulation is usually told through male figures who leave home in search of work, the lives of the apparently immobile women were also caught up in the web of this change. Marriage and migration meant that their lives, spread across homes, farms and fields, were as dynamic as the lives of the lascars and coolies who traveled from one port to another and jumped one ship to work on the other. In our own accounts of histories of circulation, home must remain an important site of investigation.

Section 6
Networks, Neighborhoods, Communities

Paulo Fontes

'The Land of Boarding Houses': Migrant Workers and Collective Dwellings in São Paulo, Brazil, 1945–1970

The journey had been long and tiring. For eleven days in that year of 1948, the young Augusto Ferreira Lima had traveled in a packed truck, sitting on an uncomfortable wooden plank that doubled as a seat. Augusto was leaving behind the poor, dry region of Alagoinhas in the interior of the state of Bahia in search of a new life and opportunities in the industries of the imposing city of São Paulo.

Augusto would never forget the rain and the cold of the afternoon he arrived. Relatives and friends had fortunately already recommended a boarding house in the city, which was where Augusto headed. The excitement was so much that despite his tiredness, he spent a long part of his first night talking with the other guests, the immense majority of whom were migrants from the countryside like him. The following day, he went to look for employment in one of the large factories in the city, where he soon found a job. For several months, he lived in the boarding house. He remembered the festive atmosphere in particular. "There was a group of *nortistas* [northeast migrants] from the *sertão* [backlands] of Piauí [a northeastern state of Brazil]," he explained. "They played accordion, tambourine – it was a crazy place. I will never forget those parties we had at night, after leaving the factory."[1]

The story of Augusto's arrival in São Paulo is not uncommon. The massive migration of workers from rural to urban regions is one of the striking facts of Brazilian social history in the second half of the twentieth century. Between 1950 and 1980, it is estimated that more than thirty-eight million people left the countryside, profoundly altering the socioeconomic profile of the country.[2] São Paulo (as the principal receptor) and the northeast (as the region of origin of the majority of the migrants) played a central role in this process. The figure of the northeastern worker escaping hunger, misery, and periodic drought arriving at the industrial metropole in search of employment and better living conditions became a symbol of migration in the Brazilian social imagination. São Paulo was transformed into a place of residence and employment for hundreds of thousands of migrants from the northeast.

The São Paulo metropolitan area in the 1950s was the setting for an accelerated and diversified process of industrialization and urbanization. The region was principally responsible for the country's elevated rate of industrial production growth. Between 1945 and 1960, as a result of governmental policies of Import Substitution Industrialization (ISI), the secondary sector grew an average of 9.5 percent a year, comprising at that time one of the fastest processes of industrialization anywhere in the world. In 1959, almost fifty percent of all factory employment in the country was concentrated in the state of São Paulo.[3] Additionally, the industrial growth of São Paulo stimulated a great expansion of the service sector in the region, increasing even more the availability

---

1 Interview with Augusto Ferreira Lima, May 18, 1998.

2 Carlos Hasenbalg, A Pesquisa Sobre Migrações, Urbanização, Relações Raciais e Pobreza no Brasil, 1979–1990 (Rio de Janeiro: IUPERJ, 1991).

3 Cf. Renato Colistete, *Labour Relations and Industrial Performance in Brazil: Greater São Paulo, 1945–1960* (Houndmills: Palgrave, 2001). See also Murilo Leal Pereira Neto, *A reinvenção da classe trabalhadora, 1953–1964* (Campinas: Editora da Unicamp, 2011).

of jobs and possible opportunities. The thousands of migrants who flocked to the capital city of São Paulo entered an expanding, highly dynamic job market. The 1950s also witnessed a major shift in the industrial structure of São Paulo, with the notable rise of the metallurgical sector as the most important and largest employer. By the end of the decade, metallurgy employed about thirty percent of all manual labor in the state. Contributing to this expansion was the growth of the automobile manufacturing sector. Sectors such as the chemical and pharmaceutical industries experienced significant growth during this period as well, while other long-established industries, such as textiles, food, and glass, lost ground.

As well as the evident economic motivation for migration, it is important not to underestimate the role of the migrants themselves as agents in this process. In many analyses, the migrants are seen only as numbers, as a labor force passively transferred from the least to the most developed regions. Northeastern rural migrants not only reflected – and were immersed in – externally determined economic forces, they were also agents of their own movement and, through diverse strategies and social networks, they contributed to the molding of the migration process. Communities of origin, families, and friends all played a determining role in this process.

Images of migration as disordered and hurried does not correspond to the experiences of the large majority of migrants. Change, decisive for the lives of those involved, was most often meticulously considered and prepared for in the best possible form, within both family and community spheres. Information about São Paulo, its employment opportunities, and the housing options were fundamental to the decision to migrate. The establishment of a communication network between migrants and their places of origin frequently guided the migratory process. Correspondence, photographs, and postcards played an important role in the provision of data and the creation of a "cultural imagination of the place of destination."[4]

The emphasis on the agency of migrants goes back to the valorization of their experiences and memories.[5] Statements by migrant workers reveal that when they reached the city, boarding houses played a particular role in consolidating and expanding contacts and were of great importance in their initial socialization in the urban environment and their connections with the world of work. Particularly between 1940 and 1970, there was an enormous expansion in the number of boarding houses which provided initial lodgings for these migrants.

In the central regions of the city, close to railway terminals and bus stations, and principally in the belt of districts and industrial municipalities around São Paulo, subletting rooms and setting up boarding houses became an attractive business for many small entrepreneurs and home owners.

This was the case in the working-class neighborhood of São Miguel, for example, on the extreme east of the city. The area possessed an enormous number of boarding houses, which were by far the most frequently used form of accommodation by new arrivals, the majority of whom were single young men. Remembering the period, Augusto Lima said that São Miguel was known as 'the land of boarding houses' in São Paulo. Linking the neighborhood to migration from the northeast, a 1948 article in the *Correio Paulistano* newspaper reinforced this image by highlighting "the singular phenomenon of [São Miguel] being one of the few suburbs where there exist boarding houses

---

4 Alistair Thomson, "Moving Stories: Oral History and Migration Studies." *Oral History* 27 (1999): 24–37, 28.
5 Alistair Thomson, among others, has emphasized the role of oral history in the analysis of migrations: "Although economic pressures frequently influenced the decisions to migrate, personal testimonies reveal a complex web of factors and influences which contribute to migration, as well as the entire process of exchanging information and negotiation through families and social networks." Alistair Thomson, "Moving Stories": 28.

and hotels, beds to rent, etc., as in the city center."[6] In his memoirs, Pastor Mário da Natividade Valladão also emphasized the presence of collective dwellings in the neighborhood at the end of the 1940s. When, in 1946 and 1947, his Baptist church resolved to start a "door to door evangelization campaign," Valladão found that there were "few families [but] many 'boarding houses,' into which were crowded numerous young men."[7]

Some of these boarding houses were actually very big. Augusto Lima remembered the Araújo boarding house, the largest one he knew. "It was in Vila Nitro Operário. Araújo was a *Baiano* [from the city] of Pilão Arcado," worked in a factory, and afterwards built this "boarding house which housed four hundred and something workers."[8] However, most boarding houses tended to be much smaller. A denunciation registered in the Department of Political and Social Order of São Paulo in 1951 against "the excessive rent" charged by Ambrozina Teixeira, owner of a boarding house on Rua Beraldo Marcondes No. 6, provides us with an idea of what this type of lodging was like:

> The woman in question ... sublet five rooms to young men, with each room having three to five beds. There are eighteen of these young men ..., the majority workers ... There is also a front room [which] according to what has been discovered is occupied by people from her family.[9]

It was common for the owners of bars and food stores to expand their businesses, transforming the least used spaces of their premises into rooms to rent and small boarding houses. Owner of a little bar at the end of the 1940s, Lídia Castelani Gomes resolved to open a small boarding house after noting the intense demand. "Every day," she remembers, "there appeared people asking for lodging." It was also common that in addition to lodging, boarding houses would provide food and offer the new arrivals basic security. The working-class neighborhoods at that time, comments Lídia Castelani, "did not have restaurants. All that existed were the small boarding houses. So, anyone who had an [extra] room provided food because there were [many people] wanting to eat."[10] At the end of the 1930s and the early 1940s, the boarding house belonging to the Bernardo family in São Miguel served "an average of eighty-eight meals to those staying there and ... another 130 extra ones."[11]

Boarding houses were points of reference for those looking for relatives, friends, and contemporaries, becoming fundamental information centers for the new arrivals. João Freitas Lírio, for example, remembers that people "would leave the [railway] station looking for the closest boarding house ... and would ask: 'Do you know so-and-so? Do you know such-and-such?'"[12] Once again revealing the sophisticated networks of contacts between migrants and their communities of origin, Augusto Lima remembered that he was always "looked for by the people from my land, by more than one hundred and thirty people. [They arrived] at the boarding house where I stayed and looked for me by my name. Everyone knew that I was there. At night, the people were sitting there waiting for me to arrive."[13]

---

6 *Correio Paulistano*, 11 April 1948.

7 Mário da Natividade Valladão, *Dá conta de tua mordomia* (São Paulo: Igreja Batista de São Miguel Paulista, 1986): 5

8 Interview with Augusto Ferreira Lima, May 18, 1998

9 Arquivo Público do Estado de São Paulo, setor Deops. Prontuário 110703.

10 Interview with Lídia Castelani Gomes, February 23, 2000.

11 Interview with Nelson Bernardo, August 7, 2001.

12 Interview with João Freitas Lírio, September 19, 2000.

13 Interview with Augusto Ferreira Lima, May 18, 1998.

Some boarding houses also became points of arrival for entire communities. Nelson Bernardo believes that many truck drivers who brought migrants "already came guided ... the northeastern-ers got off ... in front of the boarding house."[14] As mentioned above, in the first boarding house where Augusto Lima stayed, "There was always a group of *nortistas* from the *sertão* of Piauí [a northeastern Brazilian state]." When by a stroke of luck, the brother of Maria José Santos Oliveira won a prize in the federal lottery at the beginning of the 1940s, his family decided to use the money to establish a boarding house, which, due to its clientele, soon came to be known as the 'boarding house of the *Mineiros*' (in reference to migrants from the Brazilian state of Minas Gerais].[15]

In the small rooms, over breakfast and lunch, or between one beer and another after dinner, those who had just arrived in the city made their first contacts. Information and experience were exchanged.[16] The search for new employment was the principal priority, and old and new contacts were essential. Boarding houses were thus a fundamental space of socialization for workers. "In the boarding house there was a great friendship. It was through the boarding house that friend-ships were made, that people gathered and enjoyed themselves. They had fun and went on trips on the train, all together."[17]

Antônio Xavier dos Santos has similar memories from his time living in boarding houses. "The atmosphere in the boarding house was very friendly," he reports. "I myself had great friend-ships with the people from the boarding house. I would go to parties. We would go to the park on Sundays."[18]

Of course, there was a certain romanticism and idealization in the memories of life in the migrant boarding houses. Disagreements, fights, and violence were not at all uncommon in this mostly masculine environment. The popular newspapers of the time frequently reported crimes taking place in boarding houses and collective dwellings, often associated with feuds and disagree-ments involving alcohol or demonstrations of a certain standard of masculine honor. Augusto Lima reported the case "of a *Pernambucano* [from the northeastern state of Pernambuco] who stabbed a *Baiano* [from the northeastern state of Bahia] and killed him in a boarding house da Rua da Glória."[19] The *Pernambucano*, drunk, had simply not liked a joke made by the *Baiano* in the board-ing house, where they had lived for some time despite its history of brawls and disagreements. A newspaper report celebrating the project for construction of the 'Palace of Commerce,' a collective dwelling for workers in the commercial sector, provide a good idea of the bad and indeed infamous reputation which *Paulistana* boarding houses could have: "There is no doubt that the commercial workers residing in the boarding houses will find greater comfort living in an appropriate building, far from the promiscuity and the maleficence of the São Paulo boarding houses."[20]

Spending a long time in the boarding houses was very common. Coming from Babaçu, in Bahia, Antônio Xavier dos Santos arrived in São Miguel in 1950 and spent the following eight years in a boarding house, until the arrival of his mother and other relatives, when he decided to rent a house for them all to live in together.[21] João Freitas Lírio, from Camponoso, also in Bahia, spent six years

---

14 Interview with Nelson Bernardo, August 7, 2001.

15 Interview with Maria José Santos Oliveira, August 26, 1998.

16 In his studies of France, Abdelmalek Sayad found the same 'educational' nature of immigrant housing. See Abdel-malek Sayad, *Imigração ou os paradoxos da alteridade* (São Paulo: Edusp, 1998): 74–5.

17 Interview with Augusto Ferreira Lima, May 18, 1998.

18 Interview with Antonio Xavier dos Santos, February 21, 2000.

19 Interview with Augusto Ferreira Lima, May 18, 1998.

20 *Jornal de Notícias*, 8 August 1951

21 Interview with Antonio Xavier dos Santos, February 21, 2000.

in a boarding house in São Miguel before his marriage.[22] Lodging in boarding houses provided the temporariness necessary for young migrants to assess their definite installation in the new city. Marriage or the arrival of other relatives generally demanded a move and the end of their time in boarding houses, which many associated with youth and the tempestuousness of single men.

The importance of the social networks established by the migrants was evident in the environment of the boarding houses and continued to be decisive in the process of definitive installation in the city. Between the 1940s and the 1970s, a belt of worker neighborhoods was formed around São Paulo and the neighboring municipalities. The large majority of their residents were migrants from the rural parts of the country.

Despite the spatially and socially segregated character of this urbanization process, moving to the periphery could signify the chance to stop paying rent and acquiring or constructing the much-coveted 'own house.' From the point of view of the migrants, home ownership signified security and a guarantee of stability in the highly insecure and volatile environment of the large city. Given the high rents and low wages, home ownership was the guarantee of family shelter in any situation, as well as signifying a concrete investment, possible savings, and small amount of capital.

Nevertheless, for the majority of workers, the possibility of their own house in São Paulo could only be fulfilled by constructing one in peripheral lots acquired in instalments and lacking any infrastructure. Construction was slow and done in stages, achieved with their own resources and the help of relatives, friends, and neighbors, using weekends and their time off.

Not by chance, in the personal history of numerous workers, the purchase of land for the construction of their own house occurred shortly after marriage. The purchase of land obviously obeyed the criteria of price, but proximity to relatives, friends, and contemporaries was also taken into account at the time of purchasing. This helped in the maintenance and expansion of the network of cooperation and mutual aid constructed by migrants. It was also decisive in the process of building a home, which required the regimentation and aid of the largest number of people possible.

Worker neighborhoods on the peripheries of São Paulo were fundamentally marked by the collective experience of mutual aid for buildings one's own home. In this process, boarding houses played a fundamental role as initial collective housing for migrants and a space for the development of social networks and the construction of sociability. This forged much of the class formation in urban Brazil experienced in the second half of the twentieth century.

---

22 Interview with João Freitas Lírio. September 19, 2000.

Jürgen Schmidt

The Enlarged Parlor? Structures and Varieties of German Working-Class Housing around 1900

Around 1900, journalist and travel writer Karl Emil Franzos used a problematic and dubious superlative to describe the Prussian town of Erfurt, situated in the middle of the German Empire. Erfurt, he proclaimed, was the "most benchless city in Germany." In a city with, at that time, nearly 100,000 inhabitants, it was almost impossible to find a bench in a park or public place to rest, relax, or enjoy a view of Erfurt. This apparently negligible fact leads us right to the heart of our topic of home-making, especially if we look to the debate behind Franzos's observation. Ten years earlier, members of the town council had discussed the design of one of Erfurt's central and prestigious squares in front of the building of the district government (*Regierungsbezirk*). One councilman stated firmly that he was against installing new benches. He argued that the benches would just be occupied by housemaids joking and gossiping about passers-by, meaning that many ladies would not dare to cross the town square anymore. Public and private space collided here in a symbolic way. The private worlds of servants were encroaching onto public spaces; and the middle-class bourgeois elites feared that their shielded and protected family lives and lifestyles could become the subject of public chatter. The scene illustrates an important contrast between the semi-public living habits of the working classes and the middle-class intimacies associated with homes and housing. The snapshot of "benchless Erfurt" is part of a broader context of contact between the classes: processes of adaption between the working classes and middle classes, and class conflicts and separate milieu-building. Erfurt will serve in this essay as an illustrative example, but developments in other towns will be considered as well, knowing that the specificities of one town cannot stand as *pars pro toto* in a very complex process.

This essay examines working-class neighborhoods in urban spaces in German cities and describe some of the features they share.[23] First, there was the private and public dimension of housing. Home-making for working-class people meant the appropriation of public spaces and neighborhoods. Streets and the neighborhood were part of their living habits. Children and younger adults were regularly 'delegated' outside the home due to limited space within apartments. Youth socialization took place outside the home. The street was a place to learn, communicate, play, and interact. And because it was an experience shared by most families and children, theirs was an integrated, not isolated childhood. Streets were also places where young men met in groups and formed cliques. Around 1910 in Imperial Germany, a discourse about 'young rowdies' (*Halbstarke*) arose, touching on the role of 'adolescence' in the life course.

Second, women used and depended on neighborhood structures for reproductive and family work. At the grocery store, for example, women would put the daily shopping on a tab. This meant that the grocer and sometimes the neighbors would know about the family's economic situation.

---

23 See Jürgen Schmidt, *Begrenzte Spielräume: Eine Beziehungsgeschichte von Arbeiterschaft und Bürgertum am Beispiel Erfurts 1870–1914* (Göttingen: Vandenhoeck und Ruprecht, 2005); Adelheid von Saldern, *Häuserleben: Zur Geschichte städtischen Arbeiterwohnens vom Kaiserreich bis heute* (Bonn: Dietz, 1995); Gerhard A. Ritter and Klaus Tenfelde, *Arbeiter im Deutschen Kaiserreich 1871–1914* (Bonn: Dietz, 1992); Barbara Händler-Lachmann. "'n Wochenlohn die Miete': Arbeiterwohnen in Braunschweig vom Kaiserreich zur Weimarer Republik," *Archiv für Sozialgeschichte* 25 (1985): 159–81.

Publicly admitting to an empty household budget could generate feelings of shame, but it could also create a sense of a shared understanding because many families were in a similar situation. Grocers, many of whom came from similar working-class backgrounds, were dependent on these clients, a mutual dependency based on trust and mistrust. Working-class families who had been in the neighborhood for longer had a better standing in this relation than families or individuals constantly on the move. The neighborhood thus exerted influence on household budgets and consumption patterns. Similarly, the small apartments of working-class families meant that tasks such as washing were difficult to do indoors. Doing the laundry in the street also created spaces of communication outside the household. Although the male bread-winner model prevailed in working-class families, many women also needed to contribute to the household income. Working women needed the support of neighbors or older children to take care of their younger children.

Third, working-class housing was mostly crowded and characterized by a lack of intimacy and separate dwelling areas. Many so-called "half-open family structures" existed around and after 1900.[24] People not belonging to the family were part of these households as subtenants or lodgers (*Schlafgänger*). This form of living had nothing to do with solidarity; it was born of the necessity for additional household income, and it was fraught with conflict and challenges for family life. In German cities in 1890, two to six percent of all inhabitants were lodgers. In Braunschweig, a city with about 101,000 inhabitants, 800 out of 4,100 lodgers were female. Although in Berlin the percentage of households with lodgers declined from about twenty to twelve percent between 1875 and 1895, it was clear that home-making for a substantial minority nevertheless meant improvization, an abstinence of privacy, and sharing one's home with non-family members. Once the family was able to earn enough through regular work, they would try to escape this pattern.

Finally, inns and taverns were the meeting point for male workers in their leisure time, but they were also places where workers' organizations came together for political work. According to the socialist theorist Karl Kautsky, a worker "has no parlor available to welcome his friends and comrades in his home. If he wants to discuss with them common matters he has to go to the pub."[25] The inns where workers met were small and basic. They were on nearly every street, on every corner. In Berlin in 1898, there was one inn for every 135 inhabitants. Inn-life was a male-dominated world which, except for a waitress or the wife of the innkeeper, women did not frequent. The social structure of the guests depended very much on the quarter and neighborhood. In Erfurt, for example, according to police reports, people living in the immediate neighborhood would meet in the *Zum Gotthardt* pub, while the restaurant *Zur Rudelsburg* hosted mainly countrymen, railway employees, and dwellers from the cooperative building society, *Schmidtstedt*. 'Inferior public and social democratic members' came together in the *Zum alten Moritz* pub. Irrespective of the social and political structure of the guests, inns served as places of retreat for men from cramped housing and possible conflicts with spouses or children. Of course, the pubs were also places to communicate with colleagues about the working day, ask everyday questions, and play cards. Larger inns and taverns providing billiards and music became places of weekend leisure and amusement. Home-making in the working-class quarters thus surmounted the privacy of one's home.

The larger inns and restaurants played a major role for the political and social milieu of the German Social Democratic Party. Such inns were situated in working-class neighborhoods, had

---

24 Lutz Niethammer and Franz-Josef Brüggemeier, "Wie wohnten Arbeiter im Kaiserreich?" *Archiv für Sozialgeschichte* 16 (1976): 61–134.

25 Karl Kautsky (1890–91), quoted in Richard J. Evans, ed., *Kneipengespräche im Kaiserreich. Die Stimmungsberichte der Hamburger Politischen Polizei 1892–1914* (Hamburg: Rowohlt, 1989): 21.

Social Democratic newspapers on display, and provided separate rooms for party meetings and associational life. These surroundings offered a home for politically engaged workers (which could, in turn, lead to family conflicts if they neglected their private home). Especially after 1900 and in large cities, the success of the Social Democratic Party and the unions led to the professionalization of party work and the development of the relevant infrastructure. In so-called 'peoples' halls' (*Volkshäuser*), situated in Social Democratic strongholds, the political, cultural, and social life of the working-class movement and organizations was centralized. These buildings represented the strength, pride, and respectability of influential political actors who had established a home for working-class people.

It is also important to differentiate between different city types. Stable neighborhood networks were built and sustained more easily in traditional middle-sized towns, whose economic structure changed more slowly than industrial newcomer towns. Here, the city's infrastructure was often unable to cope with masses of people coming to look for work. In major cities like Hamburg or Berlin, the houses with overcrowded backyards tended to lead to anonymity. Dense networks of institutions and individual contacts shaped urban working-class quarters in the late nineteenth and early twentieth century in Imperial Germany.

Nevertheless, the homogeneity of working-class housing relations and community structures should not be overestimated. Common patterns were also crosscut by other influential factors. First, with regard to children and young people, educational reform took place in the second half of the nineteenth century, when attending school for a greater part of the day became the rule rather than the exception. In the decades leading up to 1870, it was relatively easy for parents to get a school exemption so they could send their children to work. In the decades that followed, the state put much more emphasis on schooling. Street childhood lost its significance and relevance after 1900. As Germany was a very young society at this time – in 1910, 20.3 percent of the population was between ten and twenty years old, compared with 10.7 percent in 2015 – the state and social reformers reminded working-class families of their educational duties, while also trying to win influence over young people and offer them opportunities to integrate into state and society (*Jugendpflege*). Altogether, during the course of the German Empire, the self-determined, free space of the neighborhood was confined for children and young people.

Second, at the turn of the twentieth century, workers' families began to withdraw into the privacy of their home. Neighborhoods lost their intermediate function as spaces of communication and contact. Working-class families incorporated middle-class housing habits into their lifestyles. Indeed, it was in around 1900 that better-situated working-class families began to be able to afford apartments with more than two rooms and with a parlor. A good parlor (*gute Stube*) should never be missing from a workers' house, stated a Thuringian lodging inspector in 1914. The parlor was an inimitable form of working-class home-making that illustrated a certain level of success, respectability, and no longer belonging to the unskilled, poorly paid section of the working class. Parlors were treated like sanctuaries; the family was allowed to enter this room for special events such as church holidays, family visits, or celebrations. This pattern of living was attacked from two sides: middle-class social reformers and social democrats alike saw it as a waste of space. While most families still lived and slept in the crowded other rooms of the flat, one room went virtually unused, reserved for prestigious and symbolic reasons.

However, labor organizations had to accept this housing style as the preferred way of life of their supporters. "And who but the worker should have the right to furnish his home as comfortably and nicely as possible? The worker whose home should be a shelter from the fierce struggle of life, whose home is often enough the only true recreation place," stated the Social Democratic newspaper *Tribüne* in defense of this housing style. After 1900, the Social Democratic party tried to influence workers' tastes by organizing exhibitions of ways to decorate a flat without "the bad habit of gluing small photographs and picture postcards to the wall." These exhibitions and newspapers suggested hanging "bright, cozy pictures" in the parlor – portraits by Albrecht Dürer or Hans Holbein, for example, or "atmospheric landscape paintings."

In the face of these forms of individualization – this 'my-home-is-my-castle' mentality – Social Democrats tried to uphold the political function of the home and family. The *Tribüne*, for example, declared that it was a woman's duty to abandon bourgeois advertising journals, read socialist newspapers, and remind her husband to go and vote for the Social Democratic Party. The retreat into the *gute Stube* did not mean a de-politicization of workers in general, but the direct influence of working-class quarters diminished as home-making changed.

Third, very different forms of working-class quarters existed in parallel. The structure of the neighborhood would depend on the dominant factory or industry. In 1898 in Germany, more than 140,000 company flats existed. This means that roughly two out of every hundred people employed in industry, crafts, or trade in Germany were likely to live in such accommodation. This form of housing played a role in the rapidly industrialized towns of the Ruhr valley in particular. Coal mining and steel industries tried to attract workers by offering housing. Major enterprises like the Krupp steel company in Essen erected settlements (*Werkssiedlungen)* in the aim of building a permanent workforce. Propagated by Krupp in late Imperial Germany as a master achievement and invention of social politics to solve housing problems, this form of housing had actually existed since the 1830s.[26] Although the Krupp enterprise was highly active in this form of housing politics, it only was able to offer company housing for about eighteen percent of its total workforce of 36,369 in Essen (1911). The style of the housing was very diverse. There were simple barracks designed for young, single, mobile, male workers, and ambitious cottage-style lots for more deserving staff who had been with the enterprise for a decade or more. Employees needed to have twenty-two years of seniority to even be considered for these low-density projects. Although the mass accommodation erected after 1890 by the Krupp company offered a great variety of amenities – including a beer hall – these neighborhoods would never have a participatory or emancipatory effect. Because workers' tenancy agreements were linked to their employment, losing your job meant losing your house. Political or union activities were forbidden. In *Reichstag* elections, Social Democrats had no chance of winning votes. Factory control and rules reached the home. Those living in these surroundings for a longer time, especially in the privileged cottages, felt a sense of pride at being part of one of the biggest enterprises in Europe. The term *Kruppianer* signaled a special relationship of enterprise solidarity, family-like emotions, and national importance. These forms of mass accommodation existed in other sectors as well. In the sugar beet industry, for example, it was very common for seasonal workers to reside in very poor housing conditions; the same was true of the horticulture sector. Here, extremely high mobility rates made durable socializing effects nearly impossible.

Fourth, despite social segregation in German cities, nearly all neighborhoods were lived as contact zones between workers and the lower middle classes. With a higher standard of living, workers could afford better housing and to move to more privileged, less populated areas of town. With the development of public transport and its availability for workers, too, suburbs took on a more mixed social structure of employees, civil servants, and better-off workers. The number of public transport users increased steadily: in Erfurt from about 2.2 million in 1895–1896 to nearly

---

26 For an overview, see Cedric Bolz, "From 'Garden City Precursors' to 'Cemeteries for the Living': Contemporary Discourse on Krupp Housing and *Besucherpolitik* in Wilhelmine Germany," *Urban History* 37 (2010): 90–116.

7.6 million in 1913–1914; in Frankfurt am Main from 29.2 million in 1898 to 110.2 million in 1912. This rendered the workplace and home-making even more spatially separated than before, but also more closely connected. Workers gained flexibility on the labor market, while their home-life stabilized.[27]

Finally, neighborhoods erected by building cooperatives in particular exhibited patterns of social mixing. Initiated often as private-public partnerships and joint ventures between civil society and municipalities, these cooperatives erected smaller flats with two or three rooms. They attracted the lower middle classes as well as workers. While many of these projects were based on liberal, reform-oriented ideas that aimed to connect different strata of society, certain conditions also resulted in very homogeneous milieus. In Erfurt in 1910 and 1911, for example, a building cooperative whose members mostly belonged to the middle classes and the municipal notables used municipal subsidiaries to establish a neighborhood with 326 three-room flats. More than ninety percent of the residents were workers. One-third of these apartments housed only two occupational groups: shoe makers and metal workers. These were prestigious professions in Erfurt. Situated close to the party and the people's hall, this area represented the stronghold of the Social Democratic milieu. In the 1912 *Reichstag* elections, eighty percent voted for the Social Democratic candidate (compared with fifty-three percent in the whole city). A building cooperative dominated by the local liberal and conservative urban elite had helped to create a milieu in opposition to their political affiliations.

These findings lead us back to the starting point of this essay, having explored the emergence of different forms of housing for workers and the middle classes in Imperial Germany and shown the influence of neighborhoods on working-class social structures. These processes led to the emergence of political spaces with a dominant order and culture. The 'enlarged' working-class parlor reaching the streets, the inns, and the neighborhood networks helped generate contact and communication. But it was born out of necessity, with all its possible tensions and conflicts. This was provisional home-making. Workers wanted to surmount its negative aspects (squeeze, lack of privacy, uncomfortable living conditions) as soon they could afford it, which could be interpreted as a kind of orientation toward bourgeois and middle-class norms and values. But it could also simply be the result of better financial opportunities and better urban housing infrastructure. Both forms of home-making, the enlarged working-class parlor with the positive aspects of communication and class solidarity and mutual support as well as the pride of one's own *gute Stube* could be found in working-class milieus up to and in the years after World War I. Factors such as changing lifestyles, a more individualistic way of life, rising wages, and greater scope for consumption and housing in the 1950s and 1960s increasingly meant the end especially of the first form of working-class home-making, while the other form can be seen as first step towards a retreat to the private sphere. These developments are described as the "end of proletarity" in Western Germany.[28]

---

27 See Jürgen Schmidt, "Public Services in Erfurt and Frankfurt am Main compared (c. 1890–1914): Capabilities in Prussia?" *Urban History* 41 (2014): 247–64.
28 See Josef Mooser, *Arbeiterleben in Deutschland: Klassenlagen, Kultur und Politik* (Frankfurt am Main: Suhrkamp, 1984).

Rukmini Barua

Legacies of Housing in Ahmedabad's Industrial East: The *Chawl* and the Slum

When I began my research in the former mill districts of Ahmedabad in 2011, I was confronted with a curious contradiction. Despite a significant and well documented decline in living standards in these areas following the collapse of the mill industry in the 1980s, residents marveled proudly at the transformations of the built environment.[29] They pointed out the visible improvements in the conditions of their houses and told me routinely that these neighborhoods "no longer seemed like *chawls*."

Chawls, one- or two-room dwellings often built in a row with shared facilities, were an architectural form peculiar to the mill districts of Bombay and Ahmedabad.[30] These structures emerged as the most prominent form of low-income housing for workers during the twentieth century, producing not only a singular built form and architectural aesthetic, but also engendering a distinct social space. That residents today mark their living spaces as distinct from *chawls* raises some questions: What do these transformations of the built environment reveal about property relations in the mill neighborhoods? How can we understand the process of deindustrialization and the loss of employment in the light of coeval improvements in housing? In what ways does the act of home-making reveal a community's aspirations and mobility?

To engage these questions, we must trace the history of housing in Ahmedabad's mill neighborhoods and the history of *chawls* in particular. Drawing on archival and ethnographic research, this essay traces the historical transformations of housing in the mill areas of Ahmedabad. It examines the social and legal dimensions of these built structures, the shifts in property regimes, and the imbrication of social respectability in housing arrangements.

Settling the Mill Neighborhoods

Ahmedabad gained prominence as the 'Manchester of the East' in the 1860s with the rapid expansion of the city's textile industry. As mill chimneys were beginning to sprout across the landscape at the turn of the twentieth century, industrial areas of the city grew eastwards in a semi-circle along the railway line connecting Bombay and Baroda. The first forms of workers' housing were built by mill owners and private landlords. The early built form of the *chawl*, or *chaali* as it is called in Gujarati, mushroomed around the textile mills. A fragile *kutcha* construction originally, *chawls* gained permanence over the years.[31]

---

29 See, for instance, Jan Breman, *The Making and Unmaking of an Industrial Working Class: Sliding Down the Labour Hierarchy in Ahmedabad, India* (New Delhi: Oxford University Press, 2004); B.B. Patel, *Workers of Closed Textile Mills* (New Delhi: Oxford/IBH Publishing, 1988); Manishi Jani, *The Textile Workers: Jobless and Miserable* (Ahmedabad: SETU, 1984).

30 In this article, the term *chawl* is used in both the singular (to identify the dwelling as an architectural form) and in the collective (to signify a cluster of such dwellings which were originally owned *en masse* and continue to have a cohesive social and administrative identity).

31 The term *kutcha* broadly refers to makeshift constructions, primarily of mud and thatch.

The rapid industrial growth of the city was accompanied by a phenomenal demographic increase and a host of civic and urban problems, such as sanitation, urban transport, and over-crowding.[32] Public concerns with the living conditions of the city's workers from the 1920s onwards took two forms. First, concerns arose over the deplorable conditions of habitation. Unsuitable housing arrangements were seen to lead not only to disease and a decrease in efficiency, but also to a "considerable lowering of the moral tone in relation to the sexes."[33] Second, concerns took the form of discussions around the difficulties of executing urban planning projects for the newly incorporated mill areas; disputes centered around who was responsible for the provision of workers' housing.[34] Motivated by ideals of social reform and uplift, key institutions – the Ahmedabad Mil-lowners Association (AMA), the municipality, and the Ahmedabad Sanitary Association – were involved in executing a 'shared vision of the city' in this period.[35] This translated into material interventions in the form of tenements built by the Gandhian trade union, the Textile Labour Association (TLA), cooperative housing schemes launched by the AMA, and workers' housing cooperatives. Despite these efforts, provisions for workers' accommodation remained woefully inadequate, and shelter had to be arranged in the private *chawls* and slums built in the interstices of these planned settlements.[36]

The grim conditions of workers' housing were well documented in trade union publications and the English-language press. The *Times of India* entered the public conversation on questions of workers' housing with vivid descriptions of these settlements:

> There are some hovels, the roofs of which are on a level with the road and there are others into which one cannot get admittance except by squatting on the ground and crawling. Light and air scarcely enter these habitations, and in most centers sanitary conveniences are woefully defective, if not altogether absent. Huts lie scattered about here and there and everywhere, and, where the land or tenement belongs to a private landlord, heavy rents are exacted.[37]

By the end of the 1920s, more than half of the city's population lived under these conditions. The majority of textile workers were crammed into "long rows of tenements facing each other across a narrow passage sometimes not more than six feet in width."[38] Windowless and without any drainage or facilities, these dwellings did not conform to even the very low standards of sanitation required by the civic bodies.[39] Working-class housing during this period was considered to be "unfit for human habitation in fact and law."[40] The blame for these squalid conditions was placed partly on the municipality's reluctance to take action and partly on the avarice of private builders.

---

32 Kenneth L Gillion, *Ahmedabad: A Study in Indian Urban History* (Berkeley: University of California Press, 1968).
33 Textile Labour Association (TLA), *A Plea for Municipal Housing for the Working Classes in the City of Ahmedabad* (Ahmedabad: Labour Union Press, 1929).
34 While the need for adequate housing was recognized, there was considerable disagreement between the AMA, the municipality, and the labor union over who was financially accountable for its provision. AMA Report 1927–28, 101–02; Tommaso Bobbio, "Collective Violence, Urban Change and Social Exclusion: Ahmedabad 1930–2000" (Ph.D. thesis, University of London, 2010): 49.
35 Abigail McGowan, "Ahmedabad's Home Remedies: Housing in the Re-Making of an Industrial City, 1920–1960," *South Asia: Journal of South Asian Studies* 36 (2013).
36 Report on an Enquiry into Working Class Family Budgets in Ahmedabad (Nasik: Government of India, 1928).
37 *The Times of India*, September 19, 1927.
38 TLA, *A Plea for Municipal Housing*: 15.
39 Report on an Enquiry into Working Class Family Budgets in Ahmedabad (Nasik: GoI, 1928).
40 TLA Annual Report 1928: 18.

Land in the industrial east became profitable. Landlords, it was reported, were tempted to divide existing tenements into even larger numbers, adding to the insanitary conditions. The *chawls* soon began to be known popularly by the names of the landlords, local landmarks, or the mills they were attached to. The urban landscape was transformed through the property boom of the 1930s, which encouraged the frenetic pace of *chawl* construction, profiteering by landlords, and a nearly forty-percent increase in rents.[41] The furious construction that was taking place in eastern Ahmedabad paid scant attention to legal requirements.

The Rent Control Act and the Transformation of the Mill Neighborhoods

The pace of *chawl* construction abated in the 1950s due to the imposition of the Bombay Rent Control Act of 1947. The legislation was introduced to curb the high rate of rental inflation in the post-war period and protect tenants from eviction, which accorded *chawl* housing a degree of legal stability. This provided some relief to the mill workers. However, with rent restrictions in place, the construction of *chawls* was no longer lucrative and landlords began skimping on maintenance and repair costs. *Chawl* structures became increasingly decrepit as owners neglected to provide the most basic facilities and residential upkeep. Questions of service provision grew to be ever more contentious as neither the municipality nor the *chawl* owners were willing to assume responsibility. The greater tenurial security now enjoyed by the *chawl* residents was accompanied by rapidly deteriorating material conditions.

From the early years of their involvement in everyday neighborhood affairs, the TLA's activism included a strong focus on social reform. Their attempts to ensure decent living conditions went beyond agitating or negotiating for better material conditions of housing, and included efforts to introduce certain notions of respectability, morality, and temperance. Through the 1950s, the TLA amplified their involvement in the quotidian affairs of the mill district. Cleanliness, housekeeping, and home decoration emerged as key areas of engagement. Advice on "proper elegant arrangement of household articles in rooms," "simple methods of decorating rooms and tenements," and directives towards "reform of harmful social customs" were offered.[42] This mode of home-making was centered around acquiring dignity and respectability and was presented as a way of reforming the city's working classes into responsible citizens of a newly independent India.[43]

Other more informal and precarious forms of housing emerged in the mill districts, as land owners rented out small plots of land for mill workers to build physically and legally unstable dwellings at the borders of the more established *chawls* (which allowed for easier access to water and sanitation).[44] The mill neighborhoods of the early 1950s, then, had two dominant forms of housing – the *chawls* and the slums. Reports from the mill districts suggest that the material distinctions between the two built forms were negligible. The *Majoor Sandesh*, the TLA's mouthpiece, for instance, consistently regarded local housing arrangements as sites of deprivation, disrepair, and dirt. The union's documentation of living conditions was accompanied by an underlying moral

---

41 Report of the Rent Enquiry Committee (Bombay: Government of India, 1939).

42 TLA Annual Reports 1950: 47–48.

43 TLA Annual Report 1950: 46.

44 *Majoor Sandesh*, June 2, 1951. I thank Siddhi Shah for the Gujarati translations.

judgement on life in these areas, as the TLA identified laziness, carelessness, and illiteracy as reasons for the squalor.[45] The two lines of action that the TLA pursued – one of gentle encouragement towards aesthetic reform; the other of blaming and shaming – bring into relief the relationship between the emerging hierarchies of housing and notions of social respectability.

Questions of the legality of residential structures surfaced repeatedly in the mill areas, further highlighting the hierarchies of housing. Complaints of encroachment on *chawl* premises, constructions of illegal hutments, and infringement of civic resources were routinely brought forward by *chawl* dwellers, testifying to differential claims on urban social space.[46] Slum settlements, which had already attracted much public concern, grew to be a more significant worry for the civic government and social reformers. Slum clearance was furiously debated as a strategy for relieving congestion in the industrial districts, an option that the TLA often endorsed.[47] Slum housing, while not materially greatly different from *chawl* housing, was nevertheless marked out by its impermanence. The *chawl* and the slum were being gradually delineated through everyday negotiations with the municipal authorities, landlords, and union officials.

Chawl – Slum

The 1960s witnessed a prodigious increase in the numbers of slum settlements, which was met by coercive state action in the form of demolitions and evictions.[48] While slums were identified as targets of state interventions, studies pointed out that living conditions in the *chawls* were equally bleak.[49] *Chawl* rents had stagnated at a uniformly low rate and tenants gradually began buying out their *chawls*, either as individual or joint investments. While *chawls* were briskly changing hands (though often through legally tenuous means), tenancy rights were imbued with greater heft following the 1963 amendment of the Rent Control Act. Along with a far greater protection from eviction, this amendment allowed for newer, stronger claims that tenants could stake on *chawl* properties, assigning a degree of ownership that was previously absent. The protection that *chawls* enjoyed against evictions and demolitions were clear markers of social respectability in these neighborhoods.

The Ahmedabad Municipal Corporation had ended its involvement in the provision of housing by 1974 and changed its strategy from the construction of residences to acquisition. In the official slum censuses, *chawls* were viewed as materially similar to slums, while at the same time, marked out as administratively distinct.[50] The TLA's electoral influence had waned, by this point, and the residents of the mill neighborhoods lost the institutional access that the union provided to the state agencies. New legislations, such as the Gujarat Slum Areas Act of 1973, cemented the slum as a legal category. By investing local bodies with wider discretionary powers in regulating construction and demolishing settlements, the Act precipitated a new form of precarity in urban

---

45 *Majoor Sandesh*, January 6, 1951.

46 See for instance, *Majoor Sandesh*, July 9, 1958.

47 Select AMC resolutions 1951–54.

48 AMC Revised Development Plan 1975–1985 (Ahmedabad Municipal Corporation): 13.

49 Mahesh Bhatt and V.K. Chavda, *The Anatomy of Urban Poverty: A Study of Slums in Ahmedabad City* (Ahmedabad: Gujarat University, 1979): 20. Bhatt and Chavda suggest the term 'chawl' slum' to capture the similarities between the two forms.

50 "A Report on the Census of Slums: Ahmedabad City," (Ahmedabad Municipal Corporation, 1977): 3.

living. It was against this background that the Ahmedabad Municipal Corporation began acquiring large swathes of *chawl* properties at a nominal cost across the mill areas for the purposes of slum upgradation.

As the legal and administrative demarcations between *chawls* and slums were hardening, the distinctions between the two were also paradoxically collapsing. With the Ahmedabad Municipal Corporation's policy of acquiring *chawls* for 'slum upgradation,' the *chawls'* legal status grew increasingly more fragile – with a perpetual threat of eviction and displacement, especially since the Rent Control Act no longer applied to these spaces. The attempt towards upward mobility in the mill districts through investments in housing was undermined by municipal efforts to re-designate these areas as slums. A shaky tenurial regime was produced through successive civic initiatives for upgrading slums. Envisioned objectives of these exercises included enhancing the social status of the residents and upgrading and integrating slums "into the mainstream of society."[51] Under these programs, residents contributed financially to and entered the scheme as "partners" rather than as "beneficiaries." This implication of ownership and investment, and the possibility of social mobility, however, had an uneasy relationship with actual legal rights over the land. At best, the residents retained some form of informal claims, with such settlements being protected from eviction for ten years at a time.[52] Indeed, the prospects of "transforming the slum into a colony or society" or for that matter, the increased social status that these projects were expected to engender, remained untenable with the mere provision of an informal tenure of ten years. The upward mobility that was offered through the perpetually possible, yet ever postponed, promise of secure tenancy rights remained uncertain.

Mill Closures and Contemporary Ahmedabad

The early 1980s ushered in a period of crisis for the textile industry from which it would never recover. The mill closures from 1985 onwards resulted in an extensive loss of employment, with nearly 125,000 workers retrenched.[53] Historical transformations that were occurring in this period left deep spatial traces on the industrial districts: the closure of textile mills; intermittent sectarian violence in the city through the 1980s and 1990s, which prompted distress sales and property transfers; the continued appropriation of *chawls* by the Municipal Corporation. These shifts made real estate in the mill districts both profitable and precarious.

Industrial restructuring precipitated multiple forms of insecurities in these neighborhoods. The closure of the textile mills ensured that the *chawls* that stood on mill lands were ensnared in long, drawn legal battles over ownership. Compensation for workers was fraught with complications, since the mills had declared bankruptcy and the sale of the mill lands was hampered by years of litigation and land disputes. As reparations started trickling in, however, the landscape of these neighborhoods changed dramatically. The first investment made by the former mill workers was in refurbishing the existing *chawls*. Workers, who even after fifty years of service had not been able to add a second story to their *chawls*, could now afford to invest in renovating their residences.

51 World Bank, "The Slum Networking Project in Ahmedabad: Partnering for change, Water and Sanitation Program" (2007): 2; "Parivartan and Its Impact: A Partnership Programme of Infrastructure Development in Slums of Ahmedabad City" (SEWA Academy, 2002): 35 ff.
52 AMC Resolution no. 476 dated June 20, 1996; *The Times of India*, Ahmedabad edition, March 8, 1997.
53 Breman, *The Making and Unmaking of an Industrial Working Class*: 255.

On the foundations of the original low-roofed, white-washed one- or two-room structure, two or sometimes three stories were added. The walls were tiled, cement floors were laid indoors, and most importantly as a marker of social respectability, an attached toilet and bathroom were added. A new aesthetic was being actively produced in these areas – new furniture was acquired; shelves were fitted on the walls to would display the 'good' kitchen articles and decorative items. Home-making appeared as a way of negotiating the dispossession brought on by the mill closures. Refurbishment, however, moved these residences into a zone of illegality because the requisite building permissions had not been acquired from the Municipal Corporation.

Urban restructuring through the practice of slum upgradation placed these residences in a legally tenuous zone, while industrial restructuring destabilized the historically strong claims of *chawl* residents. Simultaneously, a shift toward gentrified housing and a visible articulation of upward mobility was occurring precisely at a time when the secure tenancy rights that these areas had enjoyed thus far were being steadily threatened. When I was conducting fieldwork in 2011 and 2012, the mill districts were often referred to as "*chawl* areas" or "slummy areas" by my middle-class and more affluent interlocutors. The *chawl* dwellers themselves, on the other hand, stressed how these spaces no longer seemed like *chawls*, bringing to the fore the dissonance between how they saw themselves and how they were viewed by the affluent city. This contradiction reflects not only the changing subjectivities of *chawl* dwellers, but also hints at the long history of struggles and negotiations involved in making an urban life.

Felicitas Hentschke

'Refugees Welcome': German Civil Society and the Day of Arrival of One Million Refugees

In June 2015, the Hungarian government announced that it would build a 175 km fence along its borders to stop the flow of refugees, mainly from Syria, Iraq, and Afghanistan. Hungary did not want to take in any more refugees.[54] Thousands waited outside the closed gates to apply for asylum. The precarious situation on the ground quickly became a crisis and was hardly bearable by August and September. In addition, a picture that inflamed the mood made its way around the world during that time. This was the photo of a drowned three-year-old refugee from Syria, Aylan Kurdi. His family had fled from the Syrian war zone to Turkey at the end of August 2015 and was about to make the journey from Bodrum, Turkey, to the Greek island of Kos in a boat organized by human traffickers. The overcrowded boat capsized in the high swell of the Mediterranean Sea. The little corpse in denim shorts was washed up on the Turkish beach. This picture spread around the world and influenced public opinion in many countries. It stirred up, outraged, and strengthened the willingness of many to help.

In view of rising refugee numbers and the decreasing willingness of many countries to accept refugees, the German government predicted a refugee crisis as early as August 2015. The German idea of temporarily suspending the Dublin Regulation for Syrians for this reason spread rapidly. Many people who — coming from the southeast — had waited in vain for entry or transit through Hungary set off on foot, bypassed Hungary, and walked on to Western Europe and especially Germany. Incredible pictures of huge groups traipsing along roads and motorways went through the world press. In order to avoid an escalation between German border police and the large numbers of people marching in, German Chancellor Angela Merkel declared a humanitarian emergency at the European borders which demanded an exceptional humanitarian decision — one day after the publication of the picture of little Aylan Kurdi on September 4, 2015. She allowed thousands of refugees coming from Eastern Europe to enter Germany without the typical border controls. Supported by a strong wave of public approval, she campaigned for their friendly reception in Germany and pleaded for their rapid integration. With her repeated slogan of "We can do it," she tried to give courage and confidence.

In the first three days, about 15,000 people crossed the German-Austrian border.[55] According to EASY Gap, 650,000 refugees had arrived in Germany by the end of 2015. 300,000 people entered the first quarter of 2016,[56] of which 80,000 came to Berlin. After that, the number of arrivals dropped

---

54 The following text is primarily based on my experiences and observations as a volunteer and member of the grassroots initiative THFwelcome e.V., together with like-minded people, since September 2015 working with refugees in the former Berlin airport Tempelhof. Civil society is understood here as "individual action ... that is characterized by voluntary action, a lack of personal materially gainful intent and an orientation towards the common good." Individuals organize themselves in groups and act jointly, for example in the form of initiatives and associations. See the report on the situation and perspectives of civic engagement in Germany, published by the Federal Ministry for Family Affairs, Senior Citizens, Women and Youth, Berlin, June 2009, p. 383.

55 Georg Blume et al., "Grenzöffnung für Flüchtlinge. Was geschah wirklich?" *Die ZEIT*, August 22, 2016.

56 In 2015, 1,091,894 people were registered as asylum seekers with EASY (initial distribution of asylum seekers) and 441,899 first applications for asylum were submitted to the Federal Office for Migration and Refugees (known by its

rapidly.[57] The largest group of those who applied for asylum in Germany in autumn and winter 2015–2016 came from Syria (49.5 %), followed by Afghanistan (21 %), Iraq (10.9 %), Iran (4 %), Pakistan (1.9 %), and other countries such as Lebanon, Algeria, Morocco, Eritrea, Somalia, and the western Balkans.[58] Between 300 and 400 people were arriving in Berlin every day during the first few months, often without belongings, freezing and hungry. They had to report to the State Office for Health and Social Affairs (known by its acronym LAGeSo for *Landesamt für Gesundheit und Soziales*), then responsible for the initial registration of arriving refugees, and were distributed from there to various emergency shelters in the city, which were set up without further ado.[59] Many people came without papers. Their identity was often not ascertainable. The number of people with a reason for asylum could no longer be distinguished from those who were taking the opportunity to improve their economic and social situation. Under these conditions, the alleviation of their immediate plight came first and foremost, which affected everyone equally; reasons became irrelevant. Accordingly, this essay will no longer distinguish between immigration groups, but rather speak only of migrants in general.

The authorities were overwhelmed by the onslaught. Gymnasiums and schools, shelters for the homeless, and air domes were hastily prepared. Contracts were signed with private companies to organize these facilities, which now sprouted like mushrooms. The largest emergency shelter was planned in the former Tempelhof Airport, which had closed in 2008 and whose buildings and grounds were still largely empty. Up to 6,000 people were to be accommodated in the historic aircraft hangars. But there never were that many. At first, collective tents were set up in the huge halls, and temporary room dividers were later used to create smaller housing units for up to twelve people each. However, these residential containers had no roof, which meant that noise levels were permanently high and pigeons soiled the beds of the inhabitants. As the airport is a listed building, the operating company could not even drive a nail in the wall by law, and the installation of sanitary facilities became a major problem. For weeks, the residents were taken by bus to nearby

---

acronym BAMF for *Bundesamt für Migration und Flüchtlinge*). The difference — the *EASY Gap* — for 2015 was therefore 649,995.

57 On 18 March 2016, the EU concluded an agreement with Turkey on the re-admission of refugees and in return, in addition to financial resources, offered to seek the lifting of the European visa requirement for Turkey. In addition, the closure of the so-called "Balkan route" gradually reintroduced border controls and difficulties in applying for and obtaining asylum or acquiescence. The EU agreement with Turkey and many of the new state measures were heavily criticized by many international refugee organizations such as ProAsyl and Amnesty International.

58 The legal basis for Merkel's decision was not clear at the time. At present, there is still some debate in politics and society as to whether the German Federal Government would have been obliged under its constitution to make a different decision: carrying out effective controls of the federal borders rather than allowing uncontrolled access to migrants. There is also debate as to whether the common European border security and immigration system (Dublin III Regulation), which unfortunately was overstretched and already riddled with holes, should not have been insisted on. An entry permit for hundreds of thousands of people from September 2015 did not exist. Nor was the exception of the Asylum Act § 18 paragraph 4 no. 2 used as a basis. Instead, a "right of self-entry" from European law was used as an argument for the opening of the German border. Cf. Klaus-Rüdiger Mai, "Grenzöffnung der Flüchtlinge: Die Kanzlerin und das Recht," *Cicero*, September 22, 2017. The statistical figures are taken from the information provided by the Berlin Refugee Council: http://www.fluechtlingsinfo-berlin.de/fr/pdf/FR_Asylaufnahme_Hintergrund_04Jan2016.pdf.

59 The first step is for asylum seekers to go to the State Office for Refugee Affairs (known by its acronym LAF for *Landesamt für Flüchtlingsangelegenheiten)* for registration. There they receive their proof of arrival (*Ankunftsnachweis*). This includes taking fingerprints, a photograph, and personal details such as name, date of birth, origin, and mother tongue. They undergo a medical examination and receive some "pocket money." Then, the BAMF receives the new file, checks it, and makes a decision on the asylum application. The Foreigner's Registration Office (*Ausländerbehörde*) is responsible for issuing a visa (tolerance pending expulsion, subsidiary protection, or asylum status).

public swimming facilities to shower. Few were vaccinated and the risk of an epidemic of infectious disease such as measles or mumps weighed heavily on their accommodation as a possible public health crisis.

Humanitarian First Aid for Refugees in Berlin

Addressed by heartwarming images from the media, in which German citizens on the Bavarian border with Austria gave exhausted migrants water and blankets, people were woken up to dramatic scenes in front of the LAGeSo; the neighborhoods around the new accommodations were shaken up. According to historian Jürgen Kocka, the empathic reporting turned volunteers and thus civil society into media stars.[60] Support groups were formed, organized via an internet platform called *volunteer-planner.org*.[61] Neighborhood networks such as "New Neighborhood Moabit," "Kreuzberg Helps," and "Tempelhof Helps" spontaneously set up collection points for the essentials that the arrivals lacked: blankets and bags, baby supplies and buggies, laundry, and warm clothing. People from the neighboring districts of Kreuzberg, Neukölln, and Tempelhof also came together at Tempelhof Airport. Everyone, women and men, young and old, educated and not educated, employed or seeking work, wanted to get involved, to do something to alleviate the need. The spectrum of those who got involved was very heterogeneous. Helping was very easy: there was something for everyone to do. There was a lack of everything – we collected clothes, shoes, bags, and blankets in the neighborhoods and nearby schools and sports clubs. School bags and toys, sports equipment and books. We collected sofas, because there were no social spaces in the hangars. Mostly the inhabitants just stood around in the cold. The electrical sockets, which were concentrated at a few points, became meeting points while mobile phones were charging. The operating company Tamaja GmbH gave us volunteers a room to collect donations in kind. Often individuals came with bags full of clothing to donate and put them in front of the door. We organized the distribution of the clothing to the residents. Although the camp quickly filled up, it still lacked everything: men's trousers were often too big, the ladies' clothes inappropriate. The shoes were often too worn and could no longer be used. The shame felt by many asylum seekers was great. The volunteers also took on tasks for which the operating company or the authorities would have been responsible: we equipped the approximately 900 children with school supplies. We collected donations for Christmas presents. We organized clothing and especially underwear. We built a childcare facility, a huge scaffold with small hiding caves where traumatized children could hide if it all became too much for them. Every day, at least ten volunteers were employed in the clothing room alone to collect and distribute donations, even on Sundays, even during the Christmas season. Volunteers in other accommodation centers organized soup kitchens. The operating companies lacked personnel across the accommodation. Food was organized in canteens. It was a difficult time for mothers. They could not care for their children, who preferred to be at the childcare center, nor could they wash or cook. Many of them suffered terrible depression. The largest group

---

60 Jürgen Kocka, "Die Zivilgesellschaft als politische Potenz. Erfahrungen aus der Flüchtlingskrise," *Neue Gesellschaft/Frankfurter Hefte* 1/2 (2017): 13.

61 Volunteer-planner.org is a free and ad-free platform for coordinating volunteer services in emergency and community accommodation. The platform is constantly being developed by a group of volunteers who call themselves coders4help, an initiative to develop technical solutions for humanitarian purposes.

was made up of young men travelling alone. They tried to escape the confinement of the accommodation by walking the streets during the day.

The situation stabilized in spring 2016. The authorities were overwhelmed: the processing of asylum applications, the payment of the operating companies, and the supplies for the migrants remained unreliable. The processes were changed again and again. But fewer people came every day. No one had to freeze or sleep outside before their initial registration. Showers and washing machines were now available in the airport building. Some of the residents could afford to buy their own clothes and, above all, wash and reuse worn clothes. There were interpreters for various languages to give people official and local guidance. "Welcome classes" were set up and more and more children were able to go to school. Residents continued to help out at the clothing store, as interpreters or simply lending a hand.

And then out of this situation, we founded the small, formalized non-profit association THF-welcome e.V. for "refugee help, international understanding and civic engagement."[62] Hand in hand with the residents, the approximately fifty association members, the majority of them young people between the ages of twenty-five and thirty-five, built a café together. Some of the inhabitants were trained as baristas and worked daily behind the counter. The artists and musicians from the hangars found a space to show their skills. There were regular concerts and cultural events. Here, refugees and residents mingled. "German now," a sponsorship program, the "Asylum Library," a library with special literature for spreading German and European culture and language, moved into the café. We organized a bicycle workshop where the residents could assemble their own bicycles, a women's café where the women could share their concerns and exchange ideas. We organized sewing machines, and many women came to sew their own clothes and blankets.

But there were also tensions with the operating company. Volunteering and the management of the accommodation depended on each other. Volunteer work would not have been possible without the availability of space on site; without the volunteers, the operating company would not have been able to offer the residents a socially integrative and cultural program. It remained a tightrope walk. No one wanted to relieve the State of Berlin of its responsibilities or even the local limited liability company, which fell under its responsibility. No one should be able to profit by volunteering. We did not want our work to be welcomed but our ideas of integration and refugee assistance rejected. We were also committed to the idea of an open, humane, inviting policy with the goal of integration, as represented by the long-established Berlin Refugee Council (*Berliner Flüchtlingsrat*).[63] The rather inflammatory slogan "refugees welcome" was also meant to be taken seriously.

---

62 THFwelcome is a registered non-profit association in which a lot of creative energy is concentrated and which works together with the people arriving here so that they can escape the isolation of the emergency shelter/community accommodation at Tempelhof and shape their lives in a self-determined way. THFwelcome is as a platform for ideas and projects, exchange, and encounters. See: http://thfwelcome.de/.

63 The Refugee Council Berlin e.V. was founded in 1981 and is committed to improving the living conditions of refugees and safeguarding their human dignity. It fights for the right to asylum and refugee protection and the reduction of state discrimination in particular. The Refugee Council deals with the Berlin Senate, authorities, associations, parties and politicians in order to defend the rights of refugees. See: http://www.fluechtlingsrat-berlin.de/unserearbeit.php.

Civil Engagement Between First Aid and Integration Politics

The plight of many people in the first months following the historic decision of Chancellor Merkel on September 4, 2015, was a gift for many helpful Germans. It offered an opportunity to demonstrate openness and tolerance. It was a counterweight to the burden of the historical experience of National Socialism. Many people were moved by the community experience, the associated creation of meaning, and the idea of helping to shape social life by their own efforts. As the flow of migrants abated and structures were established, civic engagement declined noticeably. In this phase of calming, the emergence of new structures and routines, the first common ground for many Germans and Berliners who had rolled up their sleeves and made a decisive contribution to accommodating one million people at once, fell apart. The large heterogeneous community of those who made a civil society contribution to Merkel's "We can do this" crumbled.[64] Remaining were those who had experienced a holistic encounter with asylum seekers, for example through German lessons, sponsorship, or other projects, or those who were able to build up new social networks in the realm of neighborly refugee aid, which compensated for their own lack of family, professional, or social integration. Some drew on the social recognition of the gratitude on the part of those who could be helped. Others again saw it as a political task to continue to be involved in society and to have a say in public life, especially in this upheaval.

While the world looked on at Germany with admiration, the mood in the country changed. Concern about excessive demands increasingly interfered with the basic willingness to accommodate people. There was broad support for the reception of war refugees and persecuted people who are entitled to asylum under European and German law. But the call for a reduction in the number of migrants, for tighter border controls, and for the prevention of abuse became louder. It became clear how difficult and lengthy integration could be — fears of excessive immigration spread. A large middle-class group grew who became increasingly skeptical and critical of the quantity and nature of the influx without wanting to be completely isolated or concidered xenophobic.[65] And in the right-wing of the political spectrum, populist movements gained ground, often with anti-liberal, racist, and Islamophobic or xenophobic strands such as the "Patriotic Europeans against the Islamization of the West" (Pegida) or the right-wing extremist "Identitarian Movement." The right-wing party "Alternative für Deutschland" (AFD), which was only founded in 2013, experienced an enduring upswing that even brought it into the federal parliament as the third strongest party in the 2017 federal elections. The shift to the right in the party landscape had a strong impact. Those who continued to volunteer shifted the focus of their own voluntary work. They are now less concerned with securing basic needs than with integration issues. THFwelcome concentrated on the services for the residents of the hangars: German lessons, help in finding accommodation and in asylum procedures. We cooperated with sports clubs, organized visits to and put on art and cultural events. In addition to the original fifty members, THFwelcome also had a large following around it, many of whom gradually retreated, while tourists and new Berliners in particular joined in, who also knew the pictures of the initial phase and wanted to be part of this story. They were disappointed when they realized that the tasks had changed in the meantime.

---

64 As the movement in society as a whole slowly disintegrated; it has since been mainly those who were able to allocate their time flexibly who remained on the ball: students, unemployed, pensioners. Most of them are academics, among them many creative people and people from social professions.
65 This is how Jürgen Kocka describes the relationship of civil society in 2015 to its own history and its coming to terms with it. Kocka, "Die Zivilgesellschaft als politische Potenz": 14.

The Berlin Senate reacted to the loss of volunteers and tried to create new incentives for civic engagement in what is still officially called refugee aid (*Flüchtlingshilfe*).[66] As in other places in Berlin, the Tempelhof-Schöneberg district government introduced an event titled "Integration in Dialogue" to learn from volunteers for the development of integration concepts and to motivate volunteers to stay onboard.[67] In the cooperation agreements with the market-oriented operating companies for emergency and shared accommodation, Berlin has stipulated an obligation to cooperate with volunteers since 2016.[68] Such contracts promoted the linking of volunteering activities with the economy. Berlin had good reasons to strengthen this interdependence: social cohesion is strengthened through state support for local charitable activities. Volunteers act as multipliers for a positive image of migrants; they also act as bridges between different social groups among German citizens. The state cannot do without their services, it tries to support and promote them.[69] Germany has still not passed new amendments to its immigration law. Revising immigration policy has become more urgent since the "long summer of 2015," because no one can assume that the flow of migrants will abate for good.[70] The integration of all these newly arriving people of different origins is a Herculean task for both the state and society. Intensive civil society involvement and neighborly help will be indispensable if the formation of new parallel societies is to be prevented.

THFwelcome was close to dissolution in autumn 2017. The café had to close because the rooms were to be used for other purposes. The members were exhausted and there was no vision to continue working under the changed conditions at Tempelhof Airport. The work had been very successful until then. Through the association, especially the café, many former residents of the emergency shelters have managed to make the leap into a regular life on the basis of tolerance or the granting of subsidiary protection. The younger ones began their studies or completed internships and began professional training programs. The artists in particular were able to quickly integrate themselves into Berlin's art scene with their skills.

Against this backdrop, a small group of volunteers finally managed to meet the challenge and continue the association. The bicycle workshop still exists today. Former residents, who have long since moved on and live in their own apartments, still come by and say "Hello." The women's group meets every Sunday, and everyday problems are solved over a cup of tea. The last residents of the emergency shelter have had to move to the nearby community shelter "TempoHomes" on the air-

---

66 See Website of the Berlin Senate Department: https://www.berlin.de/sen/ias/presse/pressemitteilungen/2017/pressemitteilung.575377.php.

67 With the series "Integration in Dialogue," the State of Berlin wants to discuss with citizens, administration and associations, refugees and other migrants, initiatives and volunteers how long-term integration into the neighborhoods, the acquisition of housing and the labor market can be achieved. The experiences of committed civil society working on the integration and participation of refugees and migrants in the Berlin districts are an important impulse generator for the development of an overall Berlin concept for the integration and participation of refugees and migrants. See: https://www.berlin.de/lb/inmig/integration-im-dialog/informationen/.

68 Excerpt from the model contract on the operation of an accommodation and the support of the migrants living there (operating company contract): "§ 6 Cooperation with volunteers, donations. (1) The tasks of the operators include cooperation with voluntary and voluntary initiatives and the local district centers as well as their coordination and support. For this purpose, the operator provides the volunteers and initiatives with available common rooms free of charge for the implementation of integrative measures. (...) (3) The operator treats the volunteers with consideration and in partnership and strives for constructive conflict resolution."

69 Misun Han-Broich, Stärkung der Zivilgesellschaft in der Flüchtlingshilfe. Die Perspektive der bürgerschaftlich Engagierten, in: *betrifft: Bürgergesellschaft* 43, February 2013.

70 Sabine Hess et al., eds., *Der lange Sommer der Migration* (Berlin: Grenzregime III, 2016).

field — an even worse transitional solution. We are getting to know them, sewing and dancing with them, and trying to support their everyday life in Germany.

We Make History

Recently, together with colleagues from the Neighborhood Museum (*Nachbarschaftsmuseum*), another civil society initiative, and a group of migrants who have been in Berlin since 2015, I visited the now-evacuated hangars at the airport. Hangar 1 also houses the Berlin Arrivals Centre for the initial registration of newly arriving migrants and a sports area open to the public, which we built in 2016 with a great deal of volunteer work in cooperation with the operating company.[71] Migrants and residents, associations and welcome classes can meet here. Together we visited the hangars and talked about the history of the airport from its creation in 1923 until today. Wherever migration policy leads, all participants felt at this moment that their own history is connected with the history of the airport and that together we have at least added to its annuls.

---

71 Unfortunately, this still includes short-term accommodation in the hangars of the former Tempelhof Airport for newly arriving asylum seekers before they are transferred to other accommodation.

Section 7
**Being at Home in the World:
Thinking with Houses and Homes**

Milena Kremakova

Making Home on the High Seas: Bulgarian Seafarers between Ship and Shore

Once on shore I quickly start longing for the sea, yet when I am at sea, I always long for home.[1]

It was long ago, but I shall never forget my first voyage ... India, exotica, poverty, culture, elephants, the first wage spent on souvenirs for my family ... I had stepped into a deceptive magic world which I have never managed to leave. And so, my life has passed between shore and sea and I was never in my place, and I was nowhere for long.[2]

I

Although the global freight shipping industry carries an astounding ninety percent of world trade, it remains largely invisible for people on shore.[3] For Bulgaria, a small country on the southeast fringe of Europe, maritime transport has been a similarly important – and similarly invisible – industry both before and after the fall of the Iron Curtain.

As part of its post-war industrialization efforts in the 1950s, Bulgaria's new socialist government invested heavily in the development of shipping and deep ocean fishing. They quickly became not only profitable sectors that helped raise the country's Black Sea region out of poverty, but also a strategic source of foreign currency, a vehicle for political nationalism, and a lucrative and exciting international career opportunity for young men from all social strata. Under the socialist regime, the fleets were owned and managed by the state, but carried cargoes all over the world. This meant that between 1945 and 1989 seafarers were among the few Bulgarian citizens who could travel abroad.

In the 1980s, the last decade before the fall of the Iron Curtain, state socialism seemed like it would exist forever. Bulgaria had several national shipping companies with large fleets. The merchant fleets belonging to countries from the Socialist Bloc were owned and controlled by each state, and national trade quotas were negotiated within the Council for Mutual Economic Assistance. With few exceptions, ships in Eastern Europe mostly carried their home countries' flags – opposing the increasingly common global practice of open registries (also less politely called 'flags of convenience').

The events of 1989–1990 ended the economic isolation of former socialist countries. Thanks to existing global business ties and the international recognition of seafarers' education, shipping was absorbed into the global maritime market almost overnight, much faster than other industries.

---

1 Excerpt from an interview with the captain's first mate in a documentary film about the Bulgarian merchant marine, 1987.

2 Excerpt from 'Sailor on Shore', a short story awarded first prize in the Bulgarian Seamen's Trade Union's 2014 literary competition, http://seafarerstu-bg.com/union/?p=538.

3 Very few books have been written about contemporary life on board cargo ships. Among them are Horatio Clare, *Down to the Sea in Ships: Of Ageless Oceans and Modern Men* (London: Vintage, 2015); Rose George, *Deep Sea and Foreign Going: Inside Shipping, the Global Industry That Brings You 90% of Everything* (London: Portobello, 2013); Helen Sampson, *International Seafarers and Transnationalism in the 21st Century* (Manchester: Manchester University Press, 2013).

While foreign companies entered the Bulgarian maritime market and small local firms emerged, the state-owned fleets melted away like icebergs. The deep ocean fishing fleet Okeanski Ribolov went bankrupt in 1998, while its sister shipping fleet, Navibulgar, was slowly slimmed down from two hundred to twenty vessels, and eventually privatized in 2008.

To examine how this fundamental economic and political transformation affected working lives, I interviewed Bulgarian merchant seafarers born between 1935 and 1990 and examined biographical literature, fiction, news, historical records, and documentary film footage.[4] Although a lot has indeed changed since 1989, seafarers' ideas of home seem remarkably stable and unrelated to recent political, economic, and even technological changes. Bulgarian seafarers from all generations go to sea primarily to earn the money they need to build and sustain a home and family on shore (although seafarers from older generations tend to be prouder of their profession and more often see it not only as a job, but also as a vocation). Those who start out with romantic ideals of life on the high seas soon lose them in the social isolation and daily grind of hard work.

Ships are unusual workplaces: they are what Ervin Goffman called 'total institutions,' places where both work and residence take place, and in which small groups of people lead an enclosed, formally administered, and hierarchically organized life for long periods of time. Unlike involuntary total institutions such as prisons, ships are also hotels, homes, workplaces, career ladders, vehicles, and forces of nature all in one. Like in tiny remote villages, or on ships' extra-terrestrial cousins, space stations, there is much loneliness but little privacy: nobody locks their cabin, secrets immediately reach the grapevine, almost everyone is separated from their family or friends, and shared hardships forge lifelong friendships, but also spark conflicts.

Even in the twenty-first century, much of a merchant seafarer's life is spent in waiting: for better weather, for a Telex or email with orders from the shore, for the ship to arrive in port, for a new cargo, for a new seafaring certificate, for news from home. Today, unknown until recently, mobile phones, a stack of SIM cards for different countries, a laptop, and phone chargers have become necessities, but they have not managed to pacify the longing for home. 'Real life' happens on shore. Life at sea is a suspended existence: it feels intense due to the constant flow of events, but is timeless and empty because important events on shore pass you by. My fieldwork diary abounds in vivid quotes describing the mental hardships of working at sea: "There is no life at sea"; ships are "floating metal jails"; seafarers are "voluntary slaves." Their 'sea legs' walk a thin line between cabin fever and iron-sickness – becoming either overwhelmed by sea-life, or addicted to it to the point of being unable to adapt to shore life after injury or retirement.[5]

Year after year, seafarers' lives are spent mostly at sea. Similarly to other migrants who spend long periods away from home, seafarers oscillate between two spaces. Originally the antipode of home, the ship unwittingly becomes a second home. This is why making home on board a ship is an essential and sacred activity, and this is exactly why it is rarely talked about, but instead silently acknowledged and universally practiced. The boundary, or skin, separating one's home from the world is permeable and needs to be constantly maintained and reinforced through material objects and symbolic practices. As the contents of an apartment can reveal much about its inhabitants, the contents of a sailor's cabin show what material objects and what symbols humans cannot live without: a ship's cabin is the bare bones of a home.

So how do seafarers make their makeshift homes on board? What makes a ship a home?

---

4 Milena Kremakova, *Sea Change* (New York: Berghahn Books, forthcoming).
5 'Sea legs' is the ability to walk steadily on the deck of a boat or ship, and a metaphor for adjusting to life at sea.

Most seafarers' lists are like that of any frequent hotel visitor: a comfortable bed, a good sturdy desk or table (nailed to the floor), a chair. Standard ship cabins also have a sink, a mirror, and a telephone set on the wall, so the captain can always reach you even while you sleep. A few comfortable clothes suited for different climates, if you know in advance where the ship is heading; if not, you will buy some on the way. An old pair of shoes. Some books. Portable radio. When my father was young, he used to bring his guitar along to voyages. Now, the first thing he packs for a two-month voyage is a four-month supply of medication for the chronic diseases earned through forty years of work at sea. Beyond that, one can dream: of a clean kitchen with a good chef who bakes fresh bread every other morning, a tidy steward who regularly brings fresh linen, a never-ending supply of mineral water, a cozy common room. Standard cabins on contemporary vessels are equipped with what my father's generation regards as luxuries: a personal chemical toilet, mini-fridge, TV set. On some ships the crew even have Internet access.

The list of needs is potentially infinite, but cabins are small, the workday is busy, and contemporary ships squeeze out even more work and leave less time for boredom. Almost all free time is spent sleeping.

In addition to the bare necessities, even the least sentimental seafarers carry around little pieces of home. Many bring a hobby or craft to pass the time: embroidery, macramé,[6] miniature ship models, cards, chess, and backgammon are popular pastimes. Everyone brings books. But photographs are almost universally the first thing to go into the duffel bag. For young and old seafarers alike, nothing is more important than photographs. The images of parents, a sweetheart or wife, and children are the Ariadne's thread which links the traveler to his real life on shore. My father still carries in his wallet a tattered drawing I made for him as a six-year-old environmental activist: the globe, four giant stick people with different skin colors holding hands across continents, and a two-line poem in crooked capital letters. It was one of my few childhood drawings which did not feature a ship.

No less important, if less freely invoked in the polite company of a female researcher, are other two-dimensional objects of earthly desire: magazine cut-outs of women in provocative poses lurk alluringly inside built-in wardrobes in seafarers' cabins (often next to the family photos).

No cabin is complete without a wall calendar with dates crossed out. Seafarers always keep their dates up to date. These calendars always have three sheets: the top one for the month just passed; the middle one for the current month; and the bottom one for the month ahead. Obsolete calendar leaves are torn off, each is torn up neatly into four pieces, the rough-edged pieces are stacked up, and a hole is punched through so they can be hung on a nail in the wall, or stitched together with thread, to use as a DIY notebook with 144 sheets. These can be seen on any ship, anywhere around the world. Good inventions are simple and easily adopted.

Last but not least, the saints come sailing in. On January 3, 2008 the Bulgarian-flagged Vanessa, loaded with 937 tons of steel billets and 2,008 tons of wire rod coils, with ten Bulgarian crew and a Ukrainian pilot on board, sank due to hull damage during a winter storm in the Sea of Azov. Nikolai Dimitrov was the only crew member to survive the shipwreck. In his shirt pocket he carried a small hand-painted icon of St Nikola, the Orthodox patron saint of seafarers.[7]

---

6 Macramé is a form of textile produced using knotting, rather than weaving or knitting, techniques.

7 A well-researched but unsigned article on the sinking of motor vessel Vanessa, about which hardly any official information is available, can be found here: 'Bulgaria: A Case of Resignation', http://maritimeaccident.org/2009/09/bulgaria/, accessed July 20, 2018.

In the early 1980s, the captain of a Bulgarian cargo ship brought his wife and one-year-old son along on a journey. The ship was chartered in Asia and the family lived on the ship for almost two years. When the ship finally arrived in Varna and the family returned to their apartment in the city, the boy cried for a week begging his parents to take him back home – to the ship where he had spent the first two years of his infant life.

II

In Bourgas, Bulgaria's second largest port-city, every second family is a seafarers' family, and so was mine. Like most workers and their families, we lived in a council apartment. Almost all families of merchant seafarers, port-workers, and industrial fishermen, fifty-seven households inhabited identical two-room apartments in our building. Many have since moved out, but older residents still refer to our building as the sailors' high-rise. The kids from the twin block next door envied our jeans, skateboards, and chewing gum sticker collections. But we envied them, too. Their dads worked in the army or navy, came home every evening after work, and played football with them at the weekends. Our dads spent most of their time in their second home: the ocean.

My father is a merchant captain. He was born in 1950 and has worked at sea for over forty years: first in the state merchant navy, and after his official retirement ten years ago in a small private company. But time runs at different speeds at sea and on shore. My parents joke that they have been married for twelve years, since 1980. The 3,000-ton bulk cargo ship on which my father sails today is thirty-four years old and has eleven other crew. By an accident of history, he sailed on the exact same ship two decades ago, before the company was privatized and most of its fleet sold off for scrap – only then with a crew of twenty-four. In the 1990s, socialism was already in the past, but the cargo fleet was still run by the state. Perhaps because of that, merchant seafarers still had more leisure time on board. The boatswain – a hearty man appropriately named Dobrinko, 'kind hearted' in Bulgarian – was also a great craftsman. Dobrinko built a precise model of the vessel from matchsticks as a gift for my father. It gathered dust on one of our bookshelves for years until my parents got a cat.

With every visit home, I become an archaeologist digging into layers of family history sedimented on the shelves of our tiny flat.

The most garishly sea-themed objects tend to be birthday gifts. Every family member owns multiple striped sailor T-shirts. The obligatory ship's clock on the wall was a gift for my father's fiftieth birthday. An old sextant, re-purposed as a paperweight, lies on top of the household electricity bills. My father's favorite baseball cap is embroidered with a maritime crest – a modest parting gift from the merchant marine where he worked for thirty-five years. Even his tea mug sports the incantation "The captain is always right" and a caricatured pirate. The design is gaudy, but it was a gift from a dear friend.

I don't know for sure how many objects have melted into the material fabric of our home over the years, like shy, silent refugees from the various ships on which my father has worked. You have to know where to look to see them.

The bathroom cabinet with the scratched metal mirror, for example, comes from a cargo ship built in Britain in 1951 for Bulgaria's expanding cargo fleet. I had never appreciated the cabinet's innovative post-war ergonomic design, perfect for small living spaces: in fact, I first learnt its unusual history when interviewing my parents for this essay. When the vessel was sent for scrap in 1984, the crew took whatever objects they could salvage. "It was a mighty vessel, she was built properly and could have sailed decades longer," my father laments. My imagination paints the ship as a strong, healthy metal horse in a futile attempt to fathom the sadness a seafarer may feel when his ship goes to the scrapyard. "It's like seeing your house bulldozed," my father adds quietly.

Take a glimpse at the bookshelves which cover the walls of our small flat. Each is different, home-made one by one during my father's shore leave, using wooden planks left over as scraps from ship cargoes over the years.

Some of the books, a treasure trove of global classic literature and maritime novels translated into Bulgarian and Russian, came from the company library of the old merchant marine. The library lost its building in the early 2000s in the run-up to the fleet's privatization. The desolate librarians had to throw the books out. Several banana crates full of damp literary masterpieces were added to our already-crowded home book collection.

No one at home smokes and cigarettes are no longer the universal informal currency they were during state socialism, but old habits die hard and a few cartons are always hiding on top of the books. Father buys them from tax-free zones during every voyage: as gifts for friends and acquaintances, or as symbolic tokens of gratitude to strangers for small favors. A whiskey bottle hides in the piano with the same mission.

The homes of post-socialist seafarers in particular contain dusty dreams of a magical, affluent world which was once out of bounds, but is now mundane. My sister's and my childhood diaries are in leather-skinned calendar notebooks with maritime company logos on the covers and enticing Mercator maps inside. In the kitchen, grains are stored in old Nutella jars and home-made biscuits in tins of Quality Street, all of which once arrived in my father's duffel bag. The living-room shelves are full of handwritten and photocopied piano scores which my mother diligently collected for her students. The scores are glued onto cardboard from Kellogg's Corn Flakes, a gastronomic luxury which seafarers sailing to Western Europe used to bring home in the 1980s. I remember savoring these exotic, dry, crispy treats without milk as an afternoon snack. One time, my father brought so many cartons that my sister and I built a corn flake fortress in the living room.

Mother's wardrobe is full of once-fashionable clothes which could only be purchased on the west side of the Iron Curtain. Blue jeans from Liverpool, 1981; a skirt from Marseille, 1983; a leather jacket: Salamanca, 1987. On top of the wardrobe are boxes of forgotten toys: Barbie dolls, Kinder Surprise egg figurines, and other wonders once unavailable in Bulgarian shops. A white plastic water container shaped like Jesus has some holy water left in it: Jerusalem, 1998. Behind it, a cardboard box with the inscription "Navigation Maritime Bulgare" contains a set of wooden Montessori cubes which my mother made for me thirty years ago. Another shelf keeps my father's youth: a dusty collection of rock music cassettes from the 1970s and 1980s, stacks of cards with tobacco logos on their coats: gifts from shipping agents in foreign ports. An old, treasured wooden backgammon box: a wedding gift from the captain of the ship on which my father sailed when he met my mother. Dictionaries for tens of languages he never learnt properly. Books of maps, many maps.

Downstairs in the cold foyer of the concrete building, as is the Bulgarian custom, obituary posters hang on the wall. Black and white photos of deceased neighbors show dashing young men in navy uniforms, and the sad poems underneath wish them fair winds and calm seas in their final voyages.[8]

---

8 Obituary posters, known as *nekrologs* in Bulgarian, are common in Orthodox Christian regions of the Balkan Peninsula; see Borislav Gueorguiev, "Pragmatics of obituary posters in Bulgaria," *Lexia* 5–6 (2010).

III

If houses and homes are nodal points between the self and the world, then seafarers are permanently suspended between two such nodes: their home on shore and the ship where they live and work. The tragedy, but also the promise, of maritime work is that it simultaneously reinforces and breaks the uniqueness of the home as a point of ultimate reference. This bi-locational form of domesticity is unstable and stable at the same time: the two spaces are dissonant, but they also complement and interlace with each other.

In any seafarer's home you will find at least a few shells, corals, 'exotic' souvenirs, and other traces of the sea, and every cabin and suitcase treasures a few objects which signify home. But here I am not talking of the maritime symbolism which is commonplace in seaside towns the world over. Seagulls, anchors, boats, seashells, fish, waves, compasses, and blue-and-white stripes are typical decorations in street art, high-street fashion, restaurants, city crests, and company logos. Instead, many of the material objects which mark the private space of a seafarer's home are inconspicuous. More often than not, they are unassuming, transparent objects not meant as a display of identity but as building blocks built into the walls of home – like the bookshelves that cover half of our walls, like the recycled wall calendars, a seafarer's home is like a raft built from driftwood.

When I was little, my father would come home after several months at sea with a huge smile on his face and a large beard which he would immediately shave off to mark the first day of shore leave. His huge duffel bag was full of exciting and often tasty foreign gifts hidden among the old clothes and cigarette cartons, carrying the irresistible smell of ships – that peculiar mix of mold, sea salt, metal, men, and freedom. We cared little of the gifts. His return home was the biggest gift of all. But the neighbors from across the road didn't understand. They kept asking: what did your father bring you?

As a goodbye gift before each new voyage, my grandmother would give my father an aromatic geranium leaf from her balcony, its roots wrapped up in a wet paper napkin, to take with him to the ship. "A sailor must always carry a *zdravetz* leaf! How else will he remember that he is Bulgarian and that his family is waiting for him," she would say.

A seafaring life is a life in two homes at best – or a life where one never feels at home at worst. Seafarers spend their lives suspended between two fleeting worlds, always ready to leave one home at an hour's notice to go to the other. On shore, they often feel like fish out of water, constrained by four walls. But when they return to the ship, the sea stops being a space of imagined freedom and becomes a bottomless space of longing and nostalgia for the imagined idyll of home and family. Both sites of seafaring life share an intense materiality whose meanings remain hidden from land-lubbers. Material objects act as anchors for the emotional land-and-sea-scapes of seafarers' homes on shore and their cabins on board. The home-ship dyad is a two-sited museum of longing in which each site longs for the other but the two cannot meet for longer than fleeting moments.

Perhaps the seafarer's only permanent home, his castle, is his duffel bag.

Isaie Dougnon

Owning a Home in Bamako: To Be at Home after Death

For people in Bamako, the capital of Mali, life after death has been more than merely an existential question for some time. The question is linked to very practical concerns, such as building a house for your children or ensuring an individual's memory upon his death. The funeral of a politician I attended recently profoundly confronted me with the new dimensions a person's house has gained. Many people had gathered at his funeral ceremony. As the guests were leaving, I overheard two women asking a close relative of the deceased a question that caught me by surprise. "Is this his house or does he rent?" they asked. The man replied, "No, this is not his house, he rented," whereupon, in dismay, the two women, with their fingers on their lips and in a sad tone, answered, "He rented? He died without owning a house? Now that his life is over, he will soon be forgotten!"

As strange as it may appear, the need to leave behind a house reflects the intense desire of people in Bamako to build their own house as an important and ultimate act of self-fulfillment. It alludes to the anxiety and despair of those with only modest incomes who struggle to own a house in an increasingly adverse urban environment.

My essay reflects on the meaning of building one's own house in Bamako. I aim to explore how people manage to build houses of their own in economically difficult conditions. The essay is based on the research I have conducted since 2010 on the careers of civil servants in Mali. I use the term 'crises of passage' to describe the stumbling blocks an individual faces in his or her career when he or she aims to reach a level that will give meaning to their life. Buying a house is a major step in the lifecycle of a civil servant in Mali.

My analysis is also a reflection on my personal experience. A few years after I arrived in the capital in 1996, like all my friends, I began looking for a plot of land on which to start building my own house. Like the majority of people in Bamako, I was born and grew up in a rural setting and only later came to the city to work as a civil servant. My personal history weaves an emotional undercurrent into this paper. I have seen how the reflex of wanting to own a house develops once people start to work and found a family. When people are nearing retirement age, this reflex can become an obsession. I have talked to people about the psychological and moral stress of living in rented accommodation, where you are at the mercy of other people for a roof over your head. The people I interviewed emphasized the influence that home ownership has on people's behavior and beliefs. Owning a building plot already situates an individual somewhere between imagination and reality. A finished house, which one has moved into, is a place where one can contemplate one's trajectory: past, present, and future. Most importantly, being at home in one's own house is when and where one can prepare for life after death.

Building a House in Bamako

Bamako is among the fastest growing cities in the world. In less than thirty years, several dozen new neighborhoods have sprung up. Most of the houses in these neighborhoods were not built by private or public property developers. Rather, they were built by the women and men who work in Bamako, or by emigrants who, after working for some time in foreign countries, hope one day to return to Mali. Finished or not, basic or chic, these houses and the frenetic expansion of these neighborhoods express people's irrepressible desire to own their own house.⁹ Considering the low incomes of most people in Mali, there is something heroic in these endeavors.

In Bamako, the meaning of 'being at home' depends on whether the owner has built the house himself. The house underpins the owner's identity; it grants the owner the status of a full or future urban citizen. His house is like an identity card. Unlike an official identity card, however, which offers only limited or renewable validity, houses offer eternal authentication, even after the owner's death. To indicate that a person has truly become a citizen of Bamako, people say, "*abi a ka so,*" which is Bambara and, translated literally, means he lives in his own house.¹⁰ This term has only become popular during the last thirty years; it evolved out of the colonial and postcolonial system of identifying citizens through identity cards.

"I live in my own house" or "I live in another person's house" is a key piece of information citizens have to provide to the police to get their official identity card. The card certifies a person's address. The point of this question is that the applicant must state whether the house they live in belongs to them or whether they only rent it. If the person confirms that they are living in their own house, the police will include this information in the identity card, "Lives in his or her own house." However, if the person only rents the house or flat, the officer will write "lives with XYZ" and add the name of the landlord. A third category exists for those who live with their biological parents or with members of their extended family.

Our modern notion of the home clearly derives from the notion of possession in the legal and economic sense of the term.¹¹ In a legal sense, home ownership starts with the subdivision of plots by the state. Two types of ownership are created: occupancy permits and land titles. Land is inviolable property and, in many ways, is more important than the house itself. The inviolable nature of the plot, which is enshrined in the land title, is a colonial heritage and similar to the sacred and inviolable character of ancestral land in rural areas. The concept of 'home' in the capital is related to traditional ideas of the land as the place where ancestral spirits rest. This concept is key to understanding the negative image people have of flats and houses built by property developers in Bamako.¹²

The different identity card categories result in the division of the citizens of Bamako into three groups: homeowners; tenants; dependents. One of the social consequences of officially identifying people this way is that it creates power relationships where landlords feel superior to tenants.

---

9 After the village of Bamako became the capital of French Sudan at the beginning of the twentieth century, two types of houses began to compete: village-style adobe houses and modern houses (villa style). Adobe houses remain widespread due to the strong influx of rural migrants that spontaneously settled in areas in the town's periphery (from where they could easily be chased away). Adobe house are common in the old neighborhoods in Bamako's center. Such plots are large, like plots in villages, and several generations live here, together with animals such as sheep, goats, chickens, and pigeons.

10 The inhabitants of the capital feel themselves more Malian than people living outside of the capital because the city is the political, economic, and cultural capital. Bamako is also the city with the best infrastructure compared with other cities in the country. People often say, "Mali is Bamako."

11 Over the last twenty years a significant number of people from middle- and high-income groups have chosen to buy their houses through rent-to-buy schemes offered by government and private cooperatives. Although they physically own a house, these people are considered 'homeless' from a cultural point of view. This is because the state holds the property title until they pay their final instalment.

12 Social housing policy based on the construction of large, several-story buildings proved to be a dead end because people did not want to buy flats. For people, the idea of owning one's own place includes being able to walk on one's own soil. People who buy a flat say they have a roof but no house. This explains the exponential growth of Bamako. Everybody wants to own a house with a courtyard and a plot to walk on.

Freedom begins with owning a house. For as long as one rents, one has the feeling of being imprisoned by the landlord and marginalized from urban society. In the 1980s, the disparaging view of renting, its humiliating and degrading nature, became a popular theme for theatre groups and a topic of public debate. In the capital, people talked about this notion in ways that made it seem as though it was more important to own one's own house than to eat. People viewed with contempt those who decided to continue renting although they could afford to buy a house. They treated them as thoughtless, even cursed, people.

Renting is like Living in Prison

People in Bamako compare living in rented accommodation to being in prison or under house arrest. Many of the people I interviewed discussed the disagreeable aspects of renting in terms of the conditions and restrictions landlords impose on tenants. Landlords impose restrictions on the areas that they allow tenants to use within a plot. The wives of tenants are those who suffer most when, for example, owners define strict time limits on the use of the bathroom or shower. If the rent is overdue, the tenant's wife and children may face verbal abuse from the landlord.

When a young civil servant or migrant first arrives in the capital, he usually lives with a close family member or with somebody he knows. As soon as he begins to earn a monthly salary, he will be able to afford to rent a room, called an *entrée couchée*. Tenants share the toilets and a veranda. During this stage, the man is usually single, or *célibataire* in French, which is why the shared room is called a *célibatorium*. If the young tenant has a child, it will be baptized in the house of the oldest person in the village the man is from and who lives in his own house. If his wife moves in with him and his income increases slightly, he will move from the *célibatorium* to a two-room shared house also called a *salon-chambre*. Bamako's poorest citizens continue to live with their wife and children in the *célibatorium*.

Both of these forms of housing usually offer small rooms on larger plots where the landlord also lives, often in a flat that allows him to keep a close eye on his tenants. On such a plot, there can be a dozen single rooms and an equal number of double rooms. In this form of housing, tenants live at the mercy of the landlord's goodwill and whims.

Consider the account of IK:

> I came to Bamako in 1982. It took me twenty-six years to get my own house. In 1982, I first lived with a relative. I stayed with him for eight years, from 1982 until 1990. In 1990, I rented a single room with my wife. Then in 1997, I rented a two-room flat. In 2000, I rented a two-room flat with a living room and an inside shower for 25,000 F CFA [approx. 50 euros]. This was in Kalanbancoro Nèrèkoro, one of Bamako's new neighborhoods. I lived in that flat until 2013, the year I finally moved into my own house. I began looking for a plot in Bamako back in 1991. Speculators stole my money several times. I lost over 400,000 F CFA. Finally, in 1999, I was able to buy a 300m^2 plot in Niamakorokourani for 400,000 F CFA. In 2000, I began to build my house. Every month I would leave 10,000 F CFA at the builder's merchant. As soon as I had saved enough money to buy two tons of cement, I began making bricks on Saturdays and Sundays. When the builder started coming, my children and I helped.
>
> In 2013, I moved there, even though we hadn't even fenced the plot and roughcast the walls. In building, the most difficult thing is laying the floor. Making the foundation is hard, but you can do it bit by bit, but laying a concrete floor has to be done in one go. The other difficult steps are getting the door frames and tiles in, as well as painting and roughcasting. It took me over sixteen years to finish my house.
>
> For me, the problems with renting in Bamako are related to culture and behavior. People from different backgrounds and regions live together on one plot. They don't have the same customs or values. Some pay their electricity bills, others don't. When the supplier eventually cuts the water and electricity off, it punishes both those who have paid and those who haven't. Hygiene is another issue when you rent. Some tenants refuse to clean

the shared showers and toilets; they don't care if they are filthy and that leads to an unbearable stench. For me, renting a flat or a room on a larger plot means a total lack of privacy. Rooms do not have kitchens, the women all cook together in the same court. This leads to jealousy and never-ending fights, because some pots simply have better food in them than others.

This account is typical of people who have come to Bamako to work as civil servants. While they remain tenants, they count the months and years before they can afford to buy a house of their own. Tenant life, moving from one flat to the next, can last for years. Some people are over thirty before they put the first brick of their house down, others even fifty. The most important thing is to finish the house and move in before they retire or before they are physically too weak to continue the work.

Building Ensures a Life after Death

The memory of a deceased person who leaves behind a house will remain alive for generations. Houses must therefore be neither sold nor bought. Sons will teach the grandsons of the builder the principles of their grandfather who built the house in which they live. Even if memories become blurred over time, the house itself remains intact and perpetuates the memory of the builder. The house is an inheritance that creates a link between the living and the dead, between generations, places, and traditions. According to African beliefs, a person who has had the exceptional determination to build a house, will, from time to time, and even after death, return to visit his house. Every house, therefore, should have a place where the ancestors can come to drink. The ancestor's soul will return to keep an eye on the family he has founded. Families perform rituals at each anniversary of the founder's death.

These rituals of commemoration are also opportunities to renew the bonds between members of the wider family. The fact of building the first home in the capital is the root of this connection between generations and memories. Even if the descendants go on to build their own houses and leave the original house, ceremonies such as baptisms, marriages, funeral ceremonies, and the celebration of important religious feasts will continue to take place in their father's house.

For an inhabitant of Bamako there is no greater pleasure than completing his house before he retires and living there in harmony with his family. It is the affirmation of both his moral and material persona. As he grows older, he counts and counts again the number of years during which he has lived in his own house compared with the number of years he was a tenant.

Maybe building a house is, like leisure time in Europe, a condition of the urban spirit, much like the delight of living in a large city. For Bamako's honest workers, their house is their reward for their hard work, patience, and modesty. It is a moral and intellectual patience that needs time. It begins with the laying of the foundation and continues with the other decisive steps in the construction process, punctuated by breaks which may be long or short. For some, the process of building a house is so slow that they wonder whether they will live to see it finished. Because nobody has control over time, one never knows whether one will have the money to continue building. When the house will be finished and how splendid it will be depends on money, which is scarce for the large majority of Malian salaried workers. Many people therefore die before finishing their house.

All of this is linked to the emergence of a new urban culture. Urban life in Bamako is growing exponentially. It is interesting to see how this urban culture is rooted in traditional notions of land, memory, and the myth of the founding builder. As long as Bamako's inhabitants remain attached to the ancestral notion of land, they will continue to build their houses, regardless of the surroundings of their plot. It is the only way of conquering the city and earning the recognition of urban society.

Conclusion

For many inhabitants of Bamako, building their own home is a question of dignity and self-respect. Any person with at least the minimum of resources cannot morally accept the humiliation inflicted on him and the members of his family by a landlord.

However, this scramble to own a house only began recently. According to Mr. Koné, a retired primary-school teacher from Bamako who was born in 1947, people in Bamako lived in adobe house clusters built on large plots until the 1970s. In most cases, traditional chiefs granted people individual parcels of land. Except for the colonial administration, everybody built with adobe. Ten kola nuts given to the neighborhood chief were enough to get a plot of land. When such a plot was on customary land, people who had received their land from the chief and whose houses were affected by planning were resettled to other neighborhoods, which had already been divided into plots.

The idea of the modern house as a symbol of social mobility therefore only took hold as recently as 1978 and the generalized urge to live in one's own house only spread in the 1990s. Bamako has since embarked on a planning program of sub-dividing plots and accelerated urbanization, with concrete being the only authorized building material.

In the old neighborhoods of the city center, however, houses are still owned by extended families. These houses are not only for living in. They are also places where people work and, still today, house numerous small family businesses. The adobe houses in the old center and the cement villas in the newer parts of Bamako have the same role as venues for social ceremonies (birth, death, marriage, rites for the ancestors). There is virtually no difference between the two types of houses in terms of their practical and ceremonial value. Urban life in Bamako takes place more in the public than in the private sphere. Owning a house has without doubt contributed to modern individualist values such as self-confidence, personal comfort, self-esteem, the privacy of family life, and people's inner worth. However, the ceremonies and rituals, which are anchored in society and therefore regularly bestowed upon the heads of family, in most cases eclipse such values. On the inside, many of these villas in the rich neighborhoods of Bamako are village-like homes to large families. A characteristic element of these large families is their public nature. They are the places where ceremonies are held and where close and distant relatives mingle. The important role these houses play in such ceremonies reinforces the myth surrounding the ordeals the owner (whether dead or alive) has gone through to own a house. In most cases, the doors of such a house are open to the entire community and everybody is welcome. They may be closed if the owner restricts their use to his private and family life. This is not as rare as one might think.

Charlotte Bruckermann
From Ancestral Tablets to Patriotic Portraits: Remembering Kinship in Rural Chinese Homes

Living in a home, with the pervasive and ongoing rhythms of everyday activities, constantly evokes memories. Homes not only trigger recollections, but are often built, arranged, and decorated in ways that elicit or sustain memories for those dwelling within. The object world of the home can be seen as an inculcating principle that is not simply handed down by convention but arranged and created with great care and attention.

This is particularly notable when ways of life experience acute rupture. In periods of change and crisis, people must consciously position themselves anew in time and space. Such rearrangements are especially salient in China as the twentieth century brought a shift from a centralized empire to a divided republic at war, eventually reunifying as a nation under the communist government. After the People's Republic was swept up in Mao's tumultuous vision of perpetual revolution, the 1970s ushered in an opening and reform period that reintroduced markets as part of 'socialism with Chinese characteristics.' And yet despite these upheavals, kinship continues to be remembered and memorialized unabated in the home. How is memory work achieved across these historical ruptures? How do kin make claims to each other and over their houses through the home?

This essay analyses how kinship connections take material forms in rural Chinese homes. After the communist revolution in 1949, the changes to the ancestral shrines kept within the home show how kinship was contained within domestic spaces. Complementing shrines for the deceased, new photographic montages of living kin in the home evoke family histories, socialist values, and everyday labor. The high visibility of these kinship relations contrast with the secrecy surrounding written documentation related to homes, particularly genealogical scrolls and housing deeds, which are kept under lock and key in the house. Tensions between a political belonging to the socialist nation and a genealogical commitment to the personal family are thus both revealed and concealed in the home.

Housing Kinship

In the fieldsite where I conducted sixteen months of ethnographic research between 2009 and 2010, contested kinship claims to houses took center stage.[13] The mountain village of Sweeping Cliff was home to 1,200 residents. Positioned on the Loess Plateau in north-central China's Shanxi province, the village population exclusively composed of the Han ethnic majority. The region borders the

---

[13] For more detailed accounts see Charlotte Bruckermann, "The Materiality of the Uncanny: Preserving the Ruins of Revolution in Rural China," *Comparative Studies of South Asia, Africa and the Middle East* 37 (2017); Charlotte Bruckermann, "Trading on Tradition: Tourism, Ritual, and Capitalism in a Chinese Village," *Modern China* 42 (2016): 188–224.

Yellow River, often considered part of the cradle of Chinese civilization. Despite the Han ethnic dominance, most Shanxi residents speak languages belonging to a distinct Jin dialect group.[14]

This linguistic division is reinforced by the province's geography of craggy ravines dropping off into the bristling vegetation of shady valleys below. Ochre terraces with hardy agricultural crops, such as maize, wheat, sorghum, and buckwheat, cut across these gorges horizontally. For millennia, residents have carved houses into the terraces as cave dwellings, giving the architecture its characteristic vault-like rooms connected through doorways. This style of architecture has been retained in the last centuries as people increasingly move above ground. Even in the grand merchant complexes scattered across the countryside and towns since the seventeenth century, this vaulted style of building is commonplace.

The province's history of merchant wealth was part of the reason that home ownership was so contested in Sweeping Cliff. Local merchants had amassed great wealth as leaders of the salt trade and timber sales, as well as pioneering financial services. Following the communist victory, Chinese rural land was collectivized and labor was organized through brigades; the products of the fields were allocated to households on the basis of their labor contributions. The revolution thereby strengthened the house as an economic unit of consumption, while diminishing its importance as a site of production, particularly for cottage industry market goods such as cloth, paper, and garments. Simultaneously, labor, and particularly women's labor, was increasingly externalized from the home into the fields and factories. While agricultural and industrial labor outside the home was valorized, the everyday work necessary for the long-term reproduction of the workforce was rendered increasingly invisible within the confines of the domestic domain.[15]

While China's land redistribution policy has received great attention, the parallel policy of housing redistribution in rural villages such as Sweeping Cliff is less well known.[16] Unlike the temple architecture torn down in other parts of China, Shanxi province's grand domestic courtyard complexes were sectioned into bays and buildings, and distributed to veterans of the revolution. Red Army soldiers and their kin, newly formed conjugal couples, and homeless and destitute families gained access to prime real estate. Because land continues to be owned by the state today, houses have remained the main form of family property in the Chinese countryside and are transferred from generation to generation through inheritance.[17]

With the state appropriation of land, houses in Sweeping Cliff became more important as repositories for attracting wealth and fortune, both through mundane accumulation of goods and through worshiping the ancestors, gods, and other cosmological forces. Houses were legally transferred through inheritance during the Maoist era, but many were also informally bought and sold between families throughout this period. This process has continued to the present day.

---

14 For a brief history of Shanxi Province see David Goodman, "King Coal and Secretary Hu: Shanxi's Third Modernisation," in Feng Chongyi and Hans Hendrischke, eds., *The Political Economy of China's Provinces: Comparative and Competitive Advantage* (London: Routledge, 1999): 211–48.

15 Charlotte Bruckermann, "Caring Claims and the Relational Self across Time: Grandmothers Overcoming Reproductive Crises in Rural China," *Journal of the Royal Anthropological Institute* 23 (2017): 356–75.

16 For an academic review of this literature on land redistribution see Qingyan Meng, "The Land Revolution in China from an Academic History Perspective: Changes in Topics and Paradigms," *Chinese Journal of Sociology* 1 (2015): 419–46. For an evocative village study of housing redistribution based on participant observation and oral history see William Hinton, *Fanshen: A Documentary of Revolution in a Chinese Village* (New York: Monthly Review Press, 1966): 146–56.

17 Xin Liu, *In One's Own Shadow: An Ethnographic Account of the Condition of Post-Reform Rural China* (Berkeley: University of California Press, 2000): 31–57.

A number of documents pertain to the ownership of houses, most prominently pre-revolutionary lineage scrolls and post-revolutionary housing deeds. But many Sweeping Cliff residents have never seen these documents, even those of their own lineages or households, because of the politically sensitive evidence they contained. On one hand, the lineage scrolls showed the genealogical interconnections between people in the village despite the cleavages of class and status. On the other, the contracts documented illicit transfers of housing deeds during the Maoist era.

Dismantling Lineages and Domesticating Kinship

In pre-revolutionary times in Sweeping Cliff, two powerful lineages had public ancestral halls dedicated to collective worship where their lineage scrolls and ancestral memorial tablets were kept. After the establishment of the communist government, these lineage halls were dismantled to make way for more residences and a communal store. Elderly villagers recollected how the male members of the lineage used to carry food and incense offerings to the halls and kowtow in front of grand ancestral scrolls in pre-revolutionary times. These scrolls, documenting male ancestors, were unfurled and hung above the main offering table at important ritual occasions in lineage members' lives, such as births, weddings, and funerals.

The lineage scrolls survived the twentieth century and are kept today within the main lineage branch's principle homes. Nowadays, viewing the ancestral scrolls is forbidden to outsiders and even many younger male lineage members have never seen them, as the keepers of the scrolls argue that the furling and unfurling damages the scrolls. Unlike in other areas of China, where grand lineage halls have been reconstituted in the post-Mao era, the lineage halls in Sweeping Cliff were not restored, but rituals at the gravesite and in homes have become increasingly elaborate with the passing of the reform years.

When the lineage halls were converted in the early days of Maoism, most of the wooden memorial tablets were burned in large pyres. However, many ancestral tablets can still be found in people's homes, especially the tablets of deceased relatives who are still remembered by living descendants. These tablets are carefully stored in the southwest corner of the central bay of the house. As vestiges of feudal superstition, ancestral tablets were not considered objects for a public audience during the Maoist era and were hidden from view in carpentered cabinets. The ancestral tablets themselves are made of wooden rectangular plates rising horizontally from a base, similar to the stone tombstones erected on the actual gravesites of the deceased in the fields. Both the ancestral tablet and the stone tombstone carry the engraved name of the ancestor as written evidence of their existence.

During funeral processions, participants carry the casket of the deceased's body, and the casket is also preceded by a decorative sedan chair transporting her or his soul alongside their ancestral tablet and a photograph of the deceased. After the ancestral tablet is installed in the family shrine, the tablet and photograph continue to be put on public display during annual celebrations and life-cycle celebrations for the birth, marriage, or death of their kin. Through their prominent placement at these festivities, the ancestors are said to watch over their descendants. The ancestral tablets not only recollect or represent the ancestors, they also make them present in the here and now.

In a community where many elderly members cannot read, the photographs may act as mnemonic devices for recollections beyond textual inscription, as well as capturing the imagination of future generations of descendants. Unlike verbal characters, photographs are legible to anyone with the necessary contextual memory to situate their kin's face, whether through memory, experience, or narrative.

A temporal paradox inherent to the photographs of attesting to a reality that was out there, a time that existed but is now gone, stands in tension with the ancestral tablet, where a person may be gone but an ancestor potentially exists forever, or at least as long as there are descendants to worship them and continue the family line. The personalization of the ancestors through photographs therefore actively forges family devotion and helps to secure ritual subjection of a more intimately connected future generation of kin.

The Work of Photography

My fieldwork experience sharpened my attentiveness to photographs and ritual practices, and their vital importance in Sweeping Cliff home life. This was not part of a premeditated methodological plan. One of the benefits of ethnographic research is that recursive enquiry allows the fieldsite to pose its own questions and set its own priorities, such that a mundane act of taking photographs, rather than simply a technique of documentation, became a window into people's lives. My experience was intimately tied up with technological divergences as most villagers in Sweeping Cliff had never owned analogue cameras, but, by 2009, many younger people had mobile phones that could produce low-grain snapshots rather than high-quality digital images.

My camera opened doors to ritual life by eliciting invitations, particularly as I returned the favor of attendance with prints of high-resolution snapshots taken at the events. These photographs were quite different from the stylized group shots most villagers were accustomed to, and villagers appreciated my photographs of unscripted moments at these important events.

On the occasion of a senior matriarch's sixtieth birthday celebration, I was invited to take photographs of her in the main courtyard of her home, arranged with various constellations of kin. As this grandmother sat at the center of her home, various family members arranged themselves around her for each new photograph. The constellations included a photograph with her sons, with her daughters, with her sons and their wives, with her sons, their wives, and her grandchildren, as well as the impressive crowning group shot with all her direct descendants, thirty-four in total! Family members moved in and out of the arrangements, keeping in mind hierarchies of gender, age, generation, and proximity of kin to the smiling celebrant.

Family members also staged joking photographs as they jostled and teased each other in the frame. These included broad grins elicited by the word *qieeeeeezi* (literally translated as eggplant, but used like the word 'cheeeeeeeese' in English), pulling a grandson's ear for being a rascal, or squinting through an imaginary viewfinder made with index finger and thumb back at the camera. These jovial photographs contrast with the formal style of older photographs found in family homes, and yet they are still very strongly constructed and staged images, intended to capture both the boisterousness of the occasion and the personalities of the kin in attendance. The plan for these photographs was to hang them in their grandmother's home to remember this proud occasion where so many of her descendants had assembled.

These types of montages of family photographs often sat on top of the ancestral tablet box. A mirror, which according to *fengshui* wisdom deflects malign forces and repels evil intent, often protected these photomontages of close kin. These generally included group photographs of extended kin at important lifecycle celebrations, as well as family gatherings in other exceptional settings, such as visiting local tourism sites, where professional photographers often offered their services to visitors.

These photomontages notably emphasized the contributions and achievements family members made towards building socialism. Themes included family members receiving educational certificates, posing in military dress, or official pictures of colleagues and managers in their work units. Action shots were rarely included, let alone pictures of family members actually working. Nonetheless, there were frequent depictions of a romanticized peasant identity – kin overlooking a harvest hauled back to their courtyard, for instance, or sitting at a desk writing in a Maoist flat cap as part of the rural grassroots intelligentsia.

The stakes of each photographic event were probably even higher due to the rarity of contact with photographers in the past, as the pressure to create an ideal image meant that villagers took great care in selecting locations, clothing, posture, participants, and props. The montages not only documented important life stages, but also bore testament to past labor contributions in building socialism, as well as upward class mobility in terms of wealth, status, location, and profession.

Photographs provide glimpses of the past as personal memories fade. Nonetheless, when eliciting oral histories using photographs, researchers must take care to approach the photos as representations in the sense of 'presencing' – to read them in the present, rather than as access to an unmediated past. This may happen quite intuitively when contemplating staged photographs. By contrast, snapshots promise an immediacy and candid glimpse of a moment in the past, making it necessary to remember that anything within a frame cuts out critical context.

In the snapshot, the timelessness of the photograph as an object comes to be juxtaposed with the coincidental temporality of events that photographs have captured. This medium most readily evokes the power of photography to converge image and reality. Beyond its mnemonic efficacy and documentary value, the snapshot blurs the line between the framed and constructed image and the 'reality' to which it is supposed to bear witness. However, both formal and informal photography may visualize hierarchical relations, elicit group recognition, and portray sequences of events in ways that may be intentionally staged and framed, particularly for aspirational or ideal self-representation.

Making Kin for the Future

I began this essay by posing the question of how kinship is remembered and memorialized in contemporary rural Chinese homes. I have attempted to illuminate how kinship becomes materialized in and through houses to create family homes despite political upheaval and economic transformation. By turning to the history of houses and kinship in the area of Sweeping Cliff, multiple contradictions emerged in ways of recognizing, representing, and celebrating kin through the home.

The Maoist state redirected labor efforts from family and lineage interests toward collective brigades and the socialist nation. The socialist redistribution of grand courtyard complexes along meritocratic lines of contribution to the revolution was followed by decades of illicit market exchanges. Today, the house remains the main form of wealth as Sweeping Cliff families pass on their houses along patrilineal lines of inheritance to male descendants. Therefore, house ownership and genealogical commitments have not kept up the momentum of the revolution, giving farmers all the more reason to attempt to bridge their kin commitments and political allegiances. They achieve this by visualizing their adherence to socialist values, everyday labor, and the national project through the orchestration of objects in the home.

Maoism simultaneously externalized work into the fields and factories, while internalizing, even domesticating, the work of kinship, most notably drawing boundaries around networks of relations. Lineages, in particular, became contained within the realm of the home, as lineage halls were closed and ancestral worship moved to domestic shrines. However, even at the ancestral altar in the home, changes were made as the deceased were increasingly personalized through ancestral photographs.

As Sweeping Cliff kin employ multiple strategies for legitimating their presence in the house through both ancestral authority and ongoing labor, we may speak of a form of legal pluralism. By drawing on various forms of belonging, kin balance the efforts of meritocratic redistribution under socialism with the jural notion of inheritance through kinship. Although these double commitments may appear contradictory, they are both displayed and hidden in the object world of the home to great effect.

The multiple ways in which kin materialize their loyalty to both genealogical relations and the socialist nation reveal that the purpose of photographs in the home is not purely a documentary way of solidifying the past. Photographs also act on the present and future. The object world of the home does not just provide a site of memory, but produces effects through projections intended for forthcoming descendants. This reveals the unsettling balance that must be struck between making claims through a double bind placed on Sweeping Cliff families: they must stand by their productive labor in upholding the socialist nation, while simultaneously completing the ritual work that materializes genealogies though ancestral tablets and photographs, all in the interest of keeping ties to houses and ancestors for future generations.

Cláudio Pinheiro

Unhomely Afterlives: The Works and Lives of Rabindranath Tagore

In 1916, Rabindranath Tagore published the remarkable novel *Ghare Baire* (literally "At Home and Outside," eventually translated as *The Home and the World*).[18] Set at the beginning of the twentieth century, the novel explores the lives of three characters struggling with the imminence of changes in their lives and to their homes – simultaneously a house and the province of Bengal under British colonialism. The story shows the home and the world as ontologically constitutive dimensions profoundly shaken by the Swadeshi movement (the 'home rule' movement), during the explosive times of the Bengal Partition (1905–1911).

Framed by the intensity of the nationalist movements that swept across Bengal between the nineteenth and twentieth centuries, Tagore's novel deals with sentiments of dwelling and displacement, in which his characters are trapped and where actions taken in the inner and outer worlds affect both spheres mutually. *Ghare Baire* reflects not only the Indian context of that time, but the innermost aspects of the author's life. This period was particularly transformative within Tagore's work and trajectory – the inauguration of the University of Visva-Bharati in Santiniketan; the death of his wife, daughter, and son – and it was when he produced some of his most inspiring and critical writings on nationalism in both Bengali and English.[19] Receiving the Nobel Prize for *Gitanjali* in 1913 was another major event of this period, earning him international acclaim in the ensuing 'Tagore mania.'[20] This initiated, some say, a new life-phase for Rabindranath. In fact, his presence in India was quite different from the one he would experience in the West, where he had been largely unknown until then. By the time he became Nobel laureate, Tagore was renowned in South Asia for his literary works (poems, political addresses, novels, plays, and films) and for his presence in artistic and political circles. The Nobel Prize transformed him into an international author, or rather a universal figure, and reframed his global reception.

In a very short space of time, some of his works were published in several languages. This was followed by long discussions about him, the nature of his writing, and the often very poor quality of the translations.[21] He knew that the translations impoverished his original texts dramatically, to the point that they sometimes became entirely new texts, ultimately confining his person and message within the frame of Western Orientalism.

Translations and translators, mostly European, played a crucial role in recasting his image of a freedom fighter and political activist into that of a mystical poet, a man with a spiritual message –

---

18 Rabindranath Tagore, *Ghare Baire* (London: MacMillan, 1921).

19 Rabindranath Tagore, *Nationalism* (San Francisco: Book Club of California, 1917). See also Partha Chatterjee, *Lineages of Political Society: Studies in Postcolonial Democracy* (New Delhi: Permanent Black, 2011): 94–126.

20 This 'Tagore mania' began with *Gitanjali*, which hit the West starting from the UK, and where thirteen different editions were published between March and November 1913 alone. Concerning the publication of Tagore in Lusophone countries, see Sovon Sanyal, "Universalism of Tagore: The Specificities of Portuguese Reception," http://www.parabaas.com/rabindranath/articles/pSovon.html, accessed June 25, 2017. There was a truly global avalanche of translations and publications of many of his writings around the world.

21 Claudio Pinheiro, "*Las muchas encarnaciones de Tagore y los escritos de su espíritu,*" in Susanne Klengel and Alexandra Wallner, eds., *Sur/South: Poetics and Politics of Thinking Latin America-India* (Madrid: Iberoamericana Vervuert Verlag, 2016): 283–308.

an image he also helped construct. Many authors were keen to translate the works of this exotic figure who had rapidly acquired international popularity. His work built on the image of the 'universal man,' which contrasted with the ethnicization of political debate at the time surrounding the reinforced European nationalism that fueled World War I.

Moreover, translations and translators performed a process of adapting his writing, first to English and then into other languages.[22] Instead of committing with a reliable version of the original, the translations were compromised with an ontological proposal, literally recreating his texts while providing authority, legitimacy, and local recognition to the Indian poet.[23] In the first decades of the twentieth century, a desire to read and translate Tagore would signal not only an interest in the Orient and the exotic, a phenomenon very popular all over the West this time, but also an interest in the Anglo-Saxon world, including knowledge of English as a language of culture.[24]

Tagore himself expressed the disconnections between his life in India and elsewhere as different existences, a condition, he liked to say, that both he and his poems shared as part of a "perilous adventure of a foreign reincarnation."[25] Tagore did not mean the Hindu idea of reincarnation, in which a spirit can experience successive lives. Rather, Tagore used incarnation as a metaphor to illustrate different existences of his being that were simultaneous and also somehow disconnected. The metaphor has been interpreted to ratify the bi-dimensionality of Tagore's work and trajectory, referring to different co-existing selves rather than different consecutive stages of the same self. It emphasized the way his persona and literary legacy were produced and received in India and in the West as distinct and simultaneous lifecycle experiments by the same self.

His 'foreign reincarnation' also referred to sentiments of displacement which rendered Tagore homeless – the more the figure of the mystical guru acquired life, the less it seemed rooted to or identified in his existence as a polymath and freedom fighter in his homeland. Homi Bhabha's similar reading uses the concept of 'unhomely' to refer to the consequences produced by migra-

---

22 The translations made a series of adaptations that substituted a faithful interpretation for a compromise with the ontological proposal of the "Universal Harmony" that Tagore himself emphasized to his Western audience. At the same time, his translators ceded their authority and relevance to his figure and constructed spaces of utterance for the work of the Indian poet, while they themselves were becoming important authors in the field of literature. In fact, his international image was confounded in some circles with that the 'sage of Santiniketan,' a mystical poet, an oriental guru, the 'universal man.' "The translation of his 'spiritual' poems, to the exclusion of his other works and indeed his own choice in translation and self-presentation, constructed an image of a saintly spiritual person who belonged to an ashram, not to the contemporary world." Sabyasashi Bhattacharya, *Rabindranath Tagore: An Interpretation* (New Delhi: Viking, 2011): 112.

23 At the same time, his translators lent authority and relevance to his figure and helped construct spaces of enunciation for the work of the Indian poet. The majority of Tagore translators were key characters in their own countries – in cultural, political, and intellectual terms – such as W. B. Yeats and Ezra Pound in the UK, André Gide in France, Frederik van Eeden in the Netherlands, and Juan Ramón Jiménez in Spain. Many translators or writers involved in the circulation of his writing in Europe were also themselves later awarded the Nobel Prize for literature: Gide (1947), Yeats (1923), Jiménez (1956), Romain Rolland (1915), Van Eeden (1928).

24 Agustín Blanco, "Más sobre Tagore en España: una traducción olvidada (inglés-español) de Martínez Sierra," Archivum 50–51 (2000–2001): 119–48.

25 Nabaneeta Sen, "The 'Foreign Reincarnation' of Rabindranath Tagore," *Journal of Asian Studies* 25 (1966): 275–86, 275; Marion Dalvai, "A 'Foreign Reincarnation': The Controversial Afterlife of Rabindranath Tagore's *The Home and the World*," in Bevin Doyle and Brigitte Le Juez, eds., *Proceedings of the First Graduate Symposium* (Dublin: Dublin City University, 2008): 19–28.

tion, cultural relocation, and other forms of displacement, where the home and the world are not mutually exclusive dimensions.[26]

Rabindranath Tagore was then, during his lifetime, split by two different conditions and related simultaneous existences, with his Indian and Western incarnations a condition of permanent 'unhomeliness.' These two different incarnations were largely disconnected in terms of what he and his writing (sometimes the very same writing) represented to India and to the West. By the time of his death in 1941, Tagore was largely imagined as a 'mystical poet' and 'oriental sage,' as many obituaries in European newspapers described him. Nabaneeta Sen argues that Tagore himself was mesmerized by the critiques and compliments that created this image. Some scholars emphasized that the construction of this persona, of this Western spiritualized incarnation, has completely obliterated his politically compromised presence in India, creating two antithetic existences.[27] In his translations into European languages such as English, German, and French, Nabaneeta Sen suggests that all of Tagore's publications were reframed through the themes of spirituality and religion, by the clash between the West and the East.

His inaugural publication in English – *Gitanjali* – goes right to the core in this sense. The book that made him internationally famous also invented him as the interlocutor of the universality of man and representative of a type of spiritual mysticism that would condition his reception in various parts of the world, and in India itself.

This spiritual persona of the universal guru eventually transformed the author into an unhomely ghost in both places. Tagore fell hostage to his own image; the poet experienced a literary ostracism in the West through his invention as the author of an oriental mystical spirituality.[28]

Tagore Incarnation in the Tropics

Although translated into many languages, the circulation of his writing in Portuguese shows yet another interesting and more complex facet. Portugal was the only place where the poet was directly translated from the original Bengali. Between 1920 and 1940, a group of Goan intellectuals from an academic association at Coimbra (known as the 'Indian Institute') published the first translations of Indian authors directly from their mother tongues: Aurobindo, Sarojini Naidu, Chandra Bose, and others. The two most important activists within this group were Adeodato Barreto (1904–1936) and Telo de Mascarenhas (1899–1979), who played prominent roles in the cultural and political opposition to Portuguese colonialism in India. Mascarenhas was instrumental in translating Tagore directly from Bengali and publishing some of the titles in Lisbon in the 1940s, at a time when the debate on Indian independence was intensifying.

---

26 'Unhomely,' a condition more related to "uncanny literary and social effects of enforced social accommodation, or historical migrations and cultural relocations" than to "forcible evictions." A condition precisely related to how the 'home' and the 'world,' representing inner and outer (private and public) domains, are not self-excluding ideas, but complementary dimensions of the recognition of "the world-in-the-home and the-home-in the world." Homi Bhabha, "The World and the Home," *Social Text* 31/32 (1992): 141–53. For an interesting contribution on housing transitions and life course, see Andrew Beer et al., *Housing Transitions through the Life Course* (Bristol: Policy Press, 2011).
27 Nabaneeta Sen, "The "Foreign Reincarnation" of Rabindranath Tagore," *The Journal of Asian Studies* 25 (1966): 275–86; Sabyasashi Bhattacharya, *Rabindranath Tagore: An Interpretation* (New Delhi: Viking, 2011).
28 Telo de Mascarenhas, *Rabindranath Tagore e sua mensagem spiritual* (Lisbon: Edições Oriente, 1943).

In Brazil, the circumstances surrounding the publication and reception of Tagore were completely different. Like in many peripheral regions, most of the titles were originally translated from English (or other European languages). In fact, he was the only Indian author to be published in translation in Brazil until 1948.

The first title published in Brazil was *Gitanjali* (in 1914), which helped to frame how the poet would be read in many circles. His initial reception took place within the framework of spirituality, occultism, and religiosity. The Brazilian edition of *Gitanjali* included the original text by Tagore, a preface by W.B. Yeats, and illustrations of Tagore in contemplative postures, combined with symbols of occultism. In fact, the publisher, Editora Pensamento, specialized in occultism and masonry; the editor, Braulio Prego, was director of the Esoteric Circle of the Communion of Thought. Editora Pensamento was famous for esoterism, yoga, occultism, meditation, karma, alternative medicine, 'Indian philosophy,' and other themes generically associated with a mystical Orient. It published the works of authors such as H. Blavatsky, Annie Besant, C. Leadbeater, Ernest Wood, Arthur Powell, Geoffrey Hodson, Radha Burnier, J. Krishnamurti, and Yogui Ramachakara.[29]

In the same way as in other languages and countries, his popularity following the Nobel Prize was the initial motivation for translating Tagore into Portuguese. Between 1914 and 2010, just over thirty titles were translated into Portuguese, as well as 130 editions and reprints – some forty in Portugal and around ninety in Brazil. The differences between the Portuguese and Brazilian publications were stark. In Portugal, the group working under Telo de Mascarenhas at Coimbra, 're-Indianized' Tagore for a Western and ultra-colonialist audience, translating him directly from Bengali and framing his reception in Portugal through the politics of colonialism and decolonization.

Although the Orientalist fragrance of Tagore's unhomely incarnation was present in many contexts in the West, in Brazil it assumed a yet more fascinating and ironic dimension. In 1947, a book of poems entitled *Canções da Imortalidade* ("Songs of Immortality") was published in São Paulo, co-authored by Pedro Machado and "the spirit of the poet Rabindranath Tagore."[30] Although it was not his first book to be published in Brazil, it was the first fresh title authored after his death. Since then, the poet has been enjoying a productive 'afterlife cycle' in Brazil, with more than twenty books published by 2011, by the proclaimed "spirit of the poet Rabindranath Tagore."[31]

Although the literary ostracism of Tagore in the West in the 1950s also impacted Brazil, the writing of his 'spirit' experienced a very different reception. Between 1947 and 2012, the "spirit of the poet Rabindranath Tagore" published almost as many works as all the editions (and reprints) of Tagore's original writings. The peak came in the 1980s, when their publication and sale surpassed the total volume of original texts published in Brazil and Portugal combined. At that point, ironically, the 'spirit' ended up boosting the name and the sales of the "original" publications of the poet in the Portuguese language.

---

29 Adilson Ramachamdra, *Pensamento em mutação: a trajetória de uma editora. Pensamento-Cultrix 100 anos* (São Paulo: Pensamento, 2007). Claudia Poletto, *A construção e circulação de imaginários sobre a Índia no Brasil por meio da sociedade teosófica do final do século XIX até a primeira metade do século XX* (Rio de Janeiro: Ph.D. thesis, 2011).

30 Pedro Machado and Rabindranath Tagore, *Canções da Imortalidade* (São Paulo: Livraria Allan Kardec Editora, 1947).

31 Those were works of 'spiritual writing,' where the spirit shared authorship with a second (biologically) living author. For a longer explanation of this, see Bernardo Lewgoy, *Os espiritas e as letras* (Porto Alegre: UFRGS, 2000, Ph.D. thesis); Bernardo Lewgoy, "A Transnacionalização do Espiritismo Kardecista brasileiro," *Religião e Sociedade* 28 (2008): 84–104.

Similarly to his translators, the spiritual mediums who co-authored with the 'spirit' of Tagore helped to reframe the presence of the 'real' Tagore in a different arena (that of the spiritual novels), helping not only to sell Tagore's original writings, but also lending his figure a new popularity. Readers accessed Tagore based on the hallmark and the credibility of their mediums.[32] Likewise, Tagore's translations into European languages at the beginning of the twentieth century gave prestige to a poet hitherto unknown in Europe. It is a process whereby both contributed to a mutual and shared prestige and relevance.

Tagore's spiritual writings in Brazil touched on a set of subjects that are quite specific, but that reiterate, at a first glance, the agenda of the 'real' Tagore in the West: compassion, universality of man, divine love, oriental wisdom, and mysticism. The thematic agenda of Tagore's 'spirit' was also not so far from that of the political writings of Tagore criticizing nationalism, reinforcing one of the most important themes of his lifetime: the concept of *samaaj* – the idea of a universal harmony able to incorporate the ethnic and religious diversity that characterized India in opposition to the European idea of 'nation.'

Of course, it is not the intention of this essay to discuss the reality of reincarnation, or ghosts as metaphors or active historical actors, but rather to consider how the existence of Tagore's self in its afterlife in Brazil can be useful in considering how literature on the lifecycle and life course can contribute to the writing of history.

Moreover, the spiritualist reception of Tagore in Brazil offers a very interesting picture that alludes to a nationalist-spiritualist Tagore, rather than to the antithesis between these two aspects as distinct social and political existences. It can be argued that the construction of the spiritual figure not only does not invalidate, but also enters into a dialogue with Tagore's writings on nationalism. Contrary to what other scholars have argued, the Indian and Western incarnations of the poet reinforce the social existence of the spirit of Tagore in Brazil, strengthening the unity and universality of a spiritual man beyond national or ethnic boundaries. This is a remarkable aspect to reinforce in peripheral countries structured over complex societies and challenged by nation-building processes where diversity meant structural inequality. The concept of universal harmony, addressed through the 'spirit' of Tagore, found space and recognition among an audience in a country, Brazil, that was structured by inequality and compelled to find a place for diversities that were not peacefully accommodating if not through a spiritual sphere.

In a sense, Tagore's publications in Brazil and the way the author was received within the literary and religious framework created the first effective production of autonomous thought about India – detached from the encompassing framework of English as the language of culture or of the British Empire. At the same time, the publications by his 'spirit' constructed a space for the renewal and re-reading of his message of universal harmony that suggests an approximation between what has been considered the incommunicability of his Western and Oriental incarnations. The unhomely spectrum of Tagore found a perfect homeland as an afterlife cycle poet in Brazil.

---

32 There is a far more complex discussion on the idea of co-authorship in spiritual writings, where the mediums do not simply lend authority or represent receptacles of the writing of a spirit, but a shared authorship (or 'inter-authorship') in which the maintenance of the original style of that writer in life is not presupposed, but the production of a writing that introduces interferences and mutual influences of the spirit and of the medium. Readers of Tagore's 'spirit' writings are not tracing clear stylistic traits to identify what he wrote in the past with what he writes now, but identifying the content of the message. Thus, the spiritual works do not exist autonomously with the medium, "it is he who lends his charisma to mark the individuality, the value and the notoriety of the spiritual author" (Bernardo Lewgoy, Os espiritas e as letras. Ph.D. thesis. Porto Alegre: UFRGS, 2000): 143.

Reflections I

Nitin Varma
Servant Testimonies and Anglo-Indian Homes in Nineteenth-Century India

On August 21, 1818, Ramonee, a thirty-year-old woman from Patna in eastern India, appeared before the Supreme Court at Fort William, Calcutta.[1] Ramonee, who worked as an *ayah* (child's nurse, lady's maid), was called as one of the witnesses in a case brought by her former employer, Major Cunliffe. A British military captain stationed in Cawnpore (a cantonment in northern India), Cunliffe was accusing his wife Louisa of adultery.[2] A charge of adultery directed against wives, as in England at that time, allowed husbands to sue their wives' accused lovers for damages. This was usually followed by proceedings in the ecclesiastical side of the court over the separation of bed and board of the estranged couple (similar to legal separation). A full divorce was extremely rare and often the privilege of the rich and influential. This required a private act of the British parliament and usually cost a fortune.[3]

There was another problem for the British residents of India if they wished to or were capable of taking this route. The witnesses required to establish the charge – servants, other household members, friends, acquaintances, and colleagues – could not usually travel to England to appear before parliament. In 1820, a change in regulation allowed the Supreme Courts of Calcutta, Madras, and Bombay to summon witnesses and collect evidence to substantiate the allegations made by the husbands on behalf of the British parliament. The evidence and trial details were then forwarded to London for further action. The details of this particular case, including Ramonee's testimony, became available when Major Cunliffe applied for a full divorce in 1823.

A premium on morality marked a break from the *nabobs* (Europeans who made a fortune in India and often imitated the lifestyle of Indian elites) of the late eighteenth century who lived a life of excess and had several liaisons with the native *bibis* (Indian mistresses of *nabobs*).[4] The growing presence of white women in the colony in the nineteenth century provoked new anxieties and their transgressions appeared to threaten the patriarchal order; the act of 1820 was a gesture in that direction.[5] The change from white *nabobi* homes to *memsahib* households was noted in handbooks written for British subjects and servicemen in India published in 1810 and 1825.[6] Here I

---

1 I am extremely grateful to Felicitas Hentschke for her constant encouragement and intellectual input in finalizing this essay. I must also extend my gratitude to James Williams for his extremely useful feedback on an earlier draft. This essay forms part of a larger research project on the history of domestic servants in India funded by a European Research Council Starting grant project (ERC stg. DOS 640627). I am grateful to my friend and principal investigator Nitin Sinha for helping me develop many ideas presented here.
2 The details of the divorce proceedings are recorded in the annual Proceedings of the British House of Lords for the relevant years. I have been able to collect around thirty trials spanning a period of forty years (early 1820s to early 1860s) held at the Supreme Courts of Calcutta, Bombay, Madras, and Ceylon.
3 Lawrence Stone, *Road to Divorce: England 1530–1987* (Oxford: Oxford University Press, 1987); Lawrence Stone, *Broken Lives: Separation and Divorce in England, 1660–1857* (Oxford: Oxford University Press, 1995).
4 Durba Ghosh, *Sex and Family in Colonial India: The Making of Empire* (Cambridge: Cambridge University Press, 2006).
5 Joan Mickelson Gaughan, *The 'Incumberances' British Women in India, 1615–1856* (New Delhi: Oxford University Press, 2013).
6 Thomas Williamson, *East India Vade-Mecum or Complete Guide to Gentlemen intended for the Civil, Military, or Naval Service of the Hon. East India Company* (London: Black, Parry, and Kingsburg, 1810); John Borthwick Gilchrist,

A servant's gaze of an Anglo-Indian colonial bungalow, based on an ayah's court testimony

am less concerned with the new anxieties around adultery and divorcing practices, but rather with the testimonies of the servants who were summoned to court to give evidence in support of their masters' claims that their mistresses had committed adultery. Servants' testimonies do not speak directly about the nature of Anglo-Indian homes but are directed towards establishing the guilt of the mistresses and their lovers.

An attempt to reconstruct the nature of homes and master-servant relationships in early nineteenth-century India through an examination of divorce trials does not immediately appear to be a productive research strategy. So why divorce trials? Conventional historical studies of domestic

---

The General East India Guide and Vade Mecum for the Public functionary, Government Officer, Private Agent, Trader or Foreign Sojourner, in British India, and the adjacent parts of Asia immediately connected with the Honourable the East India Company. Being a digest of the work of the Late Capt. Williamson (London: Black, Parry, and Kingsburg, 1825).

relationships in Anglo-Indian households are often framed through the employer's perspective. There is substantial discussion in the literature of the anxieties of white masters with respect to their native servants who are seen as essential in the everyday functioning of Anglo-Indian homes.[7] Their dependence on and close proximity to servants reveals racial, class, and colonial tensions. *Ayahs* like Ramonee were seen as proximate to the *memsahibs* and indispensable for child rearing in the colonies, but such intimate and dependent ties were also perceived as undermining the sense of superiority and distinctiveness of the colonial master. Such closeness was further fraught by threats of dirt and disease associated with such contact. Manuals, travelogues, letters, and even diaries also limit our perspective of these domestic relationships.[8]

My research on *ayahs* relied heavily on this material initially, yet I was struck by how little could be known about women who worked as *ayahs* in European homes. There was a lot of material (textual, visual, and literary) that described how employers both celebrated and feared *ayahs*, but I could hardly assess if *ayahs* shared those views or had some other sense of this relationship. Were they sharing the sense of intimacy with the *memsahibs* and infants? Were they anxious about the violation of caste and racial boundaries? In an attempt to probe these issues further, I took the advice of social historians, and particularly micro historians, who have read the judicial archives carefully and creatively to write the history of the marginal.[9] Several recent South Asian legal historians have alerted us to the fact that case law has been largely underused in the writing of South Asian social history, and that it has great potential in reconstructing of the histories and experiences of subaltern groups.[10]

A preliminary look into the cases appearing in the civil and criminal courts of the nineteenth century showed a presence of servants embedded in the homes of their masters and beyond. The disproportionate presence of servants in published divorce trials was striking. Like other cases in which servants appear, they are not the protagonists but their presence in courts as witnesses (though in limited ways) opens up a possibility to raise new questions and offer different perspectives. In this essay, through a closer examination of one trial, I will explore the nature and functioning of the homes of white masters and native servants in early nineteenth-century India.

The Case of Ramonee

Ramonee worked briefly as an *ayah* in the household of Robert and Louisa Cunliffe. In early 1817, Louisa Cunliffe went to Calcutta by boat with two of her children who were being sent to England. It was a common practice for the children of parents based in India to attend school in England. On her way back to Cawnpore, Louisa Cunliffe was accompanied by Mr. and Mrs. Loftus and their

---

7 Nupur Chaudhuri, "Memsahibs and their servants in nineteenth century India," *Women's History Review* 3 (1994): 549–62.

8 Indrani Sen, "Colonial Domesticities, Contentious Interactions: *Ayahs*, Wet-Nurses and Memsahibs in colonial India," *Indian Journal of Gender Studies* 16 (2009): 299–328; Suzanne Conway, "*Ayah*, Caregiver to Anglo-Indian Children, c. 1757–1947," in Shirleene Robinson and Simon Sleight, eds., *Children, Childhood and Youth in the British World* (London: Palgrave Macmillan, 2016): 41–58.

9 Carlo Ginzburg, *Cheese and the Worms* (London: Routledge and Kegan Paul, 1976); Natalie Zemon Davis, *The Return of Martin Guerre* (Cambridge: Harvard University Press, 1983). For a more recent reading of a particular case see Amy Stanley, "Maidservants' Tales: Narrating Domestic and Global History in Eurasia, 1600–1900," *The American Historical Review* 121 (2016): 437–60.

10 Mitra Sharafi, "South Asian Legal History," *Annual Review of Law and Social Science* 11 (2016): 309–36.

young infant child. Loftus was taking charge as an army captain in Cawnpore and it appears that he was known to Louisa as an old acquaintance and friend. The arrival of the Loftus family with an infant required an *ayah* and Ramonee was hired through a reference working in Cawnpore. Unlike other servants of the household, Ramonee's task of taking care of the child required her to be present inside the bedroom of Mrs. Loftus during the night. During the course of the trial, Ramonee gave a vivid account of how the families organized themselves inside the bungalow. Ramonee described the bungalow, which appeared as a fairly typical *mofussil* bungalow, as a ten-room house with low ceilings. The Cunliffes occupied a sleeping room and their children slept in another room. The Loftuses were accommodated in two rooms of the house, one in which Mrs. Loftus slept with her infant (and Ramonee) and an adjoining room that was assigned to Mr. Loftus as his sleeping room. Ramonee noted that Louisa Cunliffe twice went into Major Loftus's sleeping room late into the night. On these occasions, Major Loftus would usually lift the mosquito net covering his bed and invite Louisa to sit down. They would then enter into in a conversation in a tone and language which was unintelligible to Ramonee. On both these occasions, Ramonee fell asleep and therefore could not definitely confirm when Louisa finally returned to her own room. Her evidence in the ecclesiastical court in 1818 was crucial in establishing the affair.

When the same case came up in 1823 for a divorce, the Supreme Court of Calcutta ordered the witnesses to be examined. The male servants of the household appeared in court but the different levels of intimacy and access they shared became fairly evident. The male servants in court were Nundooram, Ghonisham Etwarry, and Cocundoo, and they had all been employed for a longer period (between eight and twelve years) in roles ranging from being personal attendants, attending tables, and bearing torches. The only male servant who seemed to have some knowledge about the "private" and "intimate" details of the case was the torchbearer Cocundoo. He had accompanied Louisa Cunliffe to Calcutta when she traveled to see off her children to England. He returned with her to Cawnpore onboard a *Pinnace* (a lighter boat), while Mr. and Mrs. Loftus traveled on a *Budgerow* (a bigger, sluggish boat). They all dined together on the *Budgerow* and it was Cocundoo's task to escort Louisa Cunliffe back to her boat after dinner by torchlight. In this role, he became privy to certain encounters between Louisa and Mr. Loftus, which he later detailed in court.

Since it was clear from the proceedings of the earlier trial that Ramonee's account was crucial, she was summoned to appear in court again. But Ramonee had since left the employment of Cunliffe and could not be immediately traced. A search for Ramonee at the behest of the court (and also Mr. Cunliffe) gives us information about her life from 1818 (when she first appeared in court) until 1823 (when she was called to reappear in court). This helps us to reconstruct some of her biographical details, and would not have been possible if she was present at that time or had been traced immediately. The search was conducted through male servants of the household who knew Ramonee from work; a couple of them had accompanied her when she came to Calcutta at different stages of the case. One of the servants, who accompanied Ramonee on a boat journey from Cawnpore to Calcutta, mentioned in court that she insisted on making a stopover in Patna as she wanted to visit her "family and relations." After making this particular halt in Patna, she visited the house of Imad Khanun, a Muslim woman of repute, which Ramonee described as her home. This particular home appeared to be a sisterhood, where single women, possibly outcast women or widows, could find refuge.

After staying a couple of days at her home, Ramonee proceeded to Calcutta. In Calcutta, Ramonee stayed in the house of Mr. Hunter (an acquaintance of Mr. Cunliffe) and took up employment there. After the initial trial, the other servant left for Cawnpore but Ramonee stayed on. Working with these leads, another servant was sent to find Ramonee in Patna and he again visited the household of Imad Khanun. She mentioned that Ramonee had left her job in Calcutta and come back to Patna around 1819–1820. This was the time of a raging cholera epidemic and Ramonee had fallen ill and moved out of the house with another female servant. She could not be traced any further.

Ramonee found work as an *ayah* in the homes of Europeans. She moved within the region from Cawnpore to Calcutta, and frequently traveled back to what she described as her "home" in Patna, the household of Imad Khanun. We know little about her social and marital background. Was she ever married or was she widowed? It seems that she was Muslim or a lower-caste woman. We know very little about the circular migration of single women working for wages in early nineteenth-century eastern and northern India. This brings into focus places like Calcutta (a colonial city) and Cawnpore (a cantonment) emerging as places of 'service' that drew people from eastern India into the wage market.[11] This predominantly involved the migration of men but a category of female caregiver (*ayahs*) was also marking its presence and growing prominence. The magisterial survey of Buchanan Hamilton covering this region in the early part of the century offers little to explain their presence.[12] It seems that the figure of *ayah* in an earlier period was paralleled by a "young girl" brought under the "protection" of a family of rank and status through purchase or adoption to serve through their lives.[13] *Ayahs*, in contrast, were relatively older women working for wages and rarely had a long-term dependent relationship with the employer's family. Did the setting up of European homes in the late eighteenth and early nineteenth century with a demand for servants based on gender, caste, and religion create a market for wages for women like Ramonee? How do we situate the home of Ramonee, a sisterhood of single women mostly comprising lower castes, Muslims, and widows? It becomes fairly clear that *ayahs* did not consider themselves part of the master's home and would be employed for varying periods while also going back to places which they described as their homes. The dominant notion of servants becoming part of their master's home as subordinate members needs to be revised.

Ramonee and the other *ayahs* who appear in the legal cases rarely had long-term associations with particular households. Their working lives were marked by a series of short-term positions including extended breaks in employment. There were other instances of kin members (often daughters) substituting in times of absence or during the transfer of the employer's family to a different location. It does not seem that an *ayah's* work was a lifecycle employment as women would work as *ayahs* in several short-term engagements. It also appears that *ayahs* working in European households sought employment in other European households and there was little movement of servants between European and non-European homes. The nature of this employment seemed to be highly specialized such that *ayahs* were often hired either to take care of infants (termed a child's *ayah*) or to attend to the mistress (a lady's *ayah*). This specialized nature of the work also explained the shorter duration of employment. Some *ayahs* were specifically hired during childbirth and would be discharged within a few months of the delivery. *Ayahs* taking care of smaller children would be out of work when the children were ready to be sent to England for school, usually when they turned five. This also explains a particular personalization of authority, where *ayahs* attending the lady and the children were seen as attached to the mistress and would move with her if the mistress decided to leave the household, which often happened during divorce

---

11 Peter J. Marshall, "Company and the Coolies: Labour in Early Calcutta," in Pradip Sinha, ed., *The Urban Experience: Calcutta* (Calcutta: Riddhi India, 1987).

12 Francis Buchanan-Hamilton, *An Account of the Districts of Bihar and Patna in 1811–1812* (Patna: The Bihar and Orissa Research Society, 1936).

13 Indrani Chatterjee, *Gender, Slavery and Law in Colonial India* (New Delhi: Oxford University Press, 1999).

trials. Male servants, in contrast, were seen as under the master's command and seem to have been employed for longer periods in comparison with *ayahs*. Questions of intimacy become relevant in this context: Did these short-term engagements allow close and intimate ties to develop? Did Ramonee feel attached to the Cunliffes' child? Was leaving her job marked by emotional trauma and pain? We cannot come to a conclusive answer but at least we are alerted to the limits of these representations, which celebrate deep attachment and fondness between *ayahs* and children as the emotional foundation of Anglo-Indian homes.

Conclusion

The relevance of servants in divorce trials was based on the understanding that they were integral parts of colonial households and therefore had access to its everyday workings. In several trials, the testimonies of *ayahs* were seen as particularly crucial because they were perceived to have the most intimate access to the *memsahib*. But it is important to distinguish the levels of access servants had to the private and intimate domains. Even male servants who worked for longer periods of time were less relevant in these trials as they had less knowledge of the workings of the private domains of these homes.

The representation of the Anglo-Indian home as a stable unit of father, mother, and children attended on by a vast retinue of servants has to be interrupted by the presence of male guests and other European couples who could potentially stay there for extended periods of time. The nature of the Anglo-Indian home with the ubiquitous presence of servants in its everyday functioning and reproduction also needs to be situated alongside an understanding of how they were linked to homes of servants. The more longer-term male servants would be relatively attached to their master's home, at least for the period of employment. Yet the separation of boarding (in servant quarters) and food (the servants typically cooked their own food separately) and enduring links with their rural backgrounds meant that their idea of 'home' was not completely subsumed under the shadow of their master's home. Female servants, and particularly *ayahs*, who worked more intermittently and often changed employment due to the nature of their work, would be less integrated and often went back to the spaces they described as their homes.

Ramonee's testimony was crucial alongside other testimonies of servants, friends, and acquaintances in clinching the case in favor of Robert Cunliffe for securing a divorce from Louisa Cunliffe. In some ways this reflected an emerging template for divorce trials, in which household servants would appear in court to back their master's charge of adultery against their wives. The mistresses rarely appeared in court or brought forward their witnesses to refute these charges. The double-standard inherent in these divorce trials shaped the testimonies of servants such as *ayahs*, whose close proximity to their mistresses did not necessarily lead them to give a favorable opinion about their conduct as wives. This also reflected a lack of empathy between mistresses and servants distanced by class, racial, and even linguistic differences. A limited sense of 'familiarity' and 'friendship' that some English women developed for their female servants in England was rarely found in the colony. Yet, at the same time, these trials opened a small possibility for the servants as witnesses to register their views about their employers and even themselves and their experiences of life and work. The views about natives as generally untrustworthy and unreliable were in these particular legal moments somewhat undermined when as witnesses they became entitled and were encouraged to speak about their employers.

Reflections II

Prabhu Mohapatra, with Felicitas Hentschke and Nitin Varma

On Homes, Work, and Personhood:
An Interview with Prabhu Mohapatra

People work to make and keep a house or a home. This can refer literally to people's physical, economic, and social work on the house and home itself, but it also references houses and homes as places of safety, security, and social integration. Immediately, this marks out houses, homes, and housing as especially powerful indicators of exclusion, marginalization, and stigmatization. We speak with Prabhu Mohapatra, Professor of History at the University of Delhi, about the place and role of houses and homes in labor history.

How should we situate the home within the history of labor? Where have you encountered processes of home-making in your own work?

If we look at broad historical processes, we have some narrative trajectories of understanding how homes are created. In preindustrial Europe, home and work were deeply intertwined. To be at home was not merely to rest from work, but also to perform several productive and reproductive activities. Many homes doubled as worksites in preindustrial India too. Classically in India, the weavers worked at home. It was perhaps the same in Europe. If you see paintings or descriptions of weavers from the seventeenth and eighteenth centuries, all of them describe the man operating the loom as the woman spins or wraps the thread. Work at home not only meant a particular arrangement of labor, but also close proximity between work and home. Industrialization processes began to separate work and home, partly induced by migration, partly by the changing organization of work. Now, work was not done at home and in relation to other family members, but cooperatively and in a separated workplace. The rise of the factory crucially created a space away from the intimacy of home and designed exclusively for work.

Factory owners and workers both tried to separate and enclose home from work. We see the nineteenth century as a time of workers struggling to enforce divisions between work and home: to reduce time for work; to limit the ability of employers to intrude into aspects of their personal lives. The separation of home from work had many consequences, not necessarily all good. It led to a decline of women in the workplace, for instance. The family wage system emerged, the male breadwinner system, which reinforced a new gendered division of work. Households were separated from commodity-producing work. And this applied not only to European industrial workers.

When I studied plantations in the Caribbean, slavery was the dominant mode of production for a significant period of its history.[1] In this context, a specific arrangement between work and homes had been created. The slaves had to stay close to the manager's homes, in barracks that were allotted to them. The abolition of slavery, especially in British plantations, led to a massive flight of slaves from their employer's yard. Former slaves immediately set up independent households. Walter Rodney has shown how slaves tried to show that they can create a world apart from the world of the plantations – a world of their own.[2] This was a contradictory and conflictual process,

---

[1] See, for example, Prabhu Mohapatra, "'Restoring the Family': Wife Murders and the Making of a Sexual Contract for Indian Immigrant Labour in the British Caribbean Colonies, 1860–1920," *Studies in History* 11 (1995): 227–60.
[2] Walter Rodney, *A History of the Guyanese Working People, 1881–1905* (Baltimore: John Hopkins University Press, 1982).

but it nevertheless tells you about the human urge of the so-called slaves to create independence and autonomy by creating their own homes, even if they continued to work on the plantations as slaves or indentured laborers.

What we see nowadays is a massive return of work into homes. This characterizes the contemporary condition. Many informal settlements and many households in the urban context cannot exist if people do not have work being done in these spaces. In long and connected global chains of work and commodity productions – garments, footwear, consumer goods – home has become or re-become a site for work. We should never forget that home-making is not an exclusive historical process that exists only in relation to industrial capital and economy. It is also always a process of self-making. Like class-making, home-making is about making oneself as a person.

When you think of this book's title, To Be at Home: House, Work, and Self in the Modern World, *where would you locate home?*

It is such a fascinating subject: home as a nodal point between the workplace and the world. It is interesting to ask where do we locate the home because it begins to open up the meanings in a broader perspective. Building or rebuilding homes carry very different meanings in contexts of long-distance migration, for example, compared with those in which people stay in one place for long periods of their lives. Migration is the foundation of modern industrial societies. Industrialization has transformed social relations, especially the relations people have with their homes. This is crucial, because home or a house is not just a dwelling: it is a culturally infused space.

It is always important for us to see what systems of meanings are created when you make a home. When you make or work on something, you not only produce an object, but you also imbue the object with meanings. A similar perspective can be applied to the notion of home. Once you start to look at the sets of meanings the home carries or holds, its stability immediately breaks down. The framework of migration especially helps us see what it means to have or to not have a home. Likewise, in contexts of informality, precarious work, and the modern conditions of work, many forms and arrangements of home and home-making begin to appear. The sense of home is almost the extension of the self. If home is a cloth a person wears, we should appreciate how destabilizing the process of trying to retain a sense of the self is amid massive changes, such as migration.

Your own work explores the self-identification of the working classes, their values and distinctions from other classes. How do you conceptualize the struggle of workers to build a home?

Marx famously separated home and work on the basis of a separation between production and reproduction. Reproduction took place at home and production took place elsewhere. This separation was both intended and unintended. In many ways, workers often tried to retain the combination of work and home, while also trying to separate home and work. The process of reproduction through the wages workers earned from employment outside was always difficult. They often had to subsidize their employment earnings by working around the home. You could see it in small gardens workers built around their homes for subsistence.

I think we should ask whether this trajectory is universal. Is there one trajectory for European households and a different one for colonial and post-colonial households? Dominant narratives tend to obscure other trajectories.

In Indian history, for instance, the point of separation of home and work has been discussed in the context of middle-class nationalism. Here I might reflect on the same questions. Are there distinct forms or different ways in which different classes have conceptualized the separation of home and work? Historians have certainly argued this for the case of India.[3] What the newly emerged middle class felt about their colonial rulers was reflected in the strict separation they made between their homes and the world outside. Home became a place where they kept their cultural purity and inner sanctity. There was a civilizational demand by the colonial rulers, for women to be emancipated and come out of their homes and work. But the middle class simultaneously tried to preserve this cultural purity by cocooning the home. This had important consequences for middle-class formation. Their separation of the home from the outside world was often an elite response to the colonial capitalist transformation they were undergoing. It was based on the powerlessness they felt and on their inability to participate significantly in public spaces in which they had subordinated positions after being defeated by colonial rulers.

A different process unfolded for the emerging working class in India. This is partly because a peculiar characteristic of working-class formation in India has been in most cases exclusively single male migration. That produced alternative questions of home. Is a home where you go after work or is a home the family or household you left behind in the village? Samita Sen, a labor historian, has written very powerfully on this subject.[4] She argues that home for the workers stretched between the urban factories and the rural villages. It was the household at home in which they kept their women. You can find parallels with what happened in Europe, but also see some certain specificities. For India, industrialization solidified the idea that home remained always a temporary shelter.

There are so many variations of households and homes. Do these arrangements match popular imaginations of households and homes?

The philosopher Gaston Bachelard wrote a beautiful book called *The Poetics of Space*.[5] In this book, he talks about how different forms of secure surroundings are imagined – homes, nests, little imaginations where you can create your own space. He linked these to childhood, comfort, and questions of safety. The struggle to create security and safety is a phenomenological understanding of home-making and there are many different types of arrangements. The variation with which the home is imagined is not only a middle-class phenomenon. That different classes experience this process differently is true, but to say that other classes do not have this imagination would be wrong.

Unfortunately, the records of working-class memories or imaginations are far fewer. It is always the middle class trying to imagine what this separation of home and work means. While some great literature has been produced, I have struggled to find sources to think about this. But I have an image by Bachelard always with me. Bachelard describes how birds create nests. He quotes Jules Michelet talking about a bird pressing her heart and body in the mossy foliage and shaping the nest around it. In this process, her heartbeat goes already into making this nest. It is a brilliant image of how you make your home with your body, bringing your labor into this making of home.[6]

---

3 Partha Chatterjee, *The Nation and its Fragments: Colonial and Postcolonial Histories* (Princeton: Princeton University Press, 1993).
4 Samita Sen, *Women and Labour in Late Colonial India: The Bengal Jute Industry* (Cambridge: Cambridge University Press, 1999).
5 Gaston Bachelard, *The Poetics of Space*, translated by Maria Jolas (Boston: Beacon, 1994).
6 Bachelard, *The Poetics of Space*: 100–12.

How does home shape the personal integrity of an individual? How do people encircle the boundaries of their space of intimacy? What are the mechanism of inclusion and exclusion?

Everybody wants to create at least a shelter, but many people don't succeed. What happens when you cannot build a place where you can reproduce yourself or create a new world? What happens when you can depend only on temporary formations? How then does the self maintain integrity? We should understand how people live who never manage to make a home or who fail to make a home. We should also not forget those who decide not to make homes. Journalist Aman Sethi followed a man in Delhi and wrote a book about him, *A Free Man*.[7] This man lived in the streets. He worked intermittently. He never went back anywhere to create his home. His life story is not typical, but we can see how strong desire for safety and shelter might compete with one's desire for freedom. Home-making can be a constraint too. This is important to keep in mind.

Certain historians have shown how normative models of houses and homes, designed by middle classes, filter and shape working-class and lower-class imaginations. At the same time, some of the lifestyles and imaginations of freedom projected onto the working classes are part of the imagination of the upper classes. This is a two-way process. Insecure life at the lower end and the so-called secure life are in relation to each other not only through distinctions but also through interactions.

In India, when I work in the contemporary urban informal work sectors, I often go into homes, at least to see these homes.[8] Even in these highly insecure settlements, there are so many varieties and distinctions. In the urban spaces of Delhi, we have real squatter settlements, purely assembled out of found materials. What strikes me, even at the lowest end where workers live, is how they have tried to make a home and how they have they utilized the space. Rooms in which all family members sleep may be less than ten-by-ten feet. The massive constraint of urban space produced an economy of imagination and order of space, which is different from villages, where these urban dwellers come from. Yet, in houses like these, the utensils are shining. In a place where there is no place for art and the like, the shining utensils look like artistic pieces.

But what types of intimacies are produced in these situations? We should not think intimacy is limited to conjugal bourgeois notions of home. In India in the 1920s, when the state was massively concerned with solving the so-called housing question, working-class homes were seen as places where all kinds of unwanted mingling and interaction happened. Reformers imagined that people there lived like animals and that these homes were the sources of diseases, and that such domestic arrangements produced criminality and immoral behavior. On the basis of these imaginations, reformers wanted to provide the urban poor with new kinds of housing. In this way, working-class homes became the object of state welfare and middle-class reform action, and this continues to remain a dominant image of remaking the working class in India.

Do you think attending to personhood could be a way to craft a more politicized history of work?

Work is embedded in power relations. You cannot take these away. There is a way, like Gerd Spittler, to focus on the act of work – so, in a way, to radically depoliticize it to bring out its character.[9] This is one approach, while many, like Sidney Chalhoub, would feel that work is necessarily always

---

7 Aman Sethi, *A Free Man: A True Story of Life and Death in Delhi* (New York: W.W. Norton, 2013).
8 Prabhu Mohapatra is currently engaged in a research project on an industrial site and settlement (Wazirpur) in collaboration with Chitra Joshi, Naveen Chander, and Rukmini Barua.
9 Gerd Spittler, *Anthropologie Die Arbeit: Ein ethnographischer Vergleich* (Berlin: Springer VS, 2015).

embedded in political relations.[10] These are two slightly opposing ways of thinking about work. Sometimes the stripping away brings out elements that would not be visible if you look at it as purely embedded in networks of power alone. If you always look at the political aspects, you are somehow blind to these aspects.

However, it is important today to consider how the architecture of workers' settlements have changed over time because of the continuous, often coerced movement of workers from one locality to another. This is the life course of most workers in India now. People do not have settled homes. Yes, they hope that they will get a settled home eventually, but they typically experience their lives as a series of displacements. They come to the cities as squatter settlers, for example, often to build other people's homes – the middle-class housing and gated communities – and they try to settle down there as construction workers. But they are soon forced to move away from there into other squatter settlements. These movements continue and intensify as more and more gated communities conquer the urban space and workers find themselves continuously moving to the margins. Entire lives might be lived without ever having a settled home, but they are lived always in the hope for one. I have met many people like that. We should be using the life stories of these people to uncover home-making's possibilities and constraints. Politics remains at the center of these processes. I personally believe that the home cannot be taken away from the networks of power. Home-making should be understood in this framework. The state is still a very important player – for two centuries, the state has told us what home is, and separating out the state from people's imaginations of home is wrong. But we must not say that everything is determined by the state.

The whole history of housing and home-making should be a necessary part of a history of a political struggle of workers. How do people do it collectively? What possibilities existed earlier and how have these possibilities shifted? How do people imagine a home? How do they imagine security when the condition of life is insecure all the time or think about shelter when the whole process is creating shelterlessness? In the meanwhile, the idea of home will keep on changing like it did earlier in the eighteenth, nineteenth, and twentieth centuries.

---

10 Sidney Chaloub, "The Precariousness of Freedom in a Slave Society (Brazil in the Nineteenth Century)." *International Review of Social History* 56 (2011): 405–39.

Alf Lüdtke, with Felicitas Hentschke and James Williams

On Photography and History:
An Interview with Alf Lüdtke

How can historians and social scientists work with photographs? How can photography and photographers contribute to discussions on home, work, and the self, particularly when photographs surpass the role of just being illustrative visual material? We speak with Alf Lüdtke, historian of everyday life in the nineteenth and twentieth centuries, about historians' use and misuse of photographs.

When did you first start using photographs in your research? What role did photography play in developing your project of the history of everyday life?

My use of photographs began by accident in the 1970s. A colleague and I discovered albums of photographs from the 1900s to the 1950s in the archives of Hanomag, a metal processing company in Hanover in northern Germany. Hanomag specialized in the production of locomotives and automobiles. At the height of its production, the company employed over 25,000 workers. In the late 1970s, Hanomag went bankrupt. At this time, not only were its machines and buildings dismantled and destroyed, but also its archives. A colleague of mine and a retired engineer of the company managed to save the remaining parts of the archive and move them into Hanover's Historisches Museum.

Discovering these photographs was a pivotal moment in my research on workers and work processes in German industries. The pictures in the archive showed the factory's enormous workshops. Some of the photographs focused on the operation of lathe and milling machines, which produced engine components for cars and trucks. In one of the pictures, several dozen workers were concentrating on their work, obviously trying to demonstrate how intensely they strove to do a good job. They seemed well disciplined. But in the background, things looked somewhat different. Workers were just standing there and watching what was happening at the front of the factory hall. Some of the workers were smoking cigarettes next to the machines.

The difference between the workers in the foreground and those in the background lay in their body posture and behavior. Those working at the machines knew they were being observed and did everything to behave in accordance with the factory rules. Presumably they had been admonished to behave before these pictures were taken. But the workers in the background did not consider themselves to be in the frame. They did not feel observed. Instead of working, they took the opportunity for a break, to chat and to smoke.

This was a real eye-opener for me. The photographs helped make visible the actual behavior of working people. They transgressed the limits of workers' intimacy. The photographs allowed me to recognize people's working practices and settings with more concreteness than textual documents would have ever made possible.

The photographs invited me to look more closely. They led me to pursue an understanding of the actual work processes in industrial production. How did people handle the tools, for example? How did they operate the lathes and milling machines? In one of the albums in the archives, I found a picture showing a heavy chisel inserted into a milling machine. There was a torn piece of cloth wrapped around the grip of this chisel and fixed with a knot. I asked a retired worker about this and he told me that the work process sometimes required the chisel to be replaced with a bigger one or a slightly smaller one. To make the change swifter, the workers tied a cord around the grip of the chisel to get a better hold on it. And because the chisel became very hot and the workers did not have time to wait until it cooled, they used scraps of cloth to protect themselves from burns or from losing a hand or an arm in the machine. I found confirmation in posters of the 1920s depicting industrial health and safety measures. But it was the self-made devices for protection that most concretely showed workers' own perceptions of danger and the efforts they took to keep those at bay.

The subjects of the photographs as well as the photographic gaze itself also revealed alternative perspectives on work and workers' practices. The Hanomag pictures showed only male workers. But I found photographs of female workers too from the same industrial sector, though at another company and in a different location: Krupp's steelworks at Essen-Ruhr. These photographs focus on young women, most of them replacing those many male workers who had been drafted into the army during World War I. The pictures display joyous and boisterous females teasing each other or enjoying a few minutes of leisure time in front of the workshops during their breaks. In fact, almost all of the pictures I found of female workers showed moments and actions of non-work. Surely this focus resonates with contemporary stereotypes about gender and labor – how work is only imagined as the 'real thing' when muscular strength and a keen focus on technical skills come together. The pictorial documentations of worksites enhanced the distinctions between male and female worlds of labor.

Photographs expand the range of possibilities for the writing and depicting of history. They can help us to dig up new dimensions of everyday life that have not been seen previously.

How did other historians in the 1970s and 1980s – in Germany and elsewhere – respond to your work on everyday life: your interdisciplinary approach, your commitment to the History Workshop, your use of oral history, and your use of photographs as historical sources?

Until the 1980s, historians of Germany used photographs in their work primarily for illustrative purposes. At this time, I was developing what would become the project of the history of everyday life (*Alltagsgeschichte*). In that context, I recognized how limited and often vague available written texts were. Visual materials – that term I very much prefer to 'sources' – introduced a new round of discussion on crucial aspects of work and working life that had been ignored thus far. This made me question the seriousness with which disciplinarity is practiced, if not enforced. By this I mean that people too frequently restrict their research questions, discussions, and forms of publication to the pre-given rules of academia.

To take one example: Why did so many people more or less happily, or at least without any protest, go along with movements such as National Socialism? It was not just repression or manipulation. In fact, and as in similar cases of domination, people's livelihoods were at stake. People felt that demands and promises issued by the ruling authorities endangered their expectations, if not their most heartfelt desires. To reveal those dynamics, you must go beyond institutional records and their respective archives. It is necessary to understand how people behaved in their everyday situations. You can find hints in police material and social welfare reports, but these exclude the voices of the people themselves, for example, how they spoke to each other in family situations. The reports of undercover agents, confidants, and collaborators in other bureaucracies and agencies also offer some glimpses, but these accounts are always filtered by a bureaucratic eye or frame.

So, it became important to go beyond the established rules of historical analysis. At least since the 1940s, oral history has stepped in to complement historians' primary focus on written and printed texts. Beginning with oral interviews among the rank and file of the US military and civilians during World War II, historians in the United States launched efforts to directly record the voices of the people. A primary aim was to listen to them talking about their own lives and future expectations. However, in European settings and particularly in Germany, the danger was that people would not talk to an academic interviewer precisely because he or she is an academic interviewer. Why should an interviewee share personal opinions, feelings, and thoughts with somebody who wants to share these stories? What happens to this information when it journeys into the hands of researchers? Oral interviews have stimulated a substantial expansion of research scopes. Such increased multiplicity of voices has irritated if not levelled out rigorous disciplinarity.

How should we read and interpret photographs, particularly historical photographs? When you compare photographs with written texts, can we say that photographs are more accessible? Do you need certain skills or language to read pictures?

In many cases, I certainly think photographs are meant to simply document or visualize settings, items, or situations. I can show you a book by a photographer who documented the ruthless military assault on peaceful student demonstrators at Tiananmen Square in June 1989, for example.[11] This incident was documented with the aim of keeping memories of this violence alive in people's minds. In China, as we know, narratives of this incident are strictly regimented by the state. New generations have almost forgotten the initial cause and actual course of the conflict between the Chinese students and the government. At this point, the particular value of the photograph comes into play. These pictures provide intricate details about the setting, actions, and atmosphere at Tiananmen Square as sensed and observed by the photographer.

Pictures collect but also stimulate references: projections and associations, as well as mental images and experiences. The onlooker focuses on the depictions and sees many other sides and sights simultaneously. Simultaneity is a key aspect of visual dimension here. Pictures open. If there had been a text trying to describe a similar message, you would have to follow the lines from left to right; the linearity of the text is in a strict sense one-dimensional.

I would like to emphasize a more productive interrelationship between images and texts. Let me start with a brief remark on 'reading' pictures. For me, this is a contradiction in terms. You look on and see pictures. You see each picture at once in all its possibly different pictorial elements. It is the simultaneity of visually grasping the respective picture at one single moment.

For me, this simultaneity enhances the difference between images and written texts. I do not know whether looking at pictures is less restricted or regulated than reading a text. But the difference between reading and instantaneously looking at pictures creates an important difference that may nourish the illusion that it is easier to understand an image than a text.

But if, as you suggest, ambiguity is always inherent in photography, how can we deal with commonplace assumptions about the truthfulness and authenticity of photographs? Are written or oral sources of history more truthful?

Well, I would want to begin by expressing my skepticism about an assumption here that textual and oral sources – again, I prefer 'materials' – are reliable. Take interviews, for example. A substantial number of professional historians developed a strong skepticism about contemporary witnesses

---

11 Xu Yong, *Negatives* (Dortmund: Kettler, 2015).

and their oral testimonies.[12] Their objection, of course, was that memories have changed and will always change over the course of a lifetime.

I can add an example from my study on the Prussian police in the early and mid-nineteenth century. Between 1853 and 1857, the county office reported cases of cheating, fake scales, inedible bread, adulterations of beer, spirits, and wine, and the use of counterfeit coins. In each of these cases, the numbers were completely identical each year. I took this as proof that the scribe just copied the list of the previous year and that the county commissioner either did not take notice or did not care. Whatever it may have been, this shows that printed or written material may not be as truthful as one may think.

Nonetheless, I strongly believe that the photographic action seems to be driven by the claim for authenticity of photographic images. A photograph resonates with the desire for a *spürbare Schwerkraft der Wirklichkeit* (tangible gravity of reality) of the spectator and eventually of the photographer and that this ensures the authenticity of the depicted object or subject. In *Der Schatten des Fotografen* ("The Photographer's Shadow"), Helmut Lethen speaks of this as a context of confidence.[13] Authenticity, he argues, needs the confidence of the spectator. It is a widespread assumption that photography provides or even guarantees the authenticity of the photographed.

Photographs come with the claim of depicting and ensuring authenticity above all other mediums. This runs contrary to the *basso continuo* of modern historiography. The desire for truthfulness is nourished in part by the technology of the photography. When the shutter button of the camera is pressed, the shutter releases and clicks. This is the moment when the picture is created. At the same time, the moment freezes.

But the photograph's freezing of a specific moment can affect the perception of time and mislead historians. Let me give you a concrete example. Over the years, I had repeatedly seen a reproduction of a metal worker's portrait from the 1920s. It was of a lathe turner at work. This photograph appeared on the front cover of a widely recognized illustrated journal, the *Arbeiter-Illustrierte-Zeitung* (AIZ [Worker's Illustrated News]), in January 1929, which had a circulation then of about half a million. The photograph was inscribed with a well-known slogan of working people and trade unions. On the cover, it stood below the lathe and said: "If your strong arm is willing …," shedding the second part of this slogan: "… all wheels stand still." However, the widespread readership of the AIZ could not see the underlying blueprint, i.e. the original photograph. This picture had, of course, no inscription. More importantly, it had the turner who watched and controlled the operation of his lathe in a dark indoor site, with no one else around.

How to bridge the differences between these two pictures? By accident, I learned the name and location of this turner. We met in October 1985, almost sixty years after he had shot the picture. I asked him about the process. He mentioned that his lathe was sitting at the end of a workshop dealing with railway switches. He worked at the tools department of the switches workshop. His lathe was at the end, directly next to a high metal fence. He could employ this lathe for mounting the camera and putting up the flashlight pan. In detail, he mentioned how he had arranged things to make sure that he could be back at his lathe from starting the clock of the photographic plate to get the full blow of the flashlight. After the flash, he ran back, shut the camera, and dismounted every item.

12 See Lutz Niethammer, ed., *Lebensgeschichte und Sozialkultur im Ruhrgebiet, 1930–1960* (Bonn: Verlag, 1983). See also Harald Welzer, Sabine Moller and Karoline Tschuggnall, *"Opa war kein Nazi": Nationalsozialismus und Holocaust im Familiengedächtnis* (Frankfurt am Main: Fischer-Taschenbuch-Verlag, 2002).

13 Helmut Lethen, *Der Schatten des Fotografen: Bilder und ihre Wirklichkeit* (Berlin: Rowohlt, 2014).

But why had he made this picture? "I just wanted to show people how it was at my work station," he responded. He didn't go into any detail of the actual handling of tools and the piece he worked on. Rather, he went on by pointing to his young age and the seemingly natural result of him being the youngster on the shop floor that he regularly received the most heavy and difficult to handle items he had to work on.

The worker's memory underscored the difference between the picture he had made and the usage the AIZ derived from this. He wanted to address friends and family. There was not a minimal trace of a proletarian struggle or any resonance that might have sprung up among the workers on the shop floor. It is only the interrelationship of text (and narration) with the photographic image that can allow for multifaceted understanding and viewing.

Why do some images hold our attention over others? How come certain photos come into view or go out of view?

I think this depends primarily on the spectator. In *Camera Lucida*, Roland Barthes elucidates intriguing features of the very view of the spectator.[14] In particular, he points to the *punctum*: a minute detail in a picture that may go unnoticed by many spectators but may catch the attention of others. *Punctum* touches the direct relation of the spectator with what is depicted. It can be a carelessly strapped belt or a wrongly buttoned shirt. It helps us to emphasize the importance of the margins. Sometimes, it invites us to take a second look. It can be possible that the marginal appears less marginal and the *punctum* can destabilize inscribed codes. It is often this *punctum* that defines the relation of the spectator to the depiction. This relation decides if certain photographs come into view or go out of view.

No doubt this decision changes over time. Temporality is an important characteristic of this relation. Any person can view every image at any time. It not only has a meaning for those who employ it for their own purposes, but it is also understandable for generations to come. We shouldn't forget to consider the aspect of temporality when we deal with photographs. The moment when a picture is taken is always already past, even if it is only a second ago, two minutes ago, a few days, months, or years. In that sense, it is a reminder of destruction, decay, and death. Temporality is inherent in a photograph, in the frozen moment. That's quite a troublesome, but intriguing point. I am still very puzzled by this simultaneity of catching a moment and losing it at the same time. It tells us something beyond the moment, which we shouldn't overlook.

You bring up the subject of contextualization, perhaps historians' most useful and powerful concept and labor. How much context do we need to study a photograph?

The photographic action is part and parcel of making pictures. As much as those who are photographed or taken as the objects of photography, the context of the photographer co-shapes the momentary actions. Detailed descriptions of this context and its multiple elements and moments are crucial. Such scrutiny for context opens our eyes to both the object of the picture as well as to its actually or seemingly missing parts.

Helmut Lethen addresses another dimension of this issue. He speaks in this context of *Unheimlichkeit aus zweiter Hand* (eeriness at second hand).[15] Imagine a young woman, wading through the thigh-high water of a little creek. She turns her back to the camera. It seems to be a pleasant

---

14 Roland Barthes, *Camera Lucida* (New York: Hill and Wang, 1981).
15 Lethen, *Der Schatten des Fotografen*: 12.

moment. It is sunny. Eventually, she is refreshing herself. It looks like a classical *locus amoenus*. But if the spectator turns the photograph around, he will notice a neatly handwritten inscription. It says *Minenprobe: Vom Donez zum Don 1942* ("Search for Land Mine"). Immediately the atmosphere of the photograph changes. The horror of the actual scene becomes visible. This picture then conveys a strong sense of eeriness, if at second hand, as Lethen is suggesting. The young woman has been forced by German soldiers to step into the creek to test whether there are any land mines in the way. They accepted her death in order not to risk their own lives. So, in that sense, it's not this *locus amoenus*, but rather the opposite – and it's extremely dangerous.

I saw this photograph in a photo album belonging to an ordinary German soldier. It was collected for an exhibition in the city of Oldenburg in 2009.[16] This snapshot had been taken by an ordinary soldier for private purposes, including exchange with other soldiers. It shows us that sometimes it only needs a minimum of contextualization to place a photograph in an unmistakable historical context.

---

16 Petra Bopp and Sandra Starke, eds., *Fremde im Visier: Fotoalben aus dem Zweiten Weltkrieg* (Bielefeld: Kerber Verlag, 2009).

Reflections III

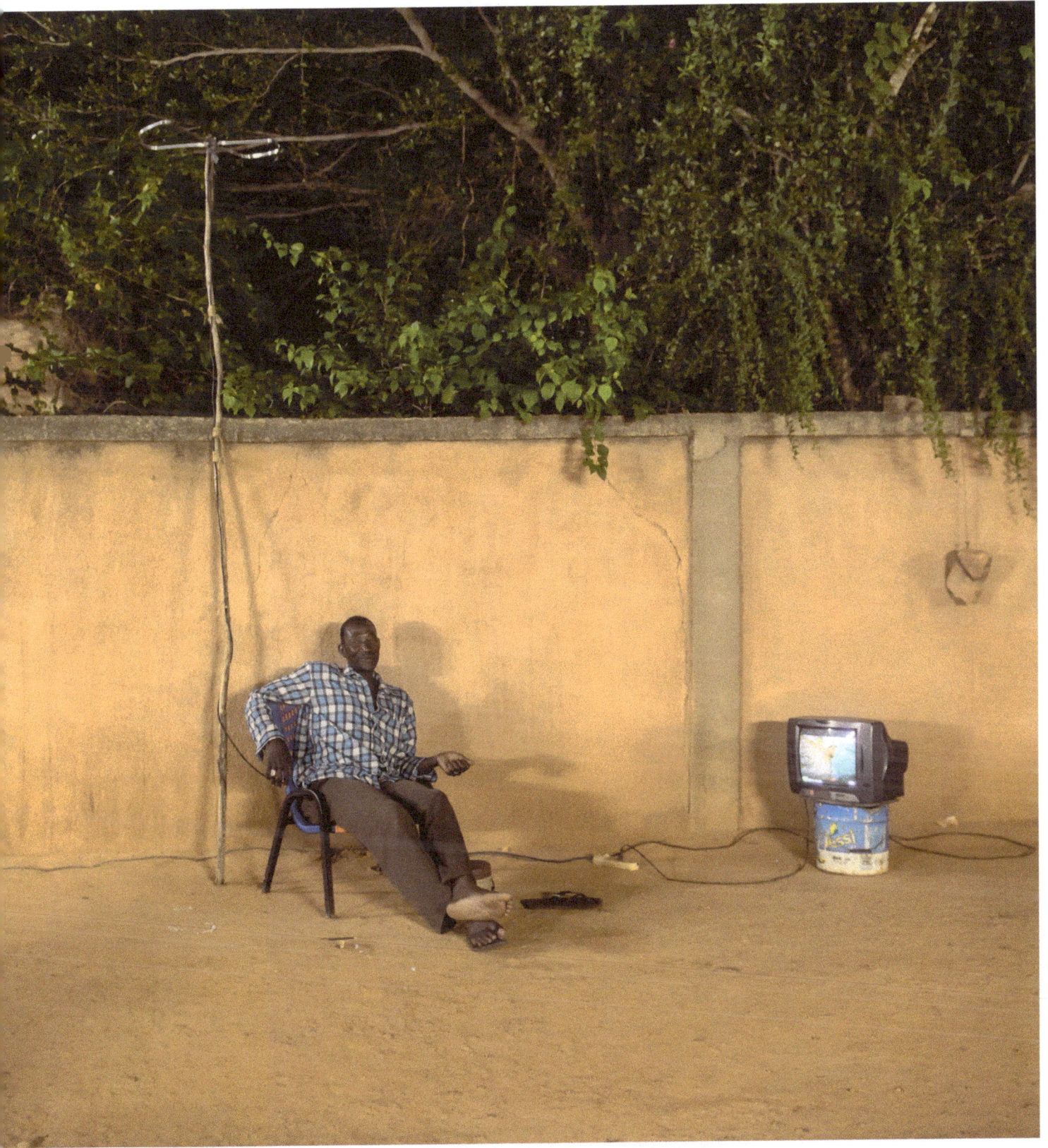

Laurent Fourchard

Why Homes Still Matter: Thoughts on Mamphela Ramphele's *A Bed Called Home*

A Bed Called Home: Life in the Migrant Labour Hostels of Cape Town was published the year before the end of apartheid. It followed a long series of anthropological and historical works that explained, explored, and criticized the centrality of the oppressive migrant labor system in the political economy of South Africa.[1] These studies made clear how successive South African governments developed a very well-known dual labor policy throughout the twentieth century. The South African government favored the stabilization of a black working class and simultaneously wanted to restrict the urbanization of black migrants, and its labor policy gave employers the chance to choose between two segments of labor according to their needs.[2] It led to a growing dissociation of two groups within the black population. On one hand, a limited black working class lived in areas made for non-white groups at the periphery of the city, the township, and were given rights of residence; most of the time they were living in family houses and had access – albeit in a very limited ways – to school and health systems. These populations were supposed to stabilize or become 'permanently urbanized.' On the other hand, there was another category of people who qualified as migrants coming from deprived rural areas (known as reserves and from the 1960s as *Bantustans*) and from different southern African countries. They were allowed to stay in cities, in the mines, or on farms on the condition that they had a job paid by a white employer. They were defined as 'temporary sojourners' or 'oscillating migrants,' had to return to the reserves once their contract was finished, and were repatriated to the reserves if they were 'unemployed' (which meant not having a recognized job three days after their arrival in a white area). They had to live in separate areas within or outside black townships in barracks or hostels constructed and owned by employers or municipalities. The obligation to carry a reference book or a pass – including a photograph, a confirmation of race, tax payments, and employment and criminal records – was extended to the black population including, from the mid-1950s, women, as one major tool to reinforce control over the mobility of migrants in order to 'freeze urbanization.' Langa, Nyanga, and Guguletu, the first generation of black townships set up on the outskirts of the city of Cape Town were typical of this policy. Guguletu was created in the late 1950s to accommodate families and permanent workers, while the township of Langa became the privileged place of migrants coming from different reserves in the Eastern Cape province. In 1960, Langa included 19,000 men among whom 18,000 were 'bachelors' – a term designating non-married males according to customary laws – accommodated in 849 barracks consisting of sixteen men each. These are the hostels that Mamphela Ramphele examines extensively, twenty-five years after their creation.

At first glance, the publication of *A Bed Called Home* in 1993 seemed to arrive too late: with apartheid ending, the negotiations between the African National Congress (ANC) and the incumbent National Party, and the preparations for the first democratic election in the country in 1994.

---

1 See in a larger production Monica Wilson and Archie Mafeje, *Langa: A Study of Social Groups in an African Township* (Cape Town; London: Oxford University Press, 1963), Francis Wilson, *Labour in the South African Gold Mines, 1911–1969* (Cambridge: Cambridge University Press, 1972).

2 Frederick Cooper, *Decolonization and African Society: The Labor Question in French and British Africa* (Cambridge: Cambridge University Press, 1995): 264, 515.

Moreover, the existing labor migrant system was collapsing. The government abolished the pass laws in 1986, lifting the requirement to carry passbooks, and black people could no longer be sent to the reserves. The requirement not to be in an urban area for more than seventy-two hours without permission was scrapped and the legislative distinction between those permanently urbanized and others was abolished. But it was precisely because it was a period of radical transformation that Ramphele's book was a timely publication. It perfectly illustrated how the prevalence of apartheid institutions was still dominating the daily lives of millions of black migrants in hostels on the eve of apartheid.

The survey in the hostels actually took place a few years before. In 1985, Ramphele accepted an invitation to come to Cape Town from Francis Wilson, a professor of economics at the University of Cape Town (UCT), who was coordinating a major research project on forms of poverty in South Africa, a project in which she soon became involved.[3] Prior to this she had had a long period of experience as a medical doctor in the rural area of Lenyenye – where she was exiled for her anti-apartheid activities in the 1970s – and set up an association for the development of the area.[4] With her background in public health and deep concern for the daily struggles of black men and women under apartheid, she began a PhD at the UCT's Department of Social Anthropology in 1986. The following year, she carried out a health survey among hostel migrants in Langa, Nyanga, and Guguletu. Her multidimensional approach – as an anthropologist living in one of Cape Town's black townships, as a feminist working with a patriarchal organization, the Hostel Dwellers Association (HDA), and as a medical doctor having developed a comprehensive approach to public health – made her book a central contribution to the anthropology not only of home but also of labor, health, and gender relations.

The notion of 'bedhold,' which first appeared in the *South African Medical Journal* in 1991, became one of the key concepts through which labor and gender relations had to be understood.[5] As Ramphele writes, "Every aspect of life here revolves around a bed. Access to this humble environment depends upon one's access to a bed; it is the basis for relationships within the hostels, between different hostels, and between hostels and places of employment. One's very identity and legal existence depend on one's attachment to a bed."[6] The 'bedhold' referred to this spatial unit which defined the parameters of 'home' in the absence of a 'household' for those who lived in township hostels. She reported on the tensions that prevailed between the formal definition of hostels as men's places and the reality of women's and children's presence there. Focusing on the relational dimensions of the bed-as-home allowed her to take some distance from dominant paradigmatic interpretations of apartheid and labor migration. The book is interestingly free of the vocabulary associated with the former approaches of the Manchester School of anthropology, which analyzed the labor system in Southern Africa within the framework of modernization theory

---

3 Francis Wilson and Mamphela Ramphele, *Uprooting Poverty: The South African Challenge* (Cape Town: David Philip, 1989).

4 She founded Ithuseng, an organization that takes a holistic approach to development. The association provides health services, child care facilities, nutrition programs, income generating cooperative enterprises, literacy training, and education programs to a population of about 120,000.

5 Mamphela Ramphele and M. Heap, "Health Status of Hostel Dwellers: Part 1. Introduction, Methodology, and Response Rates," *South African Medical Journal* 79 (1991): 697–701.

6 Mamphela Ramphele, *A Bed Called Home: Life in the Migrant Labour Hostels of Cape Town* (Cape Town: David Philip, 1993): 20.

and the so-called 'adaptation' of migrants to urban life.[7] Migrants in South Africa were qualified as 'semi-urban' because they were navigating between the rural and the urban. Anthropologists were then exploring the multiple ways in which migrants adapted to city life and so contradicting the detribalization thesis which was a common official narrative in many Southern African colonies. If this school of thought was dying out in the 1970s, the adaptation thesis has remained in South Africa, but was a possible analytical framework that Ramphele did not follow.[8] She also broke away from a radical neo-Marxist approach dominant in South African social sciences of the 1980s and early 1990s, which subsumed different social dynamics to a general process of proletarization (often qualified as incomplete) and which focused on the multiple forms of resistance to that very process.[9]

Instead she located her analysis at the crossroads of Erving Goffman's analysis, understanding the hostel as a total institution destroying the identity of migrants, and Frantz Fanon and Steve Biko's criticism of the dehumanizing colonial and apartheid regimes leading colonized people to adopt self-deprecating attitudes. As a medical doctor she calculated that the constraints of space were so severe that, on average, 2.8 people shared a bed while 'personal' space amounted to 1.8 square meters. As she states, "the lack of private space for families limits their capacity to function as a coherent unit in day to day social interaction." Following Goffman she mentioned that "people living under these specific space constraints are constantly subjected to pressure to conform," and she insisted that "hostels are institutions and not homes" having "no sense of ownership or hope of such ownership"; this particular focus was probably the clearest path-breaking innovations in understanding the concrete effects of hostels on one's self-definition and on the systematic dismantling of home as a family unit and its permanent reconfiguration under severe bureaucratic and political constraints. As such it was a radically innovative book, a fact recognized by academic reviews in South Africa and beyond, as it soon triggered new research into possible definitions of a home determined by relations with labor, family, and gender dynamics.

There are other lasting legacies in Ramphele's book. It questions two landmark issues in South African historiography: the place of women and the enduring legacy of apartheid in contemporary South Africa. The bedhold was ultimately a space of women's exploitation and not a place where compromises could be negotiated between men and women. Despite the abandoning of the pass laws in 1986, regulations in hostels remained the same: they were reserved for males with bona fide employment who were legally allowed to be in urban areas. In the late 1980s, just as during the culmination of apartheid, bedholds were allocated to men through a patronage system. Women depended on men for accommodation and did not have many other options than to acquiesce to male authority. As women feared the consequences of not complying with men's demands, subversion was very limited. Pleasing one's husband instead became an essential survival strategy for married women who wanted to prolong their stay or be allowed to live there permanently. Competition was high and multifaceted – between married and single women, between urbanized women and rural wives, and between women living in hostels and women living in the reserves. But even in this very constrained environment, Ramphele never considered these women to be mere victims.

---

7 James Ferguson, *Expectations of Modernity: Myths and Meanings of Urban Life on the Zambian Copperbelt* (Berkeley: University of California Press, 1999).

8 For a recent example, see Tom Lodge, *Sharpeville: An Apartheid Massacre and its Consequences* (Oxford: Oxford University Press, 2011).

9 Charles Van Onselen, *New Babylon, New Nineveh: Everyday Life on the Witwatersrand, 1886–1914* (Johannesburg: Jonathan Ball, 2001); Belinda Bozzoli, *Class, Community and Conflict: South African Perspectives* (Johannesburg: Ravan Press, 1987).

In this sense, the book was very much part of a growth in the 1990s of literature that challenged the idea that colonial or apartheid cities were exclusively male preserves while women were passive and stayed in the countryside where they reproduced patterns of peasant livelihoods.[10]

The book went further than merely deciphering the radically unequal relationships in the hostel. Ramphele challenged sexism not only as it manifested itself through the apartheid authorities but also – and this was a newer perception – within the anti-apartheid movements and within organizations fighting for improvements in the daily lives of migrants. The Hostel Dwellers' Association, a new association founded to exert pressure for the improvement of hostel dwellers' conditions, requested her involvement in gaining recognition of rights to family life and dignified accommodation. It did not envisage that she would challenge their patriarchal vision of excluding women from its membership. Opening membership to women was seen as a revolution. As she clearly mentioned, it would entail recognition of women as workers and as permanent residents of hostels and urban areas, threaten the legitimacy of male authority, and challenge their worldview of the place of women in the domestic sphere. Clearly, there was something deeper to be challenged beyond the bed-as-home institution: the future of women in post-apartheid South Africa. Her position challenged a strong consensus within anti-apartheid movements. When she resigned as adviser, fundraiser, and general facilitator of the association, she made it clear that the quest for transformation of gender relations was no less important than the struggle against apartheid. That decision – not easily taken – echoed her strong criticism of Cosatu's leadership, which was labelling sexism as 'bourgeois' and individuals claiming the need to transform gender relations as enemies of 'the working class.'[11] Her stance triggered a new wave of research based on what Ramphele called an 'integrated analysis' of power differentials, giving equal weight to the oppression of racism, economic exploitation, and sexism.[12]

Ramphele also knew that the social problems inherited from apartheid policies were serious challenges to be tackled by the government. She was well aware of the level and extent of poverty and inequality in the country. Exploring the conditions of migrants was also a call to look at the enduring legacy of apartheid institutions on the daily lives of the most vulnerable people in the country: the migrants and beyond them the millions of poor rural black women and men trapped in the *Bantoustans*. She identified a central issue at the core of Jeremy Seekings and Nicoli Natrass's recent interpretation: strong social inequality in post-apartheid South Africa was one of the most enduring legacies of apartheid, reflected in the division between the working and middle classes based in urban and former white areas and the rural poor in former Bantustans.[13] As the institution of the hostel was, however, slowly dying out, she anticipated that one other central issue – a

---

10 Cheryl Walker, *Women and Resistance in South Africa* (London: Onyx Press, 1990); Belinda Bozzoli and Mmantho Nkotsoe, *Women of Phokeng: Consciousness, Life Strategy and Migrancy in South Africa, 1900–1983* (London: James Currey, 1991); Teresa Barnes, *We Women Worked so Hard: Gender, Urbanisation and Social Reproduction in Colonial Harare, Zimbabwe, 1930–1956* (Oxford: James Currey, 1999); Luise White, *The Comforts of Home: Prostitution in Colonial Nairobi* (Chicago: University of Chicago Press, 1990).
11 The Congress of South Africa Trade Union (COSATU) is the federation of unions in South Africa founded in 1985, the principal ally of the ANC during the fight against apartheid and the major ally of the government since 1994.
12 For some of the first works inspired by Ramphele's publications, see for instance Melissa Steyn, "A New Agenda: Restructuring Feminism in South Africa," *Women's Studies International Forum* 21 (1998): 41–52. Carolyne White, "'Close to Home' in Johannesburg: Gender Oppression in Township Households," *Women's Studies International Forum* 16 (1993): 149–63.
13 Jeremy Seekings and Nicoli Natrass, *Class, Race and Inequality in South Africa* (Scottsville: University of Kwa-Zulu Natal Press, 2006).

housing crisis – would soon explode. There were tremendous needs due to the apartheid regime's reluctance to finance housing for the black population, and it was clear that high demand for family houses was already becoming a sensitive political issue. She indicated that 1.8 million houses needed to be built immediately and 2.8 million by the year 2000 to solve the housing shortage. She was right. Despite the tremendous effort made by the ANC government, which has no equivalent on the continent, 2.5 million units were built between 1994 and 2015. The housing crisis remains as severe as in 1993, and popular expectation has not declined but instead grown with grassroots mobilization for land and houses.[14] In the process, housing policies and housing rights became a major area of research especially among geographers and urban scholars.

One of the last legacies of the hostel as an institution is the division within the black population and the difficulty of dismantling relations based on apartheid legislation, which defined hostel dwellers as 'outsiders' and townships dwellers as 'insiders.' Even more than before, migrants were complaining in the early 1990s of being denied full urban citizenship by townships dwellers and felt that they were not fully consulted or included in existing political and organizational structures dominated by township residents. There was often aggression and sometimes collective fights between hostel migrants and townships dwellers who organized their own vigilante groups to protect against attacks by outside communities. The housing of migrants in hostels continued to define them as 'outsiders' and hampered their access to the resources of the state. Hostel dwellers were looked down upon by township dwellers who considered them as coming from remote rural areas, being poorly educated, unable to speak *tsotistal* – the argotic language of the township. Ramphele intuitively felt that this was going to be a problem. Actually, stigmatization of and violence against non-national Africans in the post-apartheid period has emerged as one of the outcomes of this triple legacy: the continued, albeit transformed, use of migrants as cheap, disposable labor in a context of structural unemployment; the racial and social stereotyping of African migrants by township dwellers rooted in the history of urban residency rights; and the indeterminacy of migrants' place in South African society produced by the South African public administration of home affairs through a massive deportation policy that regulated the presence of foreigners by removing them.[15] While Ramphele did not suspect that xenophobia was going to become one of the burning issues in the post-apartheid era, her book reminds us that, like too few empirical studies produced along that line since, the pervasive forms of xenophobia in townships in South Africa today have to be looked at through the troubled legacy of the migrant hostel as a total institution.[16]

---

14 The number of squatting areas have increased from 300 in 1994 to 2,700 and today there is still a need for 2.1 million units.

15 Laurent Fourchard and Aurelia Segatti, "Of Xenophobia and Citizenship: The Politics of Exclusion and Inclusion in Africa," *Africa* 85 (2015): 2–12.

16 Noor Nieftagodien, "Xenophobia's Local Genesis: Historical Constructions of Insiders and the Politics of Exclusion in Alexandra Township," in *Exorcising the Demons Within: Xenophobia, Violence, and Statecraft in Contemporary South Africa*, ed. Landau Loren (Johannesburg: Wits University Press, 2011): 109–34.

Contributor Biographies

Renu Addlakha is engaged in research on gender and disability at the Centre for Women's Development Studies in Delhi. Her areas of specialization include the sociology of the psychiatric profession, medical anthropology, bioethics, and disability studies.

Gadi Algazi works as a historian at Tel Aviv University. His research concerns late medieval and early modern social and cultural history, historical anthropology, the history and theory of the social sciences, settler colonialism, and frontier societies.

Eric Allina is an associate professor of history at the University of Ottawa. His areas of teaching and research include African history, the history of slavery, and Cold War era connections between African and socialist bloc states.

Rukmini Barua completed her PhD at the Centre for Modern Indian Studies at the University of Göttingen in 2016. Her research focuses on working-class neighborhoods in Ahmedabad and Delhi.

Anne-Katrin Bicher is an international curator and project manager based in Bonn. She spent six years in Johannesburg curating a project on the heritage of migrant workers in South Africa.

Alla Bolotova works at the Center for Arctic Social Studies at the European University at St. Petersburg. Her current research focuses on industrial communities and human-environmental interaction in the Arctic.

Charlotte Bruckermann works in the Department 'Resilience and Transformation in Eurasia' at the Max Planck Institute for Social Anthropology in Halle. She currently focuses on how finance drives environmental policies and livelihood strategies in contemporary China.

Sidney Chalhoub is a social historian at Harvard University. His research interests range from Brazilian slavery history to the modern history of working-class culture.

Isaie Dougnon taught at the University of Bamako before he started teaching at Fordham University in New York. His research interests include the anthropology of work, migration studies, local knowledge, rural development, and academic freedom in West Africa.

Heike Drotbohm is an anthropologist at the University of Mainz. Her research concentrates on African diasporas and transnationalism, migration, kinship and care, childhood and youth, rights and bureaucracy, and religion in the Atlantic rim.

Andreas Eckert is a professor of African history at Humboldt-Universität zu Berlin. Since 2009, he has also served as the director of the international research center Work and Human Lifecycle in Global History (re:work). He has published widely on nineteenth and twentieth-century African history, colonialism, labor, and global history.

Josef Ehmer is a professor emeritus at the University of Vienna. His research encompasses a broad spectrum of European social history, including work and the worker, the family and aging, historical demography, and migration.

Paulo Fontes is a historian of Brazilian labor and working-class culture at the Fundação Getulio Vargas in Rio de Janeiro. He works on labor migration, the role of communities in working-class formation, and the cultural aspects of organizations and politics.

Laurent Fourchard focuses on the history and socio-politics of Nigeria and South Africa at the Centre de Recherches Internationales at Sciences Po, Paris. His research fields include violence and exclusion, xenophobia, and citizenship in African cities.

Anne Griffiths is a professor of anthropology and law at the University of Edinburgh. Her research focuses on the anthropology of law, comparative and family law, African law, gender, culture, and rights.

Felicitas Hentschke works at the international research center Work and Human Lifecycle in Global History at Humboldt-Universität zu Berlin. In terms of scholarly work, she focuses on the lives of workers in the mining industry in Northern France.

Vincent Houben is a professor in the Department of Asian and African Studies at Humboldt-Universität zu Berlin. His research focuses on Southeast Asia. His research themes are colonial history the politics of postcolonial memory, and theories of non-Western societies.

Jonathan Hyslop teaches at Colgate University, New York. His work focuses on modern Southern Africa. His research interests range from labor history and the British Empire to maritime history and the history and sociology of warfare.

Milena Kremakova completed her PhD in sociology at Warwick University. She has conducted research on post-socialist transformations in Eastern Europe, maritime labor, and coastal communities worldwide. She is currently working on academic lifecycles and careers in mathematics.

Ju Li is a professor in the Department of Sociology and Social Anthropology at the Central European University, Budapest. Her work focuses on social history, labor, modern China, historical sociology, globalization, and critical development.

Alf Lüdtke is an honorary professor at University of Erfurt and his work focuses on the history of everyday life. His research interests include work as social practice, war as work, the potential of a 'visual history,' and various forms of domination, as well as people's multifaceted and self-willed activities in the modern era.

Mary Jo Maynes teaches European social history at the University of Minnesota. She specializes in the history of life course trajectories and autobiographies, as well as female labor in European textile industries, especially in France, Germany, and Ireland.

Prabhu Mohapatra is an economic and social historian at the University of Delhi. His research focuses on the economic history of India, labor history, the global history of servitude, and transnational migration.

Cláudio Pinheiro is a professor of African history at the Rio de Janeiro Federal University in Brazil and Chairman of the South-South Exchange Programme for Research on the History of Development (SEPHIS), His research interests range from colonialism and slavery to knowledge circulation and social theory.

Mamphela Ramphele is a physician, academic, former vice chancellor of the University of Cape Town, and former managing director of the World Bank. She is the co-founder of the Black Consciousness Movement, and a lifelong activist, author, and businesswoman.

Anupama Rao is a historian at Barnard College, Columbia University. Her research and teaching interests include gender studies, caste and race, historical anthropology, comparative urbanism, and the colonial genealogies of human rights and humanitarianism.

Stephen J. Rockel is a historian at the University of Toronto. He has particular interests in labor history, slavery, urbanization, colonialism, nationalism, and war throughout the African continent and beyond.

David Warren Sabean is a professor of German history at the University of California, Los Angeles. He has conducted research on family lifecycles, kinship relations, and work, and is currently examining incest discourse in Europe and America from 1600 to the present.

Jürgen Schmidt works at the international research center Work and Human Lifecycle in Global History at Humboldt-Universität zu Berlin and the Institute for the History and Future of Work in Berlin, Germany. His research specializes on the European history of workers.

Thabang Sefalafala is an economic sociologist at the Society, Work and Development Institute, University of the Witwatersrand. His research interests include sociological theory, development economics, and human resources.

Nitin Sinha is a research associate at the Leibniz Centre for Modern Oriental Studies in Berlin, focusing on topics related to the history of transport and communication, labor, ecology, and Hindi vernacular print from the eighteenth to the twentieth century.

Gerd Spittler is professor emeritus of anthropology at the University of Bayreuth, with a regional focus on Africa. He is currently working on the anthropology of work and the anthropology of material culture.

Christian Strümpell teaches anthropology at Hamburg University. His research focus is on economic and urban anthropology, particularly work and labor, caste, indigeneity, and class in South Asia.

Thaddeus Sunseri works as a historian at Colorado State University, Fort Collins. He is a historian of the ecology of beef, veterinary science, and environmental change in Tanzania and the wider world. His studies include rural migration, forest farming, and the ivory trade in colonial East Africa.

Nitin Varma is based at the international research center Work and Human Lifecycle in Global History at Humboldt-Universität zu Berlin. He is currently working on an ERC Starting Grant project on domestic servants in colonial South Asia.

Ann Waltner teaches Chinese social history at the University of Minnesota. She specializes in the history of ritual, religion, gender and feminism, and law, as well as the analysis of historical documentation.

Maurice Weiss lives and works as a photographer in Berlin. He is a member of the photographer-run agency *Ostkreuz*.

James Williams is an anthropologist at Zayed University, Dubai, interested in youth, migration, and work in contexts of urban volatility, deprivation, and post-conflict in Africa and the Middle East.

Picture Credits

Algeria, Maurice Weiss, cover

China, Maurice Weiss, p. VI

France, Maurice Weiss, p. VI

Ethiopia, Maurice Weiss, p. VII

France, Maurice Weiss, p. XIII

Turkey, Maurice Weiss, p. XX

France, Maurice Weiss, p. XXI

Saudi Arabia, Maurice Weiss, p. XXI

Niger, Maurice Weiss, p. XXII

France, Maurice Weiss, p. 10

Greece, Maurice Weiss, p. 10

Niger, Maurice Weiss, p. 11

Lebanon, Maurice Weiss, p. 36

Ukraine, Maurice Weiss, p. 36

Germany, Maurice Weiss, p. 37

Costa Rica, Maurice Weiss, p. 37

Libya, Maurice Weiss, p. 70

Ethiopia, Maurice Weiss, p. 70

Niger, Maurice Weiss, p. 71

Chad, Maurice Weiss, p. 71

Germany, Maurice Weiss, p. 100

Germany, Maurice Weiss, p. 102

Cuba, Maurice Weiss, p. 102

Costa Rica, Maurice Weiss, p. 103

Al-'Araqib, Israel, Michal Warshavsky, p. 105

Germany, Maurice Weiss, p. 134

France, Maurice Weiss, p. 135

Algeria, Maurice Weiss, p. 136

Algeria, Maurice Weiss, p. 136

Corsica, Maurice Weiss, p. 162

Ukraine, Maurice Weiss, p. 163

Chad, Maurice Weiss, p. 164

Bikini Atoll, Maurice Weiss, p. 164

Germany, Maurice Weiss, p. 190

Chile, Maurice Weiss, p. 190

Bikini Atoll, Maurice Weiss, p. 191

Portugal, Maurice Weiss, p. 191

Germany, Maurice Weiss, p. 216

Bikini Atoll, Maurice Weiss, p. 216

Ukraine, Maurice Weiss, p. 217

Niger, Maurice Weiss, p. 218

Colonial Bungalow, India, Theresa Grieben, p. 220

Germany, Maurice Weiss, p. 226

Chad, Maurice Weiss, p. 227

Ethiopia, Maurice Weiss, p. 242

Chad, Maurice Weiss, p. 242

Niger, Maurice Weiss, p. 243

Bikini Atoll, Maurice Weiss, p. 250

Bosnia-Herzegovina, Maurice Weiss, p. 251

Germany, Maurice Weiss, p. 278

China, Maurice Weiss, p. 278

France, Maurice Weiss, p. 279

Libya, Maurice Weiss, p. 279

Index